"Shoshana Fershtman's *The Mystical Exodus in Jungian Perspective* is testimony to the power of narrative and myth to heal trauma and provide meaning in our lives. Her book is a significant contribution to our understanding of the roles of Jewish myth and mysticism, the divine feminine, and archetypal psychology in the revitalization of Judaism in a post-Holocaust world. Dr. Fershtman provides us with a profound path for reconnecting with the cultural collective unconscious of Jewish life."

—**Sanford Drob**, author of *Kabbalistic Visions: C.G. Jung and Jewish Mysticism*

"The most compelling thing about this beautiful book is that the author anchors it in her own lost and re-found story of exile within the Jewish community. Her awakening and return begins at a tearfully redemptive moment when her heart opens in a temple sanctuary, and later as she slowly realizes that the broken shards of her own painful personal story were carried unconsciously throughout her exile inside a much larger, ancient Jewish story—the sacred Covenant between God and man—in psychological language, the archetypal covenant between ego and Self. Sometimes trauma is the only thing that breaks us open to this larger reality that sustains us and leads us home to ourselves—and to others who are courageous enough to share their own heartbreak. This book carries a profound message for our time of spiritual and psychological 'exile.' It shows us a way home. I cannot recommend it highly enough."

—**Donald E. Kalsched, PhD**, author of *Trauma and the Soul: A Psycho-spiritual Approach to Human Development and its Interruption*

"*The Mystical Exodus in Jungian Perspective* is a feast! With lucid and engaging prose that at times reads like poetry, Fershtman explores how the contemporary movement called Jewish Renewal revitalizes Jewish ancestral wisdom, elevating the mystical dimension and the Divine Feminine in Judaism. Fershtman weaves moving personal stories of engagement with Jewish Renewal teachings and practices seen through the archetypal lens of the Exodus story. Here we discover layers of insight—brilliant midrashic and mystical wisdom that enabled Jews to overcome millennia of collective trauma, and offers us a pathway to reconnect with the sacred in our own time."

—**Rabbi Marcia Prager**, Director and Dean of
Ordination Programs for ALEPH: Alliance for Jewish
Renewal, author of *The Path of Blessing*

"This is a book of a lifetime—both for the author and the reader. Shoshana Fershtman has documented her own and others' personal spiritual journeys of transformation in the context of the Jewish Renewal movement that taps into the cultural and archetypal dimensions of the vitality of spirit and soul—specifically Jewish but in some ways about the wellspring of renewal potentially available in any spiritual awakening."

—**Thomas Singer**, Jungian Analyst, author of *The Cultural
Complex* and *Cultural Complexes and the Soul of America*

"Dr. Fershtman has gifted us with an extraordinary book that is both vast in scope and deep in personal passion. By telling the stories of our personal passages from dislocation and trauma to belonging and wholeness, we can know ourselves as unique and precious expressions of the significant social and religious movements that are awakening our world. *The Mystical Exodus in Jungian Perspective* is a guide for consciously stepping onto the path of liberation by shining a light on the mythic and mystical dimensions of our inheritance. This book gave me a profound sense of pride, pleasure, and comfort in understanding the Jewish Renewal Movement as a vital force of healing in a world that yearns for wholeness."

—**Rabbi Shefa Gold**, author of *Torah Journeys:
The Inner Path to the Promised Land*

"There is a saying in Jewish intellectual circles that the Talmudists become Freudians and the mystics become Jungians. Shoshana Fershtman, in this highly creative work, is able to combine the best of both these worlds, the mystical and the intellectual—an outstanding achievement! Courageously sharing experiences from her own and others' lives, and drawing on the inspiration of the Jewish mystical tradition as well as aspects of … Jungian approaches to life, Dr. Fershtman has crafted a book that cries out to be read by us all."

—**Aryeh Maidenbaum, PhD**, Director, NY Center for Jungian Studies,
author of *Jung and the Shadow of Anti-Semitism*
and *Lingering Shadows: Jungians, Freudians, and Anti-Semitism*

"A beautifully written, authoritative guide to the history, evolution, and contemporary renaissance of the Jewish mystical tradition that integrates Biblical myth and personal narrative with insights from Jungian psychology. Fershtman's deep compassion and wisdom shine through the stories she tells that demonstrate how spiritual seekers may find healing and transformation by embracing their ancestral roots."

—**Estelle Frankel**, MFT, author of *Sacred Therapy*
and *The Wisdom of Not Knowing*

"*The Mystical Exodus in Jungian Perspective* is Shoshana Fershtman's work of imagination and scholarship. Through her deep immersion into the roots of Jewish mysticism, mythic traditions, and analytical psychology she allows us to see possibilities to open up spaces for holding our collective and personal healing of the 'millennial old' collective traumas and cultural catastrophes."

—**Sam Kimbles, PhD,** author of *Phantom Narratives: The Unseen Contributions of Culture to Psyche* and *The Suffering of Ghosts: Intergenerational Complexes in Analytical Psychology*

"So grateful to Dr. Shoshana Fershtman for giving us a masterful and meticulously researched integration of Jungian thought and Biblical metaphor. And that expertise is amplified by her contemporary feminist perspective. A 'must read' for spiritual seekers of all faiths."

—**Rabbi Leah Novick**, author of *On The Wings of Shekhinah: Re-Discovering Judaism's Divine Feminine*

"An important book with a potent message about the contagious nature of trauma and how it filters unimpeded through the generations. The courageous transparency with which the author interpolates within this exploration her own personal story will not only touch the hearts of the traumatized but will also deeply inform anyone engaged in the healing of trauma, whether professionally or academically. The book's creative weave of relevant studies and moving anecdotes will undoubtedly earn its place amid the annals of literature on the science and treatment of trauma, in particular in regard to children of Holocaust survivors. No less valuable, however, is the book's vivid demonstration of the power of mythology in enriching our life journeys."

—**Rabbi Gershon Winkler**, author of *Magic of the Ordinary: Recovering the Shamanic in Judaism*

"Dr. Fershtman exquisitely examines the history, mythology, and evolution of Judaism analyzing disconnection, particularly of Jews, from the sacred imagination of Judaism. Utilizing the archetypal theme of Exodus—a journey from exile to redemption—she illuminates Judaism's resurgence in the psyche. Writing reverently on the influence of trauma in Judaism, she shares poignant, liberating human stories of coming out from exile and into relationship with Jewish consciousness—journeys which reveal our spiritual essence."

—**Helen Marlo, PhD**, Professor, Notre Dame de Namur University; Psychologist; author of *The Spiritual Psyche: Intersubjectivity, Mysticism and Psychoanalysis in Clinical Practice*

"Drawing on Exodus, Jewish sources, and Jungian psychology, Shoshana Fershtman recounts her own and others' remarkable personal and collective journeys toward Jewish Renewal and a more feminine Judaism. Highly recommended."

—**Professor Henry Abramovitch**, Founding President, Israel Institute of Jungian Psychology. Co-author of *The Analyst and the Rabbi*

"I traveled through the pages of Shoshana Fershtman's book as if I was following a road map into caverns, over mountains, through deserts, and across
oceans. It is no easy journey with the troop of ancestors. Moses leads the people
out of slavery and into the promised land. They were gifted ears to hear God's
voice in a burning bush and driven into despair with Lilith through intergenerational darkness. Each chapter demonstrated a spiritual weaving of Judaism,
thousands of years of Jewish history, modern-day psychoanalysis, inner conflict, human desire, and the mystery of why the people move forward. As I continued reading, there was an emergence into a deeper realization of holiness, a
longing to unveil the infinite light of the divine within my soul. I came away
from the book with an understanding that our individual life is interwoven with
ancestral consciousness and an awareness of ritual and spiritual bonds."

—**Tu Bears**, author of *Infinite Footprints: Daily Wisdom
to Ignite Your Creative Expression in Walking Your
True Path* and contributor, *Reinventing the Enemies Language,
Contemporary Native Women's Writings of North America*

"*The Mystical Exodus in Jungian Perspective* explores how historical forces of
collective trauma and assimilation result in separation from and forgetting the
ancestral wisdom tradition of Judaism, including the mystical tradition based
in transrational consciousness. Drawing on the author's own and others' individual stories of separation and return, we see how addressing historical trauma
and its ramifications in the personal psyche creates a pathway to healing the
connection with the ancestors, with the sacred, and with what Jung called the
Self."

—**Jerome Bernstein**, author of *Living In the Borderland:
The Evolution of Consciousness and the Challenge of Healing
Trauma* and "Collective Shadow Integration: Atonement"
in *Jung and the Shadow of Anti-Semitism*

The Mystical Exodus in Jungian Perspective

The Mystical Exodus in Jungian Perspective explores the soul loss that results from personal, collective, and transgenerational trauma and the healing that unfolds through reconnection with the sacred. Personal narratives of disconnection from, and reconnection to, Jewish collective memory are illuminated by a millennia of Jewish mystical wisdom, contemporary Jewish Renewal and feminist theology, and Jungian and trauma theory.

The archetypal resonance of the Exodus story guides our exploration. Understanding exile as disconnection from the Divine Self, we follow Moses, keeper of the spiritual fire, and Serach bat Asher, preserver of ancestral memory. We encounter the depths with Joseph, touch collective grief with Lilith, experience the Red Sea crossing and Miriam's well as psychological rebirth and Sinai as the repatterning of traumatized consciousness.

Tracing the reawakening of the qualities of eros and relatedness on the journey out of exile, the book demonstrates how restoring and deepening relationship with the Sacred Feminine helps us to transform collective trauma.

This text will be key reading for scholars of Jewish studies, Jungian and post-Jungian studies, feminist spirituality, trauma studies, Jungian analysts and psychotherapists, and those interested in healing from personal and collective trauma.

Shoshana Fershtman, JD, PhD, is a Jungian analyst and psychologist in Sonoma County, California, USA. She is a member analyst and teaches at the C.G. Jung Institute of San Francisco, and served as core faculty at the Sonoma State University Depth Psychology program. She has studied Jewish mysticism with teachers from the Jewish Renewal and Reconstructing Judaism movements, and has taught extensively on Jewish mysticism, transgenerational trauma, and the Sacred Feminine. Her work as an attorney focused on advocacy for environmental and social justice and indigenous rights.

The Mystical Exodus
in Jungian Perspective

Transforming Trauma and
the Wellsprings of Renewal

Shoshana Fershtman

Routledge
Taylor & Francis Group

LONDON AND NEW YORK

First published 2021
by Routledge
2 Park Square, Milton Park, Abingdon, Oxon OX14 4RN

and by Routledge
52 Vanderbilt Avenue, New York, NY 10017

Routledge is an imprint of the Taylor & Francis Group, an informa business

British Library Cataloguing-in-Publication Data
A catalogue record for this book is available from the British Library

Library of Congress Cataloging-in-Publication Data
Names: Fershtman, Carolyn Shoshana, author.
Title: The Mystical Exodus in Jungian Perspective : Transforming Trauma and
the Wellsprings of Renewal / Shoshana Fershtman.
Description: Abingdon, Oxon ; New York, NY: Routledge, 2021. | Includes
bibliographical references and index. | that unfolds through reconnection
with the sacred"-- Provided by publisher.
Identifiers: LCCN 2020045282 (print) | LCCN 2020045283 (ebook) |
ISBN 9780367537111 (hardback) | ISBN 9780367537135 (paperback) |
ISBN 9781003083016 (ebook)
Subjects: LCSH: Judaism and psychology. | Jungian psychology. | Jewish
renewal. | Mysticism--Judaism. | Psychic trauma--Religious aspects--Judaism. |
Collective memory--Religious aspects--Judaism.
Classification: LCC BM538.P68 F47 2021 (print) | LCC BM538.P68 (ebook) |
DDC 296.01/9--dc23
LC record available at https://lccn.loc.gov/2020045282
LC ebook record available at https://lccn.loc.gov/2020045283

ISBN: 978-0-367-53711-1 (hbk)
ISBN: 978-0-367-53713-5 (pbk)
ISBN: 978-1-003-08301-6 (ebk)

Typeset in Times New Roman
by Deanta Global Publishing Services, Chennai, India

Dedicated to
Rabbi Zalman Schachter-Shalomi
and Rabbi Steven Fisdel
and to my mother
Myra Minucha Riva Rosenblum
Zekher tzadik v'kadosh livrakhah
l'chayei ha'olam ha-ba
May the memories of the righteous and holy
be a blessing for the life of the world to come

And to my beloved husband,
Jeffery Hoffman
Hincha Yafeh Dodi

Contents

Acknowledgments

This book owes its greatest debt to the work of Rabbi Zalman Schachter-Shalomi, of blessed memory, and to the rabbis and teachers of Jewish Renewal and Reconstructing Judaism. My ongoing study with kabbalistic rabbi and scholar Rabbi Steven Fisdel, also of blessed memory, shaped my understanding of the text as a guide to personal and spiritual transformation.

I offer my deepest respect and appreciation to the participants who shared their journeys of both personal and transgenerational healing—their vulnerability and sharing made this work possible. I am grateful to the San Francisco Bay Area Renewal communities whose members were the focus of the stories gathered here, including the Aquarian Minyan, Chochmat Ha'Lev, Kehilla Community Synagogue and Congregation Ner Shalom. My learning with various teachers from Aleph Alliance for Jewish Renewal and Reconstructing Judaism guided the development of my thinking. My deepest appreciation to Rabbi Margaret Holub for providing the opening for my soul to reconnect with Judaism; and to Rabbis Shefa Gold, Diane Elliot, Leah Novick, Marcia Prager, and feminist studies scholar D'vorah Grenn, and psychotherapist and author Estelle Frankel for providing support and reflection on the work; and to Rabbi Gershon Winkler for his close reading and helpful additions. Daniel Matt generously offered to review portions of Zohar-related text. My gratitude to SooJi Min-Miranda of Aleph and Rabbis Nancy Fuchs Kreimer and Maurice Harris of Reconstructing Judaism for their support and encouragement.

In addition, the support of my colleagues at the C.G. Jung Institute in San Francisco has been sustaining. Thomas Singer's wisdom and guidance has been a great gift. Carol McRae and Sam Naifeh offered professional guidance that has greatly enriched my understanding of analytical psychology. A grant from the C.G. Jung Institute of San Francisco Scholarship Committee supported the publication of the work.

I am indebted to Jungian scholar Sanford Drob for his insightful comments at key points in the development of this work, and to Jungian analysts Steve Zemmelman, Sam Kimbles, Aryeh Maidenbaum, Henry Abramovitch, Donald Kalsched, Jerome Bernstein, Helen Marlo, Paul Watsky, Michael Bala, and Kathleen Murphy for their support and engagement. The conference at Pacifica Graduate Institute on the work of Erich Neumann, organized by Israeli analyst

Erel Shalit, of blessed memory, clarified my understanding of Neumann's relationship to Jewish myth and mysticism.

I offer my profound appreciation for the generosity and insights of psychologists Flavio Epstein, Sandra Andresen, and Lisa Kully, who served as co-researchers in a two-day study from which the stories in this volume are drawn. Psychologists Jay Rice, Karen Jaenke, and Melissa Schwartz provided support in developing the work in its early stages. I am grateful to Laurel McCabe for inviting me to share the work publicly, and to Isoke Femi, Anne Coelho, Diane Camurat, Lisa Rohe, and Irene Ives for their psychological wisdom and abiding friendship. My deepest gratitude to Anne Holmes, Leila Rand and Lori Lux Tuttle for always being there with love, insight and laughter.

The brilliant, soulful, and unceasingly kind Rabbi Irwin Keller of Ner Shalom in Cotati has coalesced a community of cultural creatives and irreverent reverence that has enabled many to find our tribe after years of wandering alone in the desert. I am deeply indebted to Ner Shalom for creating a *mishkan* for the emergence and honoring of the Sacred Feminine and mystical understandings of the text, and to Judith Goleman Yael Peskin, Ellen Solot, Barbara Lesch-McCaffry, and the entire circle of wise women at Ner Shalom, for their reflections and unwavering support. My gratitude to Elaine Greenwood, psychotherapist and artist, for her transcendent artwork. Rabbi K'vod Wieder's friendship, wisdom, and kindness nurtured my burgeoning love of Judaism.

Jeane TuBears Jacobs, Cherokee-Choctaw and a little bit Jewish, an unfailing source of guidance for many decades, opened the door for my ancestors to come in and guide my journey—their presence has accompanied me every step of the way. My gratitude to Dr. Charles Gourgey, whose hospice work with my mother offered profound healing.

My first editor, Margaret Ryan, of blessed memory, offered steady support, kindness, wisdom, and humor. Editor LeeAnn Pickrell stepped in at a decisive moment and brought the work to completion with great intelligence and grace. Naomi Rose provided support and encouragement in the early stages of this journey. Editors Susannah Frearson and Alexis O'Brien have generously supported the publication of this work, and to Andy Ross for his support and guidance.

My family has offered unceasing loving support—my deepest gratitude to my brother Gerry, who accompanied me on some of the most challenging steps of the journey, to my brother Brian for his encouragement, to my parents Gil and Debra, my parents-in-law Rich and Toby for their love and faith, and to the entire Fershtman, Hoffman and Gower mishpocheh. My nieces, nephews, godchildren, and other young people in my life inspire a belief in and a commitment to a future filled with love and meaning.

Jungian analyst and author Naomi Ruth Lowinsky has been the spiritual midwife of both this work and of my finding my creative voice, for which I offer my immeasurable love and gratitude.

My husband, Jeffery Yafeh Hoffman, inspires me every day with his pure heart, musical soul, and dedication to social justice. His love, support, and encouragement have sustained me in bringing this work to fruition.

"R. Joseph learnt: ... both the tablets and the fragments of the tablets were deposited in the ark."

Babylonian Talmud Menachot 99a

The broken tablets were also carried in an ark.
Insofar as they represented everything shattered
everything lost, they were the law of broken things,
the leaf torn from the stem in a storm, a cheek touched
in fondness once but now the name forgotten.
How they must have tumbled, clattered on the way
even carried so carefully through the wasteland,
how they must have rattled around until the pieces
broken into pieces, the edges softened
crumbling, dust collected at the bottom of the ark
ghosts of old letters, old laws. Insofar
as a law broken is still remembered
these laws were obeyed. And insofar as memory
preserves the pattern of broken things
these bits of stone were preserved
through many journeys and ruined days
even, they say, into the promised land.

Rodger Kamenetz, "The Broken Tablets"[1]

Note

1 Rodger Kamenetz, "The Broken Tablets," *The Lowercase Jew* (Northwestern University Press, 2003).

Introduction

We have lost our stories,
and I believe that unless we re-dream the myths that keep us alive,
we are not going to be able to heal the planet.

Rabbi Zalman Schachter-Shalomi[1]

This book is made up of stories, my own and others; of feeling disconnected, disenchanted, and displaced from Judaism; and of the surprise of an awakening that called us into passionate reengagement with the collective memory of this ancestral tradition. These individual stories are part of a larger story of healing the separation from Jewish memory wrought by the dislocations and traumas of our millennia-long history.

These personal stories are contextualized within the larger social movements from which they emerge—social movements that fostered the reclamation of the mythic and mystical dimensions of Judaism and psychological movements that emphasized the importance of myth in the life of the psyche. These two streams come together in *Jewish Renewal*, a contemporary movement that reconnects Judaism with its mythic and mystical roots in accessible and psychologically transformative ways. Jewish Renewal created both its own unique expression of Judaism and infused the mainstream of American Jewish denominations— Reconstructionist, Reform, and Conservative—with new vitality and mystical depth.

The heart of the book explores individual and collective stories of return through the archetypal lens provided by the Exodus, which offers insight into individual spiritual development and a map for healing from collective and transgenerational trauma. We see how this timeless story is also the story of our time—of exile as a consequence of collective trauma, of hearing the call of the Beloved, and how, through following this voice, we find our way into deepening connection with our own souls, with the collective soul of Judaism, and with the sacred. Individual stories of reconnection are amplified through several expansive lenses: interpretations from Jewish mystical and other rabbinic sources, Jungian perspectives on psychological and spiritual development, and Jungian and other psychological literature on trauma.

Jewish mystics saw the passage of the Hebrew people from slavery to the Promised Land as reflective of the soul's movement from separation or exile from God to a deepening engagement with one's own truest self and with the cosmic Mystery.[2] The guidance offered by the text and the meaning found within it by generations concerned with both the preservation and deepening of the Jewish soul have much to offer present-day Jews still reeling from the collective trauma of the Shoah and the massive historical upheavals and devastations of the past two centuries. If we listen deeply, we may find that the story guides our lives, and discover how our own lives in turn amplify the story, *l'dor v'dor*, from generation to generation.

This is a book about trauma and memory. We are growing in our understanding that we survive trauma by partially or fully limiting memory of the disaster until we have the psychological resources we need to integrate the event into consciousness. The great Israeli poet Yehuda Amichai invokes the imagery of the Great Flood in understanding the necessity of forgetting in the wake of overwhelming crisis:

> The world is filled with remembering and forgetting
> like sea and dry land. Sometimes memory is the solid ground we stand on,
> sometimes memory is the sea that covers all things
> like the Flood. And forgetting is the dry land that saves, like Ararat.[3]

Reclamation of Jewish myth and mysticism in modernity

Beginning in the mid-19th century, much of European Jewish collective life was undergoing a profound transformation—a movement away from the insular communities in Eastern Europe in which Jewish mystical life had flourished, into increasing assimilation in Central European and American culture. This brought a growing material stability along with new possibilities for advancement, bought at the cost of the dominant culture's implicit requirement that Jews turn away from their traditional practices. As in our own time, the rate of attrition of Jewish spiritual practice was alarming, and many wondered whether Judaism itself would continue.[4]

The promise of increased assimilation in the late 18th and early 19th centuries was shattered by the rise of Nazism. Some great thinkers of the time turned toward reclamation of Jewish ancestral wisdom, both as a resource for understanding how to survive collective trauma and out of a need to preserve Jewish memory in the midst of the Nazi enterprise to destroy it. The significance of their work became evident in the post-World War II era. Young Jews who grew up highly assimilated or alienated from religious Judaism were able to reconnect with its depths because of the texts on Jewish mythic imagination rescued from the fires of the Shoah by these cultural historians.

Martin Buber, born in Vienna in the late 19th century, widely shared the teach-ings, stories, and practices of Hasidic mysticism practiced by Jews in Eastern Europe that assimilated Central European Jews sought to distance themselves from. In the age of the Jewish enlightenment called *Haskalah*, mystical beliefs and practices were summarily dismissed as superstition. In the early part of the 20th century, Buber's teachings inspired a generation of young German-speaking Jewish intellectuals such as Gershom Scholem and Erich Neumann to explore the mystical depths of Judaism.

Gershom Scholem was raised in an assimilated family and, recognizing the seriousness of the Nazi threat, emigrated to Palestine in the early 1930s. He dedicated his life to discovering the great mystical works of Judaism known as *kabbalah*. His work is largely responsible for creating our modern perception of kabbalah as both a discrete and profound realm of Jewish thought and establishing its central place in Judaism in both historical and theological terms.[5]

Erich Neumann, also raised in an assimilated German Jewish family, began his medical training in the early 1930s. When Nazi restrictions kept him from finish-ing his medical degree, he traveled to Switzerland to train with Carl Jung before immigrating to Palestine shortly thereafter. Considered by many as the intellec-tual heir to Jung, Neumann wrote extensively on Hasidism and Jewish conscious-ness during the final years of the war, which he chose not to publish. This work has been translated and is now available as a two-volume series entitled *The Roots of Jewish Consciousness*.[6] Neumann's decades-long correspondence with Jung is now also available.[7]

Neumann saw that the rich treasure trove of Jewish myth and mysticism car-ried great psychological meaning and the potential for transformation for Jews who could engage with it, but that depth of Jewish religious practice was largely inaccessible to many who had become assimilated. Neumann was deeply influ-enced by Buber's work on Jewish mystical Hasidic practices, and they main-tained a meaningful correspondence. Neumann also formed a close association with Gershom Scholem in the postwar era, and both men presented regularly at Eranos conferences in Switzerland along with Jung and other leading theorists on psychology, myth, and religion. Neumann's untimely death in 1961 cut short his career as the intellectual heir apparent to Jung.

The American counterculture and the reclamation of Jewish mysticism

Rabbi Zalman Schachter-Shalomi, affectionately known as "Reb Zalman," was a brilliant and creative rabbi who emigrated from Vienna to the United States with his family during the Shoah when he was still a teen. He became ordained as a Hasidic rabbi and began outreach to students on college campuses in the late 1960s. He saw that many longed for spiritual meaning but were uninterested in adopting an Orthodox approach. He developed an expression of Judaism that married Hasidic mysticism, depth psychology, feminism, and egalitarian forms of engagement. Rabbi Arthur Waskow, a social activist and rabbi involved in the development of a socially informed Judaism, popularized Buber's term "Jewish Renewal," which became formalized as a distinct expression of Judaism.[8]

Reb Zalman's work, and those it inspired, coalesced into various Renewal congregations. In 1974, his month-long workshop on kabbalah inspired the formation of the Aquarian Minyan, the first Jewish Renewal congregation on the West Coast.[9] Reb Zalman went on to found Congregation B'nai Or (*Sons of Light*), later P'nai Or (the more gender-neutral *Faces of Light*) in 1978 in Philadelphia, which later became *Aleph: The Alliance for Jewish Renewal*. Aleph shares the teachings and practices of Jewish Renewal through its affiliated communities worldwide and its ordination program for rabbis, cantors, and spiritual pastors and healers.[10]

Reb Zalman worked alongside numerous rabbis who had been deeply influenced by the works of Buber and Scholem and by the re-emergence of Jewish mysticism, including Rabbi Arthur Green, who writes widely on Hasidism and other aspects of Jewish mysticism and who became head of the Reconstructionist Rabbinical College, infusing mysticism into the training. Rabbi Burt Jacobson, who founded Kehilla Community Synagogue in Oakland, has written extensive Jewish liturgical translations and on the Hasidic master the *Baal Shem Tov*. Moshe Idel and Adin Steinsaltz continued developing kabbalistic studies in Israel, and Rabbi Jonathan Omer-man further developed and disseminated these ideas within the context of American Judaism. Daniel Matt recently completed a translation of the Zohar, the central text of kabbalah, into a multivolume series.

Reb Zalman was greatly influenced by the work of Erich Neumann. In my meeting with Reb Zalman just a year before his death, I was able to share my work researching the impact of Jewish Renewal on individuals reconnecting with Judaism. When I mentioned my training as a Jungian analyst, his whole being lit up as he began talking about Erich Neumann. "Oh, Neumann!" he said. "How I wanted to study with him!" In 1960, Reb Zalman planned to move to Israel to enter analysis with him. Unfortunately, Neumann died that year.[11]

In the chapters that follow I explore how the psychospiritual model developed by Reb Zalman actualized Neumann's vision of engaging the treasure trove of Jewish mythic imagination as a pathway to psychological growth and transformation. The journeys of individuals estranged from Judaism, who found their way back into connection with it, reveal the powerful impact of engaging with the symbolic and mythological motifs in the Jewish cultural collective unconscious.

Jung developed the idea that in addition to the personal unconscious consisting of repressed material from our own lives, our psyches are open to the collective storehouse of archetypes, which he called the *collective unconscious*. He also posited that between the personal unconscious and the collective unconscious there existed layers of familial, group, and national or cultural layers of the unconscious.[12] Jungians who worked closely with Jung and who explored the Jewish cultural collective unconscious, such as Rivkah Scharf Kluger, Erich Neumann, and Siegmund Hurwitz, provide a framework for understanding the depth perspectives inherent in the Biblical and midrashic texts. I also examine the work of a subsequent generation of Jungian analysts engaging with Judaism from a depth perspective, including Naomi Ruth Lowinsky and Sanford Drob. The disconnection from the cultural unconscious is investigated through the work of Jungian analysts Samuel Kimbles and Thomas Singer on the cultural complex. Donald Kalsched's work on trauma serves as a guide to understanding how the connection to the guiding wisdom of the psyche, which Jung called the *Self*, is injured by personal and historical trauma.

Reclaiming the Divine Feminine and social justice in Judaism

A central thread in re-engagement with Judaism is the reclamation of the Divine Feminine. This immanent aspect of the Divine, the *Shekhinah*, is central in both medieval and Hasidic kabbalah. However, until our own era, the inclusion of women's voices was not. The advent of Jewish feminist spirituality, beginning in the 1970s, profoundly altered the landscape of Judaism. Judith Plaskow explored how many women were alienated by the inherently patriarchal bias in Judaism. Drawing on the work of Rabbis Leah Novick, Lynn Gottlieb and Tirzah Firestone, I explore images of the Sacred Feminine in Biblical and mystical texts through the lens of feminist spirituality. The work of Savina Teubal bridges the ancient priestess traditions with the stories of the earliest matriarchs in the Bible. Jewish spiritual practices were also transformed by Rabbis Shefa Gold, Elliot, Jill Hammer, and others who developed forms of prayer that were more embodied and focused on the Shekhinah as the indwelling Presence. I also discuss Raphael Patai's seminal work on the Hebrew Goddess and Erich Neumann's view of the history of consciousness, which recognized the centrality of the Great Mother goddesses in early Hebrew culture.

In addition to mysticism and feminist theology, a third strand in the braid of Jewish Renewal is a strong commitment to *tikkun olam*, a concept arising from Jewish mysticism, meaning to contribute to the repair of the world. Rabbi Arthur Waskow founded the Shalom Center with his wife, Rabbi Phyllis Berman, and Rabbi Michael Lerner created *Tikkun* magazine. Lerner was mentored by Abraham Joshua Heschel, a Polish-born rabbi, scholar, and social justice activist who emigrated from Europe during the Shoah, who marched with Dr. Martin Luther King, Jr.[13] Lerner observes that social justice teachings central to the Jewish tradition were forgotten because of widespread assimilation propelled by unconscious internalized anti-Semitism. He proposes that the creation of a spiritually based political movement could transform Jewish practice and the larger culture to turn toward developing communities of meaning, offering life-sustaining alternatives to individualist culture.[14]

This psychospiritual, feminist, and socially conscious approach to Judaism realized the potential recognized by Scholem, Buber, Neumann, and others in the early part of the 20th century. The vision—that active engagement with the practices and mythos of Jewish collective memory could constellate profound psychological and spiritual development for post-modern Jews largely alienated from Judaism—was carried to the United States and realized by Reb Zalman, Rabbi Abraham Joshua Heschel, and others in the wake of the Shoah.

Stories of reawakening

This book reflects the spiritual awakenings and deepenings experienced by individuals engaging with Judaism through Jewish Renewal or other mystical experiences, who had either grown up secular or feeling that the Judaism of their youth lacked meaning. The Exodus story provides a mythic framework for understanding the journey of spiritual development from a state of alienation and disconnection—the state of exile experienced by the enslaved Hebrews—to one of expansive consciousness and connection with the sacred, symbolized by the movement into the Promised Land of a more fully realized consciousness.

As I reflected on the experiences of individuals reconnecting with Judaism in the post-Shoah era, I had an intuitive sense that their journeys, and my own, could be seen through the lens of the Exodus story. As I explored the midrashic texts associated with the Exodus journey, I saw how this story had been amplified over the course of millennia with the wisdom of people who were grappling with the same questions we face in our own time—how to maintain one's spiritual and psychological center and protect the cultural psyche—in times of overwhelming collective trauma. This collective wisdom is also, strikingly, aligned with our growing psychological understanding of how the psyche heals from trauma, both personal and collective.

The Egypt in which the Hebrews found themselves enslaved was *mitzrayim*, translated as *the narrow place*, a place of constricted consciousness. With its profoundly psychospiritual mythic cosmology Egypt may also be viewed as the womb and birth canal from which Hebrew consciousness emerged. The Promised Land corresponds to the state of realized awareness attained through the ongoing connection between our individual consciousness and the Divine Mystery.

In the following chapters, I explore the various archetypes that appear in the Biblical text through *midrashic legends* (rabbinic interpretations of Biblical texts), Jungian psychological theory, and perhaps most movingly, through the experience of individuals who found their way out of a state of alienation from Judaism to one of profound reconnection.[15] I begin, in Chapter One, "The Beloved, Knocking," with my own unexpected reconnection with Judaism and how it led me to explore the experiences of others who surprisingly found themselves re-engaged with their ancestral tradition.

In Part I, "An Historical Overview of Jewish Mysticism and Psychology," I reflect on two powerful streams of consciousness that underlie the current experience of reconnection with the mythic imagination of Judaism: Jewish mysticism and Jungian and other depth psychology approaches. The shift in collective consciousness explored in Chapters Four through Twelve is both generated by and viewed through the lenses of Jewish mysticism or kabbalah as well as Jungian

psychology and other psychoanalytic perspectives. Chapters Two and Three provide a summary overview of these extensive fields.

In Chapter Two, "Renewing Jewish Mysticism," I look at how the Jewish mystical tradition provides wisdom for healing from collective trauma and note the
ways in which historical trauma is often followed by a re-emergence of mystical cosmology. Following the Shoah, access to this healing wisdom was largely
overlooked because unprecedented assimilation had led to a state in which most
Jews were unaware of the deeper meaning at the heart of the tradition. In this
chapter, I survey the work of Buber, Scholem, Neumann, Schachter-Shalomi, and
others who devoted their lives to making the mystical tradition accessible to the
wider, non-Orthodox world. The rebirth of the Divine Feminine in the tradition
had a profound impact, through modern recognition of the central place it occupies in kabbalah (represented by the *Shekhinah*) and in the emergence of women's
perspectives through the advent of feminist spirituality after millennia of silencing. Erich Neumann's seminal work on the Great Mother archetype in the Near
Eastern pre-Hebraic traditions contributed to the awareness of the significance of
the Feminine decades before the advent of the feminist spirituality movement.
Raphael Patai's essential work on the Hebrew Goddess documents Her import
in ancient Jewish practice. I explore the Sacred Feminine in Jewish mysticism in
medieval texts such as the Zohar, in Hasidic mysticism, and in the work of contemporary feminist theologians such as Rabbis Lynn Gottlieb and Leah Novick.[16]

In Chapter Three, "Judaism and Psychology," I delve into the intersection of
Judaism, mysticism, and psychology, beginning with Freud's psychological theories and his relationship to Judaism in *fin de siècle* Vienna. Freud lived at a time
when severe restrictions on Jewish involvement in mainstream culture were just
beginning to be lifted, leading to the development of an overly rationalist and
assimilated identity among Central European Jewry that distanced itself from its
mystical roots. I then discuss C.G. Jung's recognition of the need for reclaiming
the influence of myth and symbol in psychological development and the work of
Jungian analysts Rivkah Scharf Kluger, Siegmund Hurwitz, and Sanford Drob
who articulated the depth psychological meaning of Judaism as a framework for
understanding the role of reconnecting with one's own ancestral and spiritual tradition in psychological development.[17] Erich Neumann's work, which examined
the development of consciousness, the re-emergence of the Feminine, and the
relationship with Jewish collective memory is central to the topics I consider in
more depth in the chapters that follow.[18] I also explore psychological perspectives
on intergenerational trauma and healing, developed in part through research with
survivors of the Holocaust and their descendants.

Part II, "The Rupture," considers the experience of exile in our current time
and the movement from constricted to expanded consciousness. In Chapter Four,
"Exile," I begin an in-depth consideration of the archetypal and symbolic meaning of the Exodus story, reflecting on the exile in *mitzrayim*, the narrow place,
as a state of disconnection from the sacred and from Jewish mythic imagination. Individual stories reflect the experience of growing up in families where the

relationship to Judaism was conflicted and how this conflict was internalized. By interweaving these personal stories with the mythic interpretations of the Exodus story, I probe the psychological and spiritual meaning of exile.

Part III, "The Awakening," shows how the movement out of exile takes place psychologically. In Chapter Five, "Women, Copper Mirrors, and Awakening from the Trance of Exile," I examine the midrashic legend of how the movement of the Hebrew slaves out of exile in Egypt began with the women hearing the voice of God guiding them to invite their husbands into a dance of erotic play using copper mirrors.[19] I consider this text in light of psychological perspectives on how trauma is healed through empathic holding and mirroring by one who sees and reflects back to us the potential of our larger Self. I explore the experiences of individuals who responded to a call to re-engage Judaism when their soul's longing was mirrored back to them through an encounter with a beloved teacher or inner guide.

In Chapter Six, "Moses and Awakening the Spiritual Fire," I look at the symbolic meaning of Moses in our own psychological development. How are we reawakened, as Moses was awakened before the burning bush, by a direct personal encounter with the numinous? Citing the work of Jungian analyst Donald Kalsched, I explore how trauma occludes psyche's connection with the sacred. Reflecting on the stories of individuals who felt a spiritual awakening, I consider how responding to such a call can lead to engagement with a previously unknown inner spiritual fire and how cultivating a relationship with this fire transforms our relationship with the sacred, or what Jung termed the Self.

The Hebrews' movement out of mitzrayim is catalyzed by ten plagues, which frame Chapter Seven, "Shattered Vessels, Scattered Seeds." The plagues reflect the ways in which historical trauma is internalized in the individual and in the Jewish collective psyche. Drawing on the work of Jungian analysts Thomas Singer and Samuel Kimbles, I describe the cultural complexes that develop in the wake of collective trauma. Movement out of a constricted state of consciousness requires that we work through the limitations imposed on our awareness through post-traumatic stress and internalized anti-Semitism. Each of the plagues is viewed as symbolizing a particular way in which connection to the larger reality has been occluded. How can working through these cultural complexes lead us out of the exile of constricted consciousness?

Part IV, "The Healing," explores how we find our way back into connection with collective memory. In Chapter Eight, "Serach bat Asher and Healing the Ruptured Bridge to Collective Memory," I examine the archetype of the Biblical figure Serach, who teaches that healing from collective trauma requires reconnection with the ancestors and with the larger cultural collective unconscious of Judaism. This awareness is reflected through the powerfully healing experiences of individuals connecting with their own ancestry. In the Biblical text, the ancient Hebrews encounter the figure of Serach bat Asher, who helps Moses locate the hidden bones of the ancestor Joseph, a task that has to be fulfilled before the people can leave Egypt. I explore Jung's views on the connection with the ancestors, and Jungian analyst Naomi Ruth Lowinsky's insights into the power of the ancestral psyche. The eternal nature of Serach bat Asher carries echoes of the Hebrew Goddess Asherah, the holding presence of the Eternal Feminine in Jewish lineage. This connection is explored drawing on midrashic legend and the work of Israeli cultural anthropologist Raphael Patai.

Before the Hebrews can leave Egypt, Moses must discover the coffin containing Joseph's bones. In Chapter Nine, "Joseph—Light Out of Darkness," I reflect on the archetypal meaning of Joseph who, after a series of devastating descents, eventually becomes a leader in Egypt, initiating the events that enable the survival and growth of the 12 tribes of Israel. Joseph carries a Divine light, but he also appears inflated and catalyzes envy among his brothers. His journey of multiple descents leads to a reorientation of his ego in relationship to the sacred—he becomes a vessel for the holy light, rather than being identified with it. Joseph's transformational journey helps us understand how the most painful moments of our lives often open us to the sacred and how, through suffering, we may grow into a vessel capable of holding the Divine. I explore the stories of individuals who found the spark of the Divine emerging in the most challenging moments of their lives.

As the people approach the shores of the Red Sea, they encounter Lilith, the first woman, before Eve, who fled the Garden of Eden rather than lie beneath Adam, whom she saw as her equal. In Chapter Ten, "Lilith, the Dark Feminine, and the Redemptive Power of Grief," I explore the work of Jungian analyst Siegmund Hurwitz, Rabbi Lynn Gottlieb, and feminist studies scholar D'vorah Grenn on reclaiming the disowned dark, chthonic feminine in Judaism, and consider how working through difficult emotions allows us to reclaim our wholeness. This chapter includes the stories of individuals who turn toward the disowned pain and grief in their own family lineages. Engaging and sharing these stories catalyzes a healing of their relationship to Judaism and to the sacred.

Part V, "The Promise," delves into the psychological meaning of the journey across the Red Sea and the movement toward the Promised Land. The crossing of the Red Sea, the focus of Chapter Eleven, "The Watery Initiation and Learning to Trust the Ground of Being," symbolizes the need to release our former sense of who we are and open to a new reality. Here, I explore the faith required of the Hebrew people to move into the Red Sea, not knowing whether it would part. Their journey reflects our own current challenge in finding faith following the cataclysm of the Shoah. I consider the central role of the Shekhinah, the Divine Feminine. Miriam the prophetess, leading the women in circles of chanting and celebration, reflects the non-hierarchical forms that have allowed many to re-engage with Judaism. The stories shared reflect poignant experiences of individuals trusting and allowing themselves to be held by the Divine Presence.

The story ends with the Hebrews ascent to Mount Sinai in Chapter Twelve, "The Fiery Initiation and Moving Toward the Promised Land." Symbolically, the revelation of the Ten Commandments at Sinai reflects the transformation of consciousness that has been distorted by trauma. The vessels shattered by the ten plagues re-emerge—through the spiritual discipline required by the commandments—as vessels capable of holding the transformative light of holiness. I reflect on the experiences of individuals whose lives were transformed through their engagement with Judaism, healing the conflicted relationship with the tradition they had inherited as children. The book closes with a reflection on how our engagement with Judaism transforms not only us as individuals, but also the collective itself, as we bring new expressions and interpretations to Jewish life.

It is my deepest hope that this work may provide some resonance for both Jews and non-Jews who have experienced cultural or personal trauma and dislocation and who are finding their way out of exile, toward the Promised Land of a restored connection between ourselves and the sacred Living Mystery that holds and sustains us all.

Notes

1 Susan Goldstein, "Rabbi Schachter-Shalomi Extended Interview," *Religion & Ethics NewsWeekly,* September 30, 2005, Public Broadcasting Service, https://www.pbs.org/wnet/religionandethics/2005/09/30/september-30-2005-rabbi-zalman-schachter-shalomi-extended-interview/9753/.
2 Words associated with God are capitalized, in accordance with Jewish tradition.
3 Yehuda Amichai, "In My Life, On My Life," in *Open Closed Open*, translated by Chana Bloch and Chana Kronfeld (New York: Harcourt, Inc., 2000), 111.
4 Shaul Maggid, *American Post-Judaism: Identity and Renewal in a Postethnic Society* (Bloomington: Indiana University Press, 2013).
5 David Biale, *Gershom Scholem: Master of the Kabbalah* (New Haven, CT: Yale University Press, 2018), 1.
6 Erich Neumann, *The Roots of Jewish Consciousness*, Vols. I and II, edited by Ann Conrad Lammers (London: Routledge, 2019).
7 C.G. Jung and Erich Neumann, *Analytical Psychology in Exile: The Correspondence of C.G. Jung and Erich Neumann* (Princeton, NJ: Princeton University Press, 2015).
8 R. Kamenetz, Foreword to *On Judaism*, by Martin Buber (New York: Schocken Books, Inc., 1967).
9 Aquarian Minyan history, available at http://www.aquarianminyan.org/history.
10 Aleph Alliance for Jewish Renewal, Reb Zalman history, available at https://aleph.org/reb-zalman.
11 Zalman M. Schachter-Shalomi and Edward Hoffman, *My Life in Jewish Renewal* (Plymouth: Rowman & Littlefield Publishers, Inc., 2012), 116–117.
12 Thomas Singer and Samuel Kimbles, eds., *The Cultural Complex: Contemporary Jungian Perspectives on Psyche and Society* (New York: Routledge, 2004), 3, citing diagram of the psyche as formulated by Jung, reprinted from William McGuire, *Bollingen: An Adventure in Collecting the Past* (Princeton, NJ: Princeton University Press, 1989).
13 Edward K. Kaplan, *Spiritual Radical: Abraham Joshua Heschel in America, 1940–1972* (New Haven, CT: Yale University Press, 2007).
14 Michael Lerner, *Jewish Renewal: A Path to Healing and Transformation* (New York: GP Putnam's Sons, 1994), 268–269.
15 The following texts are referenced, among others: Avivah Zornberg, *The Beginning of Desire: Reflections on Genesis* (New York: Schocken, 1995); *The Particulars of Rapture: Reflections on Exodus* (New York: Doubleday, 2001); and *The Murmuring Deep: Reflections on the Biblical Unconscious* (New York: Schocken, 2009); Howard Schwartz, *Tree of Souls: The Mythology of Judaism* (New York: Oxford University Press,

2004); Daniel Matt, trans. and commentary, *The Zohar, Pritzker Edition* (Stanford, CA: Stanford University Press, 2006).

16 Erich Neumann, *The Great Mother: An Analysis of the Archetype* (Princeton, NJ: Princeton University Press, 1955/1983); Raphael Patai, *The Hebrew Goddess* (Detroit, MI: Wayne State University Press, 1967/1978); Leah Novick, *On the Wings of Shekhinah: Rediscovering Judaism's Divine Feminine* (Wheaton, IL: Quest Books, 2008); Lynn Gottlieb, *She Who Dwells Within: Feminist Vision of a Renewed Judaism* (San Francisco: HarperOne, 1995). See also Jill Hammer, *The Hebrew Priestess: Ancient and New Visions of Jewish Women's Spiritual Leadership* (Teaneck, NJ: BenYehuda Press, 2015); William G. Dever, *Did God Have a Wife?: Archaeology and Folk Religion in Ancient Israel* (Grand Rapids, MI: Wm. B. Eerdmans Publishing, 2005).

17 Rivkah Scharf Kluger, *Psyche in Scripture: The Idea of the Chosen People and Other Essays*, (Toronto: Inner City Books, 1995); *Psyche and Bible: Three Old Testament Themes* (New York: Spring Publications, 1974); Sanford Drob, *Kabbalistic Visions: C. G. Jung and Jewish Mysticism* (New Orleans, LA: Spring Journal Books, 2010); *Kabbalistic Metaphors: Jewish Mystical Themes in Ancient and Modern Thought* (Northvale, NJ: Jason Aronson Publishers, 2009); Siegmund Hurwitz, *Lilith—the First Eve—Historical and Psychological Aspects of the Dark Feminine* (Einsiedeln: Daimon Verlag, 1992).

18 Erich Neumann, *The Origins and History of Consciousness* (New York: Bollingen Foundation, 1954).

19 Tanhuma, Pequdei, 9. See also David Ben Ha'Hasid, *Mirrors of the Women Who Ministered*, translated by Daniel Matt (Chico, CA: Scholars Press, 1982); and Zornberg, *The Particulars of Rapture*, 60–63.

The beloved, knocking

I was asleep but my heart stayed awake.
Listen! ...

Song of Songs 5:2–4[1]

I remember the dream I had the night before I got my mother's call. In it, *I am wandering desperately down long hallways, perhaps a museum. I pass by paintings on the walls, but one in particular compels me—a painting of the Rock of Gibraltar, on the coast between Spain and Morocco. I see the rock breaking apart and falling into the sea. A voice in the dream says, "My Rock of Gibraltar is crumbling."* The next morning, my mother calls and tells me she has been diagnosed with ovarian cancer, which has now spread into her stomach. I am speechless, my dream coming back into my awareness and taking on specific meaning.

That next day I had been invited by my German therapist at the time to attend a *Yom HaShoah*, or Holocaust Remembrance service, at the Jewish temple in Mendocino, near where I was living. He had been invited to speak at the service on his healing from the war. He was born into a Gentile family in Germany during the war and spent his earliest years as a refugee with his mother, fleeing from Allied bombing raids. During our work together I had not yet come into any conscious relationship with my Jewish spiritual identity, but recall having had powerful dreams of being part of a German Jewish family that was emptying our home and fleeing Nazis, although I have no immediate ancestors who were in Germany during the war.

I agreed to attend, but after receiving the call from my mother, began having second thoughts. I was concerned that being in temple might open floodgates of grief about my mother that I would not be able to contain. Perhaps my concern about attending a Yom HaShoah service for the first time in my life was related to a fear of being overwhelmed with collective grief as well.

The night before the service, I had another dream. *I was on my way to visit Jeane TuBears Jacobs, the Native American spiritual teacher with whom I had been studying for many years. In the dream, my car broke down on the side of the road. Instead of continuing the way I'd planned, I left my car on the road and walked back toward home.* The dream felt powerful and puzzling.

The Yom HaShoah observance was preceded by a one-hour meditation that I decided to attend. When I arrived, I was the only one in the sanctuary; my therapist arrived soon, and after a while, Rabbi Margaret Holub, whom I had never met, joined us. I could not remember the last time I had been in temple—likely for a wedding or Bar Mitzvah in the family. This temple was different from those of my youth; it was in a simple room in a beautiful setting near the ocean, with hand-hewn, earthy woodwork.

As the three of us sat in silence, I focused my gaze on the *ner tamid*, the eternal light suspended above the Ark that held the Torah. At the time, I was not aware of the meaning of the ner tamid but found myself drawn to the humble yet powerful light it emitted in this otherwise darkened room. At some point, I had a sense of many pairs of hands, crossed over my heart, beginning to separate, as if my heart were being unlocked in subsequent layers. As each pair of hands separated, I felt my heart opening and becoming more and more present. As the hands unlocked successive layers of my heart, I heard a voice saying, "*And it is a Jewish heart. And it is a Jewish heart.*" The words surprised and moved me deeply. Tears flowed from my eyes as I allowed myself to silently surrender to, and be transformed by, this experience.

I began to allow myself to feel my sadness and fear about my mother's illness. As I did so, I understood that I did not need to fear that my grief could not be contained, for the temple itself *was* the container, designed to hold us in the depths of our suffering. Feeling held by the temple, I allowed myself to surrender to the grief that was present in me for the first time since receiving the news.

Following the Yom HaShoah service, I walked out to my car. I discovered that I had parked the passenger wheels in a ditch off the side of the road and was unable to get out. I went back inside the temple to call the towing service. As I entered, I suddenly recalled my dream from the night before of my car getting stuck on the side of the road. It felt important to pay attention to what was unfolding. I entered the temple and found that everyone had gone except Rabbi Margaret, who graciously helped me contact AAA. Thankfully, this was before the advent of cellphones, which meant I spent an hour with Rabbi Margaret as we waited for the tow truck to arrive. As we sat together, I immediately felt drawn to her open and radiant presence, but I also felt awkward, a feeling that typified my feelings in Jewish religious settings—perhaps a holdover from my teenage years of attending temple with friends when my family were not members and burning with the shame that I literally did not "belong."

Rabbi Margaret, much to my surprise, asked directly about my relationship with Judaism and inquired about whether I felt like an outsider. I was raised in environments where if you did not "belong" to the temple, you were held at arm's distance. This feeling of exile took up residence inside me. In addition, my maternal grandparents, who had both been raised in Orthodox homes had, in the years before I was born, become messianic Jewish missionaries—Jews who believed that Jesus was the Messiah.

As a young girl, I spent a lot of time at their mission in the Lower East Side of New York, feeding the homeless in the basement soup kitchen and wandering in and out of the chapel where my grandfather led services. As I was growing up, my grandparents were often referred to as "crazy" by others because of their spiritual beliefs, which did not help my conflicted sense of shame around their orientation. Our immediate family maintained our Jewish identity, and I was raised in predominantly Jewish neighborhoods in Brooklyn and Queens, went to Jewish summer camp throughout my childhood, and went to temple for Bar and Bat Mitzvahs of friends and family. Although I was drawn to Judaism as a teenager, as a young adult I never seriously considered Judaism as a spiritual path, and instead found myself drawn to earth-based and indigenous traditions.

Rabbi Margaret's questions offered a way to talk about something taboo—to reflect on my conflicted relationship to Judaism—something I had never been invited to speak about before and certainly not with a rabbi. I shared with her, in words that I had never spoken, even to myself, feelings of being an outsider in the temple growing up, feeling embarrassed that my family did not belong to the temple, and having internalized the judgment I received toward my grandparents. As we spoke, a light turned on inside me that allowed me to view my own relationship to Judaism, a burgeoning awareness of feeling so much shame and a fear of rejection, a hidden fear that there was something defective about my Judaism—so defective that maybe I could not even call myself a Jew.

Rabbi Margaret responded by sharing her own experience of having felt like an outsider to Judaism as she was growing up. That a rabbi was sharing this with me seemed remarkable. How could a *rabbi* have felt that alienated from Judaism? I always assumed that people who practiced Judaism had always felt a sense of inclusion that I lacked.

The most striking part of her story for me was when she described being part of a Christian commune for a short time during the early 1970s. "Wow!" I thought. A rabbi who had explored a Christian path! This touched the deepest part of my sense of outsiderness—in that moment, I realized how unconsciously I felt fear and shame that my grandparents' messianic Judaism had rendered me ineligible for membership in the Jewish community. Through the generosity of Rabbi Margaret's sharing of her personal struggle with me, I felt something I had always experienced unconsciously as a wall, turn into a gate—a gate that was swinging open for the first time in my consciousness. When the tow truck arrived, I left the temple, realizing that something had profoundly shifted in me.

And it is only now, in this writing, after returning from a recent trip to southern Spain, that I wonder about the imagery my psyche chose. The Rock of Gibraltar, situated between Spain and Morocco, crumbling, losing my foundation as I contemplated my mother's terminal illness, at the same site that hundreds of thousands of Jews passed through during the Inquisition in the late fifteenth century, wrenched from the land that had been home to Jews for over a millennium.

My return to Judaism arose from my depths, unbidden. A powerful uncon-scious process overtook my life, and being a follower of my dreams and visions, I responded. About two years prior to my meeting with Rabbi Margaret, I had attended a massage therapist training at Heartwood Institute in Northern California, where I was invited to participate in a Shabbat dinner. I was honored to be included, and after dinner we formed a circle, held hands, and sang Hebrew songs together. I did not know any of the songs, but I felt them resonating within me. My tears flowed freely, and I had the sense that even though I had never learned these songs, something deep within my soul recognized them.

After the week at Heartwood, I came across the work of Rupert Sheldrake, speaking about a phenomenon he calls *morphic field resonance*. Sheldrake states that when we enter into ritual, we constellate the *morphic field* of all people through all time and space who have engaged in this ritual.[2] I found myself won-dering if, at Heartwood, I had experienced a morphic field of Jewish ancestors throughout time who engaged in the ritual of Shabbat.

I was not seeking a return to Judaism at the time. Although I resonated with the tradition as a child and a young teenager, my burgeoning feminism made it difficult to relate to the prayerbooks and services that felt overbearingly patri-archal. Instead, my spiritual longings led me first to feminist, earth-based spir-ituality and then to Native American spiritual practices, which I was honored to engage in as part of my advocacy work on behalf of tribes facing dispossession and cultural genocide. I was completely floored when my Cherokee–Choctaw (and part Jewish) spiritual teacher, Jeane TuBears Jacobs, suggested that maybe I resonated with Native American teachings because I too came from a tribal peo-ple, as I in no way related to myself as being part of a tribe.

Practicing and learning Native American rituals raised concerns of cultural appropriation. At a legal conference I attended on ecological concerns, a Native American elder instructed the non-Native people there to discover the indigenous traditions we each came from. I longed for a tradition that felt like my own, but that carried the depth of the Native American practices of unceasing gratitude, interconnectedness, humility, and blessing. When I began to practice the morning blessings in Hebrew, I was profoundly surprised to discover that such gratitude and humility are central to Jewish daily practice.

Shortly before my conscious re-engagement with Judaism, TuBears taught me a shamanic journeying practice of connecting with my ancestors. I found myself receiving visitations from my eight great-grandparents, whom I experienced as a quaternity of four couples surrounding and guiding me. All of them came from the Pale of Settlement in Poland and Russia and almost all were Orthodox, although their religious practices were never discussed in my family.

After my encounter in the temple with Rabbi Margaret, as I deepened my rela-tionship with my ancestors, I found myself seeking opportunities to engage with Jewish rituals, practices, and teachings. I began studying at *Chochmat HaLev* in Berkeley, a center for Jewish meditation, and took a yearlong course in Jewish healing, taught by Jewish Renewal rabbis and others immersed in the Jewish mystical tradition.[3]

I began attending annual nationwide gatherings or *kallahs*, organized by Aleph Alliance for Jewish Renewal. What I experienced was remarkable. In Jewish Renewal, no longer were Jewish rituals conducted in a staid and rote format. Teachers ordained by Reb Zalman, as well as Jewish feminist theologians and those inspired by the *havurah* (egalitarian self-study) movement, gave rise to a flowering of spiritual expression that reclaimed the mystical Hasidic and earlier kabbalistic traditions of Judaism as a psychospiritual practice. The use of prayers, rituals, and teachings helped participants come into relationship with the Divine and be transformed by that engagement. The atmosphere of creativity, spontaneity, depth, and authenticity was both awe-inspiring and heart-opening.

The resonance was not just with the philosophical aspect of the teachings, but with the experience of embodiment and deep feeling, so absent from much of the Judaism I had experienced as a child. I attended my first Jewish Renewal kallah gathering several months after my mother's passing. When I registered, I was asked if I was in mourning. When I said I was, I was given a black ribbon to attach to my nametag and told that in the Holy Temple in Jerusalem, mourners would enter through a separate door during the first year of mourning. I was stunned to have my bereavement honored, so unlike my experience in the secular world in which my grief was rarely acknowledged beyond the first weeks following my mother's death.

I usually tended toward theoretical learning, but my intuition guided me to take a movement workshop with Rabbi Miriam Maron. As I moved with the others in our small group, the grief began to find its way out from the darkened crevices to the surface of my body. I felt the safety to allow my tears to flow. Miriam came close and began whispering Hebrew prayers into my ear, and as I surrendered to the grief, its intensity brought me to the ground. Miriam stayed with me, covering me with gentle fabrics and prayers. Enveloped by the Hebrew blessings, I felt the presence not only of my personal ancestors, but also of my people. I could fall apart, allowing the constricted vessel in which I was trying to hold my grief stoically and alone to shatter, trusting that I was held by something much larger.

I was also moved by the depth at which those around me were stirred by the rituals, prayers, and collective ecstasy. I felt drawn to know more about these people and the journeys they had been on—what had led them to this place of profound opening, and how was it affecting them psychologically and spiritually? The stories in this book are gathered from individuals who have made their own journey from alienation to a profound and heartfelt reconnection to Judaism through engagement with Jewish Renewal practices and community.

Some years ago, I participated in a Wiccan *Samhain* (autumnal equinox) ritual guided by Starhawk, a leader in reclaiming feminist and earth-based spirituality. Starhawk is currently integrating Wiccan and Jewish practices as a "Jewitch."[4] Starhawk invited us to journey to the Isle of Apples to visit with our ancestors.

As I meditated, I experienced my boat arriving on the Isle, and I sat hopefully waiting, inviting my ancestors to come. My maternal great-grandfather, Jacob, appeared and offered me his *tefilin* (prayer phylacteries) and suggested I deepen my daily spiritual practice. I asked him for guidance on my writing about Jews reconnecting with Judaism. He smiled broadly and said, *"Tell them what was beautiful about us."*

Notes

1 Ariel Bloch and Chana Bloch, trans., *The Song of Songs* (New York: The Modern Library, 1995).
2 Rupert Sheldrake, *The Presence of the Past: Morphic Resonance and the Memory of Nature* (New York: Park Street Press, 2012).
3 Teachers included Rabbis Gershon Winkler, Tirzah Firestone, Avram Davis, psychotherapist Estelle Frankel, and Rabbi Jonathan Omer-man who, for decades, worked closely with Adin Steinsaltz, translator of the Talmud, in Jerusalem.
4 Starhawk, *The Spiral Dance* (San Francisco, CA: HarperOne, 1999). See also http://www.jewitch.org/.

Part I

An historical overview of Jewish mysticism and psychology

Chapter 2

Renewing Jewish mysticism

The angel of memory

At birth, according to Talmudic legend, as our soul descends from the eternal realms into our earthly body, an angel guides and protects us on our journey.[1] Once we are born, the angel whispers into our ear the entire reason we incarnated, the lessons we agreed to undergo to grow our souls, and the ways in which this incarnation will bring about our spiritual evolution. In another rendition, the angel teaches us the entire Torah when we are in our mother's womb. Then, once the entire story has been enfolded into our consciousness, the angel places its finger over our mouths, saying gently, "Shush." In that moment, although the pattern of our life's trajectory lives on in our unconscious, the story is lost to our conscious awareness. We only know that it happened because we feel the indentation above the center of our lips, where the angel's finger has left its imprint.

Our soul's connection with Judaism may feel this way to us—buried deeply in our unconscious, it comes to us in dreams and in moments of reverie, perhaps when hearing a Yiddish or Ladino melody or a Hebrew prayer. Like the mysterious Shulamit whose beloved calls to her in the Song of Songs, our yearning is awakened. As we answer the call, we embark on a journey that leads us to the garden of our becoming.

Many modern Jews grew up either in secular, culturally Jewish homes, maintaining certain of its customs, or in families where spiritual observance often felt rote and devoid of deeper meaning. These experiences reflect the turning away from the mythic depths that characterize modern Judaism. Having survived anti-Semitic reigns of terror throughout two millennia of European history, Jews experiencing opportunities to assimilate into central European culture in the 19th century developed a version of Judaism that was based in the values of the Enlightenment, called the *Haskalah*. Jewish theologians distanced themselves from the mystical roots of Judaism, which were devalued as superstitious and irrational. The aspiring classes of Central European Judaism sought to distance themselves from the religious practices of the Eastern European shtetls and their poorer Jewish cousins, which highlighted Judaism's difference from Christianity. The Judaism that most 20th-century Jews experienced was often a product of this rejection of the numinous, which led many to experience Judaism as lacking depth or meaning.

As we rediscover the mystical depths of the tradition, we are surprised to find that Judaism itself is not, as is often characterized, a religion made up of solely of laws and edicts, but is also hewn from the dreams and visions of the early ancestors, fashioned from numinous encounters between men and women with the living God that spoke to and guided the unfolding of their lives and destinies. The cosmology of Judaism is replete with mystical tales and its folklore filled with supernatural occurrences. This is a world of enchantment, in which every aspect of life is infused with deep spiritual significance, and in which all actions are seen as opportunities for spiritual service and growth.[2]

The following chapters seek to make meaning of the loss of soul engendered by the disconnection from the depths of Jewish collective memory. I begin by exploring how the central story of Judaism, the story of the Exodus, speaks to the soul's journey of loss and redemption.

The story of the Exodus and healing from collective trauma

Silenced by the horror of the Holocaust, Jews struggled to find a way to speak about or understand God. Rabbi Edward Feld suggests that turning to our own Jewish texts might offer us a way out of the overwhelming sense of despair and loss.[3]

Coming into a relationship with our Jewish identity and heritage in the face of the devastation of the Shoah is a fundamental task of all Jewish people. Surely there are no clear, easy, or satisfactory answers to the questions raised by the annihilation of one-third of the world's Jewish people and the decimation of Jewish culture in Europe. Yet perhaps exploring the experience of disconnection from the sacred and mythic imagination of Judaism and its resurgence in the individual and collective psyche can give us some insight into how we can continue to grow in the wake of cultural devastation.

In other epochs of mass devastation—following the destruction of the Second Temple in Jerusalem in the 1st century CE, after the Spanish Inquisition in the Middle Ages, and during the widespread reign of terror in Eastern Europe in the 17th and 18th centuries—Jews responded with an upsurge of mystical creativity that helped them maintain faith in the face of overwhelming devastation and despair. Each of these periods gave rise to a new expression of Jewish mysticism, as explored here.

In the wake of the Shoah and the profound loss of faith engendered by its unfathomable cruelty and losses, Jews had already experienced decades of disconnection from Judaism's core practices and healing myths, and were largely unable to draw on the tradition to support them in their devastation and grief. Rabbi Zalman Schachter-Shalomi, founder of the stream of Judaism that came to be called Jewish Renewal, saw that the language of the past had to be updated to speak meaningfully to modern Jews. Yet as Jews became increasingly assimilated, they had also grown through their engagement with psychology, science, social activism, feminism, and ecological and global consciousness. Reb Zalman believed that a paradigm shift was required in order to bring Jews into connection with the mythic consciousness that had become so deeply obscured and that also integrated the wisdom of secular consciousness.[4]

Some years ago, the Dalai Lama, meeting with Reb Zalman and other Jewish leaders, was interested in how Jews were able to keep their religion intact in a diaspora lasting several millennia. Reb Zalman credited the observance of the Passover Seder as central to Jewish survival.[5] During Passover, Jewish families gather in their own homes and recite the story of the Exodus. We inhabit the reality of our ancestors—recognizing that "we" were slaves in Egypt. We take personally the experience of moving from near annihilation to a miraculous reconnection with a Divine Presence we thought had long since abandoned us. This reconnection guides our steps, allowing us to leave the "narrow place" of *mitzrayim*, and enables us to take a leap of faith into the Red Sea—which miraculously parts, opening toward a Promised Land flowing with milk and honey.

The Song of Songs, a beautiful erotic poem, chanted on Shabbat during Passover, is the esoteric corollary to the Exodus story. The reclamation of the immanent feminine Presence, the Shekhinah, has been central to the revisioning of 21st-century Judaism. The feminine corresponds to the mythic aspects of consciousness, whereas the masculine is associated with logic and rationality. Modern Judaism developed an overreliance on the rational, and disavowed the mystical aspects of the tradition. As the mystical heart of Judaism is reclaimed, we move closer to bringing together the Divine lovers in the Song of Songs, weaving together the mystical and rational, creating psychic wholeness.

When we learn that there are deeper mythic layers to the Biblical text, it can open to us—the Beloved beckoning in the secret language of lovers. The Zohar, or the Book of Splendor, the central text of kabbalah, was written by Moses de Leon in 13th-century Spain. Prior to the Zohar, de Leon also wrote a text called *Pardes (Paradise)*.[6] He used the four consonants of the word *Pardes* as a guide to understanding the teachings of the Torah on multiple levels, represented by the root letters: *P, R, D, S*. The first level is the *p'shat* or literal meaning of the story. The second level, *remez*, corresponds to the allegorical meaning. The third level, *derash*, is where we amplify the text through the great teachings of rabbinic scholars and sages as well as through our own insights. The fourth level, *sod*, is the mystical or hidden meaning of the text.[7] Most of us are familiar only with the literal meaning of the story; we have neither been introduced to the treasure trove of midrashic stories that have emerged over millennia, nor to the mystical meaning in kabbalah. When we discover these deeper levels of meaning, we see that the Torah contains profound, multidimensional layers.

The central story of the Biblical text, the Exodus, is about moving from exile to redemption. This story is a vessel into which Jewish experiences of disconnection and reconnection, of exile and return, have been developed and deepened by rabbinic and mystical interpretations, or *midrash*, over the course of two thousand

years. These interpretations arise from lived experience, wisdom forged in the crucible of surviving centuries of anti-Semitic terror—the Crusades, the Inquisition,
pogroms, and ultimately the Shoah—followed by an unprecedented acceleration
of assimilation in our own time. Engaging with the teachings of our own holy
sages, we may be moved by how much wisdom and insight they shed on our
current understanding of ways to sustain a connection with the sacred in the face
of overwhelming historical forces of collective trauma and the threatened loss
of our own mythic inheritance. Remarkably, the psychological truths contained
in these midrashic teachings reflect current psychological understandings about
how we are affected by and heal from trauma. Jungian analyst John O. Wilson has
observed that people and cultures heal and recover from trauma in a phenomenon
he calls *post-traumatic growth*. Healing from personal and collective trauma is
supported by the culture's own mythic stories of recovery and regeneration.[8]

The movement out of Egypt is commemorated in daily prayers as well as in the
annual celebration of Passover. In Hasidic mysticism, this journey is also viewed
as the movement from small mind, *mochin d'katnut*, to expansive mind, *mochin
d'gadlut*; from the narrow perception that we are alone in the world to the awakened
understanding that we participate in a larger consciousness. On a personal level, it
is a map of spiritual and psychological development, a story of individuation, of
becoming one's truest self. On a collective level, it is a story about healing from the
exile of historical upheavals and growing stronger in a community of faith.

Kabbalah: myth and meaning

Kabbalah is translated as both "received" or "tradition," referring to its deriving from the oral tradition said to have been taught to Adam in the Garden of
Eden by the angel Raziel, and passed through the generations in mystery schools.[9]
Mysticism, the direct personal experience of the Divine, flowered following historical epochs in which Jews faced catastrophic change. Periods of collective
trauma were often followed by the emergence a new mystical view that sought to
make meaning out of the devastation of Jewish life.[10] As the outer forms of Jewish
life and practice were devastated, adherents were compelled to go deep within to
do the work of soul healing and seek ways to stay connected with the divine.

Gershom Scholem observes that:

> [T]he spiritual experience of the mystics was almost inextricably intertwined
> with the historical experience of the Jewish people … . The more sordid,
> pitiful, and cruel the fragment of the historical reality allotted to the Jew
> amid the storms of exile, the deeper and more precise the symbolic meaning
> it assumed, and the more radiant became the Messianic hope which burst
> through it and transfigured it…. At the heart of this reality lay a great image
> of rebirth, the myth of exile and redemption.[11]

Elliot Ginsburg notes that the writing of the Hebrew Bible, or Torah, closed with the canonization of the rabbinical writings in the 1st century. However, the ongoing act of telling the sacred story reopened almost immediately through rabbinic interpretation preserved as midrash. Because the "master narrative assumes that the divine Word is pregnant with multiple meanings," a "suite of images, arguments, readings and narratives, all rooted in the evolving Myth of the Multi-Tiered Torah" emerged through folklore, storytelling, and other forms of Biblical interpretation through the ages.[12]

Hebrew religious texts, imbued with rich mythic meaning, are "storehouses of untold riches."[13] Jungian analyst Bettina Knapp notes that the texts take numerous forms, including myths, legends, short stories, fables, parables, poetry, and drama. More than simply expressing knowledge, they evoke the *numinosum*, the feelings and sensations engendered when one experiences mystery.[14]

Jung observed, "Our psychology, our whole lives, our language and imagery are built upon the Bible."[15] Jung saw humanity in a time of metaphysical transition from religious faith to a psychological understanding of Biblical motifs. Between these two viewpoints "lies a dark valley, the valley of lost faith, alienation, meaninglessness and despair."[16] For those secure in their faith, the emergence of a psychological view of the texts is merely interesting. But for those who are alienated from its meaning, the emerging psychological approach may be potentially life-saving.[17]

Jung was addressing himself to those for whom "the light has gone out, the mystery has faded, and God is dead."[18] For these people, returning to a place of faith was not possible, nor was it clear that this was the best option. Instead, he suggested they move toward a psychological understanding of religious myth and symbol, by "melt[ing] down" myths and images from historically fixed ideas and translating them into "immediate experience."[19] He observed that Jews had "long since anticipated the development of [the study of] consciousness in [their] own spiritual history. By this I mean the … Kabbalah."[20]

Jungian analyst Edward Edinger saw the Hebrew Bible as a "grand treasury of individuation symbolism," the "ark of the covenant in which resides the power and glory of the transpersonal psyche."[21] The Biblical text reflects a continuing dialogue between God and humans, expressed through the unfolding history of the Jewish people. The story is told in a series of individual encounters with the numinous. In this motif, powerful psychological work follows the individual's encounter with the Divine and archetypal realms, achieving transformation of the ego. This is the essence of individuation, for which the Bible provides a powerful guide.[22]

Arthur Green notes that as we grapple with and live in the light of mythic paradigms contained in Jewish mythic imagination, "devotees feel themselves touched by a transcendent presence that is made real in their lives through the retelling, the re-enactments."[23]

The exile and the flowering of mysticism

In the mystical perspective, in the ancient Temple in Jerusalem, the center of Jewish collective life, the masculine, transcendent and the immanent feminine aspects of the Divine were joined in holy union.[24] This cosmic wholeness was shattered with the destruction of the Second Temple in the 1st century CE, which destroyed the foundation of Jewish collective life. Rabbis meeting in exile codified the books comprising what we now know as the Hebrew Bible, and created a system of rabbinic Judaism that enabled the continuation of Jewish life in diaspora.

In the aftermath of the destruction of the Second Temple, mysticism flowered, enabling direct experience of the Divine in the absence of a physical spiritual center. *Merkabah* mysticism, named for Ezekiel's vision of the Chariot, and the closely related *Hekhalot* mysticism, envisioned heavenly palaces that one could access in mystical states. Based in communion with angelic beings, these mystical views espoused a perspective that the chariot's descent into the depths of the soul offers a pathway for an ascent into the highest realms of spiritual understanding.

In *Hekhalot* mysticism, heaven is inhabited not by a solitary God, as we are often taught, but is comprised of seven heavens, each "filled with angels and other divine beings, such as the Messiah." In this realm, we find the celestial Temple, which mirrors the Temple in the earthly Jerusalem, "as well as an abundance of heavenly palaces, one for each of the patriarchs and matriarchs and sages, where he or she teaches Torah to the attentive souls of the righteous and the angels."[25]

Perhaps the shift of the locus of religious life from the physical Temple to the upper heavenly realms of the throne of God, and the angels surrounding it, allowed the people to transport the tradition as they were forced into exile in Greece, Egypt, and other areas in Europe and North Africa. This teaching also provided a way to understand how the descent into the depths of exile as the walls of the Temple and Jewish civilization collapsed, could ultimately lead to spiritual ascent.

Jews migrated widely in the Mediterranean following the destruction of the Second Temple in the 1st century CE, settling as far as Spain.[26] There, Jewish scholarship and mystical teachings flowered. The 500 years preceding the Inquisition in the 15th century marked the Golden Age of Spain, in which Jews, Muslims, and Christians coexisted for extended periods of relative harmony.[27] Spain was also where medieval kabbalah developed. The Zohar, or the Book of Radiance, the central text of kabbalah, was written by Moses de Leon in the 13th century, as the forces that eventually gave rise to the Inquisition were gaining strength and Jewish life was increasingly restricted. De Leon attributed the Zohar's origin to the 2nd-century Rabbi Shimon bar Yochai who, according to legend, was guided by the spirit of the prophet Elijah. Shimon bar Yochai was said to have received the teachings while spending years in a cave, hiding from the Romans who were imposing their rule over Israel following the destruction of the Temple and the beginning of diasporic existence.[28] Bar Yochai's isolation strikingly illustrates the deeply inward turn of mystics to connect with spiritual guidance in the face of catastrophic outer circumstances, an archetypal image that may have sustained Spanish Jews facing increasing anti-Semitism.

The Zohar emerged from a vibrant community of kabbalistic scholars in Spain who drew on earlier forms of Jewish mysticism that had developed over the centuries, including the *Bahir* and the *Sefer Yetzirah*, and centuries of midrashic interpretations of the Biblical texts, to further develop a mystical cosmology.[29]

The Zohar offered a mystical view of Creation, which begins with the *Ein Sof*, the aspect of God that is beyond form or comprehension. The Ein Sof emanates supernal light into the world through the Tree of Life, comprised of ten *sefirot*, or emanations. The Tree of Life is also represented as the primordial human, *Adam Kadmon*. As the supernal light moves into the upper three sefirot of the Tree, it is gestated in the womb of *Binah* (understanding), the Upper Mother. Binah gives birth to the lower seven sefirot, the building blocks of Creation. The tenth sefirah, *Malkhut* (kingdom), is associated with the *Shekhinah*, the Divine Feminine. It is through the Shekhinah that the world comes into manifestation.[30]

The Zohar revolutionized Jewish observance by reclaiming the centrality of the Sacred Feminine once expressed in the Holy Temple, viewing the Godhead as a holy couple of masculine and feminine counterparts—the *Kadosh Baruch Hu*, the Blessed Holy One, representing the transcendent Ein Sof, and the immanent aspect of Divinity manifest in Creation, the Shekhinah. According to the Zohar, the very order of the cosmos was shattered by their separation. The holy couple was first separated when Adam and Eve ate the fruit of the Tree of Knowledge of Good and Evil in the Garden of Eden. Because they partook only of the Tree of Knowledge, a representation of the Shekhinah, they separated Her from Her husband, associated with *Tif'eret*, the Tree of Life.[31] Psychologically, this reflects how the ego may arrogate to itself a spiritual experience and become inflated, rather than recognizing its connection to the Divine Source.

Adam, wandering outside after being exiled from the Garden, was met by the Shekhinah, and they went into exile together.[32] When the Temple in Jerusalem stood, the Kadosh Baruch Hu and the Shekhinah dwelt there together. When the Temple was destroyed, the Shekhinah again went into exile, this time with the entire Jewish people.[33] This separation of the Shekhinah from the Kadosh Baruch Hu correlates to the human experience of being separated from the Source.[34]

The Zohar taught that the Messiah, the emergence of a new and holy consciousness, would be brought about by the reunification of the holy couple, which could be hastened by following the commandments (*mitzvot*) with the intention of reunification. We can get a glimpse of the elevated consciousness that awaits us when the world is redeemed during the Sabbath and on certain holy days. From a Jungian perspective, this redemption alludes to the unification of the ego with the Self.

The Jews in Spain suffered another cataclysmic exile shortly after the Zohar was written. In the late 15th century, the Muslim-ruled southern part of Spain was conquered, and in 1492, Catholic monarchs Ferdinand and Isabella expelled the entire Jewish and Muslim populations.[35] Under the Spanish Inquisition, Jews were forced to convert or live as secret Jews adopting an outer appearance of Catholicism (called *conversos* or *marranos*), or be tortured or executed.

While Catholic forces consolidated their conquest of southern Spain in 1492, leading Jewish advisers such as Judah don Abravanel and others invested in the exploration of new lands and contributed to the campaign of Christopher (Cristobal) Columbus. Columbus wrote, "After the Spanish monarchs had expelled all the Jews from their kingdoms and lands in January, in that same month they commissioned me to undertake the voyage to India with a properly equipped fleet."[36] Jews fleeing Spain during the Inquisition were among the earliest settlers in the United States. In communities in the Southwest, some people who were not consciously aware of any Jewish ancestry are now recognizing that candlesticks handed down in the family for generations or family practices of candle lighting on Friday nights, are part of Jewish tradition, even though their families never outwardly identified as Jews.[37]

Some rabbis and their families fleeing Spain in the late 15th century settled in Safed, Palestine. There, Jewish mysticism continued to flower under the guidance of Rabbi Isaac Luria, who was born in Jerusalem and raised in Egypt. Luria offered a new interpretation of the Biblical story of Creation. In the beginning, all was God. In order to create the world, the Ein Sof withdrew Itself and created a space in which the world could be born. This withdrawal was called *tzimtzum*. In the space created, God emanated supernal light to create existence. God poured the supernal light into the ten sefirot, but because God's light was too powerful, each of these ten vessels shattered, causing the divine light to be scattered all over Creation. These "divine sparks" need to be uncovered from where they are concealed under the broken shards of the shattered vessels, called *kelipot*. As we uncover the holy light from beneath the shards or kelipot and return it to its Source, we participate in the healing of the world, called *tikkun olam*.[38] Luria's cosmological view reflects the awareness that the world is imperfect, and unable to contain the light of the Divine, symbolizing the world-shattering experience Jews suffered during the Inquisition.

The emergence of this new view of Creation allowed Jews devastated by the Inquisition to maintain faith in God's presence by acknowledging the flawed nature of the world and by giving humans a role in its healing. Creation itself needed human participation to attain perfection. As each of us contribute to the healing of the world, we hasten the coming of the Messiah—that is, a consciousness in alignment with the Divine patterning.

Throughout the two millennia following the destruction of the Temple, Jews in other parts of Europe also lived with great uncertainty, as periods of relatively peaceful coexistence with the dominant culture were often alarmingly upended when political and economic pressures led rulers to scapegoat Jews in pogroms, mass relocations, and other campaigns of terror. In the mid-17th century, a campaign of terror was unleashed against Eastern European Jews, and tens of thousands were slaughtered in the Chmielnicki massacres.

In the 17th century, many Jews were convinced that the Messiah had come in the person of the charismatic mystic Sabbatai Tzvi, whose followers numbered in the tens of thousands. Tzvi's appeal heightened following the Chmielnicki massacres. When Tzvi was captured in Turkey and given the choice to either convert to Islam or be executed, his conversion shattered the hopes of followers. In the aftermath of the profound betrayal many felt after his conversion, Jewish leaders anxiously guarded against the power of messianic mystical fervor.

Despite this proscription against mystical teachings among many rabbis, tremendous feelings of terror, grief, and uncertainty following the Chmielnicki massacres led others to turn toward it. A hidden esotericism was now popularized and made available to uneducated Jews through the work of the *Baal Shem Tov*, meaning Master of the Good Name (born Israel Eliazer). The Baal Shem Tov was the founder of modern Hasidism, a movement that grew rapidly among peasant Jews in the shtetls (traditional Jewish villages) of Eastern Europe in the 18th and 19th centuries. He and his followers developed practices that were ecstatic and joyous. *Devekut*, a practice of cleaving to God's presence, first developed by medieval Spanish kabbalist Abraham Abulafia, was popularized and achieved through chanting sacred wordless melodies called *nigunim*, ecstatic dance, and mystical stories that lifted the spirits of the people, enabling many without extensive schooling to experience a direct connection with the sacred.

Hasidism emphasized the cultivation of a direct connection with God through a personal relationship with the Shekhinah, the Sacred Feminine, immanent aspect of the Divine. Jungian analyst Bettina Knapp observes that practices of connection to the souls of ancestors offered a balm to many whose ancestral lineages were devastated by the massacres.[39] Hasidism also drew on the work of medieval kabbalist Isaac Luria and the teachings in the Zohar that emphasized human participation in ending exile by redeeming the shattered sparks of divinity through engaging in good deeds (*mitzvot*), charitable efforts (*tzedakah*), and deep prayer (*tefilah*). It was through such acts that the reunification of the masculine and feminine aspects of God would be achieved, leading to the coming of the Messiah, the realization of evolved consciousness.

Haskalah enlightenment and the loss of connection to the mystical depths

In the early to mid-19th century, a revolutionary fervor swept Central Europe, challenging old forms of monarchy and feudalism. During this time, reforms were passed that granted new freedoms for Jews, formerly segregated in ghettoes and limited in their ability to participate in business and social life. Although social and economic restrictions eased, the seeds of a reactionary and virulent anti-Semitism were taking hold, which would erupt into the mass murder of Jews on a scale that far surpassed previous anti-Semitic purges. These countervailing forces of history led to a powerfully conflicted identity for Jews.

Increasing opportunities for assimilation in Central Europe gave rise to the Jewish Enlightenment, or *Haskalah* movement, in the early to mid-19th century. With more opportunity to participate in the dominant culture, many Jews sought to minimize the differences that had been used to oppress them, distancing themselves from their religious and cultural identity. The rate at which European Jews were leaving Judaism in favor of a secular and assimilated identity caused reasonable concern that the Jewish religion itself would not continue. Reform Judaism sought to provide a way for Jews to maintain their religious identity while adopting the more rationalist approaches of modern life. Conservative Judaism sought to maintain observant rituals while also allowing for the realities of rampant assimilation. Yet both approaches created distance from the mystical roots of Judaism, favoring a more rationalist approach that did not appear too culturally distinct from the dominant Christian culture. In this process, the connection to the mystical depths was severed.

At the same time, in Eastern Europe, many Jews continued to live in shtetls, terrorized by the violence of pogroms and the forced conscription of young Jewish men into military service, from which many never returned. Many young Jews of this time made their way to cities and joined the growing movements for social justice in Central and Eastern Europe. Many Eastern European Jews increasingly rejected the religious messianic hopes of their Hasidic families and instead sought to bring about change through social justice movements, sparked by the secularized messianic vision of Karl Marx. Jews became central in the anarchist, socialist, and communist revolutions in the late 19th and early 20th centuries, seeking to bring about a future in which class and religious distinctions gave way to an egalitarian society.

In the years between 1880 and 1920, over two million Eastern European Jews immigrated to the United States. They were welcomed and acculturated by Jews who had immigrated in the preceding decades from Germany and other parts of Central Europe and who had built a network of Reform and Conservative temples.

Eastern European Jews often left behind the Yiddish spoken in the shtetls and the deep connection to Jewish mysticism, and most American Jews adopted either a secular or assimilated Jewish identity. Gone were the visionary and mystical states that lay at the center of Orthodox Jewish practice. Instead Jews attended synagogues that looked increasingly like Protestant churches, abandoned or minimized Hebrew in favor of English, and began disconnecting Judaism from what was perceived as an archaic past weighed down by superstitious rituals.

Scholem recognized that as Jews became increasingly assimilated, "scholars were perplexed and embarrassed" by Jewish mysticism.[40]

The Shoah

During the Second World War, from 1939 to 1945, the entire Jewish culture in Europe and two-thirds of European Jewry, comprising one-third of the world's Jewish population, was annihilated in the Holocaust. Of the nearly nine million

Jews who lived in Europe before the war, two out of every three were murdered.[41] Close to ninety percent of traditional Jewish communities were destroyed, including rabbis carrying wisdom lineages that had been in continuous existence since the time of the Roman Empire.[42]

The destruction of the European Jewish community and the near-complete loss of the Yiddish language created an irreparable rupture in the transmission of collective Jewish memory, resulting in a staggering loss of religiously and culturally identified Jews, and creating a crisis of survival for Judaism as a viable religion and as a cultural identity.[43] Historian David Biale reflects that our current period can only be compared to the "great sea change that took place with the destruction of the Temple by the Romans in the first century."[44]

The shattering of the belief in God in the wake of the Shoah left many Jews focused solely on historiographical memory. Historian Yusef Yerushalmi observes that in the mid- to late 20th century, Jews had become so separated from the deeper meaning of their rituals that there was little understanding of how these could offer solace or sustenance to help navigate the devastation and despair.

Those fleeing the Old World at the turn of the 20th century often found the past filled with memories too painful to bear. They slammed the door against the nightmares of pogroms, forced conscriptions, deprivation, and later, the unfathomable horrors of the Shoah. Yet, in closing this door, they also cut off connection to the language of their ancestors and to the mystical wisdom lineages.

Yerushalmi observes that the bridge to the collective memory of Judaism—the storehouse of its rich teachings, spiritual wisdom, and healing practice—had been ruptured. Jews had lost touch with the depths of their ancestral spiritual treasure.[45]

Jews in the postwar era also became increasingly distant from their connection to Jewish identity through social justice movements such as the Workmens' Circle. The sense of betrayal when Stalin entered into a non-aggression pact with Hitler, the devastation of the Shoah, followed by the McCarthy-era blacklist witch-hunts in the 1950s, all led many to focus instead on creating material stability and safety.

Judaism has been safeguarded from the time of the first ancestors, Abraham and Sarah, over thousands of centuries by its transmission *dor l'dor*, from generation to generation. Most Jews descend from families that just two generations ago were deeply immersed in a spiritual practice that formed the fabric of daily, weekly, and annual rituals. Spirituality infused every aspect of life. Tragically, most Jews alive today cannot trace their family lineage back more than two or three generations.

The esoteric kabbalistic approach to Judaism—based in myth and direct mystical experience—was largely forgotten or dismissed as a holdover from a time many were eager to distance themselves from, a time fraught with deprivation and trauma. Today, many Jews would be amazed to discover that their own grandparents and great-grandparents in Eastern European shtetls or Sephardic shuls were deeply familiar with an approach that had at its center a longing for the Shekhinah, the feminine immanent aspect of the Divine.

Reclaiming Jewish mysticism

Writing in the early 20th century, Martin Buber, born into an assimilated German Jewish family, was drawn to the mystical aspect of Judaism widely rejected by the reigning rationalist approach of the Haskalah enlightenment. Buber explored the inner experience facilitated by the mystical practices of Hasidism. Buber carried on the work of his grandfather Solomon, who translated midrashic literature (rabbinic interpretations of the Biblical text), making it widely available to modern readers for the first time.[46] In the foreword to a collection of Buber's addresses from the early 20th century, Rodger Kamenetz writes that Buber was "a prophet of our contemporary Jewish renewal," noting Buber's lecture in 1911 entitled, "Renewal of Judaism."[47]

In addition to philosophy, Buber also studied psychology and psychiatry with Eugen Bleuler in Zurich, a close associate of Carl Jung's, and presented to those developing Jungian psychology in 1920 at the Psychological Club in Zurich. He devoted his life to making the teachings of Hasidism available to a wide audience, and many assimilated Jews discovered the Jewish mystical tradition through his writings. His work was a profound influence on both Gershom Scholem and Erich Neumann.

Gershom (né Gerhard) Scholem was largely responsible for the recovery and valuing of kabbalah among 20th-century Jews. Born in Germany in 1897, he spent his youth immersed in the study of Jewish theology during the height of *Wissenschaft des Judentums* (Science of Judaism) rationalist approach to Jewish Studies. Whereas Buber focused on the works of Hasidism, Scholem studied and translated the classic texts of medieval Jewish mystics, which had been widely discarded by the mainstream Jewish scholars of his day.

Scholem was profoundly moved by the beauty and depth of the Jewish mystical tradition he found in the texts that were largely overlooked or devalued in the rationalist climate of the time, including the Zohar and the teachings of Isaac Luria. Aware of the looming threat of Nazism, Scholem immigrated to Palestine in 1923. There, he dedicated his life to recovering the ancient teachings that had been largely ignored by Haskalah rationalist Judaism.[48]

Scholem was influenced by his close friendship with German Jewish philosopher Walter Benjamin, who took his own life in 1940 when, after being captured by the Nazis, he chose death over deportation to the concentration camps. Benjamin explored the meaning of collective memory in the individual psyche. He understood that throughout millennia of diaspora, Jews had maintained their identity and withstood oppression by sustaining a view of collective history and memory that kept them connected to their ancestral past and to a vision of a redeemed future, in which the coming Messiah would herald a new era of enlightened consciousness.[49]

Scholem unearthed the largely lost and buried history of Jewish mystical thought and developed kabbalah as a discrete branch of Jewish textual study and as an academic discipline. Scholem made these teachings widely available for the first time, through translations into various languages. Writing in 1945, he recognized, "It is possible that what was termed degeneracy will be thought of as a revelation and light and what seemed to [19th-century historians] impotent hallucinations—will be revealed as a great living myth ... the discovery of hidden life by removal of the obfuscating masks."[50] He noted that the texts contained great treasures. "Wherever you touch, it is as if you touch gold, if you but have eyes to see."[51]

Scholem saw the development of Judaism as a monotheistic response to a previous era in which humans lived in a "pantheistic unity of God, cosmos and man." Judaism sought to definitively separate this unity into three separate realms, in which, above all, "the gulf between the Creator and His creation was regarded as fundamentally unbridgeable."[52] Kabbalah, the mystical tradition, in seeking to unify humans with the Divine, was an attempt to restore the original unity.

Following the Second World War, Scholem participated at the Eranos conferences along with Jung, Neumann, and other scholars of myth, religion, and psychology including Mircea Eliade, Victor White, Karl Kerényi, and Paul Tillich. There, Scholem shared his research with a wide audience and developed his ideas on comparative religion. His Eranos lectures were published in *On the Kabbalah and Its Symbolism* in 1965.

Erich Neumann, upon learning that Scholem was not planning on attending the conference in 1949, sent a letter to conference organizer Olga Fröbe-Kapteyn urging that money be made available for Scholem to attend. Neumann and Scholem thereafter maintained a mutually respectful relationship.[53] Scholem's personal library, maintained by the Scholem Collection at the National Library of Israel, contains many works by Jung, including some that were personally dedicated to him by the author.[54]

Speaking in 1963, Scholem reflected that the great epochs of mysticism often arose in times of historical crisis. The Jewish people had "undergone a crisis and catastrophe that are beyond the power of human words and language to express." He wondered whether a new epoch of mysticism might emerge in response to the horrors of the Shoah, but that the time needed for response was "in direct proportion to the depth of the shock."[55]

A renewed Judaism

Zalman Schachter-Shalomi was born in Poland in 1924 and raised in Vienna. He and his family escaped the Holocaust and came to the United States in 1940, where he was ordained as a Hasidic rabbi in 1947. Studying transpersonal and humanistic psychology and the psychology of religion at Boston University, Reb Zalman soon found Orthodox Judaism too constraining.[56]

Reb Zalman saw that the core mystical teachings of the Baal Shem Tov and other Hasidic masters from the 18th and 19th centuries had a great deal to offer the devastated spirit of the Jewish people suffering from losses inflicted in the pogroms of Eastern Europe in the 19th and early 20th centuries and from the horrors of the Shoah. He saw that the mystical tradition was largely unknown to most American Jews. Yet he also understood that the social strictures of orthodoxy made the mystical teachings inaccessible to counterculture youth seeking spiritual meaning.

Reb Zalman, a brilliant theorist and professor of comparative religion, drew on the insights of both Jungian and humanistic psychology, including the work of Erich Neumann and Abraham Maslow, to create an experiential approach to Jewish mysticism that was psychospiritual in nature. He saw that the practices of the mystics provided a technology of the sacred, designed to facilitate soul growth. He presented the teachings in ways that spoke to the social currents of the time—feminist, infused with the desire for social justice, and acknowledging the Eastern wisdom traditions that had opened the doors of consciousness for so many.

As he separated from the Hasidic movement, Reb Zalman continued his work introducing the postwar generation of American Jewish seekers to the treasures of Jewish mysticism and kabbalistic wisdom. He connected with Arthur Green, a founder of the havurah movement, which sought to deepen the study and practice of Judaism in collaborative communities that were feminist, ecologically aware, politically progressive, and nonhierarchical.[57] Green later headed the Reconstructionist Rabbinical College, where he infused this denomination with mystical insights. Green has written extensively on Hasidism and the relevance of their teachings to our current era.[58]

Reb Zalman also worked closely with communities in Northern California, including the Aquarian Minyan havurah in Berkeley, California. Burt Jacobson, a rabbi and scholar on the Hasidic master the Baal Shem Tov, was involved in both the creation of the havurah and Jewish Renewal movements, founding the Jewish Renewal congregation Kehilla in Oakland.

The House of Love and Prayer in San Francisco was founded in 1968 by followers of Reb Zalman and Rabbi Shlomo Carlebach, who also emigrated from Europe during the Shoah. Although not formally part of Jewish Renewal, Carlebach influenced many of the rabbis and teachers associated with it, who found their relationship to Judaism through the ecstatic communal musical gatherings at the House of Love and Prayer.[59] It has come to light in recent years that Carlebach committed serious boundary violations with several women devotees.[60]

In 1975, Reb Zalman and his followers in Philadelphia began a community called *P'nai Or* (Faces of Light). Kamenetz notes that Zalman "helped his followers integrate the feminism, ecological awareness, progressive politics, and egalitarianism of the havurah movement with a universalized Hasidic mysticism. The movement called itself Jewish Renewal."[61] P'nai Or has since become *Aleph: Alliance for Jewish Renewal.*[62] This emergent expression of Judaism drew on the mystical teachings of medieval kabbalah and Hasidism, putting insights drawn from Buber, Neumann, and Scholem into practice.

Reb Zalman observed that there have been three stages of Judaism: Temple Judaism (the time of the ancient Temple in Jerusalem), rabbinic Judaism (the religious response to the diaspora), and the present time. After Auschwitz, he believed Jews needed something different than what rabbinic Judaism could offer.[63] He proposed a paradigm shift in Judaism that was based in a revisioning of the root metaphors of Judaism. Although we are taught that religious truths are fixed, as we deepen in our discovery of the true nature of consciousness, we realize that discovery of religious truth is an ongoing process.[64] With this awareness, he suggested that we reconceptualize God and the sacred, and our relationship to it, as ever-unfolding. "Myth, too, then becomes a process, and by telling the story of that process, we see ourselves as part of that myth."[65]

Jewish Renewal continues the work begun by Scholem and Buber in re-introducing moderns to the rich treasure trove of Jewish mythic imagination. Whereas patriarchal forms of Jewish practice favor logos, mythos is associated with the feminine, intuitive aspect of the tradition. As we engage with the mythic realms, our assumptions about the root meanings of Judaism as we have known it are upended.

Entering what Jewish studies scholar Jonathan Boyarin terms the "panchronistic conversation" across the generations that is the hallmark of Jewish aggregated wisdom, we see how the mystical wisdom that emerged from the crucible of historical trauma may have something to offer us as we wrestle to find a meaningful relationship to our tradition in the aftermath of the Shoah.[66]

This task of creating a new paradigm, as Reb Zalman recognized, requires a committed community of Jewish people with "transparent or at least translucent egos" who are able to continue this transformational work over several generations.[67] This revisioning requires a sensitivity to "new mythic deep structures" upon which the new paradigm may be based.[68] It requires a thorough knowing of the tradition, balanced within the rational and intuitive. It requires a living and committed connection with a prayer and meditation practice that connects one with the living God both in solitude and community.[69]

Sociologist Chava Weissler notes that Renewal did not seek to create a new denomination, but sought to infuse spirituality into existing Orthodox, Conservative, Reform, and Reconstructionist denominations.[70] Weissler found that the quest for experiential relationship with the Divine Presence was central to Renewal, and that other than in Orthodoxy, such mysticism did not exist in any other form of contemporary American Judaism.[71]

The paradigm shift envisioned by Reb Zalman draws on and develops ancient practices that facilitate connection with the Divine, or in Jungian terms, facilitate a bridge between ego and Self. Jewish laws of ritual observance (*halakhah*) are reconceptualized from dutiful observance into an opportunity to mindfully engage in and reflect on one's spiritual experience. Rabbi Daniel Siegel writes that in *psycho-halakhic* practice, the participant and community is in a relationship of dynamic tension with existing law and practice and may modify a practice that no longer resonates to create one that does, careful to ensure that the revised practice retains the original intention.[72]

Rabbi Shefa Gold suggests that the word *mitzvot*, commonly translated as "commandments," is related to the root of the Aramaic word meaning *connection*.

Engaging spiritual practices provides a pathway to connect with Source.[73] For Gold, the litmus test for the efficacy of practice is to whether it helps one connect to "the truth hidden inside this moment," and whether it makes one more compassionate.[74] In interpreting Torah for the present time, Gold actualizes her belief that the current generation, "like each generation of Jews has done before us, must enter into the holy conversation of our tradition. It is a conversation across time and distance that dies if we refuse to hold up our end."[75]

Rabbi Arthur Green writes that the most essential teaching of the Baal Shem Tov is that "God is Being itself. All of being. *Everything* contains God. There is not a place, not a moment, not a thing, certainly not a presence that is not filled to overflowing with the Divine Presence."[76]

Rabbi David A. Cooper notes that understanding mysticism may help transform conceptions of God that keep many from engaging spiritually. Cooper observes that God is a verb—the energy that is in the continual process of unfolding and perfecting the universe. Creation is an ongoing process, in which humans participate as co-creators. As humans need God, so too does God need humans for the work of redeeming and healing that which has been broken.[77]

Jewish Renewal draws on medieval and Hasidic mysticism to facilitate a felt experience of union with Divine consciousness, creating practices accessible to those lacking traditional Jewish education.[78] Prayer, meditation, and sacred chants open the psyche to the larger wisdom that may be available when we relativize the centrality of the ego.

Elliot Ginsburg describes the transformative potential of mystical practices of meditation and chanting, citing the teachings of Kolonymus Kalman Shapira of Piasetzna, a great Hasidic rabbi who died in the Warsaw ghetto during the Shoah.[79] Shapira taught that "Only silence can heal the scars and fissures found in Speech."[80] The ancient ones used to meditate for an hour before engaging in formal prayer, allowing them to connect with this highest realm. When they engaged in worded prayer following this meditative period, "they brought down the healing light of *Atzilut*/Pure Being, and the flowing presence of Divine Love and Awe and Beauty … into their words."[81]

Ginsburg describes the potency of the Hasidic practice of chanting a wordless melody, called a *niggun*.[82] The niggun's power rests on the teaching that God spoke the world into being. "In the beginning was silence."[83] Emerging from this silence, Divine thought moved into sound and speech. The devotee who chants a niggun, "returns the favor and reverses the process—turning speech first into sound and then into silence, while bringing the separated self back to the Divine Source."[84] Ginsburg notes that the Hasidic master Rabbi Nachman of Bratslav understood that sacred dance was also a powerful act of devotion, which healed both the individual and the Shekhinah, by stimulating the flow of sacred energy and opening blocked channels in both the person and the cosmos.[85]

Rabbi Nachman also developed the practice of *hitbodedut*, in which one engages in solitary meditative practice. Rabbi Steven Fisdel, a teacher of Jewish meditation, recognizes that, "When journeying toward God, one may pass through multiple realms of reality and many levels of experience." However, one makes that journey alone. As one pursues this journey, it results in *hitbonenut*, knowing oneself. Fisdel observes that the "benefit and purpose of meditation is the evolution of the Self, the growth and development of the Soul. One evolves, by experiencing more and more, on higher and higher levels of existence."[86]

Rabbi Marcia Prager recognizes Judaism as "the path of blessing," noting that blessings have been used by Jews throughout history to sanctify life's moments.[87] Part of the reclamation of Judaism is to understand the deep holiness of the Hebrew language. Prager explains, "The Holy One 'speaks' Creation into existence, so that each letter and word is resonant with divinity."[88] Entering deeply into the mystery and power of each letter and each word, many Jews unfamiliar with or disconnected from Hebrew are able to connect with its sacred meaning.[89]

David Rosenberg observes that in prayer, heartbreak is essential to access the kabbalistic cosmos. "The reader cannot understand the text unless he or she has offered his heart to be broken on the altar of poetry." [90]

Reclaiming the Divine Feminine

Rabbi Lynn Gottlieb explains that the term *Shekhinah*, coming from the Hebrew root meaning "to dwell or abide," first appears in 3rd-century rabbinic writings, where it was used as one of the names of God.[91] The term evolved from the word *Mishkan*, which refers to the Tabernacle constructed by the Hebrews while wandering in the desert, where God could dwell among the people.[92] This presence, represented in Biblical myth as a "cloud of glory" that accompanied the Jews in their wanderings through the desert, became known as the Shekhinah, who was said "to accompany the people in exile and would appear to them whenever the people occupied themselves with the study of Torah or performed good deeds."[93]

The concept of Shekhinah evolved and by the 16th century was increasingly identified as the feminine aspect of God.[94] Jungian analyst Siegmund Hurwitz notes that the emergence of kabbalah and Jewish mysticism in the Middle Ages brought forth a world full of mythic imagery where "the feminine takes its rightful place once more and regains its due rank."[95] The kabbalistic canon is replete with stories portraying the Shekhinah as the Bride of God, and the personification of the Sabbath as the Sabbath Bride.

As the companion of the Jewish people in exile, she is also in exile from God. Her exile will end with the coming of the Messiah, when the Holy Temple will be rebuilt. However, on the Sabbath, she is joined in a *hieros gamos* (sacred marriage) with God, and we are able to experience a taste of the messianic era.[96]

In the latter half of the 20th century, feminist theologians rediscovered the centrality of the Sacred Feminine, the Shekhinah, in both medieval and Hasidic mysticism, as well as the worship of the Hebrew Goddess in ancient Israel. As a manifestation of Divine immanence, She connects us with the sacred through our bodily felt experiences and through mythic imagination. In our own time, the symbolic meaning of the Shekinah's exile represents how an overly rationalized approach to Judaism separates us from the realms of mystical and mythic experience.

The reclamation of the Sacred Feminine in Judaism in the modern era was informed by extensive 20th century archeological discoveries of the Great Goddess in the Fertile Crescent area of the Middle East. The meaning of the Hebrew Goddess was recognized by Erich Neumann in his work in the 1950s in *The Great Mother*, and further explored by Raphael Patai in the late 1960s. Patai noted that the patriarchal orientation of Judaism was culturally bound.[97] Worship of the Hebrew Goddess is recognized in the Biblical text, where the Jewish people were castigated by the prophet Jeremiah for baking cakes in the shape of Astarte's headdress for the Queen of Heaven.[98] Perhaps worship of the Hebrew Goddess continues in ways that have become lost to consciousness, such as the continued practice of baking cakes at the time of the festival of Queen Esther (Purim), whose name closely parallels that of the early Hebrew Goddess Astarte.

Kabbalistic teachings, made more widely available through the work of Scholem on medieval mysticism and Martin Buber's work on Hasidism, shone a light on the role of the Shekhinah as an equal partner with the Kodesh Baruch Hu. Ginsburg notes the recognition in the Zohar of the Shekhinah as the Bride of God was a major development in Jewish mythology, "as the very notion of such a divine Bride is the essence of myth, echoing such pairs as Zeus and Hera in Greek mythology, and El and Asherah in the Canaanite."[99] The Shekhinah, strongly resembling a Hebrew Goddess, echoes the role attributed by some to the Goddess Asherah in ancient Israel.[100]

Rabbi Gershon Winkler notes that in earlier epochs, women participated more widely in Jewish spiritual life than is widely known. "Many women were acknowledged in our history as masters of Torah, *Halachah* (guidelines for Jewish ritual observance), and Kabbalah throughout the centuries post-temple era. The Midrash also tells us that in biblical times Israel was graced with as many women prophets as male prophets." The Talmud and Midrash reference "wise women whose halachic rulings were accepted by the sages as law, and who participated in rabbinic studies and discussions. Their votes counted in these assemblies toward establishing halachic precedence." Among the original Ashkenazic communities were "women who taught men like rabbis and were actually rabbis in the original sense of the term."[101] In earlier periods of our history, women were qualified to be called up for Aliyah at the Torah, chanted from the Torah, wore tefillin, served as scribes, and recited Kaddish in the synagogue like any man. Winkler concludes, "It seems the farther back we go, the more equality existed in practice between women and men, not the other way around."[102]

In modernity, however, Judaism excluded women from positions of spiritual leadership, scholarship, and most aspects of prayer. Reconstructionist Judaism (recently renamed "Reconstructing Judaism") was founded in the 1920s by Rabbi Mordecai Kaplan. His daughter was the first Bat Mitzvah in 1922. It was not until 50 years later, in 1972, that the first woman rabbi, Sally Priesand, was ordained in the Reform movement. Yet once the door was opened, women developed nonhierarchical, embodied, and experiential approaches to study and spiritual practice, transforming the formerly exclusively male province of spiritual leadership.

Many Jewish women have felt that the patriarchal was so entrenched in Judaism that the only proper course was to reject Judaism and create other women-honoring paths. Gloria Orenstein writes of the experience of exile within her own tradition, by being excluded from traditional forms of prayer and study.[103] Yet she, and many others, felt a powerful yearning for a home within their ancestral tradition. This required a reimagination of Judaism in a way that allowed the full participation of women.

Women took their place as rabbis and scholars in the latter half of the 20th century after millennia of exclusion. Leah Novick, a Jewish Renewal rabbi, notes that despite the brilliance of the medieval and Hasidic mystical perspectives on the Shekhinah, only now are women widely participating in interpreting Her meaning.[104] Feminist rabbis, theologians and women's spiritual circles are transforming the way we conceptualize and experience this essential facet of Jewish mysticism and the tradition as a whole.

The groundbreaking work of Jewish feminist spirituality is central to the reclamation of Jewish identity explored in the chapters that follow.[105] The pioneering feminist theology of Judith Plaskow, Rachel Adler, Susannah Heschel, Alicia Ostriker, and Rabbis Lynn Gottlieb (the first woman rabbi ordained in the Jewish Renewal movement), Leah Novick, Jane Litman, Debra Orenstein, among others, enabled the long-exiled voices of Jewish women to shape textual interpretations and create new forms of observance that were sourced in the feminine. These women and other Jewish Renewal and Reconstructionist rabbis, including Marcia Prager, Tirzah Firestone, Hannah Tiferet Siegel, Shefa Gold, Diane Elliot, and Jill Hammer developed practices that facilitated direct personal spiritual experience.[106]

Gold, who has authored liturgical chants used widely in Jewish Renewal and other Jewish communities, explores the power of chant as a means to find the deeper meaning of the prayers:

> Chanting, the repetition of a sacred phrase, is a way of transforming the words of liturgy into doorways. They become entrances into expanded states of consciousness. From those expanded states, we can have access to the fullness of our power to bless and to heal, both ourselves and others. The sacred words become the lanterns by which our inner treasures, the unique medicine that we each carry, may be revealed. Rabbi Abraham Joshua Heschel says, "It is only after we kindle a light in the words that we are able to behold the riches they contain."[107]

Tirzah Firestone observes that while women were essentially written out of Jewish history, women's wisdom has been central to the continuation of Jewish life.[108] Women have nurtured the spiritual life in the home and family and often provided the livelihood that enabled their husbands and sons to study. Women's connection to the sacred was nurtured by intuitive experiences of the Divine, arising from their direct connection with life's central transitions of birth, death, and healing.[109] Although women's wisdom has not been preserved in written texts, Firestone and others are attempting to reclaim and restore the connection to the deep feminine wisdom that has been obscured by patriarchal history.[110]

Firestone sees the written Torah as masculine, whereas the mystical teachings, or hidden Torah, are based in the experience of inner receiving, a feminine approach to the sacred. The mystical path requires a wholeness born of the union of these two paths. She notes, "The feminine side of the human spirit, which has lain dormant and waiting, is reawakening from centuries of neglect, begging us to share in her riches. Together, both the mystical and the feminine paths can bring us to the necessary next step in our evolution toward wholeness."[111]

Tikkun olam and the indigenous heart of Judaism

Many involved in Jewish Renewal are committed to a path of *tikkun olam* (mending the world) by working for social and ecological justice.[112] Rabbi Abraham Joshua Heschel, a descendant of Hasidic rabbinic dynasties on both sides of his family, was born in Poland in 1907, received his doctorate in Berlin, and was ordained there as a Reform rabbi. He immigrated to America from Europe during the Shoah and was active in the civil rights movement, walking in Selma with Dr. Martin Luther King where he famously recalled, "My feet were praying."[113] Deeply impacted by the death of his mother and sisters in the Shoah, Heschel devoted his life to transmitting the depths of Jewish mysticism and the commitment to social justice into wider awareness through his writings on Jewish theology, philosophy, and social justice as a professor at both the Hebrew Union College (Reform) and Jewish Theological Society (Conservative) seminaries.[114]

Rabbi Arthur Waskow has been a pioneer in both the Jewish Renewal movement and in developing theology and practices dedicated to social justice and ecological healing. Michael Lerner was ordained by Reb Zalman and largely inspired by the work of Heschel. In his book *Jewish Renewal*, Lerner explores the politically centrist attitudes adopted by many Jewish organizations and congregations following the Second World War and in the wake of the McCarthy era. Because of the pernicious impact of the blacklist, many Jews growing up in the postwar era who were deeply involved in social justice movements of the 1960s and 1970s often did not know of the history of social justice in Jewish tradition, or even in their own family lineages.

Lerner observes that the conformist, anti-spiritual shift in mainstream Judaism contributed to the alienation of many from the tradition. Adoption of core Jewish principles of tikkun olam could lead to an "inspired politics of meaning," that would explicitly explore how the decline of meaning, spirituality, and community are linked to and assist the rise of a materialistic centered culture.[115] For progressive Jews, the creation of Jewish organizations devoted to creating a peaceful dialogue between Israeli Jews and Palestinians and dedicated to the rights of marginalized peoples has made a reconnection to Judaism possible.[116]

Rabbi Gershon Winkler reflects on another forgotten strand of Judaism—its origins as a shamanic, earth-based wisdom tradition.[117] Ancient mystical texts are becoming available that demonstrate the aboriginal roots of Jewish spirituality are more concerned with the "direct, uninhibited experience" of the Divine than with formal aspects of religion.[118] Aboriginal Judaism used the four directions to invoke sacred space and contained extensive wisdom about the healing and wisdom attributes of plants, stones, animals, and the cosmos.[119] In addition, Jewish mysticism offered guidance in relating to the spirit realm and its workings as well as a profound understanding of the nature of Reality, in both the visible and invisible realms.[120] Jewish shamanism not only involves the practices of Jewish mysticism, but also provides "a way of consciousness that perceives magic in the ordinary."[121]

Winkler observes that Judaism, originally a shamanic mystery tradition, cloaked itself in formal religious garb in an attempt to survive in a hostile climate.[122] In the eyes of the medieval Church, Jews were regarded as magicians, sorcerers, and practitioners of the occult, based on their knowledge of the mystery wisdom of kabbalah. Women were identified with Jews, as both groups were associated with magical practices, involving healing and potions, dream interpretation, and the possession of magical and mystical knowledge.[123] Anne Llewellyn Barstow writes that "witches and Jews were persecuted interchangeably. Both … were perceived as traitors to Christian society who must be eradicated."[124]

To survive, Jews had to tone down the differences, such as the active role of women (to avoid suspicion of witchcraft, attributed to all spiritually practicing women), and to hide the mystical teachings.[125] Following the Crusades, Jewish rabbinical leaders portrayed Judaism as a respectable religion that was not antithetical or threatening in any way to Christian values, in an attempt to preserve Judaism's very existence. Despite their efforts, in 1239, the Pope ordered all sacred Jewish texts destroyed, and wagonloads of handwritten books (before the printing press) were burned. Very little of the Jewish shamanic tradition survived the massive book burnings of the Middle Ages.[126]

Reclaiming the spiritual aspects of Jewish tradition that honor the earth and the natural cycles has also contributed to the development of eco-kabbalah, expressed in the writing of Rabbi David Seidenberg and the practices of groups such as Wilderness Torah.[127] In reflecting on how the teachings of kabbalah might contribute to our ecological awareness, Rabbi Arthur Green suggests that the central truth of Jewish mysticism, "that all beings are manifestations of the same one, and that the unity of being can be discovered by a disciplined training of the mind toward insight, is one that our age both longs and needs to hear."[128] In this understanding, "God is the innermost reality," where God and universe exist not as Creator and Creation, but "as deep structure and surface."[129] Rosenberg observes that in many ways, this vision aligns with that of evolutionary ecology.[130] In the mystical vision of the Zohar, the inner soul and the outer body come into balance, and the planet is restored to a balance that we cannot yet fathom.[131] Rosenberg writes, "the Garden of Eden still exists; it is in our future, depicted in the Zohar."[132]

Finding our way

Beginning in Chapter Four, using the story of the Exodus as seen through the interpretations of kabbalistic and other rabbinic midrash, I explore how Jewish Renewal teachings, practices, and community enabled those who felt alienated or disconnected from Judaism's staid, patriarchal, socially conservative, and overly rational approach to experience a new relationship to the tradition. Through spiritual practices that facilitate profoundly psychologically transformative experience, and the reclamation of the Feminine and embodied spirituality that live at the heart of the mystical tradition, many have found their way into relationship with a Judaism that had long felt closed or irrelevant to them.

Notes

1 Talmud Bav'li, Niddah 30b.
2 Joachim Neugroschel, *Great Tales of Jewish Fantasy and the Occult* (Woodstock, NY: The Overlook Press, 1976).
3 Edward Feld, *The Spirit of Renewal: Finding Faith after the Holocaust* (Woodstock, VT: Jewish Lights Publishing, 1994).
4 Zalman Schachter-Shalomi, *Paradigm Shift* (Northvale, NJ: Jason Aronson, Inc., 1993).
5 Rodger Kamenetz, *The Jew in the Lotus: A Poet's Re-Discovery of Jewish Identity in Buddhist India* (New York: Harper Collins, 1994).
6 Gershon Winkler, personal communication, July 9, 2019; citing Talmud Bav'li, Hagigah 14b.
7 Gershom Scholem, *On the Kabbalah and Its Symbolism* (New York: Schocken Books, 1965), 17; see also David Cooper, *God Is a Verb* (New York: Riverhead Books, 1997).
8 John P. Wilson, *The Posttraumatic Self: Restoring Meaning and Wholeness to Personality* (New York: Routledge, 2006).
9 Gershom Scholem, *On the Possibility of Jewish Mysticism in Our Time and Other Essays* (Philadelphia: The Jewish Publication Society, 1997), 126–131.
10 David Ariel, *The Mystic Quest: An Introduction to Jewish Mysticism* (New York: Schocken Books, 1988).
11 Scholem, *On the Kabbalah and Its Symbolism*, 2.
12 Elliot Ginsburg, Introduction to *Tree of Souls: The Mythology of Judaism*, by Howard Schwartz (New York: Oxford University Press, 2004), xxxvii.
13 Bettina Knapp, *Manna and Mystery: A Jungian Approach to Hebrew Myth and Legend* (Wilmette, IL: Chiron Publications, 1995), 1. See also Scholem, *On the Kabbalah and Its Symbolism*; and Aryeh Wineman, *Mystic Tales from the Zohar* (Princeton, NJ: Princeton University Press, 1998).
14 Knapp, *Manna and Mystery*, 1.
15 C.G. Jung, *The Visions Seminars*, Vol. 1 (Zurich: Spring Publications, 1976), 156; cited in Edward Edinger, *The Bible and the Psyche: Individuation Symbolism in the Old Testament* (Toronto: Inner City Books, 1986), 11.
16 Ibid.

17 C.G. Jung, "Concerning the Archetypes and the Anima Concept," *The Archetypes of the Collective Unconscious*, 9i, par. 120; cited in Edinger, *The Bible and the Psyche*, 11.

18 Ibid.

19 Ibid.

20 C.G. Jung, *Letters*, Vol. 2, edited by Gerhard Adler (Princeton, NJ: Princeton University Press, 1975), 155; quoted in Edward Hoffman, *The Way of Splendor: Jewish Mysticism and Modern Psychology* (Plymouth: Rowman and Littlefield, 2006), 7.

21 Edinger, *The Bible and the Psyche*, 11–14.

22 Ibid.

23 Ibid; quoting Arthur Green, "Jewish Studies, Jewish Faith," *Tikkun* 1, no. 1 (1986), 87.

24 Raphael Patai, *The Hebrew Goddess* (Detroit, MI: Wayne State University Press, 1967/1978), 84.

25 Elliot Ginsburg, Foreword to *Tree of Souls: The Mythology of Judaism*, by Howard Schwartz (New York: Oxford University Press, 2004), xliii.

26 Jane S. Gerber, *The Jews of Spain: A History of the Sephardic Experience* (New York: The Free Press, 1992), 2–5.

27 Maria Rosa Menocal, *The Ornament of the World: How Muslims, Jews, and Christians Created a Culture of Tolerance in Medieval Spain* (New York: Little Brown and Co., 2002).

28 Schwartz, *Tree of Souls*, 410.

29 Arthur Green, *Introduction* to *The Zohar, Pritzker Edition,* Daniel C. Matt, translator and commentary, (Stanford, CA: Stanford University Press, 2004), vol. I, xxxix-xliv.

30 Ibid., xlvi–liii.

31 Zohar 1:53b, vol. I, 298, fn. 1438.

32 Ibid, fn. 1438.

33 Zohar 1:203a, vol. III, 243.

34 Ibid; citing C.G. Jung, *The Collected Works of C.G. Jung*, vol. 8, *The Structure and Dynamics of the Psyche* (Princeton, NJ: Princeton University Press, 1969), 157; Erich Neumann, *Origins and History of Consciousness* (Princeton, NJ: Princeton University Press, 2014), 102–127.

35 An exhibit on the Inquisition at the Granada Jewish Museum graphically displays the instruments and forms of torture used to persecute Jews, women, healers, gays and lesbians, and others who did not conform or convert to Catholicism.

36 Gerber, *The Jews of Spain*, ix.

37 Stanley Hordes, *To the End of the Earth: A History of the Crypto-Jews of New Mexico* (New York: Columbia University Press, 2008).

38 Scholem, *On the Kabbalah and Its Symbolism*, 109–117.

39 Knapp, *Manna and Mystery*.

40 Scholem, *On the Kabbalah and Its Symbolism*, 2.

41 Helen Epstein, *Children of the Holocaust: Conversations with Sons and Daughters of Survivors* (New York: GP Putnam's Sons, 1979), 12.

42 Avram Davis, *The Way of Flame: A Guide to the Forgotten Mystical Tradition of Jewish Meditation* (San Francisco: HarperSanFrancisco, 1996), 16–17.

43 Charles Selengut, ed., *Jewish Identity in the Postmodern Age: Scholarly and Personal Reflections* (St. Paul, MN: Paragon House, 1999); Robert P. Amyot and Lee Sigelman, "Jews Without Judaism? Assimilation and Jewish Identity in the United States," *Social Science Quarterly* 77, no. 1 (1996): 177–189; Alan M. Dershowitz, *The Vanishing American Jew: In Search of Jewish Identity for the Next Century* (New York: Little Brown, 1997).

44 David Biale, "The Melting Pot and Beyond," in *Best Contemporary Jewish Writing*, edited by Michael Lerner (San Francisco: Jossey-Bass, 2001), 13.

45 Yosef Hayim Yerushalmi, *Zakhor: Jewish History and Jewish Memory* (New York: Schocken Books, 1989), 94.

46 Martin Buber, *Tales of the Hasidim (The Early Masters/The Later Masters)* (New York: Schocken Press, 1991); *The Way of Man: According to the Teaching of Hasidism* (Woodstock, VT: Jewish Lights Publishing, 2012); C.G. Jung and Erich Neumann, *Analytical Psychology in Exile: The Correspondence of C.G. Jung and Erich Neumann*, edited by Martin Liebscher, translated by Heather McCartney (Princeton, NJ: Princeton University Press, 2005), 52, fn. 215.

47 Rodger Kamenetz, Foreword to *On Judaism*, by Martin Buber (New York: Schocken Books, Inc., 1967).

48 Some leading members of the Wissenschaft wrote with interest about the Zohar and other mystical texts, but publicly expressed a general attitude of devaluation. See George Y. Kohler, "Heinrich Graetz and the Kabbalah," *Kabbalah: Journal for the Study of Jewish Mystical Texts* 40 (2017): 107–130.

49 Stéphane Mosés, *The Angel of History: Rosenzweig, Benjamin, Scholem*, translated by Barbara Harshav (Stanford, CA: Stanford University Press, 2009), 122–125; David Biale, *Gershom Scholem: Master of the Kabbalah* (New Haven, CT: Yale University Press, 2018).

50 Biale, "The Melting Pot and Beyond," 7.

51 Scholem, *On the Possibility of Jewish Mysticism*, 78.

52 Scholem, *On the Kabbalah and Its Symbolism,* 88.

53 Jung and Neumann, *Analytical Psychology in Exile,* 173, n. 390.

54 Ann Lammers, private correspondence with Zvi Leshem, April 24, 2018; cited in Erich Neumann, *Roots of Jewish Consciousness*, Vol. I, edited by Ann Conrad Lammers (London: Routledge, 2019), xii, n. 47.

55 Ibid, 10–11.

56 Rodger Kamenetz, *Stalking Elijah: Adventures with Today's Jewish Mystical Masters* (San Francisco: HarperSanFrancisco, 1997), 19. Kamenetz reflects, "In plain English, he was kicked out after an article appeared in Commentary in which Reb Zalman praised the sacramental potential of lysergic acid."

57 Ibid, 18–19. Jewish Renewal is partly attributable to the spiritual freedom afforded by structural changes in Jewish worship brought about by the creation of small collaborative learning and prayer communities called *havurot*. In these small communities, Jews studied and prayed together outside the context of traditional temples. They sought to understand Judaism in a way that held personal meaning and to create nonhierarchical relationships in which women were full participants. For an excellent history and reflection on the havurah movement, see Judy Petonsk, *Taking Judaism Personally: Creating a Meaningful Spiritual Life* (New York: The Free Press, 1996).

58 See Arthur Green, *Ehyeh: A Kabbalah for Tomorrow* (Woodstock, VT: Jewish Lights Publishing, 2002); *The Heart of the Matter: Studies in Jewish Mysticism and Theology* (New York: Jewish Publication Society, 2015); *Tormented Master: The Life and Spiritual Quest of Rabbi Nahman of Bratslav* (Woodstock, VT: Jewish Lights 1992).

59 The Magnes Collection of Jewish Art and Life, University of California, Berkeley, 2016, at https://magnes.berkeley.edu/collections/archives/western-jewish-americana/house-love-and-prayer-miscellany-1968-1977.

60 In 1998, the Jewish feminist magazine *Lilith* published revelations of widespread sexual abuse by Carlebach. Sarah Blustain, "Rabbi Shlomo Carlebach's Shadow Side," *Lilith,* Spring 1998, https://www.lilith.org/articles/rabbi-shlomo-carlebachs-shadow-side/.

61 Kamenetz, *Stalking Elijah*, 21.

62 Ibid, see also Schachter-Shalomi, *Paradigm Shift,* xxi–xxii. Schachter-Shalomi (Reb Zalman) notes that Jean Houston recognized the power of Jewish Renewal as a tool for transformation. Accepting her suggestion, Reb Zalman and his wife Eve Penner-

Ilsen founded the Wisdom School employing transformative work that "called for imaginal, meditative, introspective, interactive mimesis, journal keeping, and dream assemblies." Reb Zalman recalls that in the first year they explored "Genesis and the expulsion from Eden, sibling rivalry, dreams, addictions and the Exodus, Leviticus and shamanic technology, Deuteronomy and Ecclesiastes, Esther, Ruth, Jonah, and Job." He writes, "What an awesome night vigil it was when we wrestled with Job, danced with the whirlwind, and prayed the reconciliation prayer at dawn." Burt Jacobson, *This Precious Moment: The Wisdom of the Ba'al Shem Tov* (Oakland, CA: Kehilla, 2016), See also Kehilla Synagogue, *Rabbi Burt's Blog*, at https://kehillasynag ogue.org/category/rabbi-burt.

63 Zalman Schachter-Shalomi, "Meditations between Contractions," *Writings from the Heart of Jewish Renewal*, edited by Aleph (Philadelphia: Aleph, 2003), 7.
64 Schachter-Shalomi, *Paradigm Shift*, 303. He writes that wisdom tradition paradigms were created by mystical experiences in which "momentary flashes of Infinity … were snatched from their eternal dimension and entombed in the world of relativity in the form of religious institution and symbolism."
65 Ibid, 306.
66 Jonathan Boyarin, *Storm from Paradise: The Politics of Jewish Memory* (Minneapolis, MN: University of Minnesota Press, 1992), 128.
67 Schachter-Shalomi, "Meditations between Contractions," 7.
68 Ibid.
69 Ibid, 7–8.
70 Chava Weissler, "Meanings of Shekhinah in the 'Jewish Renewal' Movement," *Nashim: A Journal of Jewish Women's and Gender Issues* 10 (2005): 54.
71 Chava Weissler, "Jewish Renewal and the American Spiritual Marketplace," from a paper prepared for the University of Washington Samuel and Althea Stroum Lectures in Jewish Studies, 2005, 12. Quoted, with permission, from the author.
72 Daniel Siegel, "Tradition? Tradition!" in *Writings from the Heart of Jewish Renewal* (Philadelphia: Aleph, Alliance for Jewish Renewal, 2003), 4–5. Siegel notes that the psycho-halakhic process arises out of the tradition of *minhag*, which recognizes that Jewish custom has changed significantly and grown according to the custom of a particular group or culture in the diaspora. In order to merit the trust that enables one to revise traditional practices, one must first deepen one's knowledge and understanding of the tradition.
73 Gold, "Solemn Joy," at Rabbi Shefa Gold website, http://www.rabbishefagold.com/rh5763_1/.
74 Ibid.
75 Ibid.
76 Arthur Green, *Ehyeh: A Kabbalah for Tomorrow* (Woodstock, VT: Jewish Lights Publishing, 2003), 2.
77 Cooper, *God Is a Verb*, 69–74. Cooper cites the teaching of the Lurianic creation myth, that our role is not the achievement of perfect transcendence, but the participation in the healing of an imperfect world. Our work is the constant repair of our own souls and the souls of those around us. Each moment becomes meaningful, no longer seeking unattainable perfection, but fully inhabiting the imperfection and accepting the opportunity for transformation inherent within it. Ibid, 29.
78 Avram Davis, ed., *Meditation from the Heart of Judaism* (Woodstock, VT: Jewish Lights Publishing, 1999), offers an excellent sampling of writings on Jewish Renewal style meditation practices.
79 Elliot Ginsburg, "Beyond Words: Approaching Silence in Hassidic Prayer," in *Writings from the Heart of Jewish Renewal* (Philadelphia: Aleph, Alliance for Jewish Renewal, 2003), 28.

80 Ibid, 29.
81 Ibid.
82 Ginsburg, "Beyond Words," 24.
83 Ibid.
84 Ibid.
85 Ibid, 26.
86 Steven Fisdel, *The Meditation Practice Within Kabbalah* (Albany, CA: Katriel Press, 2014), 2.
87 Marcia Prager, *The Path of Blessing: Experiencing the Energy and Abundance of the Divine* (Woodstock, VT: Jewish Lights, 1998), 4–5.
88 Ibid.
89 Ibid, see also Marcia Falk, *The Book of Blessings: New Jewish Prayers for Daily Life, the Sabbath, and the New Moon Festival* (Boston: Beacon Press, 1996).
90 David Rosenberg, *Dreams of Being Eaten Alive: The Literary Core of Kabbalah* (New York: Harmony Books, 2000), 39.
91 Lynn Gottlieb, *She Who Dwells Within: Feminist Vision of a Renewed Judaism* (San Francisco, CA: HarperOne, 1995), 20.
92 Ibid, 20–21.
93 Ibid.
94 Howard Schwartz, *Reimagining the Bible: The Storytelling of the Rabbis* (Oxford: Oxford University Press, 1998), 131–162.
95 Siegmund Hurwitz, *Lilith—The First Eve: Historical and Psychological Aspects of the Dark Feminine* (Einsiedeln: Daimon Verlag, 1992), 226–227.
96 Ibid.
97 Patai, *The Hebrew Goddess*. See also, William G. Dever, *Did God Have a Wife?: Archaeology and Folk Religion in Ancient Israel* (Grand Rapids, MI: Wm. B. Eerdmans Publishing, 2005).
98 Jeremiah 44:17–19; cited in Patai, *The Hebrew Goddess*, 63.
99 Elliot Ginsburg, Foreword, xliii.
100 Ibid.
101 Gershon Winkler, personal communication, July 2019; citing Talmud Bav'li, Tossef'ta Keylim 11:3; Minchat Chinuch, No. 78. Winkler states, "One example is the 15th-century classical Code of Jewish Law, Sefer Ha'Chinuch: 'And it is forbidden to rule on Halachic issues while inebriated, and this applies to both men and women alike who are authorized to rule on halachah'" (Sefer Ha'Chinuch, No. 158). See also Shoshana Pantel Zolty, *And All Your Children Shall be Learned: Women and the Study of Torah in Jewish Law and History* (Northvale, NJ: Jason Aronson, 1997).
102 Winkler, personal communication, July 2019; citing Talmud Bav'li, Megillah 23a; Talmud Bav'li, Gittin 22b; Sif'tei Ko'hen in Note No. 6 to Karo's Shulchan Aruch, Yorah De'ah 281:3; Pit'chei Teshuva on Shulchan Aruch, Yorah De'ah 3776:4 [Note 3], and Be'er Hey'tev on Shulchan Aruch, Orach Chayim 132:2 [No. 5].
103 Gloria Feman Orenstein, "Gender Politics and the Soul: A Jewish Feminist Journey," in *Modern Jew in Search of a Soul*, edited by Marvin Spiegelman and Abraham Jacobson (Phoenix, AZ: Falcon Press, 1986), 197–214.
104 Novick, *On The Wings of Shekhinah*, 10.
105 Rachel Adler, *Engendering Judaism: An Inclusive Theology and Ethics* (New York: Jewish Publication Society, 1999); Judith Plaskow, *Standing Again at Sinai: Judaism from a Feminist Perspective* (San Francisco, CA: HarperOne, 1991); Gottlieb, *She Who Dwells Within*; Leah Novick, *On the Wings of Shekhinah: Rediscovering Judaism's Divine Feminine* (Wheaton, IL: Quest Books, 2008); Shefa Gold, *Torah Journeys: The Inner Path to the Promised Land* (Teaneck, NJ: Ben Yehuda Press, 2006); Tirzah Firestone, *The Receiving: Reclaiming Jewish Women's Wisdom* (San

Francisco, CA: HarperOne, 2014); Susannah Heschel, *On Being a Jewish Feminist* (New York: Schocken Books, 1982); Prager, *The Path of Blessing*; Deborah Orenstein and Jane Littman, *Lifecycles: Jewish Women on Biblical Themes in Contemporary Life* (Woodstock, VT: Jewish Lights, 1998).

106 Aleph, ed., *Writings from the Heart of Jewish Renewal*, which includes writings by Jewish Renewal Rabbis Shefa Gold, Leah Novick, Tirzah Firestone, Marcia Prager, Shaya Eisenberg, and Naomi Steinberg. See also Weissler, "Meanings of Shekhinah."

107 Rabbi Shefa Gold, "Chanting as a Healing Modality," available at http://www.rabb ishefagold.com/HealingModality.html. See also Shefa Gold, "That This Song May be a Witness: The Power of Chant," in *Writings from the Heart of Jewish Renewal*, edited by Aleph (Philadelphia: Aleph, 2003), 131–138; and Gold, *Torah Journeys*, 228–229; see also Rabbi Shefa Gold, *The Magic of Hebrew Chant: Healing the Spirit, Transforming the Mind, Deepening Love* (Woodstock, VT: Jewish Lights Publishing, 2013), 7–10.

108 Firestone, *The Receiving*.

109 Ibid.

110 Ibid, 3.

111 Ibid, 7.

112 Rabbi Arthur Waskow has established the Shalom Center, a project of Aleph dedicated to peace and environmental and social justice. See Arthur Waskow, Shalom Center website, available at http://www.shalomctr.org. Michael Lerner has coordinated an international network dedicated to a politics of Jewish Renewal based on healing internalized and external anti-Semitism, and pursuing peace in the Middle East employing a paradigm of healing. Michael Lerner, *Healing Israel/Palestine: A Path to Peace and Reconciliation* (Berkeley: North Atlantic Books, 2003).

113 John Lewis, *Walking with the Wind: A Memoir of the Movement* (New York: Simon and Schuster, 1998), 345–347; cited in Edward K. Kaplan, *Spiritual Radical: Abraham Joshua Heschel in America, 1940–1972* (New Haven, CT: Yale University Press, 2007), 223–225.

114 Kaplan, *Spiritual Radical*.

115 Lerner, *Jewish Renewal*, 268–269.

116 Arthur Waskow, *Seasons of Our Joy: A Modern Guide to the Jewish Holidays* (Boston, MA: Beacon Press, 1982).

117 Gershon Winkler, *Magic of the Ordinary: Recovering the Shamanic in Judaism* (Berkeley: North Atlantic Books, 2003).

118 Ibid, 11.

119 Ibid.

120 Ibid.

121 Ibid, 8.

122 Winkler, *Magic of the Ordinary*, 10.

123 Ibid.

124 Anne Llewellyn Barstow, *Witchcraze* (New York: HarperCollins, 1995), 63; cited in Winkler, *Magic of the Ordinary*, 4.

125 Winkler, *Magic of the Ordinary*, 10.

126 Ibid, 4–10. In 1553, for example, Pope Julius the Third ordered the burning of the Talmud, the Jewish people's precious legacy of seven centuries of oral traditions covering the periods between 200 BCE and 500 CE, and the cessation of its printing. On the first day of Rosh Hashanah, the Hebrew New Year holy day, the Inquisition staged a massive burning of the Talmud and other Jewish books in Rome, and subsequently in other cities across Italy. Less than a month later, over a thousand copies of the Talmud and hundreds of other Jewish books were burned in Venice. In 1559, 10,000 Jewish books were burned in Cremona, Italy, by order of the Inquisition. The

Jewish mystical classic Sefer HaZohar (Book of Splendor) only escaped the burnings by being printed at a non-Jewish print shop. Certainly, the greater tragedy was the torching of thousands of Jewish people by the Church during this period as well as before and after, but the Jewish people lost as well a great number of not only their ancient wisdom texts but, along with those, their ancient shamanic mindset.

127 David Mevoroch Seidenberg, *Kabbalah and Ecology: God's Image In The More-Than-Human World* (New York: Cambridge University Press, 2015); www.wildernesstorah.org.
128 Arthur Green, "A Kabbalah for the Environmental Age," *Best Contemporary Jewish Writing*, edited by Michael Lerner (San Francisco: Jossey-Bass, 2001), 116.
129 Ibid.
130 Rosenberg, *Dreams of Being Eaten Alive*, 34–35.
131 Ibid.
132 Ibid.

Chapter 3

Judaism and psychology

The personal experiences of reconnection that I explore in the following chapters are imbued with both spiritual and psychological meaning. Psychology is a modern discipline, while soul-making is an ancient art. Lurianic kabbalah, developed in the 16th century, shifted mysticism from a primarily cosmological exploration to a focus on the individual, offering practices for the development and healing of one's soul. This healing, or *tikkun*, was often based on the rabbi's ability to see into and understand what the student needed to develop his or her individual soul through study, meditative practice, and acting charitably in the world.[1] Religious observance became a deeply inner pursuit.

In the 18th and 19th centuries, Hasidic masters drew on the practices first developed by the medieval mystics, designing depth psychological practices that enabled their disciples to stay connected to a sense of faith in the face of overwhelming adversity and despair. Rabbi Nachman of Bratslav, great-grandson of the Baal Shem Tov, founder of Hasidism, is thought by many to have suffered from severe depression. He wrote and taught movingly, through story and prayer, about how to overcome the devastating darkness of one's soul and to find joy amid life's sorrows.[2] In the mid to late 19th century, *Mussar*, a reflective practice that enabled individuals to develop and strengthen their ethical qualities, gained favor among many Jews seeking to synthesize rationalist enlightenment ideas with traditional Jewish practice.

Although the strong pull toward assimilation in late 19th-century Western European culture led many Jews to distance themselves from their spiritual roots, the soul-making practices and teachings developed over millennia may have strongly influenced the advent of modern psychology.

Sigmund Freud developed psychoanalysis during the height of the rationalist enlightenment *Haskalah* movement. Freud's theories emerged in dialogue with an inner circle of Jewish psychiatrists. Concerned that his method would be dismissed as a "Jewish national affair," Freud fought vigorously to substantiate his discoveries as scientifically valid and forward thinking.

Freud's internalized conflict regarding his Jewish identity, reflecting the spirit of his time, is seen in his writings concerned with exposing the illusory nature of religion. Yet psychoanalysis may have been greatly influenced, either consciously or unconsciously, by Jewish mysticism.[3] Many contributors to the further developments in psychoanalysis and depth psychology in the mid to late 20th century were Jewish; several were exiles from Europe during the Shoah. Their wide dissemination of ideas and practices for reflecting on the self and developing the psyche may be viewed, in part, as a secularization of Jewish mystical thought and practice.

C.G. Jung, founder of analytical psychology, was already a renowned psychiatrist in Zurich when he began a close association with Freud in the early part of the 20th century. The two parted ways over Jung's differences with Freud about the nature of the unconscious, which Freud saw as personal. Jung developed the theory of the *collective unconscious*, a repository of the mythological and symbolic contents of human history. Jung recognized that moderns had become painfully cut off from myths and spiritual forms that in the past had provided life's meaning. Like Scholem, Jung understood the need for myth to re-fructify Western culture, which had grown overly reliant on the rational.

Jung encouraged those who trained with him to develop their connection to their own ancestral roots. This led many of the Jews who worked closely with him to discover deep psychological meaning in the Biblical text and the mythic amplifications found in midrash. In the following chapters, I draw on the insights of analytical psychologists Erich Neumann, Rivkah Scharf-Kluger, Siegmund Hurwitz, Sanford Drob, Naomi Ruth Lowinsky, and others who developed Jung's theory in relationship to the Jewish collective psyche. The perspectives of Jewish Jungian psychologists reclaiming the depths of their ancestral tradition enabled many formerly alienated Jews to find profound meaning in the texts through a psychological lens.

Jung himself displayed ignorance of the depth of Jewish tradition in the early part of his career, seeing it through the narrow lens of his Swiss Protestant upbringing. Erich Neumann sought to awaken Jung to the profound meaning of Jewish mysticism as early as the 1930s.[4] Jung's ignorance led to serious misapprehension of the dangerousness of the Nazi threat in 1933, which I explore later in this chapter.

Unfortunately, Jung was perceived by some as anti-Semitic, despite his actions in publicly addressing the threat of Nazism from 1934 onward, including providing aid to many of the Jews in his inner circle and to the Allied Forces, and his deep appreciation of Jewish mystical thought in the latter part of his life. This misperception caused many Jews to reject Jung and Jungian approaches, limiting access to a psychological healing approach that might have facilitated connection with the collective unconscious of Judaism.

As Jung engaged more deeply with the Western esoteric art of alchemy, he began to appreciate kabbalistic themes and their great wisdom. When he had a near-death experience in the 1950s, after the war, he had a life-altering kabbalistic vision. He became increasingly interested in Jewish mysticism and began an ongoing relationship with Gershom Scholem, who attended postwar conferences organized by Jung and attended by Erich Neumann at the Eranos Institute in Switzerland.

Much has been written of both the rift that developed between Freud and Jung and the work that has been done to heal the relationship between the movements they each created.[5] Although it is beyond the scope of this work to fully address this conflict, perhaps situating their work in the larger context of the powerful forces of their time will bring increased understanding.

In the postwar era, contributions of the diaspora of Jewish émigrés to the United States and England, from Nazi-occupied Europe, gave rise to new schools of psychology, including existentialism (developed by concentration camp survivor Viktor Frankl), Gestalt, transpersonal, and somatic approaches, many of which drew on Jung's approach. Humanistic psychology, developed by American-born Abraham Maslow, was profoundly influential in bringing spiritual and normative experience into psychology, also in alignment with Jung's perspective.

Zalman Schachter-Shalomi was deeply interested in psychology and strongly influenced by Erich Neumann. In the 1960s, Reb Zalman developed ties with Abraham Maslow, Ram Dass (Richard Alpert), humanistic psychologist Edward Hoffman, and others, exploring the bridge between kabbalistic and psychological practices. These various streams allowed what was formerly experienced as a split between psychology and religion to become synthesized into the psychospiritual practices of Jewish Renewal.

Freud, Judaism and the development of psychoanalysis

Freud was born in mid-19th-century Vienna, when long-established laws that limited Jewish participation in the dominant culture began to be loosened. Yet a reactionary resurgence of hatred against Jews resurfaced by the latter part of the century, in a climate that eventually gave rise to Hitler and Nazism.

Despite the loosening of strictures, Freud was denied a university post early in his career because he was Jewish, leading him to begin his private practice work developing what would become psychoanalysis.[6] Freud developed his ideas by delivering talks to a circle of psychiatrists who met regularly at the *B'nai Brith* center in Vienna. These founders of psychoanalysis were all Jewish, with the exception of Carl Jung and Ernest Jones.[7]

As mentioned previously, Freud emphasized the scientific basis of psychoanalysis so it would not be dismissed as a "Jewish national affair." The disavowal of religion was a major topic of many of his writings, in which he characterized religion as an infantile regression, a projection of "father longing" onto the deity, and a dangerous illusion.[8] Freud's distancing from religion had a major impact on both Jewish identity and culture, as modern Jews embracing Freud's ideas increasingly saw the religion of their ancestors as superstitious and lacking intellectual or psychological meaning.

In *Sigmund Freud and the Jewish Mystical Tradition*, psychologist David Bakan posited that Freud's ideas about the transference with the therapist, seeking meaning in dreams, and exploring the unconscious or hidden aspects of the psyche were based in kabbalistic thinking and practice.[9] Bakan presents a fascinating study of the intellectual and social milieu in which Freud was operating. As late as the 1880s, Jews were still being persecuted for blood libel, the incendiary accusation that Jews used the blood of Gentiles in baking matzah during Passover, a flashpoint for major pogroms against Jews throughout European history. In such a milieu, associating one's theories openly with Jewish thought and culture would likely lead to being dismissed or attacked. Bakan suggests that for these reasons, Freud presented a public persona in which he minimized or denied his knowledge of Judaism.

Bakan notes that Freud was likely exposed to the work of Adolf Jellinek, the most popular Jewish speaker in Vienna in the late 19th century, who discussed the work of medieval kabbalist Abraham Abulafia and his techniques of letting the mind move freely from one idea to another—which Bakan sees as possibly the inspiration for Freud's technique of free association. Medieval kabbalist Abraham Abulafia promoted a method of deepening one's soul by developing a close relationship with a teacher, whom one might initially see as God, to connect more intimately with God through the relational transference. Bakan suggests these ideas may have contributed to Freud's development of the idea of transference in psychoanalysis.[10] Isaac Luria, writing in the 16th century, taught that the *rebbe* could see the psychological and spiritual work that a student needed to undergo to develop and would guide him along this pathway through focused one-on-one sessions. Reb Zalman Schachter-Shalomi and psychologist Edward Hoffman reflect that this practice of *yichud*, or rebbe-student relationship, prevalent in the 19th-century Hasidic world, may have served as the model for Freud's development of modern psychoanalysis and the analyst–patient relationship.[11]

British psychoanalyst Joseph Berke also questions the assimilated public persona presented by Freud and his biographers. Freud claimed to know neither Hebrew nor Yiddish. Yet Freud's father Jacob, a Torah scholar, raised his first two sons from a previous marriage as Orthodox. Jacob became more assimilated after moving to Austria and marrying Freud's mother Amalia, who was also raised in a Hasidic Orthodox home and who spoke primarily Yiddish. Berke suggests it is highly unlikely that Freud would not have known and spoken Yiddish and, since he was a Bar Mitzvah, it is also unlikely that he was unfamiliar with Hebrew. Freud's wife, Martha Bernays, was the granddaughter of the Chief Rabbi of Hamburg.[12]

Despite his public distancing from Jewish religion, Freud maintained a strong pride and allegiance to his Jewish cultural identity. His consulting room included Jewish iconography, and he expressed his interest privately to rabbis and Jewish scholars on the subject matter of their public talks.[13] Bakan discovered, through discussion with a Jewish colleague of Freud's, that he possessed a number of books on kabbalah in German, had a copy of the Zohar in his library, and was quite interested in Jewish culture and religion.[14]

Kabbalistic scholar Jonathan Garb notes that Jewish mystical and ethical thought predated Freud's concern with the unconscious, and explored the dark forces that impeded the soul's development.[15] Both Bakan's and Garb's understanding of the wide dissemination of Jewish mystical thought and practices in late 19th- and early 20th-century Vienna raise intriguing questions as to what extent Freud was influenced, consciously or unconsciously, by these mystical teachings and insights.

If Freud was interested in Jewish spirituality, myths, and symbols, he was extremely limited by the severe anti-Semitism of his era from pursuing this interest openly. Bakan posits that Freud's focus on sexuality echoed the Zohar's use of sexual imagery to speak about the union with God. Jungian analyst Naomi Lowinsky suggests that, seen in this light, Jung's understanding of the spiritual meaning of the *coniunctio*, or the "divine marriage" in alchemy, may have been closer to Freud's focus on sexuality than has been acknowledged previously.[16] Others have suggested that Freud's focus on sexuality as central to psychological health was based on seeking to overcome the negative projections of Jews as sexual deviants, an anti-Semitic trope popular in late 19th- and early 20th-century Europe.[17]

Freud played a critical role in supporting the continuance of one of the major lineages of Hasidism that still flourishes today.[18] In the early 1900s, Eastern European Rabbi Sholom Dovber Schneerson, known as the *Rashab*, was experiencing profound despair. In the turbulent political days preceding the Russian Revolution, the Rashab was imprisoned several times by the Czar after his contemporaries (the *mitnagdim*, Jewish opponents of Hasidism) informed on him.

Freud met with him, and their work together enabled him to continue his spiritual leadership and prodigious output of books and teachings. The Rashab's successor and son, Yosef Yitzhak Schneerson, fled to the United States in 1940 from Nazi-occupied Warsaw. Yosef Yitzhak Schneerson was able to obtain the help of the US government in arranging safe passage for his son-in-law, Rebbe Menachem Mendel Schneerson, from Vichy France in 1941. Rebbe Menachem Mendel settled in Brooklyn and became widely known as the Lubavitcher Rebbe. Menachem Mendel Schneerson was a powerful mentor in Reb Zalman's spiritual development, and ordained him as a rabbi in New York in the 1950s.

When the Nazis invaded Austria in 1938, Freud and his immediate family fled to London, despite his initial protests against leaving Vienna. Freud's four sisters and their families remained there and eventually perished in the camps. Freud, already suffering from oral cancer, died less than a year after arriving in London. His daughter, Anna Freud, pioneered the development of child psychoanalysis and developed the idea of identification with the aggressor, used in understanding internalized self-hatred that may develop among victims of violence and trauma.

In the years surrounding the Shoah, many European psychoanalysts immigrated to the United States and England, establishing psychoanalytic communities that focused on the newly emerging "ego psychology." Emily Kuriloff notes that many of these analysts were profoundly traumatized by the war and the destruction of the Vienna where Freud and his work had thrived. Kuriloff observes that these early émigrés were unable to turn toward their own trauma, and in their need to hold on to all that had been shattered, reified Freud's ideas, reluctant to allow them to grow or change.[19] She cites psychoanalyst Heinz Kohut's decision, after emigrating from Nazi-occupied Austria to Chicago, to hide his Jewishness from his own son, out of a desire to protect him from harm.[20] In postwar America, a "gentleman's agreement" existed among analysts not to discuss their Jewishness.[21] Perhaps because the traumas of these analysts were too fresh and not worked through, many Shoah survivors seeking psychoanalysis in the aftermath of the war found that analysts were not always able to address their war experiences, focusing instead on issues arising in childhood in a classical Freudian approach.

In the 1950s Wilfred Bion introduced spiritual themes into psychoanalysis, offering a perspective that the psyche consists of both the conscious mind and the ultimate reality that he called "O," similar to Jung's view of the collective unconscious or objective psyche. As the field of relational psychoanalysis has developed, spiritual themes have been increasingly explored. Recently, Michael Eigen has explored the intersection of psychoanalysis and kabbalah, and notes that Bion told him privately that his entire theory was based on kabbalah.[22]

Carl Jung and the religious function of the psyche

Relying on Biblical metaphor, Freud hoped that Jung, as the prominent Gentile in his inner circle, would act as Joshua to his Moses, carrying his ideas into the wider non-Jewish world.[23] Freud and Jung ended what was a profoundly close relationship over Jung's disagreement with Freud over libido, which Jung saw as encompassing a wider range of psychic energy than sexuality, including the religious function of the psyche. Jung also differed from Freud in his view of the unconscious. Whereas Freud saw it as consisting of personal experiences that had been repressed, Jung believed that this level accounted for only one aspect, the *personal unconscious*. Jung's research into myths, symbols, and culture demonstrated that there was also a *collective unconscious*, the storehouse of all human knowledge over millennia, expressed through archetypal representations in images, dreams, symbols, and life circumstances.

The Self, or the totality of the psyche, includes the ego or conscious awareness and both the personal and collective unconscious. We access the wisdom of the Self through analysis, dreams, and numinous experiences, amplifying the meaning of the symbols that speak to us by understanding the mythological realm and engaging our imaginations. As we integrate the wisdom of the Self and increase our conscious awareness, we engage in the process of individuation, becoming more wholly our unique selves.

Jung saw that the Western world was in a spiritual crisis due to an overemphasis on the rational and the loss of connection with the meaningful myths and rituals that had always guided cultures and provided a psychospiritual foundation to life. In modernity, religion was losing its centrality in people's lives, and he decried the psychological alienation that arose in the vacuum that remained. Like Scholem, Jung recognized that we had become separated from the deep myths and symbols that imbue life with meaning.

Because myth guides our ability to come into a relationship with the Self, loss of connection to a living myth has been catastrophic in the evolution of human consciousness. A traditional people could not continue in the absence of a relationship with their guiding mythological system. Jung observed that when a traditional people loses its connection to its mythology, "it immediately falls to pieces and decays ... like a man who has lost his soul."[24] Moderns experienced the "cultural and psychological vertigo of living without a myth."[25]

The 20th century, with its two World Wars, was a time of desperate spiritual need that could only be met by the rehabilitation of religious myths that were psychologically and symbolically interpreted.[26] According to Jung, a person who believes "he can live without myth, or outside it," is relegated to a lifetime of despair:

> He is like one uprooted, having no true link either with the past, or with the ancestral life which continues within him ... He ... lives a life of his own, sunk in a subjective mania of his own devising, which he believes to be the newly discovered truth ... The psyche is not of today; its ancestry goes back many millions of years. Individual consciousness is only the flower and the fruit of a season, sprung from the perennial rhizome beneath the earth; and it would find itself in better accord with the truth if it took the existence of the rhizome into its calculations. For the root matter is the mother of all things.[27]

Jung believed that despite the challenges of modernity, religion could be reclaimed, and the continuity of myth maintained, but only if each generation was willing to reinterpret its meaning anew. A religion's "spiritual vitality depends on the continuity of myth, and this can be preserved only if each age translates the myth into its own language and makes it an essential content of its view of the world."[28]

The cultural collective unconscious

The emerging psychological concept of a cultural unconscious provides a framework for understanding the spontaneous emergence in the individual psyche of culturally specific myths and symbols. Joseph Henderson defined the *cultural unconscious* as "an area of historical memory that lies between the collective unconscious and the manifest culture pattern."[29] It may include both conscious and unconscious modalities, but draws from the archetypal realm of the collective unconscious. The images from the collective unconscious contribute to the formation of a culture's myths and rituals and promote individual psychic development.[30] Michael Vannoy Adams adds to Henderson's definition of the cultural unconscious by suggesting it includes "historical, cultural and ethnic factors" as well as the archetypal.[31]

Barbara Hannah explains that Jung described the collective unconscious as made up of succeeding layers. "The lowest level of all he called 'the central fire' (life itself), and a spark from this fire ascends through all intervening levels into every living creature."[32] Above the central fire lay successive layers, the lowest being animal ancestors in general, above which is the primeval ancestors layer, corresponding to the common ancestors of all humankind. In the next layer the latter began to split up into large groups, such as Western or Asiatic humans. The layers then became increasingly specific, narrowing to nation, clan, family, and individual.[33]

According to Hannah, "With the layer of the nation considerable differences appear."[34] Jung was struck by how necessary he found it to have some knowledge of the national layers to be able to effectively understand the individual psyche.[35] He observed that the unconscious is "immersed in a sea of historical associations," such that "history could be constructed just as easily from one's own unconscious as from the actual texts."[36] In a similar vein, Henry Corbin reflected that humans do not dwell in history, but that history dwells in humans.[37]

Siegmund Hurwitz noted that Jung expressed varying ideas on whether cultural archetypes could be inherited. Jung at one point observed that the concept of inherited archetypal pictures would be "difficult if not impossible to prove."[38] Yet elsewhere he stated that while he had "never yet found infallible evidence for the inheritance of memory images," he did not deem it "positively precluded that in addition to these collective deposits which contain nothing specifically individual, there may also be inherited memories that are individually determined."[39] Hurwitz, exploring the emergence of the Jewish mythical figure Lilith in an analysand's dream, suggested that "the inheritance of archetypal pictures could be within the bound of possibility."[40]

Erich Neumann noted that archetypes are necessarily culture-bound, because they must be represented by the art and other media of the particular culture through which they pass.[41] He observed that in each individual psyche, one's personality extends beyond personal history, back "through every stratum of history and prehistory."[42]

The discussion regarding the cultural unconscious in some ways parallels yet is also distinct from the concept of cultural or collective memory discussed in other areas of social science. Noa Gedi and Yigal Elam suggest that although the term *collective memory* is widely used in social science parlance, its meaning is not generally agreed upon.[43] They suggest it covers the areas previously designated by myth.[44] Historian Yusef Yerushalmi distinguishes collective memory from the collective unconscious, holding that collective memory requires active transmission to an individual.[45] The concept of a cultural collective unconscious suggests a possibility, hinted at by Jung, Hurwitz and Neumann, that one may access ancestral myths, images, and symbols without having been exposed to them directly, through dreams and active imagination, or through inner experience during cultural rituals and events. The ability to access images and symbols directly through the cultural unconscious creates a meaningful bridge for many who grew up cut off from their cultural and spiritual heritage.

Jung's anti-Semitic statements and subsequent repudiation

Jung headed the German Psychoanalytic Society in the early 1930s, when anti-Semitic regulations barred Jews from practicing psychotherapy in Germany. His statements made in 1933 during his tenure there reflected his gross misapprehension about the destructive impulses of Nazism and ignorance about the Jewish psyche. Jung wondered if the Nazi's use of symbols from pre-Christian German culture, such as the symbol of Wotan, might reflect an attempt to connect with the German cultural unconscious, and whether this might represent a positive development. In the following year, he wrote an article stating that Jews were not as culturally developed as Christian Europeans, because Jews had not had a land in which to develop their consciousness.[46] Following the war, Jung acknowledged to his Jewish colleague, Siegmund Hurwitz, that the article was "nonsense."[47]

Interviews with Jung's Jewish colleagues, as well as a close examination of Jung's written and oral statements, reveal that Jung seriously underestimated the evil of Nazism in the early 1930s. Jung's comments about the Jewish psyche made during his tenure as president of the German Psychoanalytic Society were given added weight because of his position and because they were printed in the society's journal, which, unbeknownst to him, included an article written by a Nazi member of the society that was hatefully anti-Semitic. Later in 1934 Jung had awakened to the evil that was at hand and began to actively work against the Nazi enterprise.[48]

Freud and Jung parted ways in 1912. Some have wondered whether Jung's deep pain at being shunned by Freud and his inner circle may have fueled Jung's harsh statements about the Jewish psyche. Some believe that Jung was self-servingly seeking to gain ground for his theories while many Jewish psychoanalysts were barred from practice in Germany.[49] Political scientist Paul Roazen notes that Jung stated that he "accepted the leadership of the German Medical Society for Psychotherapy in order to protect the profession and the Jews that practiced it" from needless suffering. Roazen acknowledges Jung's work to help German Jewish refugees establish themselves abroad.[50]

Three of Jung's close associates, James and Hilda Kirsch and Erich Neumann, fled Germany for Palestine in the early 1930s. They saw the deleterious impact of Jung's misunderstanding of both Jewish culture and his early failure to perceive the depth of evil that Nazism presented.[51] Neumann wrote in a 1934 correspondence to Jung, "I cannot comprehend why a person like you cannot see what is all too cruelly obvious to everyone these days—that it is also in the Germanic psyche (and in the Slavic one) that a mind-numbing cloud of filth, blood and rottenness is brewing." Each of them strongly encouraged him to act more consciously and compassionately. Thomas Kirsch writes that although his father, James Kirsch, Neumann and Gerhard Adler warned Jung not to make the statement about national character in 1934, he refused to listen.[52]

Kirsch also notes that Jung enthusiastically attended and endorsed a lecture that James Kirsch presented in 1930 on the subject, "A Modern Jew in Germany." Kirsch's father James and other of Jung's Jewish analysands, including Neumann, Adler, Rivkah Scharf, and Aniela Jaffé, "questioned him about his alleged anti-Semitism and none of those in analysis with him found him to be anti-Semitic."[53]

Neumann believed that Jung misunderstood the Jewish psyche because most Jews with whom he interacted were highly assimilated and disconnected from the spiritual depths of the tradition. Neumann proposed to Jung that his lack of knowledge of Hasidism contributed to his distorted perception.[54]

Aryeh Maidenbaum, a Jungian analyst, notes that the Analytical Psychology Club of Zurich adopted a restriction in December 1944 that "when possible, members of the Jewish faith should not exceed 10 percent," and that Jewish guests should be limited to twenty-five percent.[55] Maidenbaum interviewed many who were members of the Club during that time. Some reflected that a feeling of genuine hysteria existed among some of the Club's members, including fear that an invasion by Germany was imminent and that Jung would be deported to a concentration camp if too many Jews were members.[56] Aniela Jaffé related that Jung made it clear that he himself would resign if Jaffé were excluded because of the restriction. Siegmund Hurwitz who was accepted in 1950, informed Jung that he was withdrawing his application upon learning of the restriction. Jung told Hurwitz the rule had been eliminated.[57]

Jungian analyst Steven Zemmelman writes that "Jung's fascination with the psychological factors underlying the rise of National Socialism reflected blindness both to aspects of his own individual and collective shadow as well as to the Nazi commitment to persecute the Jews which spawned an entire apparatus built to assure their annihilation." The result of his involvement was that "Jung's public comments as a world-famous psychiatrist gave the Nazis validation for their demonization of Freud and the Jews and allowed them to supplement their pseudo-scientific phrenological claims with pseudo-psychological ones."[58]

By 1934 Jung came to regret his actions and statements. He provided financial and emotional support to his Jewish colleagues to help keep them safe during the war and offered to pay for Freud's passage to England, which Freud refused. Jung also worked actively with the US government Office of Strategic Services.[59] In 1943, he met with Allan Foster Dulles of the OSS. Dulles wrote that malevolent charges that Jung was pro-Nazi were entirely unfounded acts of character assassination. Dulles recounted his meetings with Jung during the war, where Jung's insight on the characteristics of the leaders of Nazi Germany and fascist Italy and "their likely reactions to passing events was of real help to me in gauging the political situation."[60]

After the war, kabbalistic scholar Gershom Scholem had reservations about participating in the Eranos conference with Jung because of his upset over Jung's statements made during the early 1930s. Swiss rabbi Leo Baeck encouraged Scholem to participate. Baeck told Scholem of his meeting with Jung upon his return to Switzerland following his internment at Theresienstadt concentration camp during the war. Baeck and Jung knew each other very well from attending joint meetings at the School of Wisdom prior to the war. Baeck was surprised by Jung's statements in 1933 and 1934, because he would never have believed him to hold any Nazi or anti-Semitic beliefs. Baeck told Gershom Scholem that although he initially refused a meeting with Jung because of rumors of his anti-Semitism, Jung came to his hotel and they spoke for several hours. Jung confessed, "Well I slipped up." Baeck felt the talk cleared up whatever had come between them and they felt reconciled. Scholem reflected that the term "slipped up" can refer "to losing one's footing on a dangerous mountain path." Sanford Drob invites readers of Baeck's and Scholem's accounts to come to their own judgment about the extent to which the story reflects Jung's acceptance of responsibility for his words and actions.[61]

At the end of the war, Jung had a vision that strengthened his interest in and relationship to the spiritual depths of kabbalah.[62] However, the schism caused by his lack of judgment in the early years of the rise of Nazism still reverberates today. The issue has been explored in depth by Jungian analyst Aryeh Maidenbaum, and addressed in the international Jungian community by analyst Jerome Bernstein and others.[63]

Jung, Jungians, and Jewish mysticism

Following a heart attack in 1944, Jung had a powerful vision of the mystical marriage between *Malchut* and *Tifferet*, two of the *sefirot* on the Tree of Life, representing the hieros gamos of the feminine and masculine aspects of God.

> I myself was, so it seemed, in the *Pardes Rimmonim*, the garden of pomegranates, and the wedding of Tifereth with Malchuth was taking place. Or else I was Rabbi *Simon ben Jochai*, whose wedding in the afterlife was being celebrated. It was the mystic marriage as it appears in the Cabbalistic tradition. I cannot tell you how wonderful it was. I could only think continually, "Now this is the garden of pomegranates! Now this is the marriage of Malchuth with Tifereth!" I do not know exactly what part I played in it. At bottom it was I myself: I was the marriage. And my beatitude was that of a blissful wedding.[64]

He experienced this vision as the most sacred of his entire lifetime. In it, Jung wondered if he was Shimon ben Yochai, the 2nd-century mystic and purported author of the great mystical text the Zohar.

Jungian scholar Sanford Drob reflects that as a lifelong student of alchemy, Jung may have recognized that many of the alchemical ideas were drawn from kabbalah as a precursor and major influence on the development of alchemy itself.

He also wonders whether Jung's deep engagement with mysticism and kabbalah may have been a way of healing his costly ignorance in the early years of the rise of Nazism. Drob cites Jung's interpretation of the Book of Job, where he concludes that perhaps God needed to incarnate as human to atone for his actions toward Job. Drob asks whether in his vision of the kabbalistic marriage, "Jung must become a Jew for the same redemptive reason."[65]

Jung was deeply engaged with Christian symbolism and ignorant of Jewish mysticism for much of his early life. He believed that Christ was a primary symbol of individuation, representing the incarnation of the God or Self energy into human ego consciousness. Jung initially viewed Judaism as less evolved because it did not accept the doctrine of the incarnation, reflecting the reigning Christian prejudice of his Protestant upbringing. Erich Neumann tried to make Jung aware of the depth psychological symbolism of kabbalah in the 1930s, but Jung was initially not receptive.[66] After the war, Jung became increasingly interested in kabbalistic mysticism. The incarnation of the Divine through the *sefirot*, as represented by Adam Kadmon, the human figure representing the kabbalistic tree of life, offered Jung an understanding of how the Self is realized in human consciousness within Jewish mystical thought.

In the postwar era, Erich Neumann facilitated a relationship between Gershom Scholem, the great scholar of kabbalah, and Jung. After speaking with Rabbi Leo Baeck, Scholem participated, along with Neumann, in gatherings convened by Jung at Eranos in Switzerland, whose purpose was to birth a new consciousness that would facilitate peaceful coexistence in the aftermath of the horrors of war.[67]

Jung's appreciation of both kabbalah and Hasidism grew greatly as he aged. On his 80th birthday, he stated in an interview: "But do you know who anticipated my entire psychology in the eighteenth century? The Hassidic Rabbi Baer from Meseritz, whom they called the Great Maggid. He was a most impressive man."[68]

Erich Neumann and the religious function of the Jewish psyche

Erich Neumann emigrated from Germany to Palestine in the early 1930s, after being denied the right to practice medicine under the Nazis. En route to Palestine, he spent many months in Zurich as an analysand of Jung. He continued a correspondence with Jung before and after the war, sharing his thoughts about Jewish consciousness.[69]

Neumann's epic work *The Origins and History of Consciousness* mapped the arc of human history, beginning with matriarchal societies that predominated the Paleolithic era for nearly 40,000 years at the dawn of human culture, followed by the ascendancy of patriarchy during the past two and a half millennia. Neumann believed the stages of human history corresponded to the development of the individual, beginning with the identification with the Great Mother that we experience in infancy and early childhood, followed by the stage of adolescence and early adulthood, where the focus is on development of the ego, which corresponds to the patriarchal age. The emerging stage of consciousness is a marriage between masculine and feminine, a central motif of kabbalah. This marriage would reflect an ongoing conscious dialogue between the ego, or rational consciousness, identified with the masculine, and the Self, or the larger unconscious, corresponding to mythos, and identified with the feminine.

On a personal level, as we develop this relationship between conscious and unconscious, we build an ego-Self axis.[70] In his exploration of Jewish mysticism, Neumann discussed the developing relationship between the ego and the Self as resulting from the connection between the various levels of soul—*nefesh* (body soul), *ruach* (emotional soul), and *neshama* (wisdom soul). We can live solely focused in our body and emotional souls, which correspond to the ego, without awareness of the wisdom soul. When we work through individual complexes, these souls can act as a conduit to the *neshama*, corresponding to the Self, without becoming overwhelmed by it.[71] This writing reflects that Neumann's development of the concept of the ego–Self axis may have its basis in kabbalistic thought.

As our conscious mind deepens its relationship with our unconscious, carrier of our dreams and our future development, we grow into our own wholeness. Neumann recognized that Jewish mystical practices provided a gateway to such an ongoing relationship but felt, like Jung, that religious symbols and practices needed to be experienced within the vessel of each person's individual psyche, because psychological approaches to religious symbolism were often not facilitated in more rationally focused assimilated religious settings. Neumann saw that Judaism had reached a crisis point with the advent of emancipation in the mid-19th century, as "Jews attempt to catch up with the Occident's development toward the individual in two generations," leading to "complete 'forgetting,' de-semitization,' to the disintegration into traditionlessness, to exceedingly isolated individuals without foundations, without historical, cultural, and psychic or spiritual continuity."[72]

Neumann's map of the history of western consciousness corresponds to the development of Jewish consciousness in our own era. Jews in the 19th and 20th centuries were emerging from an earlier collective culture in which daily life was infused with the spiritual. With widespread assimilation into the dominant cultures, Neumann witnessed Jews increasingly separating from the collective expression of Judaism, with many breaking completely from the tradition. Yet he saw within this breaking away a profound promise. He believed that a new era might emerge in which Jews would maintain a strongly developed individual ego that could also consciously engage with the myths and rituals of Judaism—myths and rituals that would strengthen, rather than detract from, their relationship to the Self. He understood that reconnecting with the cultural collective unconscious of Judaism might be powerfully affecting for Jews.[73]

Jung strongly encouraged his Jewish students to explore their relationship with Judaism. Rivkah Scharf Kluger writes that for Jews, the Hebrew Bible and kabbalistic myths make up their soul substance.[74] For Jewish individuals who have either never encountered this essential part of themselves, or have lost their bond with it, the experience of connecting with and living from their roots is essentially a psychological rebirth. "Such renewal can only come to the individual searching for the way to his or her own depth, to the inner 'well of Judah.'"[75]

Kluger explains that the symbolic meaning of being a chosen people can be understood as the decision a person makes to consecrate him or herself to God; to live according to Divine law rather than being guided only by the laws of the natural world. Psychologically, someone who enters this covenant is "placed in the situation of conflict, which is the precondition for becoming conscious."[76]

Rivkah Scharf Kluger and Siegmund Hurwitz were both close associates of Jung and wrote on Jewish themes. More recently, Gustav Dreifuss, Henry Abramovitch, Erel Shalit, Naomi Ruth Lowinsky, and Sanford Drob have explored the relationship with the Jewish mythic imagination. Their work guides the understanding of how devastating the rupture with the treasure trove of Jewish mythos has been for modern Jews, as well as how life-giving it is to reconnect with the Jewish cultural unconscious.

Judaism and psychology in the postwar era

In his autobiography, Rabbi Zalman Schachter-Shalomi wrote about how deeply influenced he was by Neumann's work, so much so that he had arranged to move to Israel to begin analysis with him in 1960. Unfortunately, Neumann died that year. Through the development of Jewish Renewal, Reb Zalman realized the promise of which Neumann spoke—a psychological approach to Judaism that enabled individuals to use the practices and teachings in a deeply personal way to bring about spiritual and personal growth—in short, Judaism as a pathway to individuation, to becoming more fully one's true self.

In the postwar era, psychology continued to grow and thrive as various schools of thought developed. Many of these grew from the work of Jews: Abraham Maslow's humanist psychology, Shoah survivor Viktor Frankl's development of existential psychology, Fritz Perls's Gestalt psychology, Wilhelm Reich's somatic psychology, and the further development of psychoanalytic theory by Erich Fromm, Theodor Reik (who also wrote on Jewish mythic themes), Anna Freud, Bruno Bettelheim, Heinz Kohut, and Melanie Klein. All these theorists (except Maslow, who was born in America, and Klein, who immigrated to London in 1926) were refugees from or survivors of the Shoah. Their work provided new frameworks for personal and spiritual growth in the postwar era that profoundly transformed the culture and understanding of our inner and outer worlds.

Another German Jewish émigré, Kurt Lewin, first developed the idea of inter-nalized anti-Semitism. Drawing on his work, Jerry Diller and others explored internalized anti-Semitism among Jews and its impact on the development of a conflicted Jewish identity.[77] Their work provides a helpful guide to the under-standing of the loss and reclamation of Jewish identity.

Is the centrality of Jews in the field of psychology a secular continuation, within the wider non-Jewish world, of a profound spiritual inheritance? Perhaps the wide dissemination of Jewish psychological insight in the wake of cataclysmic historical events reflects Isaac Luria's cosmological understanding of how holy sparks may be raised from the most painful of circumstances.

Throughout the early and mid-20th century, psychology was framed as rational and anti-religious, with the notable exception of Jung and his followers. However, with the advent of Maslow's humanistic psychology, which embraced spirituality as an important part of human experience, and psychedelic psychology—led in part by Jewish psychologists Ram Dass (formerly Richard Alpert) and Ralph Metzner—spirituality and psychology found a meeting place, largely drawing on Jung's transpersonal perspectives.

Reb Zalman, a scholar of both comparative religion and psychology, was inspired by the work of Erich Neumann, and by his engagement with Abraham Maslow and Richard Alpert. He began to knit together psychology and spirituality in a Jewish context—two worlds that had previously been sundered. As I explore in the chapters that follow, Jewish Renewal practices facilitate positive experiences of Jewish identity and its deeper meaning, creating a pathway to reconnection.

Reb Zalman devoted his life to helping Jews access the mystical heart of Judaism. The experience of what religious anthropologists call *neurognosis*—remembering something we have always known but never consciously encountered—is powerful.[78] Reb Zalman wrote, "Forgetting something is not the same as never knowing it in the first place." Despite having learned the entire Torah and then forgetting it, it nonetheless "lurks deep in our memories—all of these images point to an intricate dance between the God that is us, each individual creation, and the God that is All."[79]

Healing trauma and the transcendent experience

Much of what we know today about healing from intergenerational trauma is drawn from research done with Holocaust survivors and their descendants. Emerging work on epigenetics suggests that we each carry the imprint of traumas suffered by our ancestors.[80] In addition to exploring the personal and familial trauma generated by the Shoah, I will consider its impact on the Jewish collective psyche as well as the impact of other periods of collective trauma, including the massive pogroms and virulent anti-Semitism that brought millions of Jews to America in the late 19th and early 20th centuries.

Rabbi Isaac Luria's view, developed in the aftermath of the Spanish expulsion, that humans participate in the work of healing the creation, corresponds with current psychological ideas of post-traumatic growth. The suffering involved in trauma, although a path that we would never consciously wish for or choose, opens us to states of profound insight and awakens the possibility of transformation and redemption. Cultural stories of healing, such as the Biblical Exodus, are psychological roadmaps that can help us understand how to recover from collective and personal trauma. Although we cannot minimize the tremendous suffering involved, those who have experienced trauma may grow psychologically and spiritually in new and profound ways that are developed in order to continue to thrive in the face of soul-destroying circumstances.

John Wilson outlines three essential stages of trauma: (1) an *abyss* experience, in which the life-threatening trauma is initially undergone, and the person's world is forever changed; (2) the *inversion* experience, in which the previously perceived meaning and order within the world are completely upended, and the person's sense of the world as essentially safe and trustworthy is crushed; and (3) the *transcendent experience*, in which the person comes into a new relationship with the Divine or the "Great Mystery" and experiences tremendous soul growth.[81]

The impact of personal or collective trauma is psychologically devastating. A person is plunged into the abyss, a "metaphysical bottom of the seemingly endless chasm of emotional and spiritual darkness without relief from utter terror and fear." The abyss experience results in a "sense of abandonment by God and humanity" and a sense of utter and ultimate aloneness.[82]

After an abyss experience, a person's perceptions of reality are upended, resulting in what Wilson calls an "inversion experience" in which "the center does not hold." This stage is characterized by the symptoms called *post-traumatic stress*. The basic human trust that the universe will protect us is ripped away. The values held prior to the trauma are lost, and the person's whole sense of reality is turned upside down. Significant to our understanding of cultural trauma, Wilson notes that an internalization of the dominant culture's values may take place, and connection with our own culture can be trivialized or disowned.[83]

In the final stage of post-traumatic growth, the trauma creates a psychic opening that might not have occurred if the person had continued to live in the balanced world experienced prior to the trauma.[84] Wilson's model helps guide our understanding of our own historical moment, as we move out of the inversion period of disowning our connection with Judaism to the profound opening that reconnection with Jewish mythos may offer Jews in the aftermath of the Shoah.

Jungian analyst Jerome Bernstein explores the capacity to access the transrational dimension of reality, which he calls the "Borderland experience." Working with Native American spiritual teachers, and also with individuals highly attuned to the experiences of the natural world, Bernstein saw, "Everything animate and inanimate has within it a spirit dimension and communicates *in that dimension* to those who can listen."[85] Bernstein observes that Borderland consciousness may be experienced by those with natural psychic abilities, young children, and may also be opened up by the experience of trauma for which it can provide a powerful source of psychological support.[86]

Gathering the sparks

Gathering the shattered pieces of our familial and collective histories, we find that contextualizing these experiences within a larger, continuing story is redemptive and healing. In the following chapters, I explore stories of personal reconnection with Judaism and reflect on the import of these individual stories within the larger framework of the Jewish mythic imagination. As we gather the exiled parts of ourselves, our ancestry, and our history, we "restory" the shape of our own lives, and in that process, we may discover our connection to a holding Presence that has been accompanying us all along.

Notes

1 Jonathan Garb, *Yearnings of the Soul: Psychological Thought in Modern Kabbalah* (Chicago, IL: University of Chicago Press, 2015); *The Chosen Will Become Herds: Studies in Twentieth Century Kabbalah*, translated by Yaffah Berkovits-Murciano (New Haven, CT: Yale University Press, 2009).
2 Arthur Green, *Tormented Master: The Life and Spiritual Quest of Rabbi Nahman of Bratslav* (Woodstock, VT: Jewish Lights Publishing, 1992).
3 David Bakan, *Sigmund Freud and the Jewish Mystical Tradition* (Princeton: D. Van Nostrand Co., Inc., 1958); Joseph Berke, *The Hidden Freud: His Hasidic Roots* (New York: Routledge, 2015); Jerry V. Diller, "Identity Rejection and Reawakening in the Jewish Context," *Journal of Judaism and Psychology* 5, no. 1 (1987): 38–47.
4 C.G. Jung and Erich Neumann, *Analytical Psychology in Exile: The Correspondence of C.G. Jung and Erich Neumann*, edited by Martin Liebscher, translated by Heather McCartney (Princeton, NJ: Princeton University Press, 2005).
5 See Aryeh Maidenbaum's work on healing the split in Stephen Martin and Aryeh Maidenbaum, eds., *Lingering Shadows: Jungians, Freudians, and Anti-Semitism* (Boston: Shambhala, 1991); Sanford Drob, *Kabbalistic Visions: C.G. Jung and Jewish Mysticism* (New Orleans, LA: Spring Journal Books, 2010); and Thomas Kirsch, "Cultural Complexes in the History of Jung, Freud and Their Followers," in *The Cultural Complex: Contemporary Jungian Perspectives on Psyche and Society*, edited by Thomas Singer and Samuel Kimbles (London: Routledge, 2004), 185–195.
6 Bakan, *Sigmund Freud and the Jewish Mystical Tradition*; Berke, *The Hidden Freud*.
7 Dennis B. Klein, *Jewish Origins of the Psychoanalytic Movement* (Chicago, IL: University of Chicago Press, 1981).
8 Sigmund Freud, *The Future of an Illusion*, trans. James Strachey (New York: W.W. Norton, 1961 (orig. 1927); Sigmund Freud, *Civilization and its Discontents*, trans. James Strachey (New York; W.W. Norton, 1962, orig. 1930); *Moses and Monotheism*, trans. Katherine Jones, (London: The Hogarth Press and Institute of Psycho-Analysis, 1939).
9 Bakan, *Sigmund Freud and the Jewish Mystical Tradition*.
10 Ibid, chap. 10.
11 Zalman Schachter-Shalomi and Edward Hoffman, *Sparks of Light: Counseling in the Hasidic Tradition* (Boston: Shambhala, 2001).
12 Berke, *The Hidden Freud*, 77–111.
13 Ibid.
14 Bakan, Preface to *Sigmund Freud and the Jewish Mystical Tradition*, xviii.
15 Garb, *Yearnings of the Soul*.
16 Private conversation with Jungian analyst Naomi Lowinsky, April 2019.
17 Bakan, *Sigmund Freud and the Jewish Mystical Tradition*. See also Sander L. Gilman, *Freud, Race and Gender* (Princeton, NJ: Princeton University Press, 1993).
18 Berke, *The Hidden Freud*, 1–20.
19 Emily Kuriloff, *Contemporary Psychoanalysis and the Legacy of the Third Reich: History, Memory, Tradition* (New York: Routledge, 2014).
20 Ibid, 11.

21 Ibid.
22 Michael Eigen, *Kabbalah and Psychoanalysis* (London: Karnac Books, 2012).
23 William McGuire, ed., *The Freud/Jung Letters: The Correspondence Between Sigmund Freud and C.G. Jung* (Princeton, NJ: Princeton University Press, 1974), 196–197, Sigmund Freud, Letter to Carl Jung, January 17, 1909.
24 C.G. Jung, *Archetypes of the Collective Unconscious* (Princeton: Bollingen Press, 1959), 512.
25 Ibid.
26 Stephen Larsen, *The Mythic Imagination: Your Quest for Meaning through Personal Mythology* (New York: Bantam Books, 1990), 37–38; citing C.G. Jung, Foreword to *Symbols of Transformation: An Analysis of the Prelude to a Case of Schizophrenia*, 2nd ed., Bollingen Series XX, translated by R.F.C. Hull (Princeton, NJ: Princeton University Press, 1967), xxiv–xxv.
27 Larsen, *The Mythic Imagination*, 37–38; citing Jung, Foreword to *Symbols of Transformation*, xxiv–xxv.
28 Ibid.
29 Joseph Henderson, "The Cultural Unconscious," *Quadrant* 21, no. 2 (1988): 7–16.
30 Ibid.
31 Michael Vannoy Adams, *The Mythological Unconscious* (New York: H. Karnac Books, Ltd., 2001), 105–107.
32 Barbara Hannah, *Jung: His Life and Work* (New York: GP Putnam's Sons, 1976), 16–18.
33 Ibid, 18.
34 Ibid.
35 Ibid.
36 Ibid; citing C.G. Jung, *Psychology and Alchemy, The Collected Works of C.G. Jung*, Vol. 12 (Princeton, NJ: Princeton University Press, 1953), 83, para. 113.
37 Ibid, citing Henry Corbin, *The Question of Comparative Philosophy* (Dallas: Spring Publications, 1980), 8.
38 C.G. Jung, "Psychological Commentary on The Tibetan Book of the Dead," in *Psychology and Religion: West and East, The Collected Works of C.G. Jung*, Vol. 11, edited by Herbert Read, Michael Fordham, Gerhard Adler (Princeton: Bollingen Press, 1958), 103, cited in Siegmund Hurwitz, *Lilith—The First Eve: Historical and Psychological Aspects of the Dark Feminine* (Einsiedeln: Daimon Verlag, 1992), 173–174.
39 C.G. Jung, *Two Essays on Analytical Psychology, The Collected Works of C.G. Jung*, Vol. 7, edited by Herbert Read, Michael Fordham, Gerhard Adler (Princeton: Bollingen Press, 1953), 190; cited in Hurwitz, *Lilith*, 174.
40 Hurwitz, *Lilith*, 174.
41 Erich Neumann, *Art and the Creative Unconscious*, translated by Ralph Manheim, Bollingen Series LH1 (New York: Pantheon, 1959), 82.
42 Ibid.
43 Noa Gedi and Yigal Elam, "Collective Memory—What is It?" *History & Memory* 8, no. 1 (1996): 41.
44 Ibid.
45 Yosef Hayim Yerushalmi, *Zakhor: Jewish History and Jewish Memory* (New York: Schocken Books, 1989), xxxv.
46 Drob, *Kabbalistic Visions*, 167–177.
47 Aryeh Maidenbaum, ed., *Jung and the Shadow of Anti-Semitism: Collected Essays* (Berwick, ME: Nicholas-Hays, Inc., 2002), 211.
48 Ibid; see also, William Schoenl and Linda Schoenl, *Jung's Evolving Views of Nazi Germany: From the Nazi Takeover to the End of World War II* (Asheville, NC: Chiron Publications, 2016).
49 Schoenl and Schoenl, *Jung's Evolving Views of Nazi Germany*.

50 Paul Roazen, "Jung and Anti-Semitism," in Aryeh Maidenbaum, ed., *Jung and the Shadow of Anti-Semitism,* 9.
51 Jung and Neumann, *Analytical Psychology in Exile*, 12.
52 Kirsch, "Cultural Complexes in Jung and Freud," 190.
53 Ibid.
54 Ibid, 13.
55 Aryeh Maidenbaum, "Lingering Shadows" in Aryeh Maidenbaum, ed., *Jung and the Shadow of Anti-Semitism,* 92.
56 Ibid., 93.
57 Ibid., 93-94.
58 Steve Zemmelman, "Inching Towards Wholeness: C.G. Jung and His Relationship to Judaism," *Journal of Analytical Psychology* 62, no. 2 (2017): 247–262.
59 Schoenl and Schoenl, *Jung's Evolving Views of Nazi Germany.*
60 Joan Dulles Buresch-Talley, "The C.G. Jung and Allen Dulles Correspondence, Aryeh Maidenbaum, ed., Jung and the Shadow of Anti-Semitism, 45, citing Box 39, Allen W. Dulles Papers, Seeley Mudd Library, Princeton University.
61 Gershom Scholem to Aniela Jaffé, May 7, 1963; Aniela Jaffé, *From the Life and Work of C.G. Jung,* trans. R.F.C. Hull and Murray Stein (Einsiedeln, Switzerland: Daimon Verlag, 1989), 97-98, cited in Drob, *Kabbalistic Visions,* 192.
62 Drob, *Kabbalistic Visions*, 207–227.
63 Martin and Maidenbaum, *Lingering Shadows*, and Maidenbaum, ed., *Jung and the Shadow of Anti-Semitism*. Jerome Bernstein writes of his efforts at the Congress of the International Association of Analytical Psychology to explore these questions in the international Jungian community and to adopt a resolution establishing "a policy of non-discrimination regarding race, religion, ethnic origin, gender and sexual orientation." (Jerome Bernstein, "Collective Shadow Integration of the Jungian Community: Atonement," and "Appendix B," in *Jung and the Shadow*, 114–140 and 259–271).
64 C.G. Jung, *Memories, Dreams and Reflections*, edited by A. Jaffé (New York: Random House, 1961), 293.
65 Drob, *Kabbalistic Visions*, 211.
66 Jung and Neumann, *Analytic Psychology in Exile*. Jungian historian Sonu Shamdasani reflects that Jung was aware, as early as 1915, of kabbalistic symbology related to Western alchemy and hermeticism, but this does not appear to have significantly raised his awareness of Jewish mysticism. Shamdasani Lecture, San Francisco, California, April 2019.
67 Jung and Neumann, *Analytic Psychology in Exile*, 173–174; Martin and Maidenbaum, *Lingering Shadows*, 90.
68 Drob, *Kabbalistic Visions*, 3.
69 Jung and Neumann, *Analytical Psychology in Exile.*
70 Erich Neumann, "Narcissism, Normal Self-Formation, and the Primary Relation to the Mother," *Spring* (1966): 81–106.
71 Erich Neumann, *The Roots of Jewish Consciousness*, Vol. II, edited by Ann Conrad Lammers (London: Routledge, 2019), 82–83.
72 Jung and Neumann, *Analytical Psychology in Exile*, 47.
73 Ibid.
74 Rivkah Scharf Kluger, *Psyche in Scripture: The Idea of the Chosen People and Other Essays* (Toronto: Inner City Books, 1995), 117.
75 Ibid.
76 Ibid; citing Rivkah Scharf Kluger, *Satan in the Old Testament* (Evanston, IL: Northwestern University Press, 1967), 132.
77 Kurt Lewin, "Self-Hatred Among Jews," in *A Psychology-Judaism Reader*, edited by Reuven P. Bulka and Moshe HaLevi Spero (Springfield, IL: Charles C. Thomas,

1982), 58–70; Diller, "Identity Rejection and Reawakening in the Jewish Context," 38–47.

78 Charles D. Laughlin and C. Jason Throop, "Imagination and Reality: On the Relations Between Myth, Consciousness and the Cosmic Sea," *Zygon* 36, no. 4 (Dec. 2001): 716.

79 Zalman Schachter-Shalomi and Joel Segel, *Jewish with Feeling: A Guide to Meaningful Jewish Practice* (Woodstock, VT: Jewish Lights Publishing, 2006), 31.

80 Rachel Yehuda, *Psychological Trauma* (Washington, DC: American Psychiatric Press, 1998).

81 John P. Wilson, *The Posttraumatic Self: Restoring Meaning and Wholeness to Personality* (New York: Routledge, 2006), 169–209.

82 Ibid, 171.

83 Ibid, 180–188.

84 Ibid, 188–192.

85 Jerome Bernstein, *Living In the Borderland: The Evolution of Consciousness and the Challenge of Healing Trauma* (London: Routledge, 2005), 8.

86 Ibid, 87–96.

Part II

The rupture

Chapter 4

Exile

Loss of custom, ruin of will,
A memory of a memory
thinner than a vein.
Who will teach us to return?
To whom nothing speaks,
Not shofar, not song, not homily.
On whom nothing was wrought.
Not slaughter, not horror, not holocaust.
...
We do not want to come back.
We do not know where we are.
Not knowing where we are, how can we know
where we should go?

Cynthia Ozick, "In the Synagogue"[1]

Finding ourselves in the ancestral myth

This chapter begins an exploration of the Exodus story, in which the Hebrew people are in a state of physical and spiritual exile, enslaved in *mitzrayim*, the narrowed consciousness where access to God has been almost fully occluded. I examine the lived experiences of Jews coming of age in the postwar era, disconnected spiritually from Judaism, and reflect on their experience through the midrashic interpretations of the exile, and contextualize its psychological meaning in our own time.

The Exodus story begins: "A new king arose who did not know Joseph."[2] The Biblical story of the Exodus begins 400 years after the end of the Book of Genesis, which concludes with the reunion of Joseph with his brothers and father in Egypt. (I explore this story in depth in Chapter Nine.) Joseph, son of Jacob and Rachel, was cruelly abandoned by his brothers and sold into slavery in Egypt. The first Hebrew to enter Egypt, Joseph's personal descent both catalyzes and prefigures the collective descent the Hebrew people will subsequently make.

Joseph endured a series of trials in Egypt, was imprisoned and through his own gifts, ultimately freed, becoming Pharaoh's trusted advisor when he was able to interpret Pharaoh's dream and save the Egyptian people from famine. Joseph's prominence enabled his family, the progenitors of the twelve tribes of Israel, to settle in Egypt and survive the drought that would have surely killed them had Joseph not intervened.

Yet as the Book of Exodus opens, the new Pharaoh, who did not know of Joseph and his role in saving the Egyptian people from devastating famine centuries earlier, believed the Hebrew people had become too numerous. Because he feared their potential power, he ordered them enslaved and issued an edict that the sons of each family be killed at birth.[3] After 400 years of enslavement, the Hebrew people had lost faith in the prophetic promise made to their ancestor Abraham that they would one day be redeemed. They, like many Jews following the Shoah, turned away from a God that could allow their people to suffer unfathomable horror.

Exile and conflicted Jewish identity in our time

Jungian analyst James Kirsch, who studied with Jung in Zurich, emigrated from Germany to Palestine in the 1930s and eventually settled in Los Angeles where he co-founded the C.G. Jung Institute. Kirsch used the term *galut*, the Hebrew word for *exile*, not only in its traditional meaning of their diaspora from the Promised Land, but also to describe the experience of modern Jews separated from their own internal Jewishness.[4]

Modernity and the pressures of assimilation changed the face of Jewish existence in a way unprecedented in the long expanse of Jewish history. Unlike the Jews of the past two millennia of diasporic existence, the modern galut Jew was in exile from Judaism itself. In *A Modern Jew In Search of A Soul*, William Alex writes that the search for soul implies that the modern Jew "has either lost his/her soul or is in the process of losing it."[5] He suggests that embodied in this lost soul lies a Jewish person's "real inner sense of identity, often at variance with his outer adaptation." The impact of a person's

> loss of Jewish soul means the loss of his inner living connection and meaningful relationship to an ancient, three-thousand-year-old heritage, to an indefinable sense of being part of an ongoing historical and religious process whose contribution to world civilization, to its theology, ethics, laws, and to the overall growth of human consciousness is beyond reckoning.[6]

Jews growing up in the mid to late 20th century were often raised in homes in which profound historical undercurrents lay beneath the surface of the family's relationship to Jewish identity but were rarely consciously explored. Instead, American Jews lived with what Jungian analyst Samuel Kimbles calls a "phantom narrative" of "secrets concealed and held" that "are silently transmitted directly into the unconscious of the child."[7] These phantoms contain the underlying story of what lives unspoken in the family and cultural milieu. Children internalized the conflicts embedded in those secrets, making their relationship to spirituality and Judaism often fraught with confusion, conflict, and a despair that could not be named or discussed. Coming of age in the presence of phantoms marks the spiritual and psychological state of exile that begins this exploration.

"I'm Jewish"

My earliest memories involve my grandparents picking me up at my home in Brooklyn and driving me, always with a stop downtown at Junior's Deli, to the Lower East Side of Manhattan, where they ran a storefront chapel called Hermon House. My grandfather would preach messianic Judaism from the pulpit, and my grandmother would rewrite the words to popular songs as hymns to Jesus. My grandmother emigrated from Russia when she was a girl, and both she and my grandfather were raised in observant Orthodox Jewish homes. They both rejected Judaism in their early adulthood, turning first toward socialism and then, Buddhism and meditation in the 1950s and ultimately resonating with the teachings of *Yeshua*, the Hebrew name for Jesus. They changed their names from Abraham and Emma Rosenblum to Arnold and Emily Ross, but to each other they always remained Abe and Emma.

I remember after services, we would go downstairs into the basement where they ran a large neighborhood soup kitchen. Other than the times inside the chapel, I do not ever recall a time when my grandmother, until the end of her life, was not at the stove, preparing potato latkes, chicken, and blintzes for those in need.

My grandfather delighted in sharing a memory of me at four years old. I entered the chapel where his friend, a Protestant minister, was preaching. The minister lit up when he saw me and greeted me warmly from the pulpit: "How are you?" he inquired graciously. I replied, somewhat defiantly, "I'm Jewish!" This story reflects an awareness I had of the conflicted nature of the environment I found myself in, torn between my love for my grandparents and my sense that something about their spiritual orientation was deeply at odds with an already internalized sense of my own identity.

Throughout my childhood, I was hesitant to share my grandparents' spirituality with anyone, because I was often told that they were "crazy." I rarely spoke about them, afraid if I did people would question whether I was really Jewish. Not that my visits with my grandparents clarified much—the walls of their home were hung with paintings of Hasidic men dancing with the Torah, next to crosses and New Testament quotes from "Yeshua." It was only in the process of collecting stories of other Jewish people that I was surprised and moved to learn that the experience of conflicted identity and outsiderness was shared by many. It helped me contextualize my own experience to understand that there were many who, fleeing pogroms or as refugees from the Shoah, hid their Judaism completely. I thought of the *marranos* in medieval Spain, adopting outwardly Gentile appearances while inwardly safeguarding Jewish customs.

My Jewish identity was sourced in growing up in Brooklyn, and later Queens, where almost all my classmates were Jewish. We were not an observant family, but like many other culturally identified Jews, we held Passover Seders each year and celebrated Chanukah. Anawana, the Jewish sleepaway camp in the Catskills that I attended throughout my childhood summers was owned by the Kutsher's family resort. My father, a physical education teacher during the school year, was head of the boys camp. The camp was not religious—it primarily focused on sports—but we said the *motzi*, the blessing for bread, before each meal and attended Friday night Shabbat services led by the elder waterfront instructor, Brooks Brickman who, though not a rabbi, carried the spiritual light of a *tzaddik*, or holy person. During humid and sweltering Friday nights in the field house, which served as gymnasium, theater, and activity center, we were gathered in a dreamlike state induced by the heat and by sitting still after a week of intense activity. Brooks told us Biblical stories. I recall his tenderness as he described Hagar and Ishmael, cast out into the desert by Abraham to ensure his and Sarah's son Isaac's inheritance. Although I heard the story every year, I still felt a powerful stirring of hope when Hagar, falling into despair at Ishmael's likely death, was greeted by an angel who provided an oasis for them in the desert. I think now of the compassion this story instilled in each of us for our Arabic brothers and sisters and the pain of their struggles engendered by the family divisions begun in Genesis. Perhaps too I found solace in God's remembering a woman on the brink of total annihilation, as my own mother struggled with a crippling depression.

The proliferation of Jewish summer camps and resorts in the Catskill Mountains of New York in the mid-20th century was a curious phenomenon in the wake of the Shoah. Jewish humor, the massive menus, and the unending kosher bounty served up at the lavish resorts all spoke to an underlying anxiety and profound grief that were rarely addressed consciously in these settings. Jewish summer camp provided many Jewish children with a profound sense of belonging and bonding and inculcated positive feeling toward Jewish identity. Recent studies have reported that participation in summer camp is remarkably significant in contributing to the integration and continuation of Jewish identity.[8] The kinship I experienced at my summer camp provided a comforting sense of community that helped to counterbalance the difficult challenges I faced in my immediate family.

My father grew up immersed in Jewish cultural heritage but found Hebrew school rote and uninspiring. Although he was close with his paternal grandparents, who spoke English and ran a dry-cleaning business in midtown Manhattan where he had worked as a teen, he had little or no relationship with his maternal grandfather, who spoke only Yiddish and delivered seltzer for a living. They literally never spoke with each other. His mother, who had been raised Orthodox, was a strong woman who did not want to be constrained by the limitations set in the traditional culture. She never created a bridge between her father and mine. Although three of my four sets of great-grandparents were religiously observant Jews, almost nothing of the religious tradition was part of my childhood experience of Judaism.

When I was six years old, my parents separated. My father moved out, and my mother fell into a debilitating depression. As her depression deepened, I found solace in my conversations with God, imagining a benevolent presence watching over me. I would pray for deliverance out of the situation I was in—comforted by the sense that however the situation would resolve, even if it were with my own death—somehow, I would be held. My mother eventually moved back to the apartment where she grew up in Brooklyn, began receiving psychiatric treatment, and entered psychoanalysis for the remainder of her life. My older brother and I moved in with my father and stepmother. Separated from my mother, I still felt God's presence holding the net of connection between us. Perhaps God provided a holding presence that allowed me to maintain resiliency in the face of trauma.

As I entered adolescence, my friends became Bar or Bat Mitzvah. In my early teenage years, I began going to temple on my own, seeking the intensely personal connection I had felt earlier in my childhood. The services felt rigid and inaccessible, the congregants distant and unwelcoming to me, because as a non-member I literally did not "belong" there. Even in the Reform temple, the most liberal denomination, I was struck by the militaristic language of vanquishing one's enemies that seemed to permeate the prayerbook. Where was the tender God who had held me in the darkest times? I think of the maiden's yearning in the Song of Songs: "I sought him whom my soul loveth; I sought him, but I found him not. I will rise now, and go about the city, in the streets and in the broad ways, I will seek him whom my soul loveth."[9]

In the years that followed, I half-heartedly continued trying to find a way to engage with Judaism, but it did not open to me. My search for meaning continued in secular ways. Perhaps seeking to answer the questions my grandmother refused to respond to about her childhood in the Ukraine, and my need to comprehend the near-annihilation of my people shortly before I was born, my college studies were dedicated to understanding the culture and history of Germany that could give rise to Nazism, the history of modern Russia, and the complex interplay of European politics that led to the Second World War. I also studied the history of anti-fascist movements in the US, including the wide involvement of Jews in the counter-cultural revolutions of the early 20th century and in the civil rights, anti-war and women's movements of the 1960s and 70s.

Being Jewish in the 1980s was more confusing. Positions on the Israel-Palestine conflict were polarized between a conservative-leaning mainstream Jewish community in which there was little room for questioning Israeli policies, and a larger progressive community that viewed Israel as an expression of western imperialism. During this period, there had not yet developed strong voices in the Jewish community for peaceful approaches to reconciliation of the Israeli-Palestinian conflict.

Within the progressive movements, there was little discussion about the virulent anti-Semitism in Europe that had led to the formation of the state of Israel. Nor was there widespread awareness of the hundreds of thousands of concentration camp and other survivors languishing in displaced persons camps through the late 1940s and early 1950s, unable or fearful to repatriate to the countries from which they had been displaced, their homes and property often destroyed or confiscated by the government or neighbors, many of whom eventually settled in Israel.[10]

I focused my passion for justice in ways that felt less complicated—working to end apartheid in South Africa, on behalf of prisoners and with community organizations empowering people of color, with Native Americans on issues related to sovereignty, and with eco-activists combatting the clearcutting of the northern California old growth forests.

My search for an intimate connection with the Divine was met first through earth-based Wiccann spirituality rituals honoring the Goddess, likely related to the longing for my own mother and for the Great Mother, who was portrayed as having been trampled by Jewish monotheism, rather than, as I would later learn, part of its earliest expression. Later, as I worked with Native Americans, my spiritual longing was answered in sweat lodges and other ceremonies. In these rituals I learned to acknowledge my ancestors, and to give thanks for the blessings that came from earth and sky, the plant beings, and the four-leggeds; and to connect with the Great Spirit, a Grandfather that felt more akin to the God of my childhood than anything I had encountered in formal Jewish practice.

It would be many years before my grandmother, at the end of her life, would speak openly of her childhood experiences of near starvation and profound deprivation in the Ukraine. Only then could I begin to understand what lay behind her urgent need to feed others, and to wonder whether she and my grandfather's adoption of a Christian identity may have been related to an unconscious desire to be safe from anti-Semitic terror. I also began to question whether my grandmother's agoraphobia and my mother's depression may have been related to the trauma my grandmother experienced as a young girl. I explore these themes more fully below.

Julie's[11] story

Julie and her family attended the largest Reform synagogue in Los Angeles, which she described as the epitome of "that whole mink-coat-high-holy-day thing." Julie did not feel a sense of spiritual connection at temple. During services, she would look up at the dome in the ceiling but could not tell if the vault of the dome was truly there or just a painting. Her question seemed to reflect her inner state, wondering whether the experience was authentic or an illusion.

Beneath the veneer of materialism was profound pain that was never discussed in Julie's family. Her mother fled Germany as a child with her family and came to the United States in the mid-1930s. Julie's maternal grandfather was a very successful businessman in Germany but was never able to reestablish a business in the United States. He died of lung cancer a few years after settling in the US. He maintained his belief in God, however. When Julie's father questioned how he could still believe in God, her grandfather responded, "Leave me to my fantasies."

Her paternal grandmother, for whom Julie was named, was a deeply kind woman who suffered with severe mental illness. Her paternal grandfather left home when her father was fourteen but they didn't divorce until Julie's father was an adult to avoid stigmatizing him. Her paternal grandmother tragically took her own life shortly before Julie was born. Her father completely lost his faith in God after witnessing the suffering his own mother had endured.

Her father was scientifically oriented but maintained a strong sense of Jewish identity and interest in Jewish history. The family observed Shabbos and Passover in rote ways that made it difficult to access a sense of deep connection—her father led Passover Seders with a cow bell to keep their attention.

Julie felt that her mother believed in God, but it was not something they could ever talk about. Her mother's severe depression in the wake of her grandmother's suicide went untreated until Julie was about twelve. She recalled, "My father was pretty damaged by his mother's suicide and the loss of belief he experienced as a result of how hard her life had been. My mother was a Holocaust survivor who basically would do whatever my father said, and he didn't believe in God, so it's not even a conversation we can have now."

As a child, Julie experienced the sacred in nature, walking home from school, after a rain, when light illuminated the trees. "I miss the Santa Ana winds and that sense of that gracious wind. I never thought about going below the surface to really comprehend how important those kinds of natural things were to me, right on that six-block walk home from school."

Julie's spiritual yearnings were not witnessed or supported. Although she attended Hebrew Sunday school, she felt sad that no one ever took the time to explain to her, as a child or teenager, the spiritual meaning of Judaism. "I went through a very difficult experience in my late 20s, and when I came to a place of recognizing the profound spiritual depths in Judaism, I wondered, 'How come nobody ever told me that this was here for me before I had this really awful experience?'"

After going through this painful time, which I explore in later chapters, Julie found a meaningful connection to Judaism. She learned to read Hebrew and had an adult Bat Mitzvah when she was in her 30s. When she subsequently returned to the temple of her childhood for a nephew's Bar Mitzvah, she looked up at the familiar dome and saw that "written all around it in Hebrew, which I couldn't read as a child, was the Shema." The *Shema*, the central prayer of Judaism, speaks of the oneness of God. The first and last letters of the prayer make up the word *witness*, inviting each person to become a witness to the presence of the Divine.

Julie grew up in the conflicted milieu that characterized many Jewish families of the postwar era. The grief experienced by her mother and maternal grandparents is unfathomable, as they suffered the loss of their entire community of family, friends, and neighbors left behind in Germany. Her father could not maintain faith in the aftermath of his mother's severe mental illness and suicide and the spiritual crisis engendered by the Shoah. Yet her family continued to practice Judaism in a superficial way, because to stop practicing would mean to disavow Judaism—an unthinkable option in the wake of the memory of all those who had been killed. Yet to maintain faith in a God that had allowed the annihilation of His people was also unbearable. Prayers were uttered but not fully embodied, as rabbis, teachers, and family members held at bay the conflict and pain that they tried not to pass on to their children.

Perhaps silence and emptiness were the best they could do, surely preferable to filling the children with the rage at God and the despair that so many must have felt. Yet the children perceived the emptiness and interpreted it as meaningless-ness—as a religion that had no depth, no substance, no relevance for them. Was it truly a dome or just a painting of one? Was it a religion where mink coats and status were the only measures of one's worth? How could a child understand the desperate positioning for stability and survival that the money behind the mink coats sought to ensure? Would enough money establish a safe future for them? Would it save them from the next assault on Jews? How many in the congregation experienced the reality that only the family's hidden diamonds enabled one fam-ily's escape and another's inability to do so?

In the decades after the Shoah, many religious institutions were unable to con-vey an abiding sense of the reality of God; all Jews struggled with the question of whether God could exist and yet allow such devastation to take place. Spiritual beliefs were shaken to the core. Many temples focused instead on historical remembrances and observances.[12]

Julie, like so many other young Jews growing up in the postwar era, was left without a means to bring herself close to the heart of the tradition. She moved into adulthood without the guidance that the initiatory rituals of Judaism could offer. Julie's re-engagement with Judaism as an adult and her new perception of the deeper meaning of the dome in the temple of her youth reflected both her sadness and amazement that, like the Biblical Jacob, God was in this place and she did not know it. In the Torah, "Jacob awoke from his sleep. 'God is truly in this place,' he said, 'but I did not know it.' He was frightened. 'How awe-inspiring this place is!' he exclaimed. 'It must be God's temple. It is the gate to heaven!'"[13]

Lillian's story

Lillian, a retired psychotherapist and a founding member of a Jewish Renewal community in California, was born in New York to parents who had both rejected the observant practices of their families and instead embraced a secular, intel-lectual life. When she was a young girl, her family moved to a predominantly Gentile neighborhood in Connecticut and put her and her brother in a Catholic day school. She was separated from her grandmother, aunts, and uncles in New York, all observant Jews, with whom she felt a strong connection. The fervent spiritual longing she felt as a child could only be expressed through prayers she learned in Catholic school. Walking home from school one day with her four-year-old brother, when she was about seven, they passed a Catholic church. She said, "Let's stop and say a prayer," and together they recited the Lord's Prayer, folding their hands on the fence. "There was the sense that it was very important, and it was also very embarrassing, like we shouldn't be doing that."

The taboo against saying Christian prayers was a phantom narrative that Lillian may have unconsciously perceived. Because the Inquisition, the Crusades, and other eras of forced conversion scarred the Jewish collective psyche, Jewish practices carefully guard against Christian influences. Despite this taboo, many Jews assumed Christian names and lifestyles, some even hiding their Jewish heritage from their own descendants. Lillian's parents placed her and her brother in a Christian day school, perhaps out of an unconscious desire to create safety through assimilating into the dominant culture.

The conflict between Lillian's extended family, which maintained an observant lifestyle, and her immediate family's rejection of Judaism, lived inside of her. She recalled a Passover Seder when her grandmother, aunts, and uncles came to her home in Connecticut. She was excited about the gathering, but unfamiliar with the tradition. At breakfast with her extended family the morning after the Seder, she asked if she could have bread. Everyone "stopped dead," the awkward silence palpable. It was as if Lillian stepped unknowingly into the deep chasm that lived between her extended family's observant Judaism and her parents' decision not to transmit it to her and her brother. Her father broke the awkward silence, commanding, "If she wants bread, give her some bread!" Lillian, longing to understand and participate in the observance of the holiday, told him, "I don't want it if I'm not supposed to have it." She recalled feeling deeply confused by not knowing what was going on and upset that "nobody would really tell me."

Lillian recalled tenderly how her father's love of Judaism would occasionally peek through the veneer of his adopted secular existence. He shared Hasidic tales with her, which infused her with a love of Jewish mysticism. When they celebrated the Passover Seder every year, he would turn to her and say, "I was there," meaning he was present with all the Jews at Mount Sinai when God handed down the Torah to Moses and the Hebrew people. His words and his depth of feeling conveyed to her the numinous sense of what she imagined it might have been like to be at Sinai, with every Jewish soul who ever lived or who would yet come into being. Lillian felt a profound sense of connection, understanding that if her father was there, she must have been there too. It was shattering to her when someone told her later in her life that the women were not present at Sinai, although this interpretation has been challenged by Jewish feminists.[14]

Her parents' rejection of Judaism was based in their own painful experiences. Her mother was raped as a young woman by a rabbi. During the Second World War, her father, a journalist, publicized the plight of European Jews and was instrumental in creating a haven for hundreds of Jewish refugees in Upstate New York. His conflicted feelings about a Jewish identity were likely profoundly impacted by this experience. He showed up at Sinai, but where was God? Her parents' feelings of rage and betrayal that caused them to reject Jewish spirituality were never openly discussed. The pain that lived behind their rejection of Judaism is explored in depth in subsequent chapters.

Lillian's longing for Judaism grew, inspired by witnessing her extended family's spiritual life. At fourteen, she asked to go to Hebrew school. Her parents initially refused but relented when she threatened to convert to Catholicism if they didn't comply. She recalled, "They had me in Hebrew school the next day!" Although her parents had acquiesced, her mother became quite stern with her, saying, "You'd better be ready to leave, young lady, when I come to pick you up!" Perhaps her mother felt protective of her teenage daughter as she prepared to enter an environment where she herself had been violated.

Like many, Lillian's spiritual longings went unfulfilled by her Hebrew school experience. She recalled sitting in the temple's sukkah, participating in what felt like an empty ritual devoid of feeling. The sukkah is a temporary hut erected to celebrate the harvest and to commemorate the years spent wandering in the desert. In this celebration, Biblical ancestors are invited to dwell in the sukkah. The emptiness Lillian experienced painfully reveals the absence of connection to the ancestors and the tradition. Strikingly, as explored later, Lillian's return to Judaism occurred during another Sukkot holiday, when she was able to experience the deep meaning of the tradition in a ritual led by Jewish Renewal founder Reb Zalman.

Lillian recalled that in her confirmation class, the rabbi promised they would discuss all matters pertaining to Judaism openly, and the students were encouraged to ask questions. But when someone asked what would happen if they disagreed with the Jewish teachings, the rabbi responded that he would "take care of that," signaling that no disagreement would really be countenanced. Rather than engaging in the centuries' old tradition of wrestling with the Torah through enlightened questioning and an atmosphere open to multiple perspectives, the rabbi's glib reply had a strong impact on Lillian. His inability to support nuanced learning seemed to affirm her parents' perspective. She went out to the car where her father was waiting and said, "I quit." Her inability to hold the conflict without parental support reflected her internalization of her mother's lack of patience for Lillian to find her way within the tradition, reflected in her mother's demand that Lillian better be able to leave when her mother was ready for her to do so.

Lillian tried to continue to observe Shabbat on her own as a teenager, staying at home alone on Saturdays. Her friends, unfamiliar with Jewish culture, could not understand why she wouldn't come to the movies with them. Lillian summed up the forces that aligned against her nascent yearning for Jewish spiritual connection and expression, which she, as an adolescent girl lacking familial support, could not overcome. She recalled that she had a "tremendous amount of longing that was not recognized, or was ridiculed, or was met with anger" in her family. Her parents "had both been psychoanalyzed, and they psychoanalyzed me, and interpreted, and it would feel very *not me*, and condescending."

Lillian and her brother's attendance at a Catholic school reflects the conflict Lillian's father experienced between his strongly felt connection to God and Judaism (being there at Sinai), his love of Hasidic tales, and the desire to assimilate and succeed. His success led to his ability to influence major policy decisions, such as arranging the haven for hundreds of Jews during the height of the

Shoah. Her parents' engagement in psychoanalysis allowed them to develop in ways that would likely have gone unexplored had they maintained an observant life. Their open-mindedness helped Lillian assert herself and likely influenced her own choice of profession.

As an adult, she became a psychotherapist and discovered and co-created a form of Judaism that wove together the conflicting forces in childhood into a coherent whole—psychological depth, Jewish rituals imbued with the meaning she longed for as a child, feminist spirituality that would value women and guard against the violations her mother experienced, and free-thinking exchanges valuing multiple perspectives rather than forced conformity.

Daniel's story

Daniel's parents were socialists who eschewed religious practices and never discussed spirituality. He recalled as a child being entranced as he watched his paternal grandfather, who had emigrated from Eastern Europe, wearing *tefillin* (leather binding worn during morning prayers and reflecting one's bond with the Divine), walking up and down the hallway of his apartment. Daniel asked his father what his grandfather was doing, and his father explained that he was praying.

Daniel recalled the sacred feeling he experienced in nature as a child, enchanted by the "sound of walking in the snow, or of leaves." One day he was outside and discovered "a piece of a tree or a hunk of wood—something that I had seen and had felt some resonance with and had carried around with me for an entire day." When his mother called him for dinner, he intuitively felt that the object wouldn't be allowed in the house. "I was really torn, because there was this thing that I loved, and it had some sort of sacredness to it, and I had to leave it outside when I went in for dinner." His experience was one he had never heard anyone talk about and, therefore, assumed that something must be wrong. "In retrospect, that's tragic, but I'm also really grateful that I had a childhood filled with that sort of experience."

Daniel's paternal grandfather died when he was eight, and tragically, his father died a year later. When he reached Bar Mitzvah age, Daniel's maternal grandfather came to visit him in California from the Midwest. His mother and grandfather got into a huge fight in the car—Daniel's grandfather was strongly pushing for him to have a Bar Mitzvah, and his mother said that she wanted to leave it up to him. Having grown up with no relationship to Judaism, Daniel did not want to have a Bar Mitzvah because the ceremony had no meaning for him without any context. "It was like somebody asking me if I wanted to sail the high seas or something."

Many years later, Daniel discovered that his maternal grandfather hid his spirituality from his family, attending Sephardic temple services without letting anyone know where he was going. His longing for Daniel to have a connection to the tradition that his own children had rejected was expressed in the urgency of his request and his making a special trip to plead with Daniel to have a Bar Mitzvah. But the link had already been severed—there was not enough connective tissue for Daniel to find meaning in the ceremony.

As discussed in later chapters, his family's turning away from Judaism may have been related to unmetabolized grief. Daniel's paternal grandfather was the only one of his twelve brothers to leave Eastern Europe. Daniel's great-grandparents and all his grandfathers' brothers and their families were killed in the Shoah. This tragic loss was never openly discussed in the family. Instead, Daniel was raised in a milieu in which the connection to Jewish collective memory was ruptured, and he was left to hold the sparks of holiness in his memories of his grandfather's *tefillin* and in the sacred spaces and sounds of nature, until those sparks could be redeemed and integrated into a meaningful Jewish life.

Interruption of transmission of Jewish collective memory

Robert Bosnak, a Jungian analyst born in 1942 to a Dutch family fleeing the Nazis, shares this image from a recurrent dream: "I see the little Warsaw boy with his cap over his forehead and his hands over his head. Behind him stand the German soldiers with their guns, laughing broadly. A voice tells me in Dutch: 'All our old men have died. All the wise men are gone. Just the children are left behind. The children are bewildered.'"[15]

For those coming of age in the postwar era, the sense of continuity between the present and past generations was shattered. Personal stories of the ancestors as well as the treasure trove of Jewish collective memory were often not transmitted to the next generations. As a means of survival, the Jewish cultural collective focused on the present and the future, placing their hopes in the youth to create a new world, a new reality, unencumbered by the burdens of the past. But this focus had an unintended consequence: children lacked a framework with which to understand their innate spirituality or their place in the rich culture of their ancestors. Reclamation of Jewish identity required a turning toward, and an eventual integration of, the deeply emotional experience embedded in family legacies of grief, trauma, and triumph.

Jungian analyst Joseph Henderson noted that initiation into one's cultural heritage may be arrested. Nevertheless, initiation may occur later in life if powerful contents emerge unbidden from the unconscious. "Many modern people, because of arrested development, fail to achieve identity within the larger group and must wait for the moment when an individual self-affirmation can effectively compensate their lack. At such a moment the social archetype frequently appears as an image in dreams."[16] In subsequent chapters, I explore the spontaneous emergence of Jewish myths and symbols in the individual psyche.

Finding ourselves in the Biblical story: trauma and disconnection from the sacred

In the Book of Genesis, in the same breath that God tells Abraham that Sarah will conceive and that his descendants will be as numerous as the stars, Abraham is also told that his descendants will journey into Egypt and face great hardships.

God has Abraham engage in a mysterious ritual: He must sacrifice a goat, a heifer, and a ram, cutting them each in half. Abraham is also instructed to sacrifice a turtledove and a pigeon, but these he is to leave whole. As a great darkness falls over him, God says, "'Know of a surety that thy seed shall be a stranger in a land that is not theirs, and shall serve them; and they shall afflict them four hundred years; and also that nation, whom they shall serve, will I judge; and afterward shall they come out with great substance."[17]

After Abraham performs the ritual, God remembers (*pakod* in Hebrew) Sarah, and she conceives and gives birth to Isaac, the descendant who marries Rebecca, through whom this future emerges. The promise of the birth of Abraham's innumerable descendants is accompanied at the moment it is pronounced by the awareness of the pain they will undergo. The dividing of the animals may symbolize the splitting of the Red Sea, and the birds those descendants who would make it through the center of the sea, whole.

As the Book of Exodus begins, Abraham's vision has come into being. The people have been suffering under the yoke of slavery for the 400 years prophesied. The new Pharaoh, fearful that the increasing number of Jews might lead them to revolt against the oppressive conditions under which they are forced to live, has issued an edict that all male Hebrew children be killed at birth. The Hebrew people have been in a state of profound suffering for so long that they no longer hold any hope that things might be different. They have stopped crying out to God. They have given in to despair. And they have lost their connection to the sense that they have a destiny that is greater than the daily reality of the clay pits of Egypt, where the men perform the backbreaking work of building bricks for Pharaoh. They were bereft, as were so many Jews in the wake of the Shoah, having completely lost faith in a God that did not or could not intervene in human affairs.

Exile and post-traumatic growth

The great medieval kabbalist Joseph Gikatilla reflected that Abraham's vision revealed that from the state of enslavement, a new consciousness would arise that would enable the people to journey out of Egypt and enter into a new relationship with God. The journey in exile allows us to descend to the place where holy sparks are hidden and need to be redeemed. When these are redeemed, a new consciousness emerges.[18] Gikatilla taught that had God not placed the people in exile, they would not have willingly gone into the desert and would not have received the Torah. The suffering of exile opened the people to a new consciousness able to directly receive the light of the Divine.[19]

Chronicling the journey from despair to transformation, the Exodus is a story of post-traumatic growth. In the Book of Genesis, the people's connection to God was carried by individuals: Abraham and Sarah, Isaac and Rebecca, Jacob, Rachel, Leah, Bilhah and Zilpah and in the subsequent generation, Joseph and his siblings, comprising the Twelve Tribes of Israel. After Joseph's generation, however, the people enter their own personal relationship with God at Sinai when the Torah is given. To be ready for this transmission, each person undergoes a painful descent into profound suffering, an individuation journey, in which they are personally prepared as vessels open to receiving revelation.

As Gikatilla suggests, being open to receiving the wisdom of Torah requires that each individual personally suffer the despair and hopelessness of the exile before finding his or her way to the supernal light. Our time also requires that a new Jewish identity be forged from wrestling with the tradition in the wake of catastrophe, creating a deeply individual relationship with the Divine.

Like the Hebrews in Egypt, we too are descended from ancestors whose lives were consecrated to God. Yet coming of age following the devastation and overwhelming despair of centuries of pogroms, massive forced relocations, and the Shoah, Jewish families and institutions were unable to nurture the sparks of spiritual longing carried by the children. Like the ancient Hebrews, they had stopped crying out to God for deliverance.

Many Jews had an innate connection to and longing for the spiritual as children, but were raised in family and cultural milieus that could not support the development of what Jung termed the religious function of the psyche. Those who rediscovered their passion for Judaism had to redeem these holy sparks from where they were hidden under the *kelipot* (scattered shards) of assimilation, shame, rage, and unmourned loss.

The 18th-century Hasidic sage Rabbi Levi Yitzchak of Berditchev, who lived through times of great challenge in the Ukraine, taught that it was God's intention that the people of Israel would suffer many exiles. The exile in Egypt "was the root of all exiles, and a multitude of holy sparks awaited redemption." He observed that in the centuries that followed, the people of Israel have been exiled to the four corners of the earth, where they have raised holy sparks throughout the Creation.[20]

Individual conflicts in Jewish identity reflected a larger collective reorientation. As Jews assimilated into the new world, the tension between the opposites of traditional Judaism and assimilated identity was profound. Each side had its light and shadow. As Jung noted, we usually experience opposites as conflict. Yet, as we take the time to sit with each of the perspectives of the opposing views, we gain new insights, and the opposites can potentially come together in a *coniunctio*, or union.

Jews assimilating into American culture rejected traditional Judaism, which often felt rigid or overly patriarchal. Yet assimilation into mainstream culture cut them off from the mystical depths of the tradition. It was left to individuals to find ways to integrate these disparate pieces, redeeming the holy sparks by synthesizing the secular expressions of identity with the root metaphors of the wisdom tradition.

As individuals who experienced a profoundly conflicted relationship to Judaism discovered practices that synthesized the ancient with the emergent, they discovered a pathway for redeeming these holy sparks uncovered in the exile of assimilated identity into a new, more expansive Judaism. This renewed expression embraced feminist spirituality, inclusion of all genders and sexual orientations, egalitarian and nonhierarchical forms of learning and practice, widening inclusion of Jews by choice and interfaith families, psychologically rich experiential practices of mystical engagement, and a dedication to social justice.

Notes

1 Cynthia Ozick, "In the Synagogue," in *Telling and Remembering: A Century of Jewish American Poetry*, edited by Steven J. Rubin (Boston: Beacon Press, 1997), 233.
2 Exodus 1:8.
3 Exodus 1:9–16.
4 Ann Lammers, ed., *The Jung-Kirsch Letters: The Correspondence of C.G. Jung and James Kirsch* (London: Routledge, 2016).
5 William Alex, "An American in Jerusalem and the Search for Soul," in *A Modern Jew in Search of A Soul*, edited by J. Marvin Spiegelman and Abraham Jacobson (Phoenix, AZ: Falcon Press, 1986), 3. This volume is in the process of being reissued by New Falcon Press.
6 Ibid.
7 Samuel Kimbles, *Phantom Narratives: The Unseen Contributions of Culture to Psyche* (Lanham, MD: Rowman & Littlefield, 2014), 24; citing Nicolas Abraham and Maria Torok, *The Shell and the Kernel* (Chicago: University of Chicago Press, 1994), 140.
8 Steven M. Cohen, Ron Miller, Ira M. Sheskin and Berna Torr, *Camp Works: The Long-Term Impact of Jewish Overnight Camp* (New York: Foundation for Jewish Camp, 2011).
9 Chana Bloch and Ariel Block, *The Song of Songs* (New York: The Modern Library, 1995), 3:1–2.
10 David Nasaw, *The Last Million: Europe's Displaced Persons from World War to Cold War* (New York: Penguin Press, 2020).
11 Pseudonyms are used throughout in recounting individual narratives.
12 Yosef Hayim Yerushalmi, *Zakhor: Jewish History and Jewish Memory* (New York: Schocken Books, 1989).
13 Aryeh Kaplan, trans., *The Living Torah* (Brooklyn: Moznaim, 1981), Genesis, *VaYetze*, 63:16, 135.
14 Judith Plaskow, *Standing Again at Sinai: Judaism from a Feminist Perspective* (San Francisco, CA: HarperOne, 1991).
15 Robert Bosnak, "Echad," in *A Modern Jew in Search of a Soul*, edited by Marvin Spiegelman and Abraham Jacobson (Phoenix: Falcon Press, 1986), 33.
16 Joseph Henderson, *Thresholds of Initiation* (Middletown, CT: Wesleyan University Press, 1967), 113.
17 Genesis 15:13–14.
18 Howard Schwartz, *Tree of Souls: The Mythology of Judaism* (New York: Oxford University Press, 2004), 473; citing Joseph Gikatilla, *Gates of Light (Sha'are Orah)* (Lanham, MD: AltaMira Press, 1988).
19 Ibid; citing Gikatilla, *Gates of Light (Sha'are Orah)*, Tzofnat Pa'ane'ah; Perush ha-Haggadah 3; Em ha-Banim S'mehah.
20 Ibid, 472; citing No'am Elimelekh, Kedushat Levi ha-Shalem.

Part III

The awakening

Chapter 5

Women, copper mirrors, and awakening from the trance of exile

Let me lie among vine blossoms, in a bed of apricots!
I am in the fever of love.
His left hand beneath my head, his right arm holding me close.
Daughters of Jerusalem swear to me by the gazelles,
by the deer in the field,
that you will never awaken love until it is ripe.

Song of Songs, 2:4–7[1]

How does the journey out of the constriction of traumatized consciousness begin? According to the Song of Songs, the esoteric corollary to the Exodus story, we leave *mitzrayim* by being awakened by the Beloved. The Song of Songs, the great mystical erotic love poem attributed to King Solomon, was thought by some to be written to the Queen of Sheba.[2]

The Song of Songs is a poem of love awakened, then lost, and sought again. Following the destruction of the Second Temple in Jerusalem, when rabbis gathered to determine which texts would be included in the Biblical canon, some argued that this text should be excluded because of its deeply erotic nature. The great mystical sage Rabbi Akiva countered that not only should the Song of Songs (*Shir HaShirim* in Hebrew) be included, but that it was the "Holy of Holies" of all the Biblical texts, likening it to the innermost sanctum of the Temple in Jerusalem, which only the High Priest was allowed to enter.

Howard Schwartz quotes the Talmudic legend that the Song of Songs was given at the time the waters of the Red Sea parted, when "the heavens opened" and all its secrets were revealed. Then, "a maidservant saw at the sea things that were not seen by the prophet Ezekiel … The whole world existed for the day on which the Song of Songs was given."[3]

The Song of Songs awakens us to the possibility of love. When we suffer trauma, both personal and collective, we are wounded in our capacity to love. We may believe that we were hurt because we are unlovable. Healing our capacity to love and be loved allows us to move out of the narrow consciousness engendered by trauma.

In this chapter, I explore midrashic texts that reflect the wisdom that the path out of exile begins as we are beckoned forth by the yearning for relationship with the deeper Self. Another consequence of trauma is the loss of our connection to the inner depths, as we seek to maintain safety by cutting off feeling and our relationship to the symbolic, centering our awareness in an ego that is rational and concrete. Healing occurs when we can recover our feeling and creativity, and reawaken our imagination.

Jungian scholar Rivkah Scharf Kluger observes that the Beloved in the Song of Songs, perhaps the Queen of Sheba, represents that aspect of the Sacred Feminine that has been occluded from our collective consciousness. In the height of Jewish rationalist thinking, the connection to the depths was lost. Through the reclamation of kabbalah in our own time, we are called to follow our longing for mythos and meaning, for the eros of deep connection. We are awakened out of the trance of exile through the call of the Beloved.

Discovering the Sacred Feminine

As a girl, witnessing my mother's decline into a debilitating depression, I was strongly drawn to themes of women's empowerment. When I was a teenager, girls were just beginning to become Bat Mitzvah in Reform and Conservative temples, and I attended the ceremonies of friends. Despite this advance, there were still no women rabbis, and women were completely absent from the *bimah* (pulpit) in any role. The Judaism I encountered in temple also lacked the deeply personal connection to God that I had felt intuitively as a child. The tone of the prayer book was distant and archaic. The capitalized *He* emphasized the patriarchal tone that was sharply at odds with my burgeoning feminist self. The lack of feeling reflected the widespread psychological numbing of the post-Shoah era discussed in the previous Chapter.

I remember attending a Passover Seder at my Aunt Miriam's house after her divorce, when I was in my early 20s. She placed a Maxwell House Haggadah at each setting. In every single one, she had painstakingly crossed out each "He" and "Him" and handwritten "She" and "Her." How different this was from the Seders I attended at her house as a young child, where her strict husband, a Hungarian refugee who fled Europe as a child during the Shoah, sent my cousin to his room for singing *Dayenu* spiritedly too many times.

Something in Aunt Miriam was being profoundly liberated, and I was delighted by her new perspective. Yet I wondered if this valiant gesture could overcome the deeply entrenched patriarchal tradition. It seemed like a Band-Aid fix to a Grand-Canyon-sized hole. Would we have to rewrite each and every Haggadah by hand?

I worked at a feminist office in my late teens, before attending college, where I learned of the persecution of millions of women healers during the Inquisition. I was drawn to discovering the hidden history of the systematic repression of women's wisdom. In my 20s, I marveled to discover that there was an epoch, prior to our own, in which the Goddess was widely worshipped. Reading Merlin

Stone's *When God Was a Woman*, I was disturbed by her reflection that the patriarchal attitude of the Hebrews was a primary force in dislodging the Goddess from Her centrality in early Near Eastern religions.⁴ My ambivalence about Judaism grew stronger—clearly, I could find no home in this tradition that so denied the feminine. Notably, Stone, a Jewish woman, later wrote the Foreword to Raphael Patai's work *The Hebrew Goddess*, modifying her previous perspective and acknowledging the widespread Goddess-worshipping tradition that existed among the ancient Hebrews.⁵

Because of my increasing distance from Judaism, I was sadly unaware of the depth of reclaiming being done by Jewish feminists such as Gloria Orenstein, Jane Litman, Susannah Heschel, Judith Plaskow, Rachel Adler, and countless others meeting in small circles, creating and reclaiming women's wisdom traditions in Judaism. They sought to integrate the growing women's spirituality movement with Judaism, wrestling openly with the same questions that had led me to conclude that my only choice was to forego Judaism and seek spiritual sustenance elsewhere.⁶

I moved to a small town in rural northern California, where I worked with others to challenge the clearcutting of the majestic old growth forests and in support of traditional Navajo (Diné) elders resisting forced relocation from their homeland. Judaism was distant and seemingly unrelated to anything my life was about.

One day, as I was sitting outside Boont Berry Farm, the local health food store in Boonville, I began a conversation with a woman who was heading to a nearby retreat center and Findhorn-inspired community. She was here for a gathering of Jews connecting with the earth called *Ruach Ha'Aretz*. I grew curious as she translated—*Spirit of the Earth*. What was *that* about? I listened as the woman, who introduced herself as Rabbi Leah Novick, told me about the Shekhinah, the Divine Feminine in Judaism. Really?! Was it possible that the divided paths inside my soul might somehow be braided together?

About two years later, shortly after my heart-opening experience in Mendocino with Rabbi Margaret Holub (discussed in Chapter One), I began attending classes at Chochmat Ha'Lev, the Jewish meditation center in Berkeley. Fueled in large part by the need for spiritual support as my mother's health declined, I deepened my engagement with Jewish meditation and ecstatic practices based on teachings from the Jewish mystical tradition, kabbalah.

I was struck by an experience unprecedented in my engagement with other spiritual traditions. Coming into relationship with Jewish teachings and practices, I felt a sense of *remembering*, reconnecting to my tradition and my people as well as to ancient teachings that aligned with my innermost knowing. As I was being introduced to material I had never consciously encountered before, I was deeply moved by a sense of having already known the material, as if it were familiar to my soul. Rather than considering whether I agreed with the teachings, I felt as if ideas I had long held to be spiritual truths that I had arrived at internally were validated by the outer teachings. The feeling was not only uncanny but also profoundly emotional, as I sensed a reconnection with my ancestors and felt myself taking my place within the lineage that they had safeguarded for me. I was receiving and valuing the rich treasure of my spiritual inheritance. Religious anthropologists term this experience *neurognosis*—the process of remembering what one already knows.[7]

At both Chochmat Ha'Lev and the Aquarian Minyan in Berkeley, I was surprised to experience a profound reconnection with a renewed Judaism that was both celebratory and depthful and spacious enough to hold my grief during my mother's declining health. In participating in Shabbat services filled with deeply moving music resonant with ancestrally infused melodies, I found a place where the deep sadness I was experiencing could be held.

Perhaps I was experiencing not only my personal grief, but also the larger grief of disconnection from and reconnection with my ancestral tradition. As I prepared to let go of my personal mother, I opened to being held by the Great Mother, which I felt profoundly blessed to discover lived at the heart of Judaism as the *Shekhinah*. It was deeply comforting to feel myself woven back into the tapestry of my ancestors, a fabric which held me as I released my own mother to their keeping, in the *olam haba*, the world to come.

In my studies of Jewish mysticism, I was stunned to discover that Aunt Miriam's approach of changing God's name to She was not simply a Band-Aid, but part of a larger reclaiming of the central place that the Divine Feminine had held in the Jewish tradition for millennia.

I spoke to Rabbi Jonathan Omer-man, a renowned kabbalistic scholar, about how separate I had always felt from Judaism because of the depth of my longing for the Feminine. His response surprised me. He said simply, "Join the club!" It took me several years to appreciate this profound paradox—that my longing for the Sacred Feminine in Judaism, that had made me feel so alienated from the Judaism I encountered as a child—was, in fact, a central tenet of the Jewish mystical tradition.

Engaging in study in the Bay Area Jewish Renewal communities and attending international conferences through Aleph and *Ruach Ha'Aretz*, my relationship with Judaism healed, awakened, and deepened. Rabbi Gershon Winkler, who takes a shamanic approach to Judaism, explored how many of the names for God in the Torah are feminine, including *El Shaddai*, translated as *The Breasted One*. Rabbi Leah Novick offered teachings on the Shekhinah, the Feminine aspect of the Divine. Psychotherapist Estelle Frankel and Rabbis Tirzah Firestone, Steven Fisdel, and Jonathan Omer-man demonstrated the depth psychological meaning of the practices. Rabbis Shefa Gold, Miriam Maron, Diane Elliot, and others engaged Judaism through chant and movement, and taught embodied spirituality practices that supported the creation of an inner vessel for transformation.

The current flowering of Jewish mysticism draws largely on the wisdom of the Baal Shem Tov, founder of Hasidism, and his disciples, who recognized that people devastated by the collective trauma of the pogroms needed a deeply felt connection with God as a healing balm. To facilitate such a restorative connection to the Divine for many poorer Jews who were not formally schooled in Jewish texts, they developed practices that were experiential rather than cerebral—meditating in nature, dancing, singing—opening the pathway to God through embodied emotion. The Shekhinah, the felt presence of the Divine, was spoken of as the Beloved, the Bride, and in Reb Nachman's stories, the Lost Princess, for whom all of Israel was yearning. The Shekhinah was also central to the Zohar and other medieval kabbalistic texts as well as in the cosmology developed by Isaac Luria in the aftermath of the Spanish Inquisition.

The longing for the feminine following times of profound devastation suggests that healing occurs through connection with the deep wellsprings of wisdom contained in the mythic imagination of Jewish cosmology. When we have suffered trauma, we also find healing in embodiment and in loving relationships that offer holding, caring, and support for the emergence of our essence. This understanding is reflected in the midrash that describes the Biblical events that stir the first movements out of exile.

The Shekhinah in exile: finding the Divine Feminine in the Biblical text

The exile the Hebrews found themselves in at the beginning of the Exodus story is linked to the decline of the Feminine, the immanent aspect of the Divine. As the book of Genesis unfolds, we see the decline of women's power that was present in earlier cultures of the Fertile Crescent region. A close reading of the text reveals this deeper *herstory*.

Feminist scholar Savina Teubal demonstrates how the matriarchs in Genesis act in accordance with customs of the matristic cultures from which they emerged.[8] God's covenant with Abraham defines the future of the Hebrews as a people. Yet it is the women who decide to whom the covenant will be transmitted. Sarah's authority is reflected in her instructing Abraham to have Hagar, the mother of his first son, Ishmael, leave their home. Sarah's power ensures that the covenant will pass to her son, Isaac. Her actions accord with the codes governing a priestess's authority to both accept a concubine and to demote the concubine if circumstances required. The Bible story reflects Sarah's innate authority: In these matters, God tells Abraham, *listen to Sarah*.[9]

When it is time for Isaac to marry, Abraham's servant, searching for Isaac's true beloved, sees Rebecca at the well. According to the Zohar, the well that is prominent in the early stories of Genesis represents the Divine Presence in its Feminine aspect, the Shekhinah.[10] The sacred waters, guided by the Shekhinah, jump into Rebecca's vessels so she has abundant water to offer to both the servant and his camels. The servant recognizes Rebecca's actions as an unequivocal expression of unending *chesed*, or lovingkindness, and knows he has found a worthy partner for Isaac. Rebecca carries the energies of the Feminine Presence, overflowing with kindness.

Rebecca also acts with priestessly authority. God entrusts her with ensuring that the covenant is passed down to her second son, Jacob, rather than to the firstborn, Esau, who was Isaac's favorite. Teubal observes that Rebecca's actions evidence the matriarchal power of determining lineage—a power reflected in the continuing Jewish tradition of matrilineal descent—and reflect the matriarchal tradition in which the youngest child is the spiritual heir.[11]

When Jacob meets Rachel, it is also at a well, again symbolizing the presence of the Shekhinah. The text tells us that Jacob rolls away the stone that blocks the cistern, indicating he is opening the channel for Divine love to flow between them, and through them, to their children.

Years later, Jacob and his wives Rachel and her sister Leah, and their hand-maidens Bilhah and Zilpah, and their children stealthily leave the house of Rachel and Leah's father, Laban, because he has not dealt fairly with them. Laban discovers them preparing to leave and demands to know who has taken his teraphim. Teraphim are household statues of the Hebrew Goddess Asherah and others, understood to have been used by women in childbirth and healing.

Jacob tells Laban that he has not taken them, and unaware that Rachel, his beloved, possesses them, swears that whoever has them will surely die. Laban confronts Rachel and asks if she has them. She is sitting on a camel seat, under which the teraphim are hidden. Saying that "the manner of women is upon me" (she is menstruating), she declines to get up, and Laban leaves her alone. Teubal suggests that in safeguarding the teraphim as her own, Rachel is claiming the spiritual inheritance to which she, as the youngest, is entitled, but which has been wrongfully denied her. The priestess tradition in which the youngest receives the spiritual inheritance also explains why both Isaac and Jacob, the youngest sib-lings, become the carriers of the covenant.[12]

In Jacob's calling for the death of whoever has taken the teraphim, we can also see the powerful conflict between the two views: Rachel does not tell Jacob what she has done or the value these statues hold for her. Her life is ultimately sacrificed in the process of safeguarding these symbols of the Sacred Feminine.[13] Because of Jacob's sworn oath, Rachel, mother of Joseph and Benjamin, dies a tragically early death.

With the decline of the feminine, which carries the quality of relatedness, rela-tionships wither and harsh circumstances ensue in the next generation. Dinah, the only daughter of Jacob named in the text, goes out to see "the daughters of the land." When she does, "Shechem the son of Hamor the Hivite, the prince of the land, saw her; and he took her, and lay with her, and humbled her." Dinah is either raped or humbled by having sex without being married. Shechem's father approaches Jacob and asks for permission for Dinah and Shechem to marry, but he and his sons demand that the men of Shechem agree to become circumcised before they intermarry with the Hebrew women. They agree, and three days after they are circumcised, Dinah's brothers Simeon and Levi kill them in their weak-ened state, exacting revenge for Dinah's defilement.[14] The absence of Dinah's own voice in the story reflects the loss of feminine agency in this generation.[15]

More darkness follows. Joseph, the beloved child of Jacob and Rachel, is envied by his brothers for being the favored of their father, Jacob, who has acknowledged

Joseph's great spiritual light by giving him a coat of many colors. The brothers are shepherding in the land of Shechem, where the attack took place. Seething with envy at their father's favoring Joseph, they capture him and throw him into a dry pit. The dry pit is the antithesis of the abundant wells that flowed for their parents and grandparents.

In this generation, the feminine qualities of relatedness are nowhere to be found. The loss of Rachel, the spiritual matriarch of this generation, has profound consequences. Without her guidance, the themes of enmity and jealousy that emerged in the earlier generations between Ishmael and Isaac and Esau and Jacob now erupt into outright hostility in the violent actions of Joseph's jealous brothers. Joseph is abandoned by his brothers, alone in a dry pit, the first of many descents that he endures.

In a beautiful midrash, Rachel is seen as forever standing on the road to Bethlehem, where she died, weeping for her children, a symbol of the Shekhinah mourning for the children of Israel in exile.[16] In Chapter Nine, the journey of her son Joseph is explored, presaging, on an individual level, what the Hebrew people will go through as a collective in the time of the exile.

The Pharaohs' edict

Several hundred years after Joseph's death, the Hebrews are suffering under the crushing weight of centuries of enslavement, the men work in the clay pits, building bricks for the pyramids of the Pharaoh. The dry pit into which Joseph is hurled foreshadows the clay pits in which the people find themselves, hopeless and bereft, cut off from the loving nurturance that sustained the previous generations, seemingly abandoned by the Divine Presence. As the dryness of the clay pits suggests, the life force itself has seemingly ceased to flow.

The Exodus story begins with the ascent of a king who fears the Hebrews' growing numbers and possible gain of political power. He has forgotten Joseph's central role centuries earlier in supporting the Pharaoh of his era and saving the Egyptians from drought and starvation. The new Pharaoh issues an edict requiring that all Hebrew male children be murdered at birth. Amram, the leader of the community, the Sanhedrin, husband of Yocheved and father of Miriam and Aaron and later, Moses, instructs the men to separate from their wives, so that no children will be born, in order to keep any infant boys from being put to death.

Hearkening back to the power of the early matriarchs, Amram's daughter Miriam rises to challenge his edict, saying that it is harsher than the Pharaoh's, since to stop having children altogether would mean both male *and* female offspring would be sacrificed. Miriam's wisdom prevails—if the tradition is to continue, the way must be found. Miriam, the prophetess, holds faith in the possibility of a different future, even when to do so is seemingly at odds with manifest reality. According to one midrash, Amram, who had separated from his wife Yocheved when she was three months pregnant with Moses, listens to Miriam's plea and remarries his wife three months later.[17]

Elaine's story

The first Pharaoh's reliance on Joseph and the subsequent Pharaoh's fear of the Jews echo a familiar theme in Jewish history. Throughout the diasporic existence, when the talents of the Jews were useful to those in power, they were drawn on to support the leaders of the country, and Jews were allowed relative freedoms within the larger cultures. When the resources of the country became scarce, Jews were scapegoated as the discontent of the people was directed at them, a pressure valve that kept the people from addressing their grievances to the king or ruler. Jews were often expelled from countries in which they had made their homes and communities for centuries, or forced to convert, as happened during the Crusades and the Spanish Inquisition. The near annihilation of the Jewish people in Europe during the Shoah was the culmination of millennia of anti-Semitic hatred and propaganda used to maintain power among ruling elites by manipulating the public's animus over conditions of severe deprivation and despair and directing it at Jews.

In the tumultuous upheavals of emigration and assimilation in the late 19th and early 20th centuries, and following the devastations of the Shoah, conflicting values reflected the impact of this history on Jewish identity formation. Maintaining Jewish identity through marriage and family remained a primary focus, even as families increasingly chose to distance themselves from traditional forms of Jewish observance.

These conflicting values were evident in Elaine's family. Her grandfather was an Orthodox rabbi in Eastern Europe who had been deeply connected to the Hasidic mystical teachings when a new wave of pogroms swept Eastern Europe. In response, he rejected religious observance and turned toward socialism, with the hope that this ideology would bring about manifest change in the world and free Jews and others from the great oppression of the time. When he immigrated to the United States, he eschewed religion, and made his living teaching Hebrew school.

Elaine's family was secular and culturally Jewish, and belonged to a Reform congregation. Elaine recalled that the central value conveyed in her family was of maintaining one's Jewish identity regardless of whether one believed in the religious teachings. "It was very clear to me that I would be Jewish. And if you decided you weren't going to be Jewish, and a Holocaust came, they still killed you. So, you're stuck with being Jewish."

Her brother and sister both married spouses of other faiths, but Elaine could not, even though she fell in love with a wonderful German man when she was young. Her conditioning was so strong that she ended the relationship. "I knew I would commit suicide before I would marry someone who was not Jewish. I felt like I couldn't do that to my parents. So, all three of my husbands were Jewish, and," she remarked sardonically, "I kept making my parents happy over and over."

In college, Elaine found herself deeply drawn to the writings of Martin Buber on the Hasidic masters, which helped her connect with the mystical heart of Judaism that her grandfather had left behind. She was moved by the deep feeling and wisdom of the stories but believed this way of life had long since ceased to exist.

Elaine experienced her Jewish identity as an obligation laden with fear. When considering what led to her reconnection with Judaism, she recalled a powerful experience she had attending an Orthodox Bar Mitzvah. As a secular Jew and strong feminist, she expected to be put off by having to sit in the separate domain of the women in the balcony of the shul. Instead, she was surprised by the swell of emotion she experienced there, feeling profoundly moved by the presence of the Shekhinah, the Sacred Feminine, as the women laughed, danced, and passed babies around to be cradled in each other's arms. She felt "a sense of being at home."

Sitting among the women in the Hasidic service, Elaine was able to feel Judaism being transmitted to the children in an atmosphere of joy and celebration, so different from her own parents' relationship to the tradition based in fear. Like Miriam urging the people to continue to give birth, the Orthodox women nurtured their children with a sense of hopefulness, in contrast to the fear and obligation that suffused Elaine's family's Jewish identity.

Yehiel's story

Yehiel was born just after the Shoah and raised in an Orthodox home in a predominantly non-Jewish neighborhood in Connecticut. She recalled her mother lovingly brushing her hair while listening to radio reports of the Israeli war for independence. Her mother supported her childhood dream of one day serving as a nurse in the *Haganah*, the Israeli independence movement. Her grandfather, an Orthodox rabbi, lived with them and had an imposing study with an enormous desk by the front door of their home, where people would come to meet with him.

Yehiel grew up with an intense fear that if she did not comport herself in line with the strict rules of Orthodoxy, dreadful things would happen to her. "One of the initial cracks in this Orthodox structure occurred when I actually wrote on a Shabbat, and my hand did not fall off my body. I was terrified, and I know I was in my late teens."

As soon as she left home, Yehiel turned away from her Orthodox upbringing to discover her own values, pursuing social justice work. Ninety percent of the people working alongside her in the movement were Jewish, so she never really felt a disconnection from the values that guided their lives. "We were always very community involved, and I still feel that way—it just played itself out in a different way."

Yehiel had a synchronistic experience related to her mother's passing. She decided to close her psychotherapy practice just months before learning that her mother was ill. She was then free to leave the West Coast and move back East to help her father and spend precious time with her mother. It was an extraordinary blessing for her to give back to her mother what she had so lovingly given to her. She recalled lying in bed next to her mother and reading to her, just as her mother would read to her all summer long on the beach when she was a child. Yehiel was able to be with her mother when she died. It was Yehiel's first experience with death.

Shortly after her mother's passing, she and her father went for dinner at the home of close family friends who were Israeli, secular but proudly Jewish. Her mother's dear friend Michal lit the Shabbos candles and said the *Shehechianu* prayer (the prayer said at the beginning of certain holy days). Confused, Yehiel asked, "I thought the Shehechianu was said the first nights of holidays and at very special moments?" Michal looked directly at her and said, "Is this not a very special moment?"

Yehiel was startled. She recalled wondering, "You mean there is something in this religion that is relevant to my day-to-day life? Maybe I need to come back and rethink what this is about. And given that that my mother has just died, if this chain is to continue, I have a responsibility of linking that next link in the chain."

Michal modeled to Yehiel that Judaism could be something more than a set of rigid rules that must be followed without understanding their meaning. It was filled with ritual that could hold the sacred moments of one's own life. The loss of one's parent is an initiation into a new stage of life, and the Shehechianu is a prayer said to mark new beginnings. This moment was a new beginning for Yehiel, in which she assumed her place in the *shalshelet*, the chain of souls, carrying on the gift that her mother had so lovingly bequeathed to her.

Candles lit on Shabbos were first kindled, according to midrashic legend, by the matriarchs Sarah and Rebecca, and the tradition has continued across countless generations of Jewish women to the present day. Through Michal, Yehiel understood that this practice, this *mitzvah*, was deeply personal and connected through the generations all the way back to the beginning of the Jewish people. Learning that the practices she grew up with could be used creatively to sanctify the moments of her own life allowed Yehiel to make a choice to continue the lineage bequeathed to her through her mother's deep relatedness and love.

Mirrors of love

According to midrashic legend, the Hebrews begin to move out of exile by the women inviting the men to move out of their suffering into a dance of playful eros, using mirrors. The wisdom of this ancient story reflects current research about healing from trauma—that relatedness and mirroring of our suffering allows us to open to the new possibility of a future different from the past that has held us in its grip. The way out of exile comes first, not through heroic pronouncements, but through the gentle murmuring of love.

According to the 4th-century midrash Tanchuma, when the men were subjected to back-breaking labor in the clay pits, the Pharaoh issued a decree that they should neither lie with their wives nor sleep in their own homes. Rabbi Shimon son of Halafta said, "What did the daughters of Israel do? They went down to draw water from the Nile, and the blessed Holy One prepared for them small fish in their pitchers, some of which they sold and some of which they cooked." The women bought wine from the proceeds made from the sale of the fish. Then they women went out to the fields, where they fed their husbands.

> After they had eaten and drunk, they would take their mirrors and gaze into them along with their husbands. She would say, "I am more beautiful than you!" And he would say, "I am more handsome than you!" Thereby they would induce themselves to desire, and were fruitful and increased. The blessed Holy One attended to them, enabling them to conceive immediately.[18]

It is said that from far away, you could see the glint of light reflecting off the thousands of mirrors in the field, the sign of the fertile couplings of the young lovers. Following this night of coupling, some of the women gave birth to twins, others to sextuplets.

> Others say, twelve in one belly; others say, six hundred thousand ... This entire total came about through the mirrors ... By the merit of those mirrors—showing them to their husbands, inducing them to desire, out of the midst of the crushing labor, they produced all those multitudes.[19]

From this night of love emerges the generation of Hebrews who will leave Egypt, among them, Moses.

The midrash teaches us that when we are at our most bereft, when we can no longer envision a future for ourselves different from the limited enslaved consciousness in which we have been mired, we need someone to show us our beauty, to remind us of who we are and who we may yet become. The first act in the furtherance of liberation is imagination. And that act of imagining is brought forth in love, is brought to us by someone, either an inner or outer beloved, who sees our true essence.

When we experience trauma, we lose all sense of connection with the Divine and feel no possibility of a future that might be different from the present. At our core, we have lost touch with our own deep Self, the wisdom source that guides our unfolding growth toward wholeness. We can only see the drudgery of daily existence and have closed ourselves off to the Great Mystery. We have lost faith. Opening to the ecstatic, to the unknown, is terrifying. And yet, if we remain in this state, any possibility of growth is foreclosed, and our lives are deadened.

The midrash shows us that the only way out of this state is to be awakened by the Beloved of the soul. This love may come from another person, from a sacred encounter that awakens us to the Divine Presence, or from an inner stirring by the Beloved awakening us to the possibility that we are more than our limited egos would have us believe.

In turning toward this call of love, we allow ourselves to become undefended, to be seduced away from our vigilance and power struggles; we surrender to the erotic urgings of our souls and bodies. We allow ourselves to be seen through the eyes of the Beloved, who imagines for us a future that we had long given up on for ourselves. We loosen the tight rein of our defended egos and let ourselves play, dance, awaken to possibilities—we respond to the urgings of the heart. As Shulamit speaks in the Song of Songs:

> My beloved spoke, and said unto me: "Rise up, my love, my fair one, and come away. For, lo, the winter is past, the rain is over and gone; the flowers appear on the earth; the time of singing is come, and the voice of the turtledove is heard in our land. The fig-tree putteth forth her green figs, and the vines in blossom give forth their fragrance. Arise, my love, my fair one, and come away … My beloved is mine, and I am his, that feedeth among the lilies."[20]

As we deepen our understanding of how trauma impacts the psyche, we gain appreciation for the profound wisdom of these ancient texts. Our ancestors understood what was necessary to bring the soul out of a shattered state and to move toward healing. The movement out of exile begins when we are beheld by the compassionate gaze of one who sees us through the eyes of love and reminds us that we are more than what the trauma did to us. We realize there is more to our lives than the fear of the abyss that trauma has inflicted on us, limiting our perception of the possible. We are invited to grow beyond the limitations of traumatized thinking, to reconnect with our essence.

Julie's dream

As explored in the previous chapter, Julie's innate spirituality was not mirrored in her family. Her mother and her maternal grandparents were emotionally devastated by having to leave behind their extended families and communities as they fled Germany in the 1930s. When her paternal grandmother killed herself just a few years before Julie was born, her father was devastated and lost all faith in God. Her mother's depression deepened and went largely untreated until Julie was about twelve years old. Her family attended temple, but any spiritual feeling was absent.

Julie went through a profound descent as a young woman, which I discuss further in Chapter Nine. Afterward, she connected with Judaism through engaging with her husband, Aaron (whose story is also explored here), in a Jewish Renewal congregation. In her rediscovery of Judaism, she gained the spiritual strength to confront her inherited legacy of depression and intergenerational trauma. She had a powerful dream in September 2001, just after the World Trade Center disaster:

> *I approach my sister's house on my childhood foot-powered scooter. The house was perched above a bowl-like depression in the earth below. I tried to park the scooter without falling off the edge of the cliff.*
>
> *As I pass by another person's house, I see through a window that the people were watching a woman on television bragging about drag-racing on her motorcycle, spinning 360 degrees and that she would do a 720. I worried that the woman was going to kill herself and felt sad that she believed she had to act in such a macho manner.*
>
> *Carefully, I inch the scooter towards the front door of my sister's house, and find it became light. I am able to tuck it under my arm.*

Julie brought this dream to a Jewish Renewal rabbi and spiritual director. He invited her to continue working with the dream using Jung's technique of active imagination. As Julie re-entered the dream, she went inside her sister's house and realized that it was her own house. It had very high windows, wide vistas, and a grassy expanse outside, with trees "like an African savannah, kind of like paradise." She saw a mirror and a woman's reflection in it and realized that the woman "was me—more glorious, more primal, more priestly, self-possessed of her own inner strength and power, larger in stature and eternally beautiful." The rabbi told her that the house was her temple, a place to which she could always return.

In Julie's dream, the girl undertaking dangerous actions may reflect a counterphobic response to trauma, disregarding safety and perhaps expressing an unconscious suicidal impulse. Julie felt the dream reflected how she overrode her authentic feeling nature by trying to perform in a profession she chose to meet her father's expectations, which led to her feeling suicidal. It took years for her to overcome the guilt and shame of not living up to her father's and the culture's masculine standards and choosing instead to follow her own creative path.

In the active imagination, she sees an image of what Jung called the Self reflected in the mirror. Jung viewed the Self as the totality of the psyche, the potential of all we can become. Julie, like the men in the midrash, saw her own beauty, her radiance, reflected to her, and it was far more numinous than she had previously believed. Her rabbi offered her an image of what a temple could hold that differed greatly from her experience of a synagogue as a child. Julie continued to work with the Self figure in the dream, who could help hold and nurture her inner child, supporting her to heal the despair and loneliness she experienced growing up.

Relatedness and healing from trauma

Trauma is transmitted unmetabolized from generation to generation because it is often too painful for the survivors themselves to mourn. The trauma cannot be worked through because the experiences overwhelm the psyche. Integration of traumatic memory can occur only when we are able to experience the memory metaphorically and symbolically. When we cannot do this, we simultaneously experience hypermnesia and amnesia—the trauma is ever-present yet just outside the realm of conscious awareness, coloring all perception.

Research on the psychological impact of the Holocaust on survivors began in the 1970s and 1980s, following an initial 20-year period of shocked silence and an inability to turn toward the massive collective trauma. Jungian analyst Angela Connolly notes:

> The concentration camp experience represents an evil so appalling that we too, when we turn to face it, suffer psychic unbalance ... Some hideous impression of Auschwitz is in every mind, far removed from conscious thought but *there* ... and anything connected with it, anything that starts it into consciousness, brings with it a horror too large and intensely personal to confront safely.[21]

We live in a time when every Jewish person is given the task of integrating and healing from the traumas of the past—the Shoah and its impact on the Jewish collective psyche, and other family histories of anti-Semitic terror and subjugation. We recover and redeem shards of our ancestral memory through engaging images that emerge from the unconscious. Working with a compassionate witness who sees our brokenness, we can begin to recover these lost parts of ourselves.[22]

The essence of trauma is not that some injury occurred, but that there were no loving arms to hold us and to help us integrate and make meaning of the event.[23] We are cast adrift into an experience of shame, self-loathing, self-doubt, and existential angst—we are alone. This is the state of exile. The midrash reflects the understanding that a loving presence is necessary for us to survive massive trauma with our souls intact. The women restore the experience of a loving other to the traumatized psyches of their men.

Trauma is inherently humiliating; being witnessed in our pain may feel excruciating. We feel as if we must hide our true self and may go to incredible lengths to avoid the experience of being seen by another.[24] The play between the women and men invites the deeply wounded soul to be seen, to move through the terrifying fear of humiliation, and to begin to allow oneself to enter true connection with another. This is the first step toward ending the exile of the separate self that results from trauma.

The women and men are both subject to profound degradation in slavery, the men through being forced to perform brutally difficult work; the women, by the edicts that control their bodies and murder their children. The mirror play allows humiliation and shame to come to the surface, and it offers an invitation to see oneself through a different lens.

The women remember and redefine themselves as they are seen through the eyes of the Divine, as beautiful. In teasing the men that they are more beautiful than them, they playfully give voice to the shame that the men live with, the internalized voice of the Pharaoh, and invite them to speak back to that voice, asserting their own beauty and individuality. As the men and women boast playfully together, they find the beauty in themselves and each other, leading to a sacred union between them that regenerates the life force of the community—a force that transforms the people from humiliated slaves to lovers who see themselves, and each other, as Beloved.

As our ancient sages recognized in the midrash, it is through imaginative play that the women and men recover from the brutalizing effects of trauma and remember the essence of who they are, enabling them to embrace the fullness of life.

Reclaiming God in her image

The movement out of exile is brought about through the actions of the women. Previous periods of profound collective devastation have been followed by a rebirth of mysticism and a re-emergence of the Shekhinah, the Sacred Feminine. And, for the first time, in our era *women* are reimagining the meaning and expression of Judaism. The widespread role of women in Jewish ritual leadership is unprecedented. It is through their involvement that many who had been alienated from the patriarchal tradition have found their own reconnection.

Women's growing involvement is a holy spark that is being redeemed within new expressions of Judaism. With the shattering of the Old World, women became active in life outside the shtetl and other traditional settings. In Eastern European Jewish culture, women often earned and managed the family's money, freeing the devout men for study and prayer. Jewish women, equipped with managerial skills, led movements for social and economic justice in American sweatshops and in the burgeoning labor movement of the early 20th century.[25]

Jewish women were central in the development of second-wave feminism in the 1960s and '70s. Judith Plaskow writes of the tension that women felt between their feminist and Jewish identities. Many felt so alienated from the patriarchal texts and practices that they left Judaism altogether. Those who stayed set about the profound task of remaking Judaism in the image of the Feminine aspect of the Divine.

Supported by the emerging archeological evidence of the widespread Goddess tradition in the Fertile Crescent area of the Middle East, and as Raphael Patai has demonstrated, in Hebrew religious observance itself, many began to see that the patriarchal bent of Judaism was just one expression—an expression of a particular era and ethos. They saw the possibility that a further stage of Judaism lay ahead—as Jewish mystical texts also recognized—in which the feminine and masculine aspects of the Divine would be balanced.

The emergence of new forms of Judaism grew from women taking their place as rabbis and community leaders in the Reform, Reconstructionist, and Conservative movements, and as scholars in the Orthodox tradition. In the Jewish Renewal movement, women were central in developing liturgy, rituals, and approaches to Judaism that were deeply feminine in form—nonhierarchical, embodied, experiential, and based in relationship and deep feeling.

And it was women, denied access to Judaism's core for millennia, who picked up the tradition, shook it out, and watched as the holy sparks cascaded outward, to be captured and redeemed. They held up a mirror to the men and showed them the treasures they had found. "I am more beautiful than you," they said. And the men countered, "No, I am more beautiful." And so it went, back and forth, in an erotic dance new and ancient, as interpretations of Torah expressed new visions, beautiful silk-screened *tallit* designs were crafted, medieval meditation techniques were rediscovered, the poetry of the Zohar explored. A proliferation of songs, chants, and ecstatic movement blossomed into a new Judaism, eager to discover what lay beyond the *mitzrayim* of trauma.

Notes

1 Ariel Bloch and Chana Bloch, trans., *The Song of Songs* (New York: The Modern Library, 1995).
2 Rivkah Scharf Kluger, *Psyche in Scripture: The Idea of the Chosen People and Other Essays* (Toronto: Inner City Books, 1995), 92.
3 Howard Schwartz, *Tree of Souls: The Mythology of Judaism* (New York: Oxford University Press, 2004), 277–278; citing Song of Songs Rabbah 1:11.
4 Merlin Stone, *When God Was a Woman* (New York: Harcourt Brace & Jovanovich, 1976).
5 Merlin Stone, Foreword to *The Hebrew Goddess*, by Raphael Patai (Detroit, MI: Wayne State University Press, 1967/1978).
6 Kluger, *Psyche in Scripture*; Rivkah Scharf Kluger, *Psyche and Bible: Three Old Testament Themes* (New York: Spring Publications, 1974); Sanford Drob, *Kabbalistic Visions: C.G. Jung and Jewish Mysticism* (New Orleans, LA: Spring Journal Books, 2010); Siegmund Hurwitz, *Lilith—the First Eve: Historical and Psychological Aspects of the Dark Feminine* (Einsiedeln: Daimon Verlag, 1992).
7 Charles D. Laughlin and C. Jason Throop, "Imagination and Reality: On the Relations Between Myth, Consciousness and the Cosmic Sea," *Zygon* 36, no. 4 (Dec. 2001): 716.
8 Savina J. Teubal, *Sarah the Priestess: The First Matriarch of Genesis* (Athens, OH: Swallow Press, 1984).
9 Genesis 21:12.
10 Zohar 1:135b.
11 Ibid, 45.
12 Ibid.
13 Genesis 31:19–35.
14 Genesis 34.
15 Genesis 34:1–31, Tamara Cohn Eskenazi, Andrea L. Weiss, eds., *The Torah: A Women's Commentary* (New York: URJ Press, 2008), 190–195.
16 Zohar 1:203a, Vol. III, 243.
17 Avivah Zornberg, *The Particulars of Rapture: Reflections on Exodus* (New York: Doubleday, 2001), 68–70.
18 Tanhuma, Pequdei, 9. See also David Ben Ha'Hasid, *Mirrors of the Women Who Ministered*, translated by Daniel Matt (Chico, CA: Scholars Press, 1982); and Zornberg, *The Particulars of Rapture*, 60–63.

Awakening from the trance of exile 93

19 Ibid. See also Zohar, Vol. IV, Shemot 2:4a, 12–13.
20 Song of Songs, 2:10–16.
21 Angela Connolly, "Healing the Wounds of our Fathers: Intergenerational Trauma, Memory, Symbolization and Narrative," *Journal of Analytical Psychology* 56, no. 5 (2011): 607–626, 610; citing Terrence Des Pres, *The Survivor: An Anatomy of Life in the Death Camps* (New York: Oxford University Press 1976), 170.
22 Stephen K. Levine, *Trauma, Tragedy, Therapy: The Arts and Human Suffering* (London: Jessica Kingsley Publishers, 2009).
23 Robert Stolorow, *World, Affectivity, Trauma: Heidegger and Post-Cartesian Psychoanalysis* (New York: Routledge, 2011).
24 John Steiner, "Seeing and Being Seen: Narcissistic Pride and Narcissistic Humiliation," *The International Journal of Psychoanalysis* 87, no. 4 (2006): 939–951.
25 Elaine Leeder, lecture given in Cotati, California, 2017.

Chapter 6

Moses and awakening the spiritual fire

From the night of coupling by the banks of the Nile, the generation that will leave Egypt is born. Among them is the great leader Moses. Moses grew up assimilated into a culture not his own. He spent years wandering in the wilderness to find his own connection to the Divine. His encounter with the *numinosum*, the awesome spiritual presence, came to him unbidden as he walked along the hillsides. Responding to the great light within the burning bush, Moses was called to his life's path.

Moses, the greatest prophet, was also paradoxically the most humble man among the Hebrews. In him we may see the unattainable ideal of the Self, and the humility of our ego in the face of it, our own inadequacy as we attempt to give voice to the ineffable. Moses's role as deliverer of the people out of exile and toward the Promised Land reflects the journey each of us takes when we respond to the voice of the soul, calling us to greater vistas than the narrowness we had come to regard as reality. In this chapter, I explore Moses's journey and its resonance in the experience of individuals finding their own reconnection with the Divine within Judaism.

The female lineage bearers

Moses journey, from the time of his birth through his ascendance as a great leader, is supported and sustained by the women around him, and by his unique relationship with the Shekhinah. The heroic masculine emerges from and is nurtured in the matrix of the feminine. The Zohar teaches that the Shekhinah was hovering over the marriage bed of Moses's parents, Amram and Yocheved, and dwelt with Moses all his days. "From Amram, who clung to the blessed Holy One, issued Moses— from whom the blessed Holy One never departed, to whom *Shekhinah* clung constantly."[1] Moses's title, *ish ha-Elohim*, is interpreted as "husband of *Shekhinah*."[2]

The actions of seven women make the Exodus journey possible. The midwives Shifrah and Puah defy Pharaoh's decree and safeguard Moses at birth. Yocheved, Moses's mother, places him in a basket of reeds to ensure his survival. Moses's sister Miriam, whose passionate pleas for continuing the lineage made his birth possible, watches over him as his basket floats up the Nile. He is lifted out of the water by Batya, Pharaoh's daughter, who raises him with the help of Yocheved, his mother, who becomes his nursemaid.

The Shekhinah's attendance at his conception and birth reflects the hero motif of one whose parents are both Divine and human. Both Yocheved and Batya raise Moses, in accord with the archetypal pattern of the hero with two mothers.

Tzipporah, Moses's wife, saves his life through the circumcision of their son. As Tzipporah ensures the covenant passes to future generations, Moses is able to fulfill his destiny as deliverer of the Hebrew people. Serach bat Asher, whose role I examine in Chapter Eight, carries the secret knowledge of the ancestors that enables Moses to guide the people out of Egypt.

Moses in the wilderness

Moses is the greatest leader in Biblical text. Surprisingly, we may also see him as being not unlike ourselves, growing up alienated from the tradition into which he was born and having to adapt to the dominant culture to survive. The first pivotal moment in Moses's separation from the Egyptian culture comes as he encounters an Egyptian killing a Hebrew slave. Moses responds with great outrage and, in fury, kills him. The Pharaoh calls for Moses to be punished by death. Moses flees to the wilderness, where he sits down by a well. There he meets seven daughters of a Midianite priest, and helps them get water from the well to water their flocks.[3] The sacred waters of life begin to flow once again.

Moses marries the Midianite Tzipporah and lives among her people. Kabbalists say that during this extended period of solitude, Moses was schooled in the esoteric mysteries. When we separate from the collective, as Moses does in the wilderness, we embark on the path of individuation—discovering who we are, separate from the family and the society into which we are born and to which we have become acculturated. Many journeys of individuation involve a period of retreat or separation so that we can hear the voice of the inner Self speaking, a voice that might otherwise be drowned out by the cacophony of cultural and familial demands. In the quiet of the wild places, we may be able to hear the "still small voice" within.

Moses spends many years as a shepherd on the mountain where he can separate himself from the conditioning of the house of Pharaoh and begin to hear the voice of his own soul. Moses must develop and mature, growing in strength so he will be ready to lead the people. He must become someone who will not simply react, as he did in slaying the Egyptian. Instead, he learns how to respond wisely and with restraint, through bringing himself into alignment with the Divine Will, becoming Its instrument.

One day, when walking along the mountain path, Moses sees a bush on fire. He stops, surprised to see the fire does not consume the bush. He hears the voice of God calling to him, telling him to take off his shoes because he is standing on holy ground. Something numinous is occurring. Moses responds, "*Hineni*" ("I am here"), the same words used by Abraham to indicate his complete receptivity to God. Saying "Hineni" acknowledges one's willingness to be present to what

God, the voice of the Self, asks of us, even though we may struggle mightily with what we receive. It is an agreement to undergo the difficult trials of initiation and individuation.

Prior to Moses's encounter with the burning bush, the people's hope of deliverance was stirred when the most recent Pharaoh died after Moses fled to the wilderness. The midrash also reveals that the people's hope is reawakened when the women hear and respond to the voice of God telling them to meet the men on the banks of the river with fish and wine. Perhaps when the Israelites witness Moses's slaying of the Egyptian, something happens. Moses's response to the slaves' mistreatment catalyzes a new awareness in the people. They remember that they are more than slaves. They are children of Abraham and Sarah who formed a covenant with God. It now becomes clear that slavery is a human construct that can be overthrown. The shackles can be lifted. There is a higher authority to whom the people are connected.

After centuries of silence, the people again begin crying out to God. The Biblical text tells us that their cry came up unto God, and awakened God's compassion.[4] The relationship between God and the people is one of mutuality—the people must call out to God for God to respond. "When God heard their groaning ... [He] remembered His covenant with Abraham, with Isaac, and with Jacob ... And God saw the children of Israel, and God took cognizance of them."[5]

The great Hasidic master Rabbi Nachman of Bratslav taught his students a practice to use when they were in a state of complete despair. He taught them to go out into the wilderness and to cry out to God, to give voice to their deepest grief and pain. This practice teaches us that to feel God's presence, we must first connect with our own despair, our longing, our deep need for God, and to communicate these laments in some way, so that God can hear our cries. As this story teaches us again and again, the relationship between humans and Divine requires our active participation. When we cry out from the depths of our hearts, from the intensity of our longing, God hears and remembers us.

God reveals Himself (here in the transcendent masculine aspect) at the burning bush to Moses as the God of his father and ancestors, signaling the prophecy given to Abraham that his descendants would move beyond the suffering they currently endured. Despite the long period in which the people have felt separated from the Divine, God has witnessed their hardships and heard their cries and has now come to deliver them from slavery "unto a land flowing with milk and honey." God tells Moses that he is to go to Pharaoh and demand to bring His children forth from Egypt.

As Moses approaches the burning bush, he asks who he should say has summoned him. God responds, tell them "*Ehyeh Asher Ehyeh.*" Translated as "I Am that I Am Becoming," the words simultaneously encompass the past, present, and future tenses of the verb "I am" (I am, I have been, I will be).[6] Often translated in English texts as Yahweh or Jehovah, in Hebrew the tetragrammaton of four Hebrew letters, *Yud Hei Vav Hei*, or *YHVH*, is used to reflect that the true name of God cannot be spoken—the infinite reality of the Divine cannot be reduced to words.

Rabbi Arthur Green observes that the name that God speaks to Moses—*Ehyeh Asher Ehyeh*—is sometimes translated as "I shall be." This "means nothing less than the truth that God is Being itself."[7]

As we open to the Divine, the Self, the numinous, speaks, either through visions or dreams. It shows us a new and unfamiliar way. Our footsteps are guided by opening to the great Mystery. Rather than directing our path with desires and intentions solely from the conscious level, we begin to open to what life presents and learn to dance with it. Jungian analyst Edward Edinger saw this dance as the "creative point where God and man meet, the point where transpersonal energies flow into personal life … the central source of life energy, the fountain of our being which is most simply described as God."[8]

Ruth's story

Ruth was raised in Central California in a family of socialist intellectuals dismissive of spirituality. Yet Ruth's ancestors in Eastern Europe were Hasidim descended from two great spiritual lineages—one connected with the founder of Lubavitch Hasidism, Shneur Zalman of Liadi, and the other from the renowned Talmudic and kabbalistic scholar, the Vilna of Gaon—two renowned sages who strongly differed over their approaches.

As a child, Ruth cleaved to the small sparks of holiness she received from her parents and others around her as precious gifts that helped her understand the spiritual reality beyond the physical. When she was about four years old, she asked her mother about God. Her mother said, "God is in everything." Ruth delighted in this explanation and, as a child, felt God's presence everywhere.

Her family was deeply intellectual, culturally Jewish and secular, carrying the family lineage of wisdom in a non-religious way. They attended the Reform temple where the rabbi recognized her love for Judaism, suggesting that perhaps someday she would become a rabbi. This was a profound mirroring for her as a young teenager in the 1950s, when women were not yet being ordained. She was deeply disheartened by the fractious temple politics that led to her rabbi's resignation and turned away from Jewish practice after this disillusioning experience.

In her early adulthood, Ruth apprenticed with a Native American spiritual teacher and learned to pray by invoking the four directions and acknowledging the sacredness of the earth. Like many of her generation, connection with other spiritual paths helped her find meaning and a relationship with the sacred. When she told her teacher that she wished she had something of this in her own tradition, the teacher replied, "Your tradition knows about holy ground. Look at Moses." This was a profound moment for Ruth; she realized that she could "take off her shoes and feel the Divine Presence" in Judaism. Ruth later reconnected with Judaism through encountering a highly intelligent rabbi strongly committed to social justice. This rabbi carried the integrity of the rabbi she had known in childhood.

She still found the Native American practices, such as praying to the four directions, meaningful, but she felt conflicted about continuing them after embracing Judaism, wondering whether the four directions prayer violated the proscription against having other gods. When she discovered that kabbalah teaches about the directions and the elements, she was able to strike a balance. "I still occasionally pray to the directions, but I don't do it on Shabbos!"

Awakening the spiritual fire

On the mountain, Moses encounters the spiritual fire of transformation, a numinous experience that shifts him out of ordinary consciousness and awakens him to his spiritual purpose. No longer living solely in the personal realm, he now carries the destiny of the Jewish people.

When we experience the Divine Presence in our own lives, it may herald the beginning of an individuation process, in which the psychic center shifts from the conscious personality, or ego, to a relationship between the Divine, or the Self, and the personal. Edward Edinger sees Moses as the way-shower who brings our conscious mind into relationship with the Self, the totality of who we are becoming.[9]

Moses represents what Jung called the *transcendent function*, leading us out of the narrow place of consciousness centered only in the ego, to the expansive Promised Land of connection with the Self. The continuing process of bridging these two aspects of consciousness is what Jung referred to as *individuation*— becoming one's true self.

Jungian analyst Donald Kalsched notes that the soul becomes present when the Divine and human worlds come together.[10] A spiritual awakening may happen in a powerful moment, often a synchronistic one, in which our everyday consciousness tears open to reveal the archetypal pattern guiding our lives. We awaken to the Self, that aspect of us that carries the spark of the God-image, the spiritual dimension of existence.

For Jews who grew up in secular families that rejected spirituality altogether, or in observant families in which spirituality was not shared in a way that could be meaningfully internalized, the awakening to this archetypal pattern in the context of Judaism can be both powerfully surprising and deeply familiar. When the archetypal pattern of our lives opens to us in uninvited and uncanny ways, we may experience this breakthrough as synchronicity. The world is speaking to us and showing us that we need to pay attention, for we are in the presence of the great Mystery.

Synchronicity occurs when the outer world offers independent affirmation of our internal psychic experience. The boundary between inner and outer is transcended. Edinger observed that synchronistic experiences "are most likely to occur when the archetypal level of the psyche has been activated and they have a numinous impact on the experiencer."[11] Through such an experience, we glimpse a larger story that is unfolding through us. We may become aware of the creative matrix of which our lives are an expression. We come into relationship with the

Divine Mystery and allow ourselves to become partners in its, and our, unfolding. When we experience synchronicity, we gain a glimpse into the archetypal realm and we understand that we live in a meaningful universe.

The images that appear to us are often numinous, filled with a holy light. Rudolf Otto coined the term *numinous* to describe objects or images that are infused with a holy character, in the sense of being awesome and overwhelming to our ordinary consciousness.[12] Otto, a German Lutheran, wrote about the philosophy of religion in the early 20th century. His writing informed Jung's understanding of the numinous. Jung became deeply interested in what he called *synchronistic* experience, which he saw as resembling "numinous experiences where space, time, and causality are abolished."[13]

Otto's interest in the holy grew from a powerful experience he had while attending synagogue services in Morocco in 1911. Zalman Schachter-Shalomi explains that Otto was so overcome by his experience of holiness that he sought ways to express it in psychological terms.[14] Otto described the experience as holding within it both *mysterium fascinans*, the awe that draws us closer to the Divine Mystery, and *mysterium tremendum*, the fear we experience as we come closer and closer to God—fear that we may be consumed by God, that we might ultimately fall into the abyss of non-being. In Hebrew, the word *yirah* means both *awe* and *fear*, both *mysterium fascinans* and *tremendum*. *Yirah* is seen as one of two gateways of connection to the holy, the other being through love. The encounter with the numinous is often terrifying, as we open to a consciousness much larger than that of our personal egos. Reb Zalman likened Otto's experience of the awesome power of holiness to that of Moses at the burning bush.[15]

The fire that Moses encounters is a manifestation of God's presence in the earthly realm, a meeting of spirit and matter, a unification of the transcendent and immanent realms that prefigures the great meeting that will follow at Sinai. The fire is a spiritual flame that guides our engagement with the great Mystery of life. As we draw near to it, it illuminates the darkness that once shrouded the unconscious realms and invites us in.

Rejection of Jewish identity may impede the development of connection to an authentic core because access to the religious center of the psyche may also be rejected. On a collective scale, recent centuries of anti-Semitism, assimilation, and genocide have resulted in a period of unsurpassed rupture in the historical transmission of Jewish identity.[16] How then does someone who grew up in a milieu where the connection to the Divine has been either denied or repressed begin to find their way back into relationship with the holy? For many Jews who have rejected a Jewish identity, a synchronistic numinous experience may catalyze and subsequently guide the individuation process.

Daniel and the soul's menorah

Daniel, whose secular childhood was discussed in Chapter Four, was taken completely by surprise when, as an adult, he saw the Lubavitcher Rebbe (the leader of the Hasidic movement Chabad) lighting a giant Chanukah menorah with a cherry picker on television. Unexpectedly overcome with emotion, Daniel burst into tears. He recalled "weeping and weeping … It completely broadsided me—I had no idea what was going on."

Daniel began exploring Judaism more actively the following year, attending Rosh Hashanah services at a Jewish Renewal congregation in Berkeley. As the service began and people started praying, he was not sure why he had come; everything felt unfamiliar. Then, at some point during the service, he had a sudden awareness—"Oh my God, this is why I am who I am, this tradition, these prayers, this *everything* is how I got to be who I am, and how did I not know that before now? And then, that was it." He began what has become a lifelong journey of a deepening reconnection with Judaism.

The great Hasidic master Reb Nachman of Bratslav taught that the deeper meaning of Chanukah is the opportunity to light "the inviolate spark of Judaism" that lives inside each Jewish person, even one who has forgotten his or her connection. This spark is akin to the single untouched vial of oil found inside the Holy Temple that had been desecrated by outside forces. The oil was used to light the menorah, symbolizing the Temple's rededication to holiness.[17] The menorah is one of the central symbols of Judaism, representing the numinosity of the sacred fire first experienced at the burning bush.

Daniel experienced a transcendent moment of opening to Judaism when he witnessed the lighting of the menorah. The significance of the transmission through the leader of the Chabad Hasidism reflects a symbolic reconnection with the lineage that was broken when Daniel's parents turned away from the tradition. As I will explore further in a later chapter, the loss of Daniel's paternal great-grandparents and all their children, except for Daniel's grandfather, was never consciously mourned in his family.

The Lubavitcher Rebbe carried the sacred love for Judaism that Daniel saw reflected in his paternal grandfather's prayers. The rabbi's deep honoring of the tradition conveyed in performing this sacred act broke Daniel's heart open to the beauty of Judaism. He experienced a revelatory moment when his innate spirituality found a home in the Jewish ritual. William James stated, "A man's character is discernible in the mental or moral attitude in which, when it came upon him, he felt himself most deeply and intensely active and alive. At such moments there is a voice inside which speaks and says, '*This* is the real me!'"[18]

Jews raised without a spiritual connection to Judaism may experience a sense of amazement to discover the Beloved speaking in the language and rituals of their ancestors, calling them home in a way that is at once completely foreign and achingly familiar. Writing of the havurah movement, which invited Jews to create collaborative communities to develop study and ritual, Judy Petonsk notes that the impulse behind the movement was the need "to understand this Jewishness stirring inarticulately within us if we were to become whole persons. The Jewish stories were our stories, a lens through which we could understand the world and ourselves. To become more Jewish was to become more ourselves."[19]

Finding speech after the Shoah

At the burning bush, Moses asks incredulously, "Who am I, that I should go unto Pharaoh, and that I should bring forth the children of Israel out of Egypt?" Moses is slow of tongue and afraid that he lacks the skills to speak on behalf of the people. God assures Moses that God will be with him and that his brother Aaron will help him speak. Moses's concern that he will not be able to carry God's message teaches us that we may move out of exile by giving language to our experience, even when language seems wholly inadequate to address the enormity of what we have suffered or are suffering.

Eva Hoffman describes her interior world as a child born to Holocaust survivors.[20] Born in Poland in 1945, Hoffman grew up with war as "the heavy ground of being, the natural condition to which the world tended, and could at any moment return."[21] She spent much of her childhood waiting for the war "to manifest itself again … waiting for danger and destruction, which were the fundamental human condition, to trample the fragile coverlet of peace."[22] She anticipated the death of her parents because all the other adults who had once made up her family were dead. "Life itself, for children born into families like mine, could seem a tenuous condition, a buffeted island in the infinite ocean of death."[23] Hoffman recalled listening to her parents and their friends utter the first communications about the war, their "speech broken under the pressure of pain."[24]

> The episodes, the talismanic litanies, were repeated but never elaborated upon. They remained compressed, packed, sharp. I suppose the inassimilable character of the experiences they referred to was expressed—and passed on—through this form. For it was precisely the indigestibility of these utterances, their fearful weight of densely packed feeling, as much as any specific content that I took in as a child. The fragmentary phrases lodged themselves in my mind like shards, like the deadly needles I remember from certain fairy tales, which prickled your flesh and could never be extracted again.[25]

Hoffman wrote that for the second generation, those born in the wake of the Shoah, "the Event that preceded us was fundamental enough to constitute an overwhelming given and a life task."[26] This generation shares reference points that "have to do with our location in the dark topography of the Shoah and with the stages of a long and difficult reckoning—with our parents' past and its deep impact on us; with our obligations to that past, and the conclusions we can derive from it for the present."[27]

Edward Feld notes that finding faith after the Holocaust is a challenging task for most Jews.[28] Many Jews completely rejected God, feeling betrayed and abandoned or failed by One that could not or would not prevent the annihilation of His chosen people. The Shoah became a "repressed memory," too painful to speak about. George Steiner writes, "The world of Auschwitz lies outside speech as it lies outside reason."[29]

Feld believes that finding meaningful language is the central task of the post-Shoah generation. "Surely we must find the syllables of a religious language that would speak to our time even if what we say is like a child's first utterances. For the overwhelming events we have seen demand speech; our inner being clamors for it."[30] The reclamation of the sacred is a critical task for Jews because, Feld notes, "the obliteration of all that was holy" had been "at the center of the Nazi enterprise."[31]

Feld shows how the religious imagination of Judaism can provide the salve for healing the Jewish psyche. Jewish theology was borne of many cycles of death and rebirth following historical tragedy, and it developed in response to a perceived need to recreate a spiritual life following destructive events. The Hebrew Bible itself was written during the Babylonian exile, following the destruction of Jewish civilization in Jerusalem in 589 BCE.[32] The experience of loss and tragedy lies at the heart of the Biblical stories, not just thematically but also in the historical context in which they were written down. Exile made it imperative that the teachings were remembered. Just as each generation has had to find its voice, Feld urges that the current generation must also speak.[33]

In every generation, as we each connect with our inner Moses, the way-shower, we begin to find words to express our experience of the numinous. As we do, we open to possibilities beyond the constricted consciousness imposed by trauma.

Lillian's story continues

Lillian, whose secular upbringing I discussed in Chapter Four, recalled that her father grew up poor, speaking primarily Yiddish as a toddler, just after his family came to the United States. "When he was three years old, he broke his leg, and he was hospitalized for six weeks, during which time nobody visited him, and he came home speaking English and refused to ever again speak Yiddish."

Lillian's father graduated from college and became a newspaper columnist. He succeeded by assimilating—changing his surname, moving to a predominantly gentile neighborhood in Connecticut, and even placing his children in a Catholic school. Yet his connection to Judaism was profoundly stirred during World War II, when he learned about the Nazi genocide. He used his role as an influential newspaper columnist to advocate for American involvement in the war. Due in large part to his advocacy, a haven was created in upstate New York that enabled a thousand Jews to be admitted into the US during the war.

Lillian recalled her great surprise when, in the 1950s, "our family went to Germany and my dad started speaking Yiddish to all the customs people, and he couldn't stop." She was deeply moved as she saw him reclaim his *mamaloshn*, his mother tongue, abandoned as a young child. Here is the father who assured Lillian that he too was at Sinai, a Jew, in spite of his assimilationist choices. He was a Jew who stood by other Jews, who acted bravely to save those lives he could save, to awaken the American people to the horrors of the Shoah, and who advocated fiercely for American intervention in the war to save Jewish lives.

Recalling this story enabled Lillian to forgive the ways in which her father's turning away from Judaism had impacted her, understanding that he too suffered from a sense of abandonment as a young child. As the first child in his family born on American soil, his connection to the Old World ways was more attenuated than his more observant parents and siblings, and the thin thread of his connection to Yiddish was severed by the trauma of his separation from his family during his hospitalization.

An independent spirit then took root, one that led to increasing secular and assimilated identity, until such time as he was moved by the horrors of the war to proudly reclaim his Jewish identity and to act. This independence allowed him to act effectively in the world in which he was able to yield power. Visiting Germany in the 1950s, the language of his early childhood returned spontaneously and forcefully, the language of so many who had burned in the fires of the Shoah.

The inner Pharaoh

Jungian analyst Donald Kalsched reflects that when we experience trauma, a protective figure may emerge in the psyche to shield us from further injury. Yet soon this protective figure eventually becomes an inner persecutor, ever vigilant against potential dangers. The protector/persecutor keeps us from spontaneous expression and action. We live in the grips of a complex that keeps us afraid and quiescent.[34] Our inner Pharaoh will not let us go.

The inner Pharaoh corresponds to the oppressive Pharaoh as he appears in the Exodus story. It is important to distinguish this particular Pharaoh and the role he plays in the story from the larger history of Egypt and its great leading Pharaohs.

Moses's parents ensured his survival by hiding his identity and allowing him to be raised by Pharaoh's daughter Batya in the palace. Moses is raised by both Batya and his mother Yocheved acting as his nurse. He occupies two worlds—that of Pharaoh and that of his own people. When we are subject to oppression by the dominant culture, we develop a "double consciousness." We are aware of the way that the dominant culture thinks, while also aware of our own perspective. It is only by inhabiting this dual consciousness that our survival is ensured.

Having suffered from anti-Semitic attacks for millennia, Jews have a strongly developed dual consciousness, which may account for the strength of Jewish analytical thought and perception. We learn to perceive when there is danger in the air, when we may become the target of the dominant culture's aggression or hostility toward us. We develop ways to be unobstructive, compliant, to not draw too much envy or wrath. In so doing, we may find ourselves too timid to speak our own truths. Yet eventually, if we are to become our truest selves, we must risk stepping outside of the safe confines of the dominant culture. In time, the protective benefits of living in the Pharaoh's home are too limiting for Moses, who must find and liberate his true self along with his people.

Aaron's story

Aaron's father was still a boy when he, his sister, and his parents narrowly escaped from a small German town in the late 1930s, leaving behind a large Jewish community that was annihilated in the Holocaust. His mother was born in America into a poor, non-practicing Jewish family during the Depression. Her identity was so suppressed that she didn't even know she was Jewish until she was five and overheard girls whispering she was "J-e-w-i-s-h." She turned to them and said she knew how to spell. She met Aaron's father at the end of World War II, when she was 17 and passionate about going to Palestine to help defend it. Aaron recalled that his father, who had survived both the Nazis and beach landings and jungle fighting in the South Pacific, was not supportive of that idea. He persuaded her to raise money instead. His mother, who was never fully accepted by his father's more affluent German Jewish family, became a lifelong leader in Hadassah, a Zionist women's organization.

Aaron grew up in a New Jersey suburb in the 1950s and 1960s. His family was excluded from the local country club and had to join "swim clubs" of Jews, Italians, and other non-WASPS. His experience of Judaism was permeated with fear. He thought of God as "the God of the cookie jar," watching your every move to see if you took an extra cookie. His family attended a Conservative synagogue and observed rituals at home, "but no one was *talking about Judaism*." The synagogue experience was also frightening. "To the end of his life, my father sat on the cantor's side of the *shul*, so he didn't have to watch the rabbi who, to my father, was a very scary man."

As a child, Aaron found a meaningful spiritual connection in a rich internal world where he "could pull the veil and be quiet somewhere and talk inside, and that was sacred, that was my sacred space." After his Bar Mitzvah, he felt "a full court press" from his parents to "keep me Jewish." He went on a teen tour in Israel, which felt oppressive due to numerous constraints imposed by Orthodox chaperones.

He experienced the insular Jewish neighborhood he'd grown up in as stifling, with its conservative values and focus on material wealth. "Everyone I knew was Jewish. What I wanted to leave was the upper-middle-class background where everybody just had too much, and everybody was very racist." In college, he married his ex-Catholic girlfriend, and had little relationship with Judaism or Jewish ritual. He soon divorced and remarried a woman from an influential Jewish family, attempting to conform to the family script of who he was supposed to be. They joined a Reform temple, where Aaron had a rabbi who was young, remarried, and who played ball and had a more relaxed approach. Aaron could "see himself" in the rabbi, a new experience.

Aaron's second marriage ended and he met Julie (whose story I discussed in Chapters Four and Five), and together they moved to the West Coast and joined a Reform synagogue. Aaron appreciated the way in which the more relaxed approach of the Reform service allowed him to connect with Judaism; however, it was not deeply moving for him spiritually.

Aaron received a recording of Reb Zalman and Rabbi Shlomo Carlebach from his mother. They were leading a *fabrengen* (a spirited Hasidic-style event of spiritual teachings and melodies) in Berkeley.[35] He recalled, "Shlomo's talking, Zalman's talking, about how you don't have to be learned, but you have to have a *taste*." Afterwards, he and Julie attended their first Jewish Renewal service in 1996 at Berkeley Hillel. "There were fewer than 15 people in this room, and it just washed over me! At the end of that sweet, *sweet* service, we were in Jewish Renewal, totally. I had come home!"

The joy, vibrancy, and ecstatic experience of the Renewal service touched his capacity for profound inner experience that he had as a child. Aaron and Julie both came from families that had escaped from Germany in the 1930s, and both carried the legacy of terror and loss that overlaid their family's relationship to Judaism. When they met each other, they were able to hold and nurture their shared love of the spiritual.

Aaron's father carried a great deal of resentment for Aaron's marriage to a non-Jewish woman, his rejection of conservative values and the long separation between them. Yet when Aaron married Julie, he was moved to see how the in-laws could easily relate to each other because of their shared history. His father was able to tell Julie how proud he was of the life that Aaron was living, once he had fully re-engaged with Judaism.

Aaron grew up in a psychic field infused with the unmetabolized terror of the Shoah, and with his father's experience as a combat veteran. He experienced constrictions on his freedom and spontaneity that were an unconscious response to terror. Many Jews growing up in families whose ancestors endured traumatic violence in Eastern Europe, or in families whose lives had been shattered by the Shoah, focused on creating survival and material stability. Seeking refuge in those areas of life over which they could exercise control, many reacted with an intense striving for economic stability and material status that might insulate them from attack.

Like Moses, Aaron had to separate from the milieu in which he was raised to listen for the voice that came from the Self. His life was a circambulating journey to loosen the grip of the inner Pharaoh's demands of cultural conformity that his parents imposed to attain some sense of safety. When he experienced Judaism in a form that enabled his innate spirituality to find expression, he was able to fully inhabit the tradition of his ancestors that had been constricted through the experience of profound trauma. With perspective, Aaron was able to appreciate that his parents' conservatism was a response to the traumas they had suffered.

Parents raising children in the wake of collective trauma sought to protect the everyday lives of their children from the dangers that might live behind the easygoing scenes of stickball and pastrami sandwiches—shadows of storm troopers and village pogroms from which the children must be shielded. Their terror was transmitted through the preoccupation with safety and with security, suffused with fear. Occasionally, the prospect of anti-Semitic terror bubbled through the limited safety of assimilated identity—in the Lindbergh and John Birch campaigns, in the McCarthy hearings, in the closed offices and country clubs, in the shadows of Southern lynch-ings and Klan robes and fires. Young Jews flocked to Mississippi during the civil rights era, fueled by their passion for justice. Perhaps only their parents or grandpar-ents truly understood the self-protective impulse behind their involvement.

As Moses's position of privilege allowed him to see the injustice visited upon the Hebrew slaves, young Jews coming of age in the postwar era had the privilege of viewing injustice from a safer distance than many of their parents and grand-parents. Some were aware of prejudice suffered in their own family histories of exclusion and marginalization from the dominant culture. Others were not aware of this history because their families protectively shielded them from it.

The Jewish values of concern for others and healing the world, the kabbalistic vision of *tikkun olam*, were expressed by many Jewish youth during the explosive activism of the 1960s and '70s, often causing a divide, as Aaron experienced, from parents who had adopted conservative values to ensure safety for their fami-lies in the aftermath of the Shoah and the McCarthy era. The youth passionately cast off the outer Pharaoh of oppressive institutions. The work of depotentiating the inner Pharaoh of internalized anti-Semitism engendered by transgenerational trauma necessitated further introspection and awakening.

Moses and the sacrifice of the "too small" self

God tells Moses that those who sought to take his life for attacking the Egyptian slave master are now all dead, and it is now safe for him to return to Egypt. Moses begins the journey back with his wife Tzipporah and his sons. In one of the most shocking and mysterious passages in the text, as he makes his way down the mountain and prepares to return to Egypt, God seeks to kill him. The text is ambiguous—either God seeks to kill Moses, or one of his sons. He is saved by Tzipporah, who takes a flint and circumcises their son, symbolizing that she and Moses are placing themselves and their descendants in a lineage covenanted to God. Perhaps Moses must come into awareness that he is not acting solely on his own, but as representative of the covenant that flows from God's bond with Abraham and Sarah and their descendants. With this, God lets Moses and his sons live.[36] Moses understands that he is acting as a vessel of the Divine Will, through which the consciousness of the people will be transformed.

Perhaps Moses falters out of fear that he is not up to the task, still acting in the grip of the too small self. Perhaps God is letting Moses know that if he acts hesitantly, he will surely die. His task requires that his faith be unshakable. As he falters on the way down the mountain, Tzipporah's love and wisdom saves him. Tzipporah, like the matriarchs before her, ensures the transmission of the lineage to future generations.

The entrenched consciousness of collective trauma is difficult to overcome. It will take a series of cataclysmic plagues to shake off the yoke of the inner Pharaoh and convince the psyche that a new way lies ahead. As the plagues intensify, the journey out of *mitzrayim* becomes unavoidable. The choice is clear—resist change and perish, or move forward into the terrifying unknown.

Notes

1 Zohar 2:11b, Vol. IV, 52.
2 Ibid, fn. 225.
3 Exodus 2:11-21
4 Exodus 2:23
5 Exodus 2:24
6 Exodus 3:14.
7 Arthur Green, *Ehyeh: A Kabbalah for Tomorrow* (Woodstock, VT: Jewish Lights Publishing, 2002), 2.
8 Edward Edinger, *Ego and Archetype: Individuation and the Religious Function of the Psyche* (Boston: Shambhala, 1992), 104.
9 Edward Edinger, *The Bible and the Psyche: Individuation Symbolism in the Old Testament* (Toronto: Inner City Books, 1986), 45.
10 Donald Kalsched, *Trauma and the Soul: A Psycho-spiritual Approach to Human Development and Its Interruption* (New York: Routledge, 2013).
11 Edinger, *Ego and Archetype*, 292.
12 Rudolf Otto, *The Idea of the Holy* (London: Oxford University Press, 1923, 1967), 5–7.
13 C.G. Jung, "1952 Interview with Mircea Eliade," in *C.G. Jung Speaking: Interviews and Encounters*, edited by W. McGuire and R.F.C. Hull (Princeton, NJ: Princeton University Press, 1977).
14 Zalman Schachter-Shalomi, *Wrapped in a Holy Flame: Teachings and Tales of The Hasidic Masters*, edited by Nataniel M. Miles-Yepez (San Francisco: Jossey-Bass, 2003), 72–73.
15 Ibid.
16 Yosef Hayim Yerushalmi, *Zakhor: Jewish History and Jewish Memory* (New York: Schocken Books, 1989), 94.
17 Yehoshua Starrett, *Chanukah with Rebbe Nachman of Breslov* (Jerusalem: Breslov Research Institute, 2002), 75.
18 Erik H. Erikson, *Identity: Youth and Crisis* (New York: W.W. Norton & Co., 1968), 19; citing William James, *The Letters of William James*, Vol. I, edited by Henry James (Boston: The Atlantic Monthly Press, 1920), 199.
19 Ibid, 36–37.
20 Eva Hoffman, *After Such Knowledge: Memory, History, and the Legacy of the Holocaust* (New York: Public Affairs, 2004), xv.
21 Ibid.
22 Ibid.
23 Ibid.
24 Ibid, 11.
25 Ibid.
26 Ibid, 28–29.
27 Ibid.
28 Edward Feld, *The Spirit of Renewal: Finding Faith After the Holocaust* (Woodstock, VT: Jewish Lights Publishing, 1994), xi–xii.
29 George Steiner, *Language and Silence: Essays on Language, Literature and the Inhuman* (New York: Athenaeum, 1986), 123.
30 Feld, *The Spirit of Renewal*, xii.
31 Ibid.

32 Ibid, xii.
33 Ibid.
34 Donald Kalsched, *The Inner World of Trauma: Archetypal Defences of the Personal Spirit* (New York: Routledge, 1986).
35 Shlomo Carlebach also emigrated from Europe during the Shoah. He developed music that influenced a generation. Although not formally part of Jewish Renewal, he influenced many of the rabbis and teachers associated with it. In 1998, the Jewish feminist magazine *Lilith* published revelations of widespread sexual abuse by Carlebach. See Sarah Blustain, "Rabbi Sholomo Carlebach's Shadow Side," *Lilith*, Spring 1998, https://www.lilith.org/articles/rabbi-shlomo-carlebachs-shadow-side/.
36 Exodus 4:24–26.

Chapter 7

Shattered vessels, scattered seeds

Years ago, during a Friday night Shabbat service at Chochmat Ha'Lev in Berkeley, I found myself dancing to the ecstatic music, marveling at the joy that suffused the room. Who would imagine dancing at a Friday night service? Certainly not anyone who had grown up in the stilted, hushed temple rooms where even the movement of a chair scraping the floor drew disapproving glances. Yet here, the room was exultant. As I looked out at the jubilant faces, I sensed the presence of the ancestors, watching us from above, delighting in seeing us on the other side of the Shoah, reconnecting with the ecstasy the tradition had always held, but which few modern Jews experienced. The tears, the joy, the fear, the grief—all flowed through us, as we connected with the powerful energy of reclaiming the sacred.

I wondered whether we were perhaps experiencing a healing in the Jewish collective psyche. Our parents and grandparents had survived the traumas of recent Jewish history, mostly by shutting down the connection to mythos and focusing on the conscious tasks of survival. Perhaps we, the next generations, had enough distance from the intensity of the trauma to begin to allow the thawing of feelings long frozen. In the thawing we were able to allow the grief and tears to flow, to acknowledge the suffering and the terror, and to discover the healing and redemptive power of the teachings our ancestors had gifted us, a treasure trove for us to open as we were ready.

As Jungian analyst Donald Kalsched has recognized, following the experience of personal trauma a figure may emerge in the psyche that seeks to protect us from future harm. This figure advises us to stay quiet, to not attract attention, to be compliant, to not make waves. This may work strategically when we are in a setting, perhaps even in our own families, in which we may be criticized or attacked for being our true selves. As we grow, this protective figure becomes an inner persecutor—what I have called the inner Pharaoh—keeping us from bringing our light, our divine spark, into the world. John Wilson observes that following an abyss experience, we seek to maintain safety by adapting to the ways of the dominant culture, often causing us to lose or act counter to our own identity. We adopt a false self, a persona that keeps us safe in an inhospitable world.[1]

Jungian analysts Thomas Singer and Samuel Kimbles explore how these same phenomena operate on a larger cultural scale. When a culture or group feels itself under attack, it may develop archetypal defenses, called *cultural complexes*, of the group spirit that not only seek to protect the group from further harm but may also result in the group becoming closed and rigid in its thinking. "A traumatized group presents only a 'false self' to the world, and the world cannot 'see' the group in its more authentic and vulnerable identity."[2] How do we begin to free ourselves from these calcified states?

The mystics teach that the Hebrews entered into exile because it was necessary to free the divine sparks that were trapped in the far-flung places of the world and, perhaps also, in the depths of the heart. Rabbi Isaac Luria's cosmology was developed after the Jews were expelled from Spain, following a Golden Age of 500 years of relatively peaceful coexistence with Christians and Muslims. Luria offered a new myth of Creation that sought to maintain faith in the abiding presence of the Divine amid the cataclysmic upheaval and terror people were experiencing.

Luria taught that when God created the world, supernal light was poured into the ten vessels, representing the ten *sefirot* or building blocks of creation. Yet the light was so great, and the vessels not yet worthy of containing them, that the vessels shattered into pieces. The great light was scattered throughout Creation, and it is the work of the holy person, or *tzaddik*, to discover the holy sparks from beneath the *kelipot*, or shards, of the broken vessels and redeem them to their true purpose. In this way, humans are actively involved in the redemption of Creation. When enough sparks are redeemed, we will attain a state of messianic consciousness, a transformed Creation infused with holiness.

The Hebrew word for exile, *ga'lut*, is rooted in the Hebrew word *ga'luy*, for "reveal" or "uncover," a meaningful insight when reflecting on the Lurianic myth of discovering the holy sparks in exile. Reb Zalman recognized that Luria also spoke of these shards as seedpods that needed to burst open to release the seed (divine spark) within. The seedpods held within them both the protective force that contained the seed until it was ready to sprout, as well as the nurturance that the seed needed to draw on until it was ready to sustain itself.[3]

This image provides a powerful symbolic understanding of the transformation of intergenerational trauma into post-traumatic growth. The generations that survived the massive pogroms and devastations of Eastern Europe and the Shoah underwent severe psychic wounding, dislocation, and unfathomable suffering. The survivors of these cataclysmic events created seedpods that served two profound purposes. They safeguarded the material well-being of the children, providing a ground of being in which the future generations could root and flourish. They also contained nourishment that guided these seeds in their growth. Yet often challenging coping strategies were developed in the fight for survival.

Jews were in the midst of a paradigmatic reorganization of consciousness in the 20th century. Reb Zalman observed that previous conceptions of God and Judaism could not be easily transplanted in the soil of the new reality. A complete shift of consciousness needed to occur to ensure that a new Judaism could come into form that met the realities of the current era. At first, this shift looked like a turning away from the old worldview—the breaking down of the orthodoxy of the previous generations.

Yet, in the rejection of orthodoxy, new forms of vitality were discovered: (1) a feminist sensibility that allowed for the full participation of women in Jewish ritual life; (2) an inclusion in the larger culture and a dedicated ethic of working for justice for all peoples; and (3) a development of psychological awareness and insight that synthesized psycho-spiritual development. The seedpods that appeared to fall far from the ancestral tree of Judaism were, in fact, freeing up life energy that fed the emergence of a new form of Jewish spiritual observance that incorporated the advances of the modern era. As the seeds of the new generation took root in the earth, Judaism underwent a profound and radical paradigm shift.

Following the Shoah, a complete reorientation of the sacred became necessary for the continuation of faith. Reb Zalman noted that the idea of an all-powerful God "out there" in the cosmos that would intervene on behalf of the Jewish people and rescue us from annihilation could not be sustained. Like the mystics following other cataclysmic eras of Jewish history, he recognized that for Judaism to be renewed, it needed to go inward, to find a sense of God as immanent within our own psyches and within Creation.[4] Drawing on the wisdom of the Zohar, we see that God suffers *with* us and longs, as we do, for the healing of the shattered Creation.

The journey out of *mitzrayim*, the narrow place, represents a rebirth into a new state of consciousness. In the Biblical story of the Exodus, the shattering of the limited consciousness of enslavement occurred as the ten plagues completely altered the reality the people had previously known.

The plagues represent a total remapping of the personal and collective psyche. Whereas we may have previously believed that the negative voice of subjugation and constriction, represented by Pharaoh, constituted reality, we may now reach a critical moment in our lives, either through crisis or synchronicity, where a larger reality reveals itself to us. Through listening to and following this new awareness, we come to understand that our previous conceptions were a limiting prison.

The ten plagues

During and following the encounter at the burning bush, God instructs Moses to tell Pharaoh that God will bring a series of increasingly destructive plagues upon the Egyptians. God also tells Moses that he will harden Pharaoh's heart so he does not succumb to the power of these devastating events. Why must Pharaoh's heart be hardened?

The Biblical text offers a stunning truth about how to move out of the grip of the inner persecutor. When we are visited with plagues of suffering, Pharaoh's heart—our defenses—harden, and those defenses become more entrenched. When the inner Pharaoh fears that change is afoot, it tightens its hold and does not cede power willingly. It cajoles and schemes to keep its power at any cost. In the end, freedom from the traumatized defenses is possible only with the depotentiation of this enslaving energy and a rebirth into a new consciousness.

As the ruler that has reigned in our psyche senses its defeat, it seeks to bargain, to maintain some kind of control, some portion of its rulership. Yet the true force of our being and our becoming does not bargain. The complete defeat of Pharaoh is necessary so that we do not and cannot cling to an illusion. We must completely release the hold of the constricted self. When we face an opportunity to move out of a narrow belief system that has held us prisoner, we often face a moment that requires quick and decisive action. As the Hebrews did at the Red Sea, we must move forward into the unknown, no matter how unlikely it seems that the Sea before us will actually part. The way out of mitzrayim opens for those with the courage to move toward it. Staying stuck in old ways may mean death for the awakening self.

The plagues represent a necessary turning toward the suffering that lays beneath the calcification, the feelings that we have had to numb in order to continue to live in constricted consciousness. Turning toward this suffering is transformative—it frees us from the grip of the inner Pharaoh and allows us to move out of mitzrayim toward a new and more spontaneous existence, held by our relationship with the Divine energy that guides our unfolding.

Luria taught that in the beginning, all was God, and God had to withdraw Its energy to make a space in which the world could unfold. This withdrawal is called *tzimtzum*. Reb Zalman teaches that we may experience this *tzimtzum* as a loss of God's presence in our lives.[5] Yet it may be that at times when we cannot feel God's presence, we are letting go of old forms, and God is taking up residence within us to unfold anew.

For the largeness of the Self to incarnate, we often must let go of fixed images (idols) of who we believe ourselves to be and let the I that is becoming, become. In this process we often lose treasured parts of our fixed identities, involving a painful process of ego death. Marriages fail, the meaning of our work falters, families splinter. And in the midst of the shattered fragments, we gather the precious sparks of ourselves and begin to allow a new, larger vessel to form, a vessel that is stronger and capable of holding complexity, pain, grief, regret, and sorrow—*as well as* the largeness and joy of the Self.

The Biblical text reflects how this process often unfolds in our lives. We may choose to stay stuck in patterns that bring comfort in the here and now—at the cost of our own flowering. It may take a cataclysmic event to wrench us out of stuck patterns. The unfolding may need to shatter the small self for a larger vessel to come into being that can contain more of our essence. We are psychologically plagued. Once we have developed an ongoing relationship with the unfolding Self, as the Hebrews did at Sinai, such catastrophic awakening may no longer be necessary. Instead, we ourselves undertake the ongoing work of nurturing our development, as the Hebrews learned to do as they wandered through the desert and made their way into the Promised Land, which I discuss in subsequent chapters.

In this chapter, I explore the earlier stories of those growing up in Jewish homes in the aftermath of the Shoah, using the lens of cultural complexes represented by the plagues. By plumbing the deeper forces behind the confused and conflicted feelings about Judaism that have largely lived in the unconscious, we may discover the sparks of holiness that lay hidden beneath the surface.

Kabbalistic view of the plagues

In kabbalah, the world is comprised of ten supernal energies, the *sefirot*. Rabbi Steven Fisdel observes, "From Divine Thought and Will emanates the desire to have the world exist and be blessed." This is achieved through a process initiated "within the Divine Intention that unfolds step-by-step progressively until the physical Universe is manifested." The entire Emanation, "the Creative Process that emerges continually from the Divine, has ten specific stages." Nine of these are subtle and preparatory to the manifestation of the energy in the physical reality through the sefirah of Malchut, associated with the Shekhinah.[6]

In each of us, the blueprint of the world is also replicated in our subtle bodies, represented as the Tree of Life in human form, the *Anthropos*, symbolized in kabbalistic thought as Adam Kadmon. The upper three sefirot correspond to highly spiritual energies most closely connected to the Divine Source, beginning with *Keter*, meaning Crown, residing slightly above the center of the head, where the Divine emanation enters our awareness. At the right side of the head (corresponding to the right side of the brain), we find the sefirah of *Chokhmah* (wisdom); the left side of the brain corresponds to *Binah* (understanding). These three upper sefirot allow us to receive, understand, and gestate guidance from the Divine Source until we are ready to begin to manifest the energies in our lives and our relationships. This Divine wisdom is gestated in the womb of Binah, the upper Mother, who gives birth to the lower seven sefirot in the emotional and physical body.

This supernal energy moves down through the lower sefirot to a level where we can consciously experience it as emotional and bodily wisdom. *Chesed* (lovingkindness), *Din* or *Gevurah* (discernment), and *Tiferet* (beauty) comprise the triangle formed between the right and left shoulders and the heart, respectively, and correspond to our ability to give and receive love. It is through our hearts that we understand the meaning of the Divine Emanation. *Netzach* (ambition), *Hod* (humility), and *Yesod* (bonding) comprise the triangle between the right and left hips and the pelvis, respectively, and correspond to our ability to give form to the Divine Emanation through our own creative expression and our relationships. *Malchut* (kingdom) is the root sefirah, corresponding to the Shekhinah, the Divine Presence, manifested in the world. We may see this sefirah as the Ground of Being itself, in which the energy that has moved down through the Tree becomes manifest.

In kabbalistic texts, an imbalance in the sefirot may cause each sefirah to manifest its shadow side. This state is called the *Sitra Achra*, the other side of the holy, in which the positive energy that manifests from the Divine Source is recruited into the service of evil. Similar to Kalsched's description of Hell as an endless neurotic suffering, we can become stuck in the world of the Sitra Achra, such as when we are locked in an addiction to a substance or to an organizing system of negative beliefs that manifests as severe depression or anxiety. The Sitra Achra represents the *shadow* in Jungian terms, or unintegrated aspects of the unconscious.

In the mystical view, the plagues are brought about by the Shekhinah, in Her avenging aspect, to correct the cosmic imbalance that has been caused by the state of enslavement. The Shekhinah unleashes a series of plagues that will transform the negative energies and return the Jewish people to a state of psychic wholeness. The plagues are like the forest fire that not only destroys but also liberates the seeds, preparing the way for new growth. In this work, the divine spark that is trapped within the kelipot, or shards of the shattered vessels, is redeemed and returned to holiness.

Hasidic Rabbi Yosef Jacobson sees the plagues as expressions of the ways in which the sefirot have become corrupted when we are out of alignment with our highest potential.[7] Each plague corresponds to a negative expression of the attribute of a particular sefirah. As we bring awareness to the suffering that this distortion has caused in our lives, we are given the opportunity to repair and come into relationship with the possible higher manifestation of that sefirot's energy.

This perspective calls to mind the practice of *merkavah* mysticism from the 1st century CE, in which one descends in the chariot (*merkavah*) through the realms, clearing the obstructions that block the path to the Divine. As these are cleared, we become open vessels to receive the flow of Divine energy.[8] The Baal Shem Tov taught that to ascend to the highest levels, we must first descend, go to the depths of ourselves, to attend to that which needs healing, to prepare ourselves to become vessels or chariots for the Divine flow or *shefa* that is available to each person. The Tree of Life, which is replicated in each human psyche, can attain great spiritual heights, but only after we have worked through psychic blockages, creating a receptive soil for deep roots capable of holding such ecstatic experience.

Exile is the state of feeling separate from our deepest selves, from those we love, from God, and from life. As we become aware of the complexes that keep us in this state of disconnection, we are already opening to the awareness of the possibility of something greater than the psychological prison in which we have been trapped. Conscious suffering allows for transformation of unconscious patterns that have been inherited or adopted. By becoming aware of the anguish these patterns have caused us, we also become aware of the possibility of leaving exile and moving toward the more fulfilling life that increased awareness brings.

Jacobson's view of the plagues and cultural complex theory offer helpful maps to make sense of the impact of centuries of anti-Semitic trauma on the Jewish psyche. By exploring the various complexes that arise in the collective psyche in response to trauma, we come to understand how these forms of suffering have not only protected us from the overwhelming effects of the traumas, but also simultaneously kept us in a narrow place where awareness of the Divine has been occluded.

Samuel Kimbles developed the idea of "phantom narratives," cultural stories that haunt the collective psyche of a people who live with unmetabolized trauma. The phantom grows out of secrets that are concealed and silently transmitted to the child's unconscious.

> The child haunted by a phantom becomes a living tomb, in which an unspeakable drama, experienced as traumatic by someone else, lies buried yet alive, exerting its disruptive influence … Along with the transgenerational transmission of a secret, the child inherits the unspoken imperative to preserve intact the integrity of that secret.[9]

Within cultures, the phantom operates in the background, becoming the water in which we swim, the air that we breathe, an "unthought known," a present absence.[10]

The plagues function to shatter the limited vessels in which Judaism was housed because of cultural complexes. Exploring each of the plagues as a cultural complex, we see how working through it allows energy that has been suppressed to be freed to give birth to a renewed consciousness. As the seedpods crack open, they bring awareness to the limitations created by the cultural complexes. The freed seeds can now be nourished in the fertile soil of the renewed tradition, and new expressions of Jewish life may begin to flower.

Water into blood—facing our grief

In the first plague that is visited upon the Egyptians, the waters of the river Nile are turned into blood. This plague corresponds to the foundational sefirah of Malchut, associated with the Shekhinah, connecting us to the ground of being. When we experience trauma, our connection to the source of life, our ability to trust life, is severed. We live in a state of disconnection and often unspoken despair.

The Nile is the source of life for both the ancient Egyptians and Hebrews. Yet for the Hebrews, it has also been the source of death, as the edict of the Pharaoh demanded that newborn Hebrew children be drowned in its waters.[11] By the time of Moses, there had been so much death, so much suffering, that many had lost any hope of redemption. The people had stopped crying out to God. Yet as God spoke to the women, they began to rekindle the eros with the men at the banks of the Nile and awaken the possibility of a future.

The plague that turned the water of the Nile into blood symbolizes the awareness of the Hebrew infants who had been killed, forcing both the Egyptians and Hebrews to come to terms with the great suffering the people experienced. This plague reminds us that for our lifeblood to return, for our connection to the source to be renewed, we must bring to consciousness and mourn the unbearable losses we have endured. The holding presence of the Shekhinah, or Divine Mother, is awakened, healing us in those places where the transmission of maternal love has been constrained by trauma.

As discussed earlier, Julie's mother was a child when she fled Germany with her parents in the 1930s, leaving behind their entire village, including extended family, all of whom were murdered in the Shoah. Julie's paternal grandmother suffered from severe mental illness and killed herself shortly before Julie was born. Julie's mother, who never consciously grieved fleeing Germany as a child, and the loss of extended family and community, became profoundly depressed after her mother-in-law's suicide, and progressively worsened until she was stabilized on medication around the time Julie was around twelve years old.

Julie described growing up in a psychic field that was permeated with the grief of her grandmother's suicide and the unmourned losses of extended family and friends. Julie grew up feeling deeply aware of the sadness that haunted the family, but the devastating losses were never discussed. Nor was she able to talk with her family members about their feelings regarding religion or God.

Julie reflected on the meaning of a small box she had, its lid imprinted with an image of a whole bird and another half bird. She spoke about the shattering of her grandmother's life, which she saw as the half bird, the half-lived life, and her own wholeness, which she accessed through consciously grieving her family's unmourned losses. Tucked away inside the box was a heart, symbolizing her ability to fully feel both the love and loss from her grandmother's legacy and to honor her truncated life by embracing the fullness of her own.

Julie's healing required a descent into the depths of the family's unmetabolized trauma to feel the grief that had gone into the unconscious. In subsequent chapters I examine how healing from the trauma that had haunted her and her family facilitated an opening to the sacred. Alessandra Cavalli notes that the traumatic events of previous generations destroy the inner world of the trauma survivor and are passed down to subsequent generations as a sense of the "deadly," a mental void that is experienced as meaninglessness.[12] When parents are unable to process the trauma, a psychic field of what psychoanalyst Wilfred Bion describes as "nameless dread" surrounds the children.[13] In turn, the children experience the parents as being unable to provide a reliable matrix in which they can work through the trauma. To heal, they must bring the trauma into consciousness in a supportive, healing environment, where it can be named, mourned, and integrated.

Before the Hebrews, who have experienced the traumatic deaths of their children in the rivers of the Nile, can leave Egypt, they must bring the mourning to consciousness, so the blood can be available for new life. They must find their connection to the Shekhinah, the mothering presence that will allow the tears of their broken hearts to flow, to cleanse the river of blood with their collective tears. They must also allow Lilith, who rules the depths of the psyche, to lead them to the deepest places of grief and reconnection, a journey explored in Chapter Ten.

The Shekhinah makes us aware of the places where we have become disconnected from the Source. By bringing these soul-destroying patterns to consciousness, our life force may begin to flow more freely. As we collectively face the devastating experiences that threatened to destroy the very fabric of Jewish life and culture, our tradition teaches us that we are held by the presence of the

Mother, who is with us in exile. In the darkest and loneliest experiences, we may find we are not alone.

Frogs—loss and reclamation of the imagination

In the second plague, God rains down swarms of frogs upon the land of Egypt. Frogs correspond to the second sefirah of Yesod, which represents the ability to create, to bond and connect, to bring forth the visions received from Divine inspiration into manifestation. Mythologically, they symbolize transformation—shape-shifting from eggs to tadpoles to frogs. Because they live comfortably in water, on land, and can leap in the air, they represent the ability to dwell in multiple states of consciousness. Psychologically, they represent what Jung called the *transcendent function*, the ability to link conscious and unconscious levels of awareness. When we open to the unconscious, we can access dreams, visions, and the mythopoetic language of the soul. Our conscious awareness is continuously fed by a stream of living waters that help us to develop and live in a state of ongoing growth and unfolding.

Research with survivors of the Shoah and their descendants notes that one of the principal factors in the intergenerational transmission of trauma is the incapacity of the survivors to remember, to mourn, and to symbolize the trauma.[14] This incapacity serves a vital defensive survival function originally, but once the acute crisis is over, the survivors remain cut off from their own unconscious depths, which carries the medicine that might enable them to heal. The plague of frogs makes us aware of the loss of connection with the unconscious, with the mythic imagination of Judaism itself, and with the redemptive healing quality of the transcendent function.

Daniel's parents rejected religious Judaism and adopted a rationalist worldview dedicated to social justice. The loss of Daniel's entire extended paternal family in the Shoah was never openly discussed or mourned. (I explore in more detail the losses in Daniel's extended family in Chapter Ten.) Growing up in a home where the spiritual was exiled, Daniel was left without a means of accessing the inner world of Judaism. It took him decades to contact this world himself, which came to him unbidden as he erupted into sobs while watching a television broadcast of a Lubavitcher Rebbe lighting the Chanukah menorah. The menorah symbolizes the rededication of holiness after the Holy Temple had been desecrated by secular forces. The power of this moment reflected the numinosity of Daniel's own reconnection with this sacred Jewish symbol and experiencing, bodily, his own connection to the religious depths, after a childhood and young adulthood spent in a state of rationalist exile. For Daniel, the Lubavitcher Rebbe carried the luminosity of the great tradition of Hasidism, the spiritual tradition of his paternal ancestors, lighting a spark that connected him with his own depths and with his unmourned and unacknowledged family legacy.

Psychologically, the plague of frogs awakens us to the places where the transcendent function has closed down and calls for renewal. The frogs represent the development of our own capacity for symbolic meaning making. In moving toward this engagement, the world transforms from the narrow consciousness of the traumatized self to a new awareness of a life filled with awe and possibility.

Gnats or lice—internalized anti-Semitism

The third plague, swarming gnats, sometimes translated as lice, corresponds to the third sefirah of Hod, associated with humility. Jacobson suggests that this plague makes us conscious of unhealthy submission or internalized shame:

> In this type of submission, where one thinks of himself as a worthless inconsequential creature, the perception of the self as useless dust develops into lice that demoralize and debase one's life. Like lice, this type of humility sucks out a person's blood, depriving him of his vitality and energy-flow.[15]

When we suffer trauma, we experience tremendous rage at the violation of our souls. Yet, when this outrage falls on deaf ears or catalyzes more of an attack against us, we learn to suppress our rage over time and turn it inward. We attack ourselves instead. When Jews were overtly persecuted as a community, they could readily recognize the source of shame as coming from the dominant culture. Paradoxically, as Jews became more assimilated, individuals turned contempt inward, against themselves.[16] This internalized contempt created a splitting of the self, where one part became persecutor and the other persecuted.[17]

Both Yehiel and Aaron experienced Judaism as something terrifying. This reflects what Wilson calls the inversion experience following trauma, where people blame themselves for the trauma and seek to conform their behavior to the dominant culture to stay safe.[18] One's own self or culture is seen as the problem and so one seeks to distance oneself from it. This is the experience of internalized cultural shame.

Yehiel experienced her grandfather, an Orthodox rabbi who lived with her family growing up, as frightening. She shared a disturbing dream in which his study in the front room of her home was "*a science fiction kind of place with the bookshelves, where the books were this huge, and if you turned the pages they would have started crumbling ... On the other side of the living room was the kitchen and my parents' bedroom, and I knew that if I could get through the living room and into the kitchen where my mom was, I'd be safe.*" But she feared that her grandfather, who followed God's edicts literally, might have harmed her, because she could not be sure that God would not issue an edict against her.

Yehiel's family was one of only a handful of Jewish families in the Connecticut neighborhood where she grew up. Yehiel's fear that an edict would be decreed against her reflects an unconsciously carried terror of arbitrary decrees that her ancestors faced in the pogroms of Eastern Europe and that others faced during the Shoah, and echoes the Biblical story of the Pharaoh's edict calling for the killing of the Hebrew male babies. Her conflation of this fear with her grandfather's strict observance caused her to fear her grandfather.

In Aaron's family, his father's escape from Nazi Germany and the fear of persecution was projected onto the temple rabbi, who was experienced as frightening. Aaron's father's family left the small village in Germany where they had lived in the late 1930s. Aaron reported experiencing God in his childhood as an omnipresent force watching for any violation. Growing up in the shadows of this trauma, fear of the Nazi's unbridled authority was projected onto God and the rabbi.

Both Yehiel's and Aaron's fathers' projection onto rabbis as sources of terror reflects the inversion experience in which rather than fearing the oppressor, one views one's own difference as the source of danger. The idea of internalized anti-Semitism was first developed by psychologist Kurt Lewin in the mid-20th century. Lewin astutely observed that as assimilation increased, Jews gained social status by forgoing those aspects of identity that were notable sources of difference. The subtle but pernicious process of assimilation included the development of self-deprecation and distancing themselves from appearing too different.[19]

Conformity is prized and being different is experienced as dangerous. If Jewishness is the source of this difference, then we may turn against that aspect of ourselves that is seen as generating the pain of not "fitting in." We reject our own Jewishness and all things associated with it. Thus, the hidden cost of assimilation is the increased tendency toward feeling shame, experienced unconsciously as self-hatred, for that which marks us as different.

Psychoanalyst Jay Frankel explores what happens "when we have lost our sense that the world will protect us, when we are in danger with no chance of escape." In response, we try to disappear: "Like chameleons, we blend into the world around us, into the very thing that threatens us, in order to protect ourselves. We stop being ourselves and transform ourselves into someone else's image of us. This happens automatically."[20]

The alarming rate of attrition of those observing Jewish practices, while maintaining a Jewish "cultural identity," may be seen in part as a consequence of this internalized shame. In the early and mid-20th century, there was a high level of overt anti-Semitism in America. Jews were scapegoated, shamed, and excluded. Jewish communities struggled to maintain an intact identity, to create schools and temples and organizations to support Jewish learning and kinship. Today, after decades of hoping that anti-Semitism in America was largely past, we are witnessing the fomenting of long-dormant anti-Semitic tropes, resulting in unprecedented acts of violence against the Jewish community.

The tendrils of anti-Semitism are subtle, weaving themselves in small but pernicious ways into each individual. Many may feel fiercely proud to be Jewish but have adopted lifestyles in which the expression of our Jewishness is minimal. We may experience a sense of awkwardness or conflict in our identity. We may have grown up in homes in which our families were "culturally" Jewish but did not engage in religious practice. Or if spirituality was practiced, it was done in a way in which much of the difference from the dominant culture was minimized.

Rejection of our Jewishness takes place at a profoundly deep unconscious level, where we may choose the path of assimilation because it creates less of a sense of *dis-ease* than holding onto that which makes us different from the dominant culture. The landscape of internalized anti-Semitism is the realm of the inner Pharaoh, who persecutes with messages designed to protect us from danger by circumscribing the realms in which we can express our Jewishness. We might find ourselves slightly changing our accents or tones of speech in our interactions in predominantly non-Jewish settings and may be surprised to see how freely our Jewishness flows when we are among fellow Jews. Or, we may project our shame at being Jewish onto other Jews, embarrassed when we notice someone exhibiting behavior that has been negatively projected onto Jews and from which we seek to distance ourselves. In studying Jewish identity, psychologist Jerry Diller found that Jews often feel conflicted in their sense of Judaism, reacting to Jewish settings or themes with anger or embarrassment.[21]

After almost two millennia of being the disempowered "other" in European culture, Jews in America were offered what cultural anthropologist Jonathan Boyarin calls a "devil's bargain"—to identify as "white" as an indirect exploitation of racism. That is, Jews were able to identify as white if they tacitly agreed that blacks and other people of color occupied the position of "other." Its cost was a loss of alliance with other ethnic groups and a sharp curtailment of "the sphere in which we are free to continue being and to become Jewish."[22]

Repression of Jewish language, speech, dress, forms of discourse, and spirituality has come at a great cost to the authentic experience and expression of the Jewish psyche.[23] The unspoken agreement in America required not so much that Jews act Protestant, but that they cease being "too Jewish."[24]

Lillian recalled her parents' views: "My parents had a great concern that we not grow up looking or acting Jewish, and so we moved to Connecticut and they enrolled me in a school where there were no other Jewish children. I felt completely like a freak and had no idea until I got to college that there were people like me who are verbal and who are liberals. I was just stunned, completely stunned, to find this out."

The plague of gnats or lice awakens us to the immense suffering and shutting down of authentic expression caused by internalized shame. This awareness helps free us from the narrowing of identity in which we have been caught and invites us to reclaim the wider range of our authentic being.

Swarming flies—the distortion of healthy ambition

In the fourth plague, swarms of flies attack Egypt. This plague corresponds to the sefirah of Netzach, our capacity to move forward in the world. The flies represent the disruption of our healthy ambition. When our ambition is aligned with our true nature and recognized as flowing from the Source, we can freely manifest our gifts and sharing them with others. Yet when we have been harmed by anti-Semitic hatred and projections, we may respond by seeking acceptance through conforming to the dominant culture, replacing our own moral compass with group values and norms. This plague (swarming flies) reflects ambition that is out of balance, running rampant, and causing great destruction.[25]

Julie grew up in Los Angeles in the 1960s, attending the largest temple in the city, and felt alienated by the status anxiety and material focus of the Jewish culture within which she was raised. Developing insight into this type of conformity as a response to deep fears of annihilation and disempowerment allows for the development of a different relationship with aspects of Judaism that may have felt off-putting. Underneath this overemphasis on the material lay a complex economic and social history of the Jewish experience.

Jewish immigrants at the turn of the 20th century came from a world awash in the powerful political movements of the day: socialism, communism, anarchism, the push for social democracy, and transformation of despotic czarist regimes. Many Jews were able, because of the loosening of social strictures, to move more freely in the world. Frustrated with their ancestors' view that prayer would bring the Messiah, they rejected traditional Jewish practice. They may have lacked compassion for the reality that prayer was often the only avenue available to parents whose existence was constantly threatened by violent pogroms and massacres.

In the United States, the horrendous conditions Jews faced as new immigrants working in sweatshops and living in substandard tenement housing led many to participate in the movements that worked for safe and equitable working conditions, rights to fair housing, equal rights for women, access to healthcare and birth control, and cultural expressions of freedom, such as free love, an end to private property, and social ideals of communal economic life. Many women rejected the sexism of Orthodoxy that limited their participation and became active leaders in the movements for labor justice and women's rights.

The Red Scare and Palmer raids immediately following World War I led to the deportation of hundreds of Jewish activists, including the brilliant writer and activist Emma Goldman. Viewing Goldman's pamphlets on free love and labor rights, written in Yiddish, is a powerful reminder of how deeply embedded in Jewish community these movements were.

Despite the forces that threatened imprisonment or deportation for activism, many continued their efforts, resulting in the hard-won reforms of a unionized labor force. The proud tradition of social activism among Jews was dealt a crippling blow by the signing of the Hitler-Stalin non-aggression pact in 1939, causing a great sense of betrayal among those who believed in and worked toward realizing the socialist utopian views of the Bolshevik revolution. This pact, along with revelations of the persecution of Jews in the Soviet Union both during and after World War II, led to a profound disillusionment with socialism and communism among many.

The heartbreak following the Shoah coupled with the pernicious rise of McCarthyism broke the spirit and silenced the voices of many who had been passionately dedicated to social justice as a messianic movement that had, for many, replaced traditional Jewish observance. The brutal repression of the McCarthy era forced many progressive or liberal Jews to turn away from overt expressions of social activism. The fears that were catalyzed by the Shoah doubtless contributed to the silencing of these voices of dissent. If Germany—the bastion of assimilated Jewish intellectual and cultural expressions in the late 19th and early 20th centuries, which had fostered the great intellectual advances of Marx, Freud, and Einstein—was not immune to the ravages of anti-Semitism, how could one be sure that the United States was safe? The choice to become more assimilated and more focused on material stability was borne not only of a desire for financial stability, but also for the safety that assimilation and wealth might offer.

Many American Jews experienced a schizophrenic existence in which the outer reality reflected an economically comfortable milieu, even as they unconsciously guarded against a gnawing sense of dread, a remnant of the recent genocide that their parents, grandparents, and great-grandparents may have experienced. This legacy taught Jews to keep one eye on the door at all times, never knowing when the hospitality of the land on which they dwelt might give way beneath their feet, opening into a chasm of terror. And although American Jews have experienced an unprecedented period of relative safety over the past decades, the recent riling of anti-Semitic tropes in social media and an upsurge in anti-Semitic violence has called that sense of safety into question.

The swarm of flies paradoxically provides us with an opportunity to heal our relationship with a Judaism that may seem over-concerned with material security. We can understand our ancestors' fears that may have driven them to focus on creating a stable foundation for the future. It was left to their children and grandchildren to begin to unpack the attics and basements of both stored and repressed memories and experience the pain, suffering, grief, and hope that lived there. As they did so, many Jews were surprised to find that underneath the rhinestone surface of an assimilated Judaism lay the true gems of deep spirituality and an ancestry rich with meaning.

Murrain—the broken heart

The fifth plague by *murrain*, an infectious disease that brought about the death of cattle, represents the killing off of the instinctual self. In kabbalah, *Tiferet* is the heart center, the center of the self. It joins the upper worlds of the most spiritual sefirot (*Keter*, *Chokhmah*, and *Binah*) with the seven lower worlds of the physical and emotional body.

The connection between mind and body is necessary for us to heal from trauma. Otherwise, the powerful feelings contained in our bodies do not come to consciousness. In Hebrew, reversing the Hebrew letters of the word for *Pharaoh* gives us the words *ha oref*, corresponding to the nape of the neck. According to Isaac Luria, the inner Pharaoh sits facing our throat, cutting off the channels of sustenance: the trachea, esophagus, and the blood vessels, sucking the vital energy and blocking the flow from the upper sefirot into the body, where the spiritual energy could be received and manifested.[26]

Luria taught that Moses had difficulty speaking because the exile happened, in a spiritual sense, at the level of the throat. Moses had to find his voice to overcome the Pharaoh and the inner exile. Only then could he lead his people out of slavery and into connection with their own voices and true spiritual selves. When we are traumatized, all our psychological resources go toward vigilantly maintaining safety. An inner Pharaoh sets up its rulership in the back of the neck overseeing all that goes on from a position of fear and constant anxiety, monitoring all aspects of existence and ever ready to signal *danger*. In this process we lose access to our innate bodily intelligence, muffled as it is by hypervigilant static.

Trauma is transmitted intergenerationally, from parent to child, in thousands of incremental interactions that make up the child's experience of attachment. If a parent or caregiver is suffering from post-traumatic stress, the fear, disconnection, and overwhelm are transmitted to the child on a bodily level. The parent's disconnection from her or his own bodily signals may impede the ability to attune to and respond to the child's needs. The child grows up with a sense that the mother or caregiver is not present, is unresponsive and unavailable to meet her or his needs. In turn, the child experiences the world as unsafe and unresponsive, triggering a new cycle of traumatic psychic organization.

The endless array of subtle interactions that occur over the course of childhood and adolescent development can coalesce into a pattern of feeling life itself to be untrustworthy, requiring constant vigilance. Split off at the neck, the conscious mind presses down the felt sense of trauma to the body and the unconscious, where it exists in a state of internal exile.

Ruth recalled that her maternal great-grandmother died when her grandmother was a young child, and her grandmother did not know how to raise Ruth's mother with maternal nurturance. Instead, the family focused on the intellectual and rational areas of daily life. Ruth's opening to Judaism occurred when she understood the meaning of standing on holy ground in the Jewish tradition. Connecting with the Divine Presence embodied in the Creation, the Shekhinah, allowed Ruth to feel held, helping her to shift from her head into her body and connect more meaningfully with her embodied heart center.

In its healthy manifestation, Tiferet represents the masculine aspect of the Divine that unites with the Shekhinah. Gathering the energies of the upper spiritual sefirot with those that are experienced on an emotional and bodily level, Tiferet brings these energies into manifestation through uniting with Malchut, the Ground of Being. Moses must remove his shoes, so he is fully aware he is standing on holy ground when he encounters the burning bush—to feel his connection with his own body as it connects with the body of the earth, the Shekhinah, the Indwelling Presence in all things. Moses's reconnection with his own embodied self is the starting point of the journey out of mitzrayim.

The plague of the murrain reminds us of the painful work entailed in reawakening the Jewish heart. This journey of reconnection brings us to the depths of the grief, terror, and rage that has gone untended in our family histories and in own lives. The impact of the Holocaust on all Jews was cataclysmic. Jews who had emigrated from Eastern Europe before the Shoah, in the late 19th and early 20th centuries, were also deeply affected, leaving behind immediate and extended families, neighbors, and friends who were later murdered. Gloria Freund, who chronicles the histories of Jewish communities in Eastern and Central Europe, reflects, "Any American Jew who says they didn't lose family in the Holocaust just doesn't know."[27]

The Baal Shem Tov once asked, Why does the prayer say that God's words are written "upon the heart," and not *inside* the heart? He responds that it is only when the heart is broken that God's words can enter us.[28] As we allow ourselves to feel our broken hearts, the words of the Divine can enter us and transform our deepest suffering. As we open the stream of heart energy that has been constricted, we allow the flow from the upper sefirot into the body. We are no longer silent, no longer cut off at the neck.

Boils—destructive anger

The sixth plague corresponds to the sefirah of Gevurah which, when it is in the right balance, governs our ability to discern, make judgments, and set healthy limits. When imbalanced, we are in a state that corresponds to the sixth plague of boils, which developed when embers from a hot furnace were hurled over the land. This plague is a symbol of cruelty and rejection. Jacobson observes, "When our inner capacity for rejection turns into hate, bitterness and cruelty, the embers of our soul become a destructive force. Like boils, they infect our lives and the lives of people around us."[29]

In families that have been devastated by trauma, the blocked flow of love between parents and children is one of the most grievous casualties. In Jewish families, relationships between our grandparents and our parents, our parents and ourselves, and perhaps even between ourselves and our children have been impacted by anti-Semitic trauma.

Our ancestors, having fled pogroms and the horrors of the *Shoah*, sought to ensure safety for their children. Yet often the impact of the trauma caused deep scars in the psyche—profound depression and despair that often went under-ground, and a hypervigilance and preoccupation with security and safety. The language of love was transmitted in material ways, through food, support, and encouragement to succeed. But often the ability to express love through words, through touch, through relatedness may have been lacking.

Hannah recalled being deeply moved by her experiences at the temple as a young girl. She recalled being entranced by the gorgeous stained-glass window in the sanctuary of her youth. She experienced the central panel that was supposed to represent God: "I kept looking at that .... That's what God was. It's like this amorphous energy of color and light and beauty. So that was the experience of the Divine. And one that I can still tap into." Yet Hannah could not speak to her family about her mystical experience of the Divine. Her father was pragmatic and strictly rational. Her mother engaged in rituals but could not articulate the feeling or meaning that they held. It was decades before Hannah found a community that could nurture this early felt love of the Divine in a Jewish context.

As I will describe in more detail later, Hannah's mother had grown up with a father who maintained an Orthodox Jewish practice, but who was extremely abusive to his wife and children. He had been profoundly traumatized by witnessing his own mother's murder in a pogrom in Russia. Because of her own father's cruelty, Hannah's mother was psychologically defended against the kind of ego surrender that is required to fully experience the sacred. Such surrender threatened to open into an abyss of family trauma that had never been worked through. Hannah sensed the presence of the trauma as a nameless dread which was carefully avoided.

Many of us have family members who have been so hurt by the traumas that their families have suffered that the flow of love becomes impaired, and violence or aggression from the unhealed trauma is acted out upon loved ones. Constant anxiety about other people's intentions is dealt with through efforts to control others by manipulating their emotions or exploiting their vulnerabilities. The widely caricaturized portrait of the overbearing Jewish mother, made famous in the fiction of Philip Roth and other mid-century Jewish male writers, may be more compassionately understood when we see her through the lens of survival anxiety engendered by centuries of oppression and terror.

Tragic consequences of unhealed trauma have often gone unspoken. Mental illness, family violence, and other dysfunctions in Jewish families remained taboo subjects that often went unnamed and unaddressed out of concern that exposing these difficulties would invite further anti-Semitic attacks from the outside world. The pressure to assimilate and appear to be good kept many from discussing the pain they experienced at home. As we begin to release the divine sparks from under the kelipot created by trauma, opening up awareness of this hidden suffering is necessary to heal the pain that many experienced as transgenerational trauma acted out in physical, sexual, or emotional abuse.

The hatred that is visited upon oneself or one's ancestors may fester under the skin like a boil, erupting into cruelty. For some who have been traumatized, hatred that has been inflicted on them, if not worked through, may be unconsciously acted out on other family members. The intensity of the hatred and cruelty is devastating to their children and other loved ones because it unconsciously transmits the collective force of the virulent anti-Semitism that the perpetrator suffered. Bringing awareness to the distortion that the boils represent may allow those victimized by such cruelty to reconnect with self-compassion and self-worth. Perhaps the awareness will allow forgiveness of oneself and others, or at a minimum, understanding of the forces that brought about their cruel behavior.

Hail—narcissistic wounding

The seventh plague of hail corresponds to the sefirah of Chesed, the flowing stream of lovingkindness. The plague of hail symbolizes the disrupted state in which loving emotions are frozen. The hail that fell in Egypt had fiery flames within it, which Jacobson sees as symbolic of a "cold and icy individual" who is also aflame with "self-love and ablaze with egotistical passions," what we commonly refer to as narcissism.[30]

Trauma can result in the development of a narcissistic defense, in which a person appears inflated or grandiose, striving for recognition from others to compensate for an underlying sense of inadequacy or shame, or a lack of a sense of a coherent self. Trauma survivors may develop narcissistic defenses to cover up an underlying emptiness that keeps them from experiencing intrusions from the outside world that feel threatening to the fragile psyche.[31]

Impairment of healthy boundaries may also manifest in parents' projection of the need for success and achievement onto their children, in order to assuage internalized feelings of shame and self-doubt. This projection may be experienced by children as a tremendous pressure to fulfill the parents' desires and expectations at the expense of their own soulful self-expression.

Aaron described the overbearing pressure he felt from his parents to conform to their conventional suburban Jewish lifestyle, a lifestyle they adopted after escaping from Germany in the 1930s. Aaron felt the unconscious heaviness of the Shoah weighing on him—the pressure to continue the lineage and to fulfill his parents' expectations. This demand was felt by many children of families fleeing the Shoah, who carried the weighty expectations of fulfilling the dreams not only of their parents, but also for the members of the extended families and communities left behind that perished.

Aaron responded to the unbearable pressure by rebelling, marrying a non-Jewish woman, and moving far away from home, which created a deep rift in his relationship with his family. He felt punished for not living up to their projections onto him, which included pressure to enter into and sustain the family business and participate in weekly extended family gatherings. In this environment, he felt that his own nature was neither recognized nor nurtured.

Failure of the parents to accurately see and mirror the true self of the child leads to a profound rupture in the child's psyche, as the child must abandon her or his true self in order to receive the love that the parents are offering to those aspects that meet their expectations. The creation of a false self leaves the true self in a state of exile and profound suffering.

Some of the most painful manifestations occur when the ability to give and receive love within the family has been shut down due to trauma and shame. Those who defend against powerful feelings of internalized shame may become inflated, projecting the shame they feel onto others, becoming critical and harsh, especially toward those closest to them. It is often difficult to understand why those upon whom we rely for love, support, and a foundation of trust in the world are often unable to fulfill these needs. We may have received material stability while simultaneously feeling profoundly unsupported emotionally.

Trauma and centuries of anti-Semitism have taken root in our psyches and in intergenerational patterns of relating. By understanding that these patterns have their genesis in trauma, we may develop compassion for those whose capacity to love has been severely impeded, and we may feel the pain that this causes them as well as us. We can also have compassion for ourselves and understand that we are all deserving of love, even if we did not experience its free flow into our lives as children. We can finally begin to explore the places where we are blocked in our capacities to love and respect others.

This profound and difficult work takes dedication, insight, and time. Often these patterns have been passed down through many generations and may take generations to heal. Many of us can notice a profound difference in the experiences of our parents with their parents and how much they had to overcome to give us what they could. As we learn to reparent ourselves and parent our children with more awareness, we learn how to heal these patterns so we do not pass them on to succeeding generations. In the Passover Seder, we say a prayer that each generation be able to move further into freedom than the previous one. This is the hope that healing intergenerational trauma holds.

The upper sefirot—loss of the spiritual

The upper branches of the Tree of Life are most directly linked to the Divine emanation. The spark of Divine truth is received through the uppermost sefirah of Keter (crown); is transmitted conceptually through Chokhmah, the sefirah pertaining to wisdom; and is gestated in the sefirah of Binah, understanding, before taking shape in our awareness and our actions through the lower seven sefirot. The last three plagues correspond to the disconnection from these upper sefirot, resulting in our inability receive, access and make use of Divine guidance. In healing this obstruction, we begin to reawaken our connection to Source.

Locusts—loss of connection to the Spiritual Mother

The sefirah of Binah is a manifestation of the Divine Feminine as the *Imma Ila'ah*, the Higher Mother, a womb for the Divine transmission, helping us gestate and understand its significance. From her womb of understanding, Binah gives birth to the lower seven sefirot through which the Divine Emanation is manifested. The eighth plague of invading locusts symbolizes the loss of connection to the matrix of meaning. We cannot decipher the spiritual insights we are given.

Jews reeling from the devastation of the Shoah were unable to provide matrices of meaning in which the trauma could be fully held and healed. Rabbi Edward Feld writes movingly of the spiritual and emotional devastation suffered. "In less than ten years French, Dutch, Belgian, Danish, Greek, Czech, Polish, Hungarian, Romanian, Italian, Latvian, Lithuanian, Ukrainian, and of course, German and Austrian Jewry ended, and the litany can go on. All of Europe, stretching from the Atlantic well into Russia, was decimated of its Jews."[32]

Along with the death of millions, Jews suffered a cultural genocide. The epoch of Jews in Europe, a history spanning 2,000 years and the entire Yiddish culture, ended. Feld weighs the enormity of the loss:

> The fabric of European Jewish life, of scholars and poets, of Talmudists and story tellers, of theologians and violinists, of thespians and comics, is gone. The fecund symbiosis of Jewish culture and the German language, the world of Freud and Buber, of Kafka and Einstein, is aborted. And the Eastern European Jewish community—the Maskilim and Hasidim, socialists and Hebraists, rabbinic masters and secular novelists of the largest Jewish community the world has ever known, are gone. The Bund and the Musar Yeshivot whose clashing sounded the voice of Jewish renaissance are both now stilled.[33]

Feld observes that any Jew of European origin now living in North or South America, Israel, or Australia has had some family member killed in the Shoah. In addition, North African and Middle Eastern Jews were profoundly impacted by the war. "Almost every Jew alive has been touched in a deeply personal way that almost makes each one of them a survivor." The decimation of entire lineages of Jewish cultures, developed over centuries, has been spiritually devastating. "No longer are hundreds of Yiddish poets and novelists upbraiding their people, telling their stories, teaching them how to live and love. A vital religious center was swept away as well: nine of every ten rabbis living at the time died."[34]

Strategies that had been used by Jews in the past to escape campaigns of genocidal terror, such as bribery and self-governance, were used by Nazis to further their genocidal campaign. Even conversion, which had been the central goal of previous campaigns of terror against the Jews, such as in the Inquisition, was not an option. Because all Jews, regardless of religious affiliation, were slaughtered, this martyrdom (sacrificing one's life to maintain one's faith) was not a victory. Feld observes that the only act of resistance left was to seek to maintain connection to our reverence for life and our dignity in the face of unending horror and debasement.

> We meet such an intense reality of evil in the Holocaust that we are forced to incorporate a new and different understanding of what humanity is capable of … We now know the depth of humanity's capacity for evil. We are different because of the Holocaust, terribly different … The range of human possibility, the depth of evil revealed by the Nazis, goes beyond anything previously imagined. Indeed, the inability to imagine anything so horrible limited the victims' ability to defend themselves.[35]

For many coming of age in the wake of the Shoah, Judaism was experienced as lacking depth or meaning. Yet when we understand that the elders of the community who had survived—parents, rabbis, Jewish educators—were themselves reeling from the overwhelming horrors of the Shoah, we can see why they were unable to provide young seekers with any meaningful response to their questions about suffering.

Hannah's family was profoundly traumatized by her grandfather witnessing his own mother's murder in a pogrom and her grandfather's subsequent descent into mental illness and abusive behavior. When Hannah learned about the Shoah, it raised startling questions for her about the meaning of life and the fate of the soul in the afterlife. Perhaps the undigested intergenerational trauma in her own family led to her deep search for meaning. She recalled seeking answers from her rabbi and Hebrew school teachers who offered unsatisfyingly vague answers about how one's good deeds survive after death. Jewish spiritual leaders and teachers were unable to respond to questions about the meaning of life, God, death, and Heaven in the aftermath of the Shoah. Answers that sustained the community in the past were rendered meaningless in the wake of unfathomable horror.

Reb Zalman recognized the emotional agony, which so many suffered after the Shoah, that made it impossible to find meaningful answers within Judaism. "After the Holocaust we all became defiled by so much death. Rage at God at times unconscious and repressed was seething in our teachers below the surface."[36] Those who longed for spiritual connection sought out holy teachers from other traditions who were not consumed with the anger so many Jews felt. Connection to spiritual meaning through the sefirah of Binah was foreclosed by the invading locusts of despair, rage, terror, and overwhelming grief. Acknowledging the immensity of the task of religious leadership in the postwar era helps us understand the powerful emotional forces that made it difficult for rabbis, teachers, and spiritual leaders to transmit a meaningful Judaism to young people in the years immediately following the Shoah.

In subsequent chapters I explore how the reclamation of Judaism requires a healing with the matrix of meaning that Binah represents, and the cultivation of both internal and communal spaces in which spiritual wisdom can gestate.

Darkness—loss of connection to God the Father

Chokhmah is the sefirah of wisdom, where the Divine Will that is transmitted through Keter is first received and comprehended. The plague of enveloping darkness corresponds to the loss of connection to the Source of enlightenment. This plague disrupts the ability of Chokhmah to receive wisdom and symbolizes the shattered relationship between the Jewish people and God after the Shoah.

Theologian Richard L. Rubinstein writes poignantly of the death of God after the Holocaust: "The bodies of my people went up in smoke at Auschwitz. The God of the covenant died there." The Yiddish poet Jacob Glatstein reflected, "We received the Torah at Mount Sinai and in Majdanek we gave it back."[37] Recognizing our limited human capacity to know whether or not the supernal God is dead, Rubinstein makes this clarification:

> We live in the time of the "death of God." ... Buber ... spoke of the eclipse of God ... The thread uniting God and man, heaven and earth, has been broken. We stand in a cold, silent, unfeeling cosmos, unaided by any purposeful power beyond our own resources. After Auschwitz, what else can a Jew say about God?[38]

In past epochs, suffering was refracted through a scriptural lens from which one could derive meaning, such as seeing suffering as a testing of one's faith, as happened to Job. The Shoah collapsed all previous categories of meaning-making. Rubenstein notes:

> To see any purpose in the death camps, the traditional believer is forced to regard the most demonic, antihuman explosion in all history as a meaningful expression of God's purposes. The idea is simply too obscene ... The full impact of Auschwitz has not yet been felt in Jewish theology or Jewish life. Great religious revolutions have their periods of gestation. No man knows the hour when the full impact of Auschwitz will be felt, but no religious community can endure so hideous a wounding without vast inner disorders.[39]

After the Shoah, the sense of a Living Presence that mediated one's very existence gave way to a devastating sense of aloneness, catapulting individuals into a world without a sense of a compassionate witness, without meaning. In psychoanalytic theory, the "third," usually represented by the father, allows the developing child to move from the dyadic relating of mother and infant to a triadic relationship that includes the world. In times of massive trauma, the relationship to the witnessing other, the living third, is lost. Instead, the child senses the absence of a caring Father God or even a witnessing community.

Julie's family completely lost their faith in God after her mother's extended family and community were annihilated in the Shoah. Looking at the domed ceiling of the affluent temple she attended, Julie could not read the words on the dome ceiling, the words of the Shema, affirming that God is One with all Creation. With no one to help her decipher the meaning of the religious symbols and teachings that surrounded her, she could not feel or receive God's presence.

For Jews in the post-Shoah era, a relationship and ongoing conversation with the living God, the omnipresent third, has been profoundly ruptured. The third allows an individual to solidify a sense of self, purpose, and belonging, which is gradually internalized. When we experience traumas that shatter this sense of abiding presence, we are left with, in the words of psychoanalyst Samuel Gerson, "the absence of that which made life comprehensible." When this sense of a living third is lost,

> the container cracks and there is no presence beyond our own subjectivity to represent continuity. It is a world constituted by absence where meaning is ephemeral and cynicism passes for wisdom; a world in which psychic

numbness is the balm against unbearable affects, where feelings of ennui and emptiness replace guilt and shame, and where manias of all sort masquerade as Eros.[40]

The plague of enveloping darkness invites us to become more consciously aware of the devastating impact of the Shoah and other forms of collective and personal trauma on our capacity to make meaning of our world and our lives in spiritual terms. In subsequent chapters, I explore how opening to the collective unconscious through turning towards our suffering and grief, has allowed many to begin to heal and open to a personal relationship with God.

Death of the firstborn—loss of the soul child

We heard villages lock their gates,
We heard our language burn in a great fire,
And we urged it, the fire, to take
The tongue of our despair.
From yellow hearts we rescued no poems.
Nor can we purchase poems from the dead
Among whom we live in suburban verses.

Richard Chess, "Yiddish Poets in America"[41]

The uppermost sefirah is Keter, or Crown, the portal through which Divine guidance is transmitted and received. The final plague, and the most devastating, is the death of the firstborn. This plague corresponds to the loss of transmission through the sefirah of Keter. When the pathway between the personal and transpersonal is cut off, we are unable to feel our connection to the Divine. We lose our connection to the soul of Judaism itself, to Jewish collective memory, and to our own *neshama*, our soul.

When we experience trauma, we may unconsciously create a false self to meet the expectations of the outside world—a persona disconnected from the true self that resides at the core of our being. Donald Kalsched refers to this true self as the "Adam-self." Our task in healing trauma is to rediscover the "aboriginal soul-carrying part of the self" and live from the place of our true longing.[42]

For Jews, the loss of the connection to the Adam-self carries a double meaning—a disconnection both personal and collective. God's relationship with the Jewish people began with the creation of Adam from *adamah* (soil), of humans brought forth from the ground of living earth, animated with God's own breath. Yet as we have seen, the cataclysmic disruptions of the recent past have cut off connection with Jewish collective memory, the storehouse of riches in the form of Jewish mythic imagination. The plague of the death of the firstborn reflects the devastating loss of transmission, *l'dor v'dor*, of Judaism from one generation to the next.

Trauma experienced in Jewish families was often not metabolized and was experienced by those growing up in the post-Shoah era as a confused and conflicted silence. Often the weightiness left the children feeling alienated toward Judaism because they could not find meaning in what was being conveyed to them.

Daniel recalled being deeply moved as he watched his grandfather davening in the hallway of his home. As noted earlier, his grandfather had left behind his parents and twelve brothers, all of whom were murdered in the Shoah. Perhaps Daniel could feel the intensity of connection that his grandfather felt in keeping the traditions of his family alive in his daily prayers. Yet Daniel's own parents both rejected Judaism and embraced secular social justice pursuits. When his paternal grandfather passed away when Daniel was eight and his father died a year later, he was left without any connection to the paternal lineage of his ancestors. When his maternal grandfather pleaded with him to have a Bar Mitzvah, he had no context in which to find meaning in the initiation ritual into a tradition about which he knew so little.

The near annihilation of European Jewry and the lineages of Jewish wisdom have left us in a time of unprecedented historical rupture of the bridge to Jewish collective memory. As historian Yusef Yerushalmi has noted, this loss of connection to our mythic inheritance is a symptom of the complete unraveling of beliefs and practices that once allowed Jews to draw on the past to create a living present infused with holiness and spiritual meaning.[43] A deep and abiding Jewish culture had developed over the course of millennia in Europe, especially in the Pale of Settlement, including parts of Poland, Ukraine, and Lithuania.

Access to the Yiddish idiom, including an entire worldview that permeated Jewish life in the shtetl, was lost to the generation born on American soil. This loss assumed catastrophic consequences after the rapid assimilation of the early 1910s and 1920s, when many American Jews chose not to teach their children Yiddish in the hopes of helping them adapt to American culture. Just years later, almost the entire Yiddish-speaking world of Eastern and Central Europe was destroyed in the Holocaust. Assimilation resulted not just in the loss of a language, but also in the loss of a worldview in which the mystical and the rational are not separate; the loss of an identity in which one knew who one was in relationship to self, community, and to the Divine. The loss of this anchored self in the context of one's culture has been shattering to the Jewish psyche.

Joachim Neugroschel notes that Jewish mystical stories reflect a continuous interaction in which human and divine imagination play together in a perpetual dance of Creation.[44] He suggests that our current view of kabbalah as a discrete branch of Judaism may be a product of our time. Prior to the 19th-century Haskalah movement, the separation between rational and mystical did not exist. Instead, Jewish mystical stories "show that divine and supernatural forces are quite human and natural; or vice versa: that the human and the supernatural are really integrated in a cosmos that allows for anything in the human or divine imagination."[45]

For the generations born in the United States, the loss of Yiddish culture and language and the turning away from Jewish spiritual practice led to the eradication of rituals in which a connection to Jewish collective memory could be developed. Not only was access lost to the culture, but also to the living transmission of Torah, Talmud, rabbinic midrash, and kabbalistic teachings about the meaning of life, God, family, and the framework for developing a Jewish identity. The loss of connection to the matrix of meaning, to the sense of a witnessing and compassionate presence, and to the transmission of Jewish collective memory gave rise to the profound feelings of alienation and exile that I examined in earlier chapters.

Understanding the reasons behind this profound loss of meaning may allow us to heal this sense of alienation and exile. In so doing, we may begin to reclaim our place in the chain of souls as both receivers and transmitters of Jewish collective memory.

Leaving mitzrayim

Trauma can shatter the world in a way that necessitates the creation of a new reality—a process that involves what Reb Zalman calls a *paradigm shift*.[46] In the following chapters, I explore how deepening awareness of the cultural complexes symbolized by the plagues may help us move out of constricted consciousness toward psychological and spiritual rebirth.

Before the Hebrews leave Egypt, Moses advises them to ask the Egyptians for jewels of silver and gold before making the journey across the Red Sea. God causes the Egyptians to look with favor on the Hebrews and grant their request. Egypt, the narrow place, is also spoken of as a metaphorical womb, in which the Hebrew people grew from a small tribe into a great nation. Perhaps the mythological richness of Egypt gave birth to the new mythic manifestation of Judaism. When we are ready to be born, the womb becomes too small and, as the living waters part, we must enter a new world. The plagues represent the death of a particular way of being, the contractions that announce that a way of life must be released, so that a new life can begin.

Like the Hebrews receiving the gold and silver of Egypt, the generations newly settling in the United States were profoundly enriched by their engagement with the wider culture. Reb Zalman observes that this time was one in which the seed-pods were germinating the seeds of a paradigmatic shift in Judaism.

In each epoch, a new expression of Judaism is birthed, one that expresses the zeitgeist of its time. This is a hallmark of Judaism's adaptability and capacity for survival over millennia in diaspora.

The first rabbi of the State of Israel, the great mystic Rav Kook recognized that our understanding of God is transformed over time as consciousness grows and develops, even in times of devastating loss. Because God is beyond any human conceptualization, even the denial of God that may appear to be heresy, "when clarified is actually the highest level of faith. Then the human spirit becomes aware that the Divine emanates existence and is Itself beyond existence. What appeared to be heresy, now purified, is restored to purest faith … The Infinite transcends every particular content of faith."[47]

Following the intense suffering of the plagues, we gather at the edge of the Red Sea, waiting to see if a new path will open. A renewed Judaism in the post-Shoah era is born out of wrestling with questions of faith and meaning in the wake of unprecedented catastrophic loss. The new birth is shaped by forces that initially seemed at odds with Judaism as it had been previously known—new awareness sourced in feminism, social justice activism, psychological insight, and scientific understanding. As I explore in the following chapters, opening to this rebirth of consciousness requires bridging our connection to the ancestors as well as turning towards and bringing healing to our own personal and collective suffering.

Notes

1 John P. Wilson, *The Posttraumatic Self: Restoring Meaning and Wholeness to Personality* (New York: Routledge, 2006), 180–188.
2 Thomas Singer and Samuel Kimbles, eds., *The Cultural Complex: Contemporary Jungian Perspectives on Psyche and Society* (New York: Routledge, 2004), 19.
3 Zalman Schachter-Shalomi and Netanel Miles-Yépez, *God Hidden, Whereabouts Unknown: An Essay on the "Contraction" of God in Different Jewish Paradigms* (Boulder: Albion-Andalus Books, 2014).
4 Zalman Schachter-Shalomi, *Paradigm Shift* (Northvale, NJ: Jason Aronson, Inc., 1993), 266–268.
5 Schachter-Shalomi and Miles-Yépez, *God Hidden, Whereabouts Unknown.*
6 Steven A. Fisdel, *Roots and Branches: The Dynamics of Kabbalah's Tree of Life* (Albany, CA: Rabbi Steven Fisdel, 2019), 28.
7 Yosef Y. Jacobson, "The Ten Plagues in Our Personal Life," *Ascent of Safed*, 2002, http://ascentofsafed.com/cgi-bin/ascent.cgi?Name=j1462Plagues.
8 Steven Fisdel, private conversation, 2016.
9 Samuel Kimbles, *Phantom Narratives: The Unseen Contributions of Culture to Psyche* (Lanham, MD: Rowman & Littlefield, 2014), 24–25; citing Nicolas Abraham and Maria Torok, *The Shell and the Kernel* (Chicago, IL: University of Chicago Press, 1994), 140.
10 Kimbles, *Phantom Narratives*, 26; citing Christopher Bollas, *The Shadow of the Object* (New York: Columbia University Press, 1987).
11 Exodus 1:22.
12 Alessandra Cavalli, "Transgenerational Transmission of Indigestible Facts: From Trauma, Deadly Ghosts and Mental Voids to Meaning-making Interpretations," *Journal of Analytical Psychology* 57, no. 5 (2012): 597–614.
13 Ibid., 598; citing Wilfred Bion, *Learning from Experience* (London: Heinemann, 1962).
14 Angela Connolly, "Healing the Wounds of Our Fathers: Intergenerational Trauma, Memory, Symbolization and Narrative," *Journal of Analytical Psychology* 56, no. 5 (2011): 607–626, 610.
15 Jacobson, "The Ten Plagues."
16 Gershen Kaufman and Lev Raphael, "Shame: A Perspective on Jewish Identity," *Journal of Psychology and Judaism* 11, no. 1 (1987): 30–40.
17 Ibid.
18 Wilson, *The Posttraumatic Self*, 180–188.
19 Kurt Lewin, "Self-Hatred Among Jews," in *A Psychology-Judaism Reader*, edited by Reuven P. Bulka and Moshe HaLevi Spero (Springfield, IL: Charles C. Thomas, 1982), 58–70; Jerry V. Diller, "Identity Rejection and Reawakening in the Jewish Context,"

Journal of Judaism and Psychology 5, no. 1 (1987): 38–47; Sander Gilman, *Jewish Self-Hatred: Anti-Semitism and the Hidden Language of the Jews* (Baltimore: Johns Hopkins University Press, 1986).

20 Jay Frankel, "Exploring Ferenczi's Concept of Identification with the Aggressor: Its Role in Trauma, Everyday Life, and the Therapeutic Relationship," *Psychoanalytic Dialogues* 12, no. 1 (2002): 101–139.

21 Diller, "Identity Rejection," 42–43.

22 Jonathan Boyarin and Daniel Boyarin, eds., *Jews and Other Differences* (Minneapolis, MN: University of Minnesota Press, 1997), xi.

23 Ibid.

24 Ibid.

25 Jacobson, "The Ten Plagues."

26 Moshe-Yaakov Wisnefsky, *Apples from the Orchard: Gleanings from the Mystical Teachings of Rabbi Yitzchak Luria-the Arizal on the Weekly Torah Portion, from Sefer HaLikutim*, (Malibu, CA: Thirty Seven Books, 2008), www.chabad.org/kabbalah/articl e_cdo/aid/379830/jewish/The-Butcher-in-the-Throat-Part-2.htm).

27 Louise Steinman, *The Crooked Mirror: A Memoir of Polish-Jewish Reconciliation* (Boston: Beacon Press, 2013), 4.

28 Estelle Frankel, Radio Interview, KPFA, Spring, 1998.

29 Jacobson, "The Ten Plagues."

30 Ibid.

31 Shmuel Gerzi, "Trauma, Narcissism and the Two Attractors in Trauma," *International Journal of Psychoanalysis* 86, no. 4 (2005): 1033–1050, 1042.

32 Edward Feld, *The Spirit of Renewal: Finding Faith after the Holocaust* (Woodstock, VT: Jewish Lights Publishing, 1994), 84–85.

33 Ibid.

34 Ibid.

35 Ibid., p. 93.

36 Ibid.

37 Jacob Glatstein, "Dead Men Don't Praise God," in *Selected Poems of Jacob Glatstein*, translated by Ruth Whitman (New York: October House, Inc., 1972).

38 Jerry Diller, *Ancient Roots and Modern Meanings* (Jacksonville, FL: Bloch Publishing, 1997), 239; citing Richard Rubinstein.

39 Ibid, 241.

40 Samuel Gerson, "When the Third is Dead: Memory, Mourning, and Witnessing in the Aftermath of the Holocaust," *International Journal of Psychoanalysis* 90, no. 6 (2009), 1341–1357, 1343–1344.

41 Richard Chess, "Yiddish Poets in America," in *Telling and Remembering: A Century of Jewish American Poetry*, edited by Steven J. Rubin (Boston: Beacon Press, 1997), 453.

42 Donald Kalsched, *Trauma and the Soul: A Psycho-Spiritual Approach to Human Development and Its Interruption* (London: Routledge, 2013), 106–107.

43 Yosef Hayim Yerushalmi, *Zakhor: Jewish History and Jewish Memory* (New York: Schocken Books, 1989), 94.

44 Joachim Neugroschel, *Great Tales of Jewish Fantasy and the Occult: The Dybbuk and Thirty Other Classic Stories* (New York: Overlook Books, 1997), viii–ix.

45 Ibid.

46 Schachter-Shalomi, *Paradigm Shift*.

47 Daniel C. Matt, *The Essential Kabbalah: The Heart of Jewish Mysticism* (San Francisco: Harper San Francisco, 1995), 35; citing Abraham Isaac Kook, *Orot* (Jerusalem: Mossad ha-Rav Kook, 1961), 124–128.

Part IV

The healing

Chapter 8

Serach bat Asher and healing the ruptured bridge to collective memory

I wear you like a necklace with one lost stone ...
There is no place on earth where you don't see me
Your spirit inhabits my bones ...
Naomi Ruth Lowinsky, "I See You in the Foothills, Oma"[1]

When we lose our connection to the cultural psyche due to collective trauma, we feel alone, adrift, disconnected from the Source and from our own spiritual identity. No longer woven into the cultural fabric, we may feel ourselves hanging on by a thread to our heritage, or we may feel like we have lost the thread entirely.

The plagues shattered the previous world order and opened the space for a new reality to come into being. After awareness of contemporary "plagues" shatter the structure of our former reality, we are freed to move in new ways. And, as the ancient Hebrews did, we may find our way in the unknown through connecting with the wisdom of our ancestors.

Before the people can leave Egypt, an ancient promise must be fulfilled. As the Book of Genesis concludes, Joseph, whose story I detail in the following chapter, reunites the twelve tribes of Israel in Egypt. In the final lines of the Genesis, Joseph tells his family, "When God has taken notice (*pakod yifkod*) of you, you shall carry up my bones from here."[2] Joseph knows that there will be a time when God "remembers" the Hebrew people and delivers them out of Egypt.

The task of finding Joseph's bones carries great symbolic meaning: To move out of a state of alienation and exile, we must find and carry with us the bones of our ancestors, our link to cultural collective memory. By the time of the liberation from Egypt, 400 years have passed since Joseph's death. No one knows how to fulfill the covenantal task; no one knows where Joseph's bones are buried. Broken in spirit by seemingly endless brutality, they have all given up hope that the day would ever come. Not unlike our own time, the link with the past seemed irrevocably broken.

In the midst of the seemingly insurmountable challenge, an ancestor emerges who guides Moses to find the bones of Joseph. Serach bat Asher, the daughter of Asher, Joseph's brother, was alive at the time Joseph was buried and is still alive at the time of the liberation from Egypt. This chapter explores how Serach serves as a guardian of collective memory, coming when the people are ready to move toward liberation out of *galut*, the spiritual exile.

The ruptured bridge

Our longing to connect with our past often takes us down a road ravaged by the storms of time, littered with great fallen trees that make passage seemingly impossible. Even if we know about the once thriving village of Jewish life in Eastern or Central Europe where our ancestors lived, we cannot return the way other immigrants can, because the village or town no longer exists, its inhabitants annihilated in the fires of the Shoah.

We live in a time when the transmission through this *shalshelet*, this chain of souls, has been profoundly ruptured. We long for the past, yet many of us grew up in families in which the connection with the past was rarely discussed—often shrouded in a gray fog of repressed grief and suffering that was too potent to name. We may have been keenly aware of the presences of family members whose pictures filled the hallway, their sepia-toned faces calling out to us from the Old World, both haunting and intriguing us, betrothing us to a history that courses through our blood, but for which we were often not given words or stories. We may feel a deep longing for those stories—stories that can fill in the gaps of our own becoming—our personal creation myths that orient us in time and space, that give us a sense of our essence.

Many Jewish families turned away from actively transmitting Jewish collective memory by disengaging from Jewish rituals and practices. Personal memories were often not shared. As children or grandchildren of immigrants, our natural curiosity about our family history may have been met with a stony silence or an injunction to move away from such charged topics that carried within them too much pain. "Don't talk about the past." "Why would you want to know about that?" "That's not for children." "Let's talk about something happy." "No need to dwell."

Many Jews of today, when invited to "remember," feel a profound lack of connection to either the Torah or the practices that were, just one or two generations ago, the lifeline of their families. And many know so little about their own families that it takes a conscious awakening to realize just how deeply the river of tradition ran for millennia, until the mighty river, then a stream, became a trickle that ran out just before it reached this bend in the riverbed.

Yet we may still feel the irrevocable sense of loss. Even if we long to connect in some way to our Jewishness, we feel overwhelmed at the prospect. Too much has been lost or was never transmitted. We may have never learned Hebrew. Some of us rarely, if ever, went to temple. Many may think, "I am not like those other Jews, who really know about Judaism. I would just be pretending. It's embarrassing; people will know I don't belong here." In our shame, in our ignorance, we retreat, we withdraw, we carry on with our lives even as we also carry within us an untended flickering, now sputtering, light that longs for the oxygen of our attention. When we occasionally feed it, caressing the sepia photograph of our great-grandmother, feeling the delightful gargle of a Yiddishism in our throats, we feel the light spark, and for a moment, it dances.

And we may be surprised to discover that, even when the connection to our personal and collective histories is difficult to trace, the ancestral psyche speaks to us in the dreamtime, in the imaginal realm. If we listen with our hearts, we may find a way to cross the ruptured bridge of memory. Reconnecting with our histories, we can make sense of our identity as Jews. As we listen for the voices of our ancestors, we may begin to weave ourselves back into the fabric of our collective story.

Serach bat Asher

In the Exodus story, the pathway to the ancestors is fiercely and lovingly tended by one of our earliest grandmothers, Serach bat Asher, daughter of Joseph's brother Asher. Moses must find the bones of Joseph; otherwise the people will not be able to leave Egypt. No one can help him, as no one alive knows where Joseph's remains lie—until Serach bat Asher, who was alive 400 years before, shows him where her uncle is buried. Serach connects the Hebrews enslaved in Egypt to their birthright—she reminds them that they are children of Abraham and Sarah who pledged a covenant with God. She reminds them that their deliverance was fore-told, giving them faith that their redemption is assured.

Serach plays several pivotal roles in the Exodus. When Moses first comes down from the mountain after his encounter with the burning bush, the people are skeptical. They consult Serach, the holder of communal memory, to see if they should, indeed, place their faith in him.

Serach is "the repository of the secret of redemption"—she alone recognizes and confirms Moses as the one who is fulfilling God's covenant with the people.[3]

Initially, Serach is unmoved when told of the miracles Moses has performed. Yet when she hears Moses say, "God has surely taken notice of you (*pakod pakadti*)," she confirms that he is destined to lead them out of Egypt. She recalls that God "remembered" (*pakod*) Sarah and blessed her with the birth of her son, Isaac, assuring her and Abraham that they would have descendants as numerous as the stars in the sky. Serach was also present when her uncle Joseph, on his deathbed, had his family promise that "when God has taken notice (*pakod yifkod*) of you, you shall carry up my bones from here."

Biblical scholar Avivah Zornberg observes that the terms *pakod* and *pakod yifkod*, meaning that God "remembers" or "takes note of," are rarely used. Their usage marks an event in which the transmission of the covenant between God and the Jewish people is taking place.

As the people accept Moses, the process of liberation begins, and the ten plagues culminate in Pharaoh's relenting and finally allowing the Hebrews to leave Egypt. As Moses has the people gather their things, along with the gold and riches from the homes of the Egyptians, he sets out on his own task—recovering the bones of Joseph.

Moses spends three days and nights searching, without success. He despairs, until Serach bat Asher guides him to the banks of the Nile. She recalls witnessing the Egyptian magicians and astrologers sinking Joseph's metal coffin into the depths of the river, so its waters would be blessed. They advised Pharaoh that as long as Joseph's bones remained hidden, the Hebrews would never leave Egypt.[4]

Varying accounts are offered as to what happens next. In one telling, Moses places a shard, on which he has written the unutterable name of God, into the Nile, causing Joseph's leaden coffin to rise from the depths. In another, Moses takes a chalice that once belonged to Joseph and throws it into the river Nile, summoning the coffin to the surface.[5] With Joseph's bones gathered, Moses and the people can now make their way to the Red Sea.

Serach bat Asher carries the link to the past and opens the portal to the future. Her time is not linear. She waits centuries; she is not diminished by historical adversity. When we are ready, she presents the guidance needed to reconnect with that which appears to have been irretrievably lost. She is accessed through intuition, through the hidden oral tradition. By following her guidance, the buried wisdom of the ancestors rises to the surface, rekindling the connection to the mythic imagination of the people. We remember that the ancestors dreamed us into being and that they dwell with us and within us.

Serach represents the feminine feeling-based aspect of familial connection. When Joseph is first sold into slavery, his brothers fear telling their father Jacob that he has gone missing, afraid the news would devastate him. The brothers knew that only Serach could approach her grandfather. With her harp and beautiful, soothing voice, Serach sat with Jacob for long hours, comforting him. At times he wondered aloud, "Is it possible? Sometimes I wonder if perhaps Joseph is still alive." And Serach wondered with him, "Perhaps so, Grandfather. Perhaps so."

Many years later, when the brothers learn that Joseph is not only still alive, but also vice-regent of all Egypt, they are again afraid to tell their aged father. They fear that this news may kill him as well—carrying with it not just the shocking joy of discovering that Joseph is alive but also the overwhelming grief of all the years of separation. The brothers decide once again that only their niece Serach can deliver the news to Jacob. And so Serach sits again with her grandfather, with her harp, gently singing to him that his long-cherished dream of Joseph being alive is indeed true.

We too, like Jacob, may wonder whether our connection to our loved ones is irrevocably broken. We may have lost hope, feeling that the link to our ancestors is too tenuous, that the weave of the fabric has grown too thin, that we cannot and will not find the thread that connects. And maybe too, there is a part of us that wonders if the ancestors are sitting right there with us, within reach if only we could remember how to call out to them. And maybe Serach is sitting with us as well, strumming her harp and consoling us with her gentle voice, saying, "Perhaps so, perhaps so."

Journeys with the ancestors

Like the matriarchs and patriarchs of Genesis, our personal ancestors may symbolize wholeness, occupying a realm we may visit for restoration of our connection to our lineage, going all the way back to our Biblical foremothers and
forefathers. Lawrence Sullivan, in a study of cross-cultural healing, recognized
that in many cultures ancestors represent archetypal wholeness. Because we as a
collective have a shared history of profound trauma, some personal ancestor stories are painful and carry the grief that has often not been worked through in our
lineages. These stories of grief and suffering are explored in Chapter Ten. In this
chapter, we recount stories of the ancestors as symbols of wholeness.

For many years before engaging with Jewish spiritual practice, I studied
indigenous shamanism with Jeane TuBears Jacobs, a Native American teacher
of Choctaw and Cherokee and, surprisingly, Jewish ancestry. Her grandfather,
Simon Levi Jacobs was a furrier who married her Native American grandmother.
With TuBears's guidance in a shamanic journeying class, I was invited to travel
to either the upper (spiritual) or lower (animal ally) worlds, or to the middle world
where the ancestors dwelt.

I was drawn to a hut in the midst of a forest in the middle world, where I found
my ancestors waiting. My only great-grandparents still alive when I was a child
were my maternal grandfather's parents, who I met only once or twice. I recalled
feeling a sense of intense light in their presence. In my journeying, I imagined
feeling the spirits of all my great-grandparents surrounding me, like a mandala,
around a *mikveh* or ritual bath, and felt them bathing me in sacred waters, preparing my soul for a journey.

Over the months and years that followed, I entered into the forest hut and
invited their presences again and again. At the time, I had no conscious connection to Jewish spiritual practice. But what unfolded in my life was a spontaneous
emergence of a deepening love for, and understanding of, Jewish spirituality and
teachings. I met with them many times over these years and in powerful meditations received their healing wisdom and guidance.

In a meditation, my maternal great-grandmother Rivkah, whom I had met
briefly when I was a child, showed me something of her life. I recently learned
that her maiden name was Cohen, suggesting that she may have descended from
the priestly class of *Kohanim*. She immigrated from the Pale of Settlement to the
United States in the early 1900s. She revealed the bright spiritual light that had
once lived within her shtetl and told me, "We are keepers of the light. We are
transmitters of light. The light goes back, to the beginning … to *Gan Eden* (the
Garden of Eden)." She showed me the powerful collective soul of the communities of Eastern Europe, the brightness of the spiritual light they carried, the depth
and strength of it. In the meditation, I can see the light emanating from a unified
field of souls, powerfully shining.

Then she presented the darkening of the light, the destruction of so many souls,
so many carriers of light, in the Shoah. The devastation is unfathomable. And we,

on the other shore, post-Shoah, open to receive the transmission from our ancestors, as they offer it to us. She then raised her hands and offered me the priestly blessing, this *kohain*, and I felt my body, each sefirah, filling with light—blinding, powerful light. She declares, "This is your birthright."

She tells me how my grandfather's (her son's) turning away from Jewish observance devastated her and my great-grandfather. And she says that my understanding of the turning away and the return, the *teshuvah*, is important in helping others find their way back to what matters. As noted in Chapter One, my great-grandfather Jacob, Rivkah's husband, appeared to me in an early meditation to guide me in this writing on Jewish identity. And now I see the two of them, beaming their light to me, to us, their beauty, their strength—these lineage bearers, transmitting the light from Gan Eden, from Sinai, *l'dor v'dor*, from generation to generation, maintaining, remembering, observing, sometimes sacrificing life itself to protect this light, so that it continues to be transmitted.

Ruth's story continues

As I have detailed previously, Ruth grew up in a family where secular intellectual pursuits were prized and connection to her Hasidic and other mystical lineages was diminished. For Ruth, connecting imaginally with her ancestors restored a depth of feeling and spirituality that had been missing in her childhood family.

Ruth reflected on the lack of transmission of maternal warmth and holding in what Jungian analyst Naomi Lowinsky calls the *Motherline*, the link between women and their mothers and grandmothers going back generations.[6] Ruth's maternal great-grandmother died when her grandmother was only three years old. Because her grandmother was never nurtured by her own mother, she was unable to raise Ruth's mother with much tenderness or maternal holding. Ruth experienced her own mother as emotionally shut down, focused on intellectual, masculine pursuits. Ruth, a deeply feeling woman, had difficulty valuing her own depths and intuition, her own spiritual nature.

Ruth remembered asking her mother about holiness when she was about three years old. Her mother told her the mystics believed that God was in everything. Ruth delighted in imagining God wherever she looked. As a teenager, she discovered Martin Buber's *Tales of the Hasidim* and was profoundly moved by the holy light surrounding the rabbis in the stories. She felt she had found her spiritual home and was devastated when her parents told her that the type of observance spoken of in the stories no longer existed.

Ruth first encountered Reb Zalman in Berkeley in the 1960s and saw "angels at the ends of his hands." As she reclaimed her Judaism, she began studying in the Jewish Renewal rabbinic pastor program. Over time, she found herself connecting with her own ancestors who, she was moved to discover, were the same Hasidim she loved in the tales Buber wrote. She traced her lineage back to the founder of

Lubavitcher Hasidism, Shneur Zalman of Liadi, for whom her uncle was named, and to the Vilna Gaon, a brilliant 18th-century Talmudic and kabbalistic scholar.

When she began studying the Tanya, the holy kabbalistic text written by Rabbi Shneur Zalman, Ruth felt the presence of her ancestors surrounding her. Her great-grandfather was a *shadken* (matchmaker) descended from a lineage of rabbis. Ruth felt herself receiving the flow of spiritual light that was her inheritance and felt the ancestors' support as she deepened into the experience of reclaiming her own spirituality.

In meditations, Ruth visualized all the women in her ancestral lineage loving her, completely accepting her in ways that her own mother was unable to. This connection with her ancestors healed the lack of relatedness she had experienced in her own family, instilling in her a sense of love, comfort, and belonging to a lineage of profound spiritual depth reaching back many generations.

Lillian's story continues

Lillian recalled going to an Orthodox service with her grandmother when she was a girl, sitting in the women's section and listening to the cantor's beautiful voice, which elicited a longing in her for the soulful depth of Judaism. She felt that the love with which her observant grandmother and paternal aunt and uncle had treated her transmitted the essence of the tradition without words. Only later did she realize that her parents had forbidden her extended family from talking with her about Judaism.

In a meditation some years ago, she imagined going into her refrigerator from her childhood home, where she found a double helix. She understood that these were her ancestors arranged in the form of a strand of DNA. In a meditation with her ancestors, she experienced connecting with many of them who appeared as a group made up of both men and women. She climbed up on them and melted into them, feeling very safe and protected. She experienced herself becoming "potential," in an embryonic state prior to taking form. Her female ancestors "told me that I was going to be born."

For Lillian, the connection to both her living ancestors and to those who appeared in her meditations symbolizes a wholeness that supported her healing from the profound spiritual alienation she felt growing up in her assimilated, secular family. The image of the ancestors in the family refrigerator speaks to the frozen ancestral connection, due to her immediate family's inability to transmit her lineage to her.

When she connected to these ancestors in a meditation filled with bodily warmth, her spiritual potential came to life, her essence replenished. The image of the DNA helix on ice is a powerful one. Like the Hebrews who waited 400 years for Serach to guide them to Joseph's bones, Lillian's visions reflect how our own connection to the ancestors waits for us until such time as we are ready to turn toward them and receive their blessings.

Yehiel's story continues

In a meditation Yehiel healed the distance that she had felt from her grandfather throughout her life. She described him as an Orthodox rabbi who looked like the Baal Shem Tov without the *streimel* (fur hat) and a *kohain*—a member of the priestly class. He brought his family to the United States from Lithuania in 1923. Yehiel's father had his Bar Mitzvah on the sea journey to America.

Her grandfather represented many of the things that caused Yehiel ultimately to turn away from Judaism—not being allowed to question anything about the tradition and being excluded from participating in many rituals because she was a girl. Yet he also transmitted strength that no matter what adversity Jews have faced over millennia, they have found ways to survive, which in turn has helped her endure periods of hardship in her own life.

As an adult, Yehiel engaged in Jewish Renewal rituals, where she was encouraged to take her role as a priestly kohain, something she was forbidden to do as a woman in the Orthodox lineage in which she was raised. She felt conflicted about taking this role, unsure whether her grandfather would be happy or horrified.

In the meditation, Yehiel experienced her grandfather handing her a golden *yad* (a hand-shaped pointer used to read Torah) and telling her, "Go read Torah, girl!" Receiving his blessing lovingly dissolved the seemingly insurmountable *mechitzah* (a barrier separating men from women in Orthodox temples) that had lived inside her psyche since childhood.

The ancestors—deep roots of psyche

Recalling the deeply meaningful relationship with her own grandmother who was killed in Auschwitz, Jungian analyst Naomi Ruth Lowinsky writes:

> Whether we hear them or not, the ancestors call us. They throng the air, rustle the leaves of trees, and whisper our names. They wander into memory, dream, and family story, reminding us of parts of ourselves we've neglected, forgotten. They live in precious objects they've handed down to us—a necklace, a pair of candlesticks, a painting. They wake us in the night with terror fingers, reminding us that we must die, must join them in the realm beyond. They orient us, tie us into our lineage, weave our thread into the tapestry of myth, and connect us to our roots and to our place in the generations. For, as Jung says, they are "older and wiser" than we. "They are *axis mundi*, spirit stone, portal to the *mundus imaginalis*."[7]

As we work with the ancestors who appear to us in our dreams, in our family stories, in our imaginings, we open to the storehouse of riches of the cultural collective unconscious. Reconnecting with Judaism is a pathway of remembering, of finding ourselves in the soul chain of our ancestors, both Biblical and personal. Biblical ancestors model both the profound complexities of human experience and engagement with the Divine, showing us how to walk in the human and spiritual realms simultaneously, with humility and grace. At an archetypal level, a young person is initiated into the spiritual life of her people through connection with the ancestors.[8]

Closer to us than Abraham and Sarah, Isaac and Rebecca, are the stories of our personal ancestors. When we engage with the accounts of their lives, we begin to untangle the knotted web of story into which we were born. We come alive to tales of our aunts and grandmothers, our mothers, fighting to define their own lives, overcoming patriarchal systems that limited who they could love and who they could become. And of our grandfathers, fathers and uncles, holding their dignity in the face of systemic blows of shaming and disempowerment.

We respond deeply to stories of our grandparents struggling with their own parents over impassioned beliefs in a utopian future, straining against the strictures of Orthodoxy. And within these stories, new insights arise—the longing of parents to impart their wisdom to their children, the refusal of the children to receive it. Stories of reconciliation, later in life, when animosity turned to tenderness in the face of death, hearts softening toward those who we thought would never lose strength. We imbibe these stories with the lox and bagels, the sticky Passover wine, the brisket. We are hungry for them.

This past holds not only the memories of trauma, but also the powerful essence of the lifeblood of Judaism. Many of us have ancestors who were holy people, teachers, steeped in tradition. As we connect with their energy, which moves through our own blood, we begin to feel grounded in the tradition and allow ourselves to claim it as our own, even if we grew up in homes in which not a single Hebrew prayer was uttered.

Many traditional prayers in Judaism begin with the phrase "by the merit of my ancestors." Perhaps this prayer provides a doorway. Even if we do not know the words of the prayer, or can barely hum the melody, the merit of our ancestors who prayed, who kept the mitzvot, who lived lives of holiness, allows us to find our way back into connection to the tradition that is our inheritance. Claiming our place as descendants of our ancestors, we experience a sense of belonging that arises out of a matrix of holy connectedness. We exist because our ancestors prayed and dreamed us into being.

Ancestral and collective memory

Jung believed that our ancestors dwell with us and are an active part of our psyches. He saw that the profound alienation suffered by moderns stemmed from their egocentric view that focused on the present, cut off from the deep reservoir of the past that lies just beneath the surface of consciousness.

I feel very strongly that I am under the influence of things or questions which were left incomplete and unanswered by my parents and grandparents and more distant ancestors. It often seems as if there were an impersonal karma within a family which is passed on from parents to children. It has always seemed to me that I had to answer questions which fate had posed to my fore-fathers, and which had not yet been answered, or as if I had to complete, or perhaps continue, things which previous ages had left unfinished.[9]

Overcome by his own profound sense of alienation and despair, Jung began a healing process that involved creating a stone tower at Bollingen. In the tower, in retreat from modernity, he became intimately aware of the presence of his ancestors. He wrote that in the tower, he had the sense of living in many centuries simultaneously. He felt that his ancestors' souls were:

> sustained by the atmosphere of the house, since I answer for them the ques-tions that their lives once left behind. I carve out rough answers as best I can. I have even drawn them on the walls ... It is as if a silent, greater family, stretching down the centuries, were peopling the house. There I lived in my second personality [referring to his eternal Self] and see life in the round, as something forever coming into being and passing on.[10]

Jung observed that awareness of our origins bridges the past and the future. Without anchoring ourselves in the deep wisdom of our ancestors, we are "without root and without perspective, defenseless dupes of whatever novelties the future may bring," unable to discern the real from the counterfeit. Culture is grounded in the continuity of history, which "reconciles all opposites and also heals the conflicts that threaten the gifted child."[11]

Jungian analyst Marie-Louise von Franz observed that as one comes into rela-tionship with the fullness of psyche, "having one's ancestral souls behind and supporting one, instead of being cut off from them, is of absolutely essential importance." Being "connected with historical continuity ... from inside, with one's ancestral soul" connects us to the archetypal foundations of the psyche. Tribes cut off from their ancestral continuity by outside influences lose their will and fall into decay.

Von Franz reflects on the focus of many creation myths on long genealogies, including those recounted in the Bible: "The reading and learning by heart of such long catalogues of ancestral kings and Gods therefore has probably to do with the fact that it is a sacred ritual action by which man connects himself with the conti-nuity of the past. It is the countermagic against dissociation."[12]

The cultural memory of a people is transmitted to individuals through practices that connect the personal to the collective. Prayer, rituals, and teachings create gateways to "figures of memory"—significant events and individuals in the col-lective past.[13] Historian Jan Assman notes that observing a sacred calendar and rituals of holy days form "islands of a completely different temporality suspended from time [in which] a collective experience crystallizes, whose meaning, when touched upon, may suddenly become accessible again across millennia."[14]

Cultural historian Pierre Nora recognized that inhabiting collective stories from one's culture creates "vessels and vehicles of memory," an inner space where cultural identity takes form and deepens.[15] By engaging in ritual, we cultivate an internal locus where our sense of identity develops and deepens over time. Participating in Jewish rituals weaves us into the fabric of the cultural psyche, a shared landscape of mythic imagination.

In the mid-19th century, Abraham Geiger and others created the Jewish Reform movement at a time when Judaism was facing startling rates of attrition as Jews assimilated into modern central European cultures. Geiger understood the power of ritual to link individuals with the past, allowing them to place themselves in a lineage and create a meaningful Judaism for future generations. He saw the individual power of imagination that enabled each person to transcend corporeal reality to access the past in a personally meaningful way.[16] He recognized that "memory transposes the self beyond the present, we 'bear within that which is past.'"[17] The inner world of spirit "shows us that knowledge is an activity of memory and imagination that recalls a meaningful past and projects potential future worlds."[18]

> The power of the religious expression of life lies not merely in individual feelings but especially in the living relationship of the individual to the community standing upon the same ground: in the firm grasp of a great, richly remembered past, and in the joy of being led from such a past into a new future.[19]

Geiger recognized that each generation reforms the communal prayer service to make it meaningful in its own time. "Reform is not revolution but a rich dialogue with the past in order to link the present with a future 'standing on the same ground.'"[20] Engaging in traditional observance of the weekly Sabbath and the annual cycle of Torah and holy days allows us to develop a personal and communal reflective space in which we contemplate our connection to the ongoing story of our people, sharing in an experience that has been transmitted across millennia.[21]

Cultural studies scholar Jonathan Boyarin recognizes that this sense of "panchrony," or conversation across the generations, is woven into the fabric of Judaism. In the Talmud, rabbis dialogue across the centuries in an ever-living conversation of ethical and psychological insight about the meaning of life, both practical and spiritual. The continued unfolding of Jewish identity relies on this panchrony, speaking with the ancestors and listening for their responses. "In a panchronistic world, all Jewish generations were, in a sense we find difficult even to comprehend, contemporaneous with one another."[22]

When this collective memory is not actively transmitted, we experience profound loss of soul. Boyarin recognized that traditional panchronistic consciousness was suppressed under the force of massive historical and cultural pressures. Jews have lost communal spaces and communities in which culture was transmitted and shared, have lost tradition, and have experienced genocide, resulting in "the destruction of an imagined national collective, the loss of a 'people.'"[23] Healing requires a reconnection with the ancestors, modeled by the panchronistic conversations of the Talmud.[24]

Serach bat Asher and the transmission of Jewish memory

Serach bat Asher, the guardian of Jewish memory, is a powerful archetype for our time of profound soul loss. Like the Hebrews in ancient Egypt, we may have lost our faith and connection to the past. Yet, when the soul is ready to awaken, Serach is present, providing the guidance we need to find our way back into relationship with the ancestors. How do we begin to hear the voice of Serach carrying the messages of our ancestors? How can she find us—we who have been so cut off from the transmission, who do not even know that she is there for us to call on? Perhaps she comes to us, unbidden—perhaps our ancestors are seeking *us*, in response to our own longing for them.

As the people made their way across the Red Sea, Serach witnessed the journey. As we too make our way out of mitzrayim, as we step onto the pathway that opens to the larger story of who we are, we may feel the presence of the ancestors supporting us. We may discover our connection to a lineage that has withstood enormous adversity to pass onto us the gift of spiritual wisdom, insight, and perseverance. As we lean into their strength, we find our own.

Echoes of the Hebrew Goddess Asherah

Jacob offers Serach a blessing in return for her sitting with him and mending his broken heart: "May you live forever and never die." The midrash offers various accounts of Serach's longevity—she enters Eretz Yisrael with the Hebrew people, and is still alive in the time of King David. We are told that Serach entered Heaven when she was a thousand years old. She enters Heaven alive, never having to experience the pain of death, an honor granted to only two others in Jewish tradition—the great archangel Enoch and Elijah the prophet.

According to another legend, her grave is in Linjan, a small village near Isfahan, Iran, near a 2,000-year-old cemetery and small synagogue. Some Jewish Persian mystics believed that she died in Isfahan, where a gravesite was dedicated to her, in the 12th century:

> She is the bearer of an oral tradition and of secret knowledge, a power of life and redemption. In this capacity she seems to function as an eternal figure, rather like a female counterpart to Elijah, who will reveal the hidden time of the final redemption when he heralds the coming of the Messiah.[25]

As an eternal figure, Serach resembles the archetype of Asherah, the Great Mother Goddess worshipped by the earliest Hebrews. For many centuries Asherah was worshipped as the Divine partner of YHVH. Serach bat Asher may represent how the spirit of the Great Mother abided with the people in exile and guided them toward redemption.

In 1985, I traveled to Israel for my older brother's wedding. Immersed in my struggle with Jewish patriarchalism, I believed there was no room for the Sacred Feminine within the tradition. And so I was completely stunned by a small exhibit at a granary museum. There, amid the otherwise banal exhibits on agricultural history, was an entire wall filled with female figurines. The museum sign identified them as "Fertility statues," but having immersed myself in feminist spirituality over the previous decade it was clear to me—these were Goddesses! But who were they? The question stirred my soul at the deepest level.

Israeli anthropologist Raphael Patai's work explores the long history of the worship of the Hebrew Goddess Asherah, present in the earliest stages of Judaism and continuing robustly through the time of the Holy Temple in Jerusalem. Her worship was widespread in villages and in sacred tree groves throughout the lands of Samaria and Judea that made up ancient Israel. Asherah is a Great Mother Goddess like those found throughout the Near East in the time that Judaism developed. Small figurines were planted in sacred groves, symbolizing the peoples' prayers for fertility for their crops and for their families. Women in childbirth clutched Asherah figurines for strength and protection.[26]

Raphael Patai suggests that Serach's father Asher's name may come from Leah's calling out to Asherah while attending her handmaid Zilpah's birth of her son. Leah exclaimed "'Happy am I! For the daughters will call me happy.' And she called his name Asher."[27] Asher and Asherah share the same root as *ashrei*, the Hebrew word for happiness.

Few are aware of the Hebrew Goddess who was worshipped alongside the Masculine aspect of God for centuries. Raphael Patai's work explicates the rich history of Asherah and other Hebrew Goddesses who are acknowledged in the Biblical text, and the ongoing tug of war between those who worshipped Her and the efforts to end Her long reign.

King Solomon built the Holy Temple in Jerusalem, inspired in part by his love of the Queen of Sheba. In Jewish cosmology, the Queen of Sheba carries the profoundly mysterious and compelling aspects of the Dark Feminine. In the Temple, light and dark, masculine and feminine, hidden and revealed, were joined in a *hieros gamos*, or sacred marriage. Patai observed that the Solomonic Temple stood in Jerusalem for 370 years; and for no less than 236 years, or two-thirds of that time, "the statue of Asherah was present in the Temple, and her worship was a part of the legitimate religion approved and led by the king, the court, and the priesthood and opposed by only a few prophetic voices crying out against it at relatively long intervals."[28]

The 16th-century kabbalistic master Rabbi Yeshayahu ben Avraham wrote, "The Asherah was beloved by our ancestors."[29] Asherah worship was symbolized by poles that were sunk deep into the earth, reflecting Her generative function as the ground from which all life springs. In the mystical tradition that emerged in the Middle Ages, the Shekhinah was seen as the carrier of the Divine Feminine energy. In kabbalistic thought She is associated with Malchut, kingdom, the sefirah representing the ground of being itself. Rabbi ben Avraham observed the kinship between Asherah and Shekhinah when he noted, "The Shekhinah is drawn mostly to the realm of trees."[30] The central image of kabbalah is the Tree of Life, perhaps an echo of the Asherah tree groves where the sacred was honored in ancient rituals.

Because all cosmological systems tend toward wholeness, Biblical injunctions against Asherah worship and the suppression of the Feminine aspect of the Godhead could not be sustained. The kabbalists replaced the worship of Asherah with the Shekhinah, the manifestation of God's presence in the world. According to the Zohar, the Sacred Feminine once represented by Asherah was subsumed within and continued to live in the energy of the Godhead, represented by the second letter, the *Heh*, of the tetragrammaton, YHVH, representing Shekhinah.[31]

Erich Neumann recognized that during the Paleolithic era, for almost 40,000 years before the rise of Judaism, the Great Mother was the central figure of Divinity. As Judaism developed, it brought with it a new consciousness—that of the Divine as beyond any representable form, transcendent, encompassing all. The people may have believed that worship of Asherah in the form of poles and pillars may have kept them linked to an older time in which God could be reduced to an image, a view that they were seeking to transcend. Perhaps to move forward into the unknown, the people believed that they had to outgrow their Mother. Yet even as Asherah worship was prohibited, the sacred tree assumed its place as the central image in Judaism, the cosmic Tree of Life, in the menorah, and as the Torah herself—the *Eitz Chaim*, rolled on pillars of acacia wood, sacred to Asherah.

We live in a time when the patriarchal stage of consciousness can no longer be sustained. Overvaluing the transcendent, we have forgotten that the earth itself is Divine, bringing us to the unfathomable reality that the continuation of life for many species, including our own, is in jeopardy. The perilous nature of our time requires us to honor the Divine immanent in the Creation. I recall when I first became aware of that Divine immanence. Walking amid the ancient redwoods along the beautiful Navarro river in northern California, I saw each plant, each tree, bursting forth with life, with numinous Godliness, like that of the burning bush itself—the flame inside the living Tree of Life, that holy immanence of the Shekhinah, called by our mothers, *Asherah*.

Elaine's story continues

Elaine recalled the meaning of a mortar and pestle that belonged to her maternal grandfather. When her mother was dying, the two of them were going through the family treasures and Elaine asked, for the first time, about the mortar and pestle. She'd always assumed it had belonged to her father, who was a pharmacist. Her mother told her that her maternal grandfather had brought it with him from the

Ukraine, to grind poppy seeds. She recalled that her grandfather had studied to be a rabbi in the Ukraine, but by the time he came to the United States, he had become a socialist and only wanted to teach Hebrew.

Elaine shed tears of gratitude that the deeper meaning this item held was revealed to her while her mother was still alive. Her tears communicated both the potency of this simple object as well as the tenuousness of her connection to the past, recognizing how easily the deep significance of an item can be lost forever. Ground poppy seeds are traditionally used to make *hamantaschen*, cookies eaten at Purim, commemorating Queen Esther's victory in saving the Jewish people from destruction in ancient Persia. Elaine was moved that this seemingly mundane object held great resonance, as a remembrance of the shtetl life her grandfather had left behind. That he would carry a mortar and pestle with him across the ocean suggests its meaningfulness to him as well, perhaps stemming from his desire to maintain the traditions of Purim and other holiday observances.

Hamantaschen are said to represent the hat of Haman, the enemy of the Jews whom Queen Esther helped vanquish. Yet the triangular-shaped hamantaschen may also carry a deeper imprint of the ancient Sacred Feminine. The women of the Hebrew Bible "baked cakes for the Queen of Heaven." Items associated with the Great Mother Goddess often were triangular, representing the vulva or uterus. Esther, Queen of Persia, may also represent an aspect of the Hebrew Goddess Astarte, the Queen of Heaven. In the last days of Elaine's mother's life, this ancestral ritual related to celebrating the feminine in Judaism in her maternal lineage was transmitted to her, healing the bridge to her ancestral memory.

Ancestor healing

Serach bat Asher carries the energy of the Divine Feminine, providing the holding presence of the "mothering other" that we need to enable us to piece together the shards of our broken families and history.[32] Serach joins us as we do the work of healing our family complexes.

As Serach sits with Jacob as he waits for the return of his son Joseph, Serach carries our own ancestors' longing for us, as we once again turn toward them. Seeing our family complexes in the light of a larger history, we begin to have compassion for the choices our older family members have made. We begin to see life from their perspectives, understanding that the weight of history they were each asked to carry was simply too great to bear, and in turning toward survival, they provided a pathway for our own lives to unfold. We begin to accept that their burden is also ours to carry, and as we take the bundle of pain from their shoulders and gently begin to unwrap it, we allow ourselves to feel their grief, terror, shame, and loss as we begin to find our place in the shalshelet, the great chain of souls. As we do our grief work, we discover the gift—that beneath the powerful unexpressed feelings lies a torrent of love and light, our inheritance as well, that flows forth from Eden, flooding our lives with grace and opening the flow to our descendants.

Serach abides until we are ready to awaken. When we do, she provides us with the teachings that link us to our ancestors. Even if we never consciously received the transmission, never went to temple or learned Hebrew, we can listen to the voices of the ancestors whispering to us in our dreams and can open the Torah of our hearts to our inherited essence. As we do, Serach is there to help us connect back to the Tree of Life, the ancestral tree on which we are all branches. Drawing on the strength of the ancestors that flows out through the trunk and through us, we begin to bear fruit.

As we create a bridge from the ancient world left behind and bring its meaning and resonance into the present, we may experience a sense of profound loss and longing. Yet we may also experience a powerful influx of meaning and healing as we receive the spiritual light of the inheritance that is passed down through us, reminding us of what we already carry in our bones.

Notes

1 Naomi Ruth Lowinsky (2014) "Self-Portrait with Ghost: The Art of Lament and Redemption," *Jung Journal: Culture & Psyche* 8, no. 3: 37–65, 40.
2 Genesis 50:24–25.
3 Avivah Zornberg, *Particulars of Rapture: Reflections on Exodus* (New York: Doubleday, 2001), 30.
4 Mekhilta, Beshalach, 2; cited in Simcha Paull Raphael, *Living and Dying in Ancient Times: Death, Burial, and Mourning in Biblical Tradition* (Boulder, CO: Albion-Andalus, 2015), 44; Howard Schwartz, *Tree of Souls: The Mythology of Judaism* (New York: Oxford University Press, 2004), 379.
5 Mekhilta, Beshalach, 2, and Midrash Ha'Gadol, end of Genesis cited in Raphael, *Living and Dying in Ancient Times*, 44–45.
6 Naomi Ruth Lowinsky, *The Motherline: Every Woman's Journey to Find Her Female Roots* (Skiatook, OK: Fisher King Press, 1992/2009).
7 Lowinsky, "Self-Portrait with Ghost," 38.
8 Emma Jung and Marie-Louise von Franz, *The Grail Legend* (Boston: Sigo Press, 1970), 75. Emma Jung and von Franz recognized that a connection to the ancestors was necessary for a young person to be initiated into the spiritual life of a people.
9 C.G. Jung, *Memories, Dreams, Reflections*, edited by Aniela Jaffé (New York: Vintage, 1989), 233.
10 Ibid, 235–237.
11 Marie Louise von Franz, *Creation Myths* (Boston and London: Shambhala, 1995); citing C.G. Jung, "The Gifted Child," in *The Collected Works of C.G. Jung, The Development of Personality*, Vol. 17 (Princeton, NJ: Princeton University Press, 1954), para. 250.
12 Von Franz, *Creation Myths*, 309.
13 Jan Assman, "Collective Memory and Cultural Identity," *New German Critique* 65 (1995): 128–129.
14 Ibid.
15 Yosef Hayim Yerushalmi, *Zakhor: Jewish History and Jewish Memory* (New York: Schocken Books, 1989), xxvii; citing Pierre Nora, ed., *Les lieux de mémoire, I: La République; II–IV: La Nation* (Paris, 1984 et seq.); and Nora's introductory essay to vol. I, entitled "Entre Mémoire et Histoire: la problématique des lieux," in *Realms of History: Rethinking the French Past*, edited by Lawrence D. Kitzman, translated by Arthur Goldhammer (New York: Columbia University Press, 1996). Citing Pierre

Nora's work on French collective memory, Yerushalmi writes that "Nora's conception of 'lieux de mémoire' corresponds closely to what I have called … 'vessels and vehicles of memory.'"

16 Ken Koltun-Fromm, "Historical Memory in Abraham Geiger's Account of Modern Jewish Identity," *Jewish Social Studies* 7, no. 1 (2000): 112; quoting Abraham Geiger, *Das Judentum und seine Geschichte*, translated by Ken Koltun-Fromm (Breslau, 1864).

17 Ibid, 113.

18 Ibid.

19 Ibid, 114; quoting Abraham Geiger, "Nothwendigkeit und Maass einer Reofrm des judischen Gottesdienstes," in *Nachgelassene Schriten I*, edited by Ludwig Geiger, translated by Ken Koltun-Fromm (Berlin, 1875), 205.

20 Ibid, 115; quoting Abraham Geiger, "Unser Gottesdienst," *Judische Zeitschrift fur Wissenschaft und Leben* 6, no. 2 (1868).

21 Assman, "Collective Memory and Cultural Identity."

22 Jonathan Boyarin, *Storm from Paradise: The Politics of Jewish Memory* (Minneapolis, MN: University of Minnesota Press, 1992), 128.

23 Ibid.

24 Ibid.

25 Moshe Reiss, "Serach bat Asher in Rabbinic Literature," *Jewish Bible Quarterly* 42, no. 1 (January–March 2014), 49.

26 Raphael Patai, *The Hebrew Goddess* (Detroit, MI: Wayne State University Press, 1967, 1978).

27 Genesis 30:13.

28 Patai, *The Hebrew Goddess*, 50. Patai notes, "The worship of Asherah was introduced into the Jerusalem Temple by Solomon's son, King Rehoboam, in 928 BCE and worshiped for 36 years, until King Asa removed it. Restored by King Joash in 826 BCE, it remained for a full century, until King Hezekiah removed it. After an absence of 27 years, Asherah was back again, when King Manasseh replaced her in 698 BCE. She remained in the Temple for 78 years until King Joshiah removed her. Upon Joshiah's death 11 years later, she was brought back, where she remained until the Temple's destruction 23 years later in 586 BCE."

29 Gershon Winkler, personal communication, July 2019; citing *Sefer HaSh'lah, Vai Ha'Amudim*, Chapter 17.

30 Ibid.

31 Zohar, I, 1:149a, 270–271.

32 Nanette C. Auerhahn and Dori Laub, "The Primal Scene of Anxiety: The Dynamic Interplay Between Knowledge and Fantasy of the Holocaust in Children of Survivors," *Psychoanalytic Psychology* 15, no. 3 (1998): 360–361.

Chapter 9

Joseph—light out of darkness

And if I say, "Surely the darkness shall envelop me,
and the light about me shall be night;"
Even the darkness is not too dark for Thee,
but the night shineth as the day; the darkness is even as the light.
For Thou hast made my reins;
Thou hast knit me together in my mother's womb.

Psalms 139:11–13[1]

For many, reconnection with Judaism begins as a solitary journey. We separate from the collective versions of Judaism that do not fit us, or we separate from secular families in which our spiritual light was not recognized. Often, the journey takes us into the depths through a period of difficulty, a dark night of the soul, in which we find, unexpectedly, the light of the Divine opening to us. In this chapter, we explore the life of the Biblical Joseph. Reflecting on his life's journey, we see a model for how we may reconnect with the sacred even when separated from our ancestral lineage.

After the major migrations of the late 19th and early 20th centuries, after the dislocation of our ancestors from Jewish worlds into modernity, after the *Shoah*, after the loss of *Yiddishkeit*, alone in the depths, like Joseph in the dungeons of Pharaoh, we may open to receive Divine guidance through the dreams and visionary messages that come to us. Listening deeply, we learn how to live with integrity, and how to develop our inner trickster to survive adversity. We come to understand how we grow through suffering.

Joseph and the Exodus

Four hundred years prior to the Exodus, Joseph, son of the beloveds Jacob and Rachel, lay on his deathbed in Egypt surrounded by his family. In their youth, Joseph's brothers scapegoated him and threw him into a pit, from which he was sold by passing traders into slavery in Egypt. Joseph began his solitary descent into Egypt. He experienced transformation from enduring profound suffering and adversity. Through the wisdom he gained, he moved out from the lowest point of his descent, leaving the dungeons of Pharaoh to assume a role of great power in Egypt. He was then able to bring his entire family to dwell there, where they grew from twelve tribes to a nation at the time of the Exodus some four hundred years later. Through the many travails he suffered, Joseph gained great wisdom—wisdom that enabled him to save his people from starvation and annihilation.

Despite overcoming these many trials, Joseph, at the end of his life, foresees the tremendous hardships his descendants will yet face, as well as their eventual liberation, a collective journey that mirrors his solitary descent and redemption. Facing death, Joseph tells his family that in the future, God will redeem the people of Israel and lead them out of Egypt to the Promised Land. He shares the wisdom gained from his own suffering to assure them that even when things appear hopeless, God will not forsake them.

In the last lines of the Book of Genesis, Joseph tells his family, "I die; but God will surely remember you, and bring you up out of this land unto the land which He swore to Abraham, to Isaac, and to Jacob." Joseph swore to his children, "God will surely remember you, and ye shall carry up my bones from hence." Joseph died at 110 years old, and his family embalmed him and placed his body in a coffin in Egypt.[2] In a midrashic tale, Joseph tells his family that they must "surely carry my bones with you from hence, for if my remains are taken to Canaan, the Lord will be with you in the light … Also take with you the bones of your mother Zilpah and bury them near the sepulchre of Bilhah and Rachel."[3]

Four hundred years later, as the plagues descend and the people are preparing to leave Egypt, Moses assumes the task of finding where Joseph is buried. The people cannot leave without fulfilling this promise made to Joseph to take his bones with them. With the help of Serach bat Asher, Moses locates and summons Joseph's coffin from the depths of the Nile, grateful that he has been able to fulfill the oath sworn by Joseph at his deathbed.

Through all the years wandering in the desert, from the time they left Egypt until their arrival in the Promised Land, the Hebrew people carried with them two arks—one containing Joseph's bones and the other carrying the Torah given at Sinai. When asked by passersby why they carried two arks, the people responded that the one, Joseph, fulfilled all that was written in the other.[4]

Joseph's life is a living Torah. Understanding it shows us how to live a life of integrity. He models how we may maintain a connection to the sacred despite the seemingly unbearable suffering that can overtake our lives. Joseph undergoes a series of descents, first thrown by his brothers, overtaken by envy, into a pit in Shechem, from which he is sold into slavery in Egypt, then into the dungeons of Pharaoh where he experiences complete despair and hopelessness.

Joseph's is a shaman's journey of ego death and rebirth. He dies to his small self and is reborn into a leader who follows the path that God shows him. He fulfills his destiny, not on his own behalf, but on behalf of his people. Joseph represents the true meaning of *kabbalah*, which is wisdom that is *received*. Unlike the direct transmission from God that his ancestors received, or the written Torah that would guide his descendants, Joseph's connection with the Divine was cultivated through listening to dreams and a sense of inner knowing that guided him.

He models what Erich Neumann notes is the most decisive stage of spiritual experience—the challenge to the conscious mind to come into relationship with the overwhelming mystery of the unconscious, which often occurs through an encounter with the numinous. Such experience can profoundly overwhelm the ego, yet overcoming that danger strengthens the "steadfastness of consciousness. The soundness of an ego that can be transformed, yet not broken … leads to a revolution of the personality, to the renewal of consciousness and to the completion of man."[5]

Exiled and separated from his people, Joseph develops the ability to engage with and not be overwhelmed by the numinous. From his individuated perspective, he is able to catalyze a process of *teshuvah* (repentance) for his brothers, facilitating their development into their wholeness. The twelve brothers, progenitors of the tribes of Israel, reclaim their own spiritual light and depth. The Hebrew people, who grow from the twelve tribes to the nation that leaves Egypt, undergo a prolonged period of descent and suffering that prepares each of them to come into an individuated relationship to the Divine, each becoming a spiritual vessel that can receive the transmission at Sinai. Their collective journey is prefigured by Joseph's solitary one, demonstrating how we may each cultivate our capacity to become a vessel for holiness.

In our own time, many Jews have felt alienated from their familial expression or rejection of Judaism, or have felt exiled in their families for following their own inner guidance. Some, like Joseph, found in the darkness a personal relationship with God that sustained them. Many who developed a renewed relationship with Judaism through Jewish Renewal, Jewish feminism, and other approaches that recovered the lost light of the tradition, brought that light back into their families and communities and shared their matured understanding with the larger collective. Like the ancient Hebrews in the desert carrying the bones of Joseph, we feel how the ancestors live in *our* bones, in our DNA. We are their descendants, and also the future ancestors transmitting the lineage to the next generations.

Once the Hebrew people leave Egypt and reach the Promised Land, they bury Joseph's remains at Shechem, the place where Joseph was first thrown into the pit and abducted into slavery. "God spake to the tribes, saying, 'From Shechem did ye steal him, and unto Shechem, shall ye return him.'"[6] With this sacred act, Joseph's journey comes full circle, and the promise of redemption that he foretold is fulfilled.

The loss of the mother and the descent into darkness: the dry pit

Joseph, his eleven brothers, his sister Dinah and other sisters who remain unnamed in the text comprise the progenitors of the tribes of Israel. Joseph is the eldest son of Jacob and Rachel. As a youth, Joseph receives a coat of many colors from his father, which ignites great envy among his brothers, perhaps symbolizing Jacob's awareness of Joseph's unique beauty and his role as the one who would ensure the transmission of the covenant passed down from his grandfather Abraham.

God comes to Joseph in his dreams. Early in his life, Joseph shares the dreams without reflection. As he matures, he learns to sit with a dream and decipher its true meaning. As a youth, Joseph has two dreams that he tells his brothers. In one, *they are all binding sheaves in the field. Joseph's sheaf stands upright and the brothers' sheaves bow down to it.* The brothers respond, "'Shalt thou indeed reign over us? Or shalt thou indeed have dominion over us?' And they hate him yet the more for his dreams and for his words." In the second dream, *the sun and moon and eleven stars bow down to him.* He shares this dream with his brothers and father, and his father Jacob says, "Shall I and thy mother and thy brethren indeed come to bow down to thee to the earth?"[7]

In truth, the dreams were prophetic, but Joseph had not yet developed the wisdom to understand the voice of the Self that was speaking through him. Instead, his brothers and fathers experience him as inflated, which catalyzes his brothers' envy and enmity.

Jacob sends Joseph to see how his brothers, who are tending sheep in Shechem, are faring. Seeing him approach, the brothers say to each other, "Behold, this dreamer cometh. Come now therefore, and let us slay him, and cast him into one of the pits, and we will say: An evil beast hath devoured him; and we shall see what will become of his dreams."[8] Reuben, the eldest, convinces them not to slay Joseph. Instead, they steal his colorful coat and throw him into a dry pit. Midianite traders passing by abduct Joseph from the pit and sell him into slavery in Egypt.

In this generation, we see the continuation of the sibling rivalries that existed in earlier generations—Ishmael being cast out and Isaac receiving the covenant; Jacob receiving the birthright over Esau. In previous generations, the brothers reconciled, but in Joseph's, the rivalry grows malignant, resulting in his near-death and abduction into slavery.

By the time of Joseph's generation, the presence of the Feminine, which has played such a powerful role in the stories of Sarah, Rebecca, Leah, and Rachel, begins to decline. As discussed earlier, Rachel secreted the teraphim out of her father Laban's home. When confronted by Laban asking for their return, Rachel, who is sitting on the statuary, refuses to get up from her seat, saying she is in "the woman's way."[9] Jacob, presuming without inquiring, denies that anyone has them and says that if anyone does, they will surely die an early death. He unknowingly condemns his beloved to death out of ignorance or proper regard for her commitment to the Sacred Feminine.

Rather than give up the teraphim, Rachel invokes her womanhood as a shield against having to reveal them. In this period of the ascendant masculine, Rachel pays for this act with her very life, dying giving birth to Joseph's brother Benjamin. Joseph grows up without the guidance of a loving mother who could have helped him ground his spiritual light in a related way. Without the support of his mother, he loses connection to the ground of being. He experiences a split, where his true self goes into hiding. His false self, inflated and grandiose, irritates and alienates his brothers. Joseph is cut off from the feeling of connectedness to his own family and is without support or solace. He is profoundly alone.

Joseph's brothers, enraged by his inflation, respond to him with hatred and envy, throwing him into a pit, described in the text as a dry well. According to the Zohar, the well is a symbol of the Shekhinah, the place where lovingkindness has overflowed at the meeting of Isaac's servant and Rebecca, and between Jacob and Rachel.[10] In the generation of Joseph, instead of flowing forth lovingkindness, the well is dry, symbolizing the loss of the feminine qualities of eros and relatedness. Joseph is thrown into the dry pit at Shechem, the same place in which his sister Dinah lay with the prince of the region. We are never told how Dinah felt, whether or not she engaged in a consensual encounter. Dinah does not define her own destiny. The brothers take it upon themselves to exact harsh retribution upon the men of Shechem. It seems that the brother's aggression continues in their cruelty towards Joseph.

The disconnection from the feminine in Joseph's generation leads to a loss of relatedness among the brothers. They devolve into envy and competitiveness—there is an absence of love. In families that have experienced trauma, power often overtakes love as the central way of relating. Positioning oneself, protecting oneself, staving off attack, cutting others down to size—all are symptoms of a family in which the capacity for love has been profoundly injured. Only by pursuing his path of individuation, by enduring his own descent to find the strength of his soul-essence, can Joseph develop the capacity to bring healing and true relatedness back to the family.

Joseph's brothers see the shining light within Joseph and seek to destroy it, hoping to garner their father's favor for themselves instead. Yet in disowning and projecting their own light onto Joseph, they lose touch with the Divine spark they each carry within and retreat into bitterness and spite. Because they cannot see the good as existing within themselves, the brothers seek to destroy it outside themselves. Ann and Barry Ulanov reflect on how envy keeps us disconnected from our own spiritual core:

> When we envy we are not willing to find and live within our own self, with all the hard nasty work that that involves. Instead we want to seize another more glittering self ... We hunger and desire to be a person of substance, but we are unwilling to nurture the only substance we can ever possess—our own.[11]

We reject the self that lives within us, "the ordering center of our whole psyche. Rejection of the self keeps us envious, and envy keeps us rejecting. Our ego's task is to build relation to this larger center of the self which acts, as Jung says, like a god-image within us."[12] Joseph's descent catalyzes a lengthy process of wounding and exile to make possible the redemption of his family, the twelve tribes of Israel, and the nation they will become.

Joshua's story

Joseph's exile provides a framework for understanding the suffering we may undergo when we are wounded in our own families. As a child, Joshua shared a strong spiritual bond with his father. Like Jacob adorning Joseph with a coat of many colors, Joshua delighted in being wrapped, with his sister, protectively under his father's *tallit* (prayer shawl) while his father would pray, the three of them singing and praying together. Passover Seders at his bubbe's (grandmother's) house, with his extended family, were filled with joy, as family members offered different melodies for the various songs.

Joshua's mother, who had converted to Judaism to marry his father, became a Unitarian after they divorced when Joshua was six years old. Joshua looked forward to his Bar Mitzvah. Immediately after the ceremony, however, his mother announced she was moving to another town with his sister. Joshua felt that that the significance of his Bar Mitzvah and his commitment to Judaism was somehow tied to her leaving. "I'd just had this tremendous experience of coming into adulthood, and then she left."

Joshua lived in a low-income rural area, where the neighborhood kids were not Jewish and did not understand Joshua's relationship to his tradition. He felt separated from the more affluent Jewish kids with whom he had attended Hebrew school. Feeling lost and alone, he began using marijuana daily, which totally obliterated the spiritual connection he had experienced as a child. He recalled, "I felt so tired of being different from the people I hung out with and different from my community—my sister was the only other Jew in my school, and she left with our mother."

Without the regular Hebrew school attendance required for the Bar Mitzvah, or family or peer support, he had difficultly staying connected to Judaism. "I was living in a trailer park. One of the people who rode the same bus I did asked me if I wanted to get high. I saw that as the opportunity to leave behind the Judaism that was making me so different and to connect with people who were my peers, so that summer I spent all of my Bar Mitzvah money on pot."

He refused his father's invitations to go to *shul*. "I just couldn't go to that sweet sacred experience. When my dad would go to *shul*, I would sit in my living room and get high and watch Saturday morning cartoons—that became my Shabbat practice! I totally lost my religious connection and replaced it with just shutting down."

His father asked him to leave, to separate him from the other young people in the trailer park, because his marijuana use had gotten so bad. He went to live with his mother and sister. When he got clean at 17 years old, he had already assumed a secular identity. He stopped calling himself Joshua. "I turned off any Jewish connection and took on a completely different persona. I wasn't Christian, and if people would ask me, I would say I was Jewish, but I just didn't have any sense of Jewish identity." He noticed that he felt a tremendous amount of anger and sadness at relinquishing his heritage. "Coming back to that moment now, I realize I had a lot of grief there that I hadn't talked about to anyone."

Like Joseph, Joshua's loss of his mother left him without the support he needed to nurture the inner light. He descended into a profound state of aloneness without connection to what had previously sustained him spiritually. It took Joshua years to reconnect with his Jewish spirituality. As he did, he recovered the spark of holiness he had experienced as a child with his father in *shul* and with his extended family. Eventually, he felt called to train to become a teacher of Jewish meditation. He shared a dream he had during a retreat that was part of his training.

> *I'm standing on a concrete platform and people are giving me these tools. They're kind of like hole punchers; they're big and there are two of them. I start pushing them down into the ground, and the concrete starts to shatter underneath my feet. Underneath it, it's just miles down to where the earth is. The concrete's actually shattering beneath my feet, and the underlying mesh that holds the concrete together is falling away.*
>
> *As this starts to happen, I see a door there and I go towards it, and someone helps me through the door and says, "You've got to make sure to lock that." So I put a lock on the door and put caution tape over it. And then that same person says, "You know there's an easier way to go down." I walk toward a set of stairs, and the dream ends.*

Joshua consulted with a Jewish Renewal rabbi and scholar of Jewish mysticism, who told him the dream reflected the tools he was being given through Jewish meditation and prayer practice. The rabbi suggested the concrete represented the way he'd been in life up to this point, and the tools he had used to protect himself. But as he looked beneath the concrete, he saw the ground was falling away. The stairs symbolized that he was being invited to begin a safe descent.

The experiences Joshua had at the meditation teacher-training retreat led to the shattering of a concretized way of being that was now ready to change. He saw that locking the door meant not returning to his old ways if he was going to move forward in his life and develop the tools he needed to connect with others and with his own spirituality. He recognized that he had previously relied on his intellect and had not been connected to his emotions or his body. Joshua recognized how those patterns were beginning to transform.

Like Joseph, Joshua's loss of relationship with his mother during his adolescence resulted in a disconnection from his core sense of self. That disconnection can devolve into a sense of grandiosity, such as Joseph experienced, or in a dissociative retreat into addiction, the road Joshua had taken. Even after getting sober, Joshua continued to defend against his feelings through relying on his intellect. On a collective level, Jews have relied on thinking and achievement in response to trauma, often staving off powerful feelings stored in the emotions or the body.

Yet with the development of his meditation and prayer practice, Joshua was able to tend to his feelings and to reconnect with the whole of his being. The stairway provided a pathway along which Joshua could reconnect with the ground of being, descending slowly and consciously, rather than plummeting. As we grow spiritually, we no longer have to be abducted, as Joseph was when he was thrown into the pit. Instead, we can choose to engage consciously with the depths. Joshua's dream reflects the path of individuation through a chosen descent, rather than passively remaining in a stagnant state of isolation.

Joseph's journey into Egypt—suffering in service of the soul

Joseph is abducted from the dry pit and sold by Midianites into slavery in Egypt. In the midrashic text *Sefer HaYashar*, written in the early 17th century and perhaps drawn from earlier extant texts, the depth of Joseph's suffering and terror is revealed.[13] The Midianites gather Joseph from the pit and sell him to the Ishmaelites (descendants of Abraham and Hagar's son Ishmael), who transport him as a captive to Egypt.[14] He is so frightened that he may not survive the journey—that he may literally die of terror. Screaming and wailing, his cries go unheard. At one point, the caravan stops, and Joseph sees the spirit of his deceased mother, Rachel, at the spot where she died in childbirth. There, "Joseph cried aloud upon his mother's grave, and he said, 'O my mother, my mother, O thou who didst give me birth, awake now, and rise and see thy son, how he has been sold for a slave, and no one to pity him.'"

Joseph hears Rachel's voice respond to him from beneath the ground, assuring him that God is watching over him and will not leave him:

> "My son, my son Joseph, I have heard the voice of thy weeping and the voice of thy lamentation; I have seen thy tears; I know thy troubles, my son, and it grieves me for thy sake, and abundant grief is added to my grief. Now therefore my son, Joseph my son, hope to the Lord, and wait for him and do not fear, for the Lord is with thee, he will deliver thee from all trouble. Rise my son, go down unto Egypt with thy masters, and do not fear, for the Lord is with thee, my son."[15]

Rachel's comforting words alleviate Joseph's terror and give him the strength to endure the great suffering to come. An embodiment of the Shekhinah, Rachel compassionately witnesses the pain and suffering of Her people. In another midrash, we learn that her spirit dwells on the road to Bethlehem, eternally weeping for her children. Here, she assures Joseph that God is with him, and that his suffering has a larger meaning, if he will endure it.

Joseph begins to trust that his suffering is in the service of something greater. He is able to see himself as an instrument in God's larger design, even though he does not understand what that is. The formerly inflated ego opens to the suffering, recognizing that it is guided by the Self. Now the nature of Joseph's journey has changed. Understanding that his suffering has a larger purpose, and that he is seen and held by his beloved mother, Joseph surrenders to the descent.

Julie's soul-shattering renewal

For Julie, the call to return to Judaism came at "a moment of deep depression and total crisis in my life." After many years of training as a medical professional, she quit, for the first time not following the script of what she was "supposed" to do. She had no sense of who she really was. Her marriage was failing, and her husband did not support her choice to leave her career.

Julie's mother was a Holocaust survivor who had let her own father and her husband decide her life's course. In breaking with this patriarchal worldview and finding her own true path, separate from her husband's and parents' expectations, Julie experienced a shattering of her ego and a descent into the depths. She recalled this "time of complete tearing and ripping of all the veils that I didn't even know that I had."

Julie drew an image of being crumpled on the floor, lying prostrate. She reflected, "I was suicidal; it was a really bad time. I was brought to my knees and crumpled in the fetal position." Looking at the picture she mused, "It kind of looks like some people's prayer position. I felt, in that silence that there was something beyond the whole way that I contextualized my life and that's the moment! That's the beginning of the whole rest of my life!"

Looking up, she noticed a wooden box on her bookshelf that once contained the sewing machine that her great-aunt had sent from Germany before the outbreak of the war. Both the side and the front of the box were stamped with large letters NOT WANTED, meaning it could be sent out of Germany.

Julie's mother had narrowly escaped the Shoah, and became severely depressed following her mother-in-law's (Julie's paternal grandmother's) suicide. Julie tried to fit into the family mold by succeeding professionally. As she connected with her essence and let go of the life she had believed she was supposed to live, she felt a despair that connected to the unmetabolized grief in her family. The sewing machine, sent from Germany as her aunt left during the rise of the Nazis, represented the trauma of being exiled, of being "not wanted," but it also meant the sewing machine could be passed on to her. Julie worked with the paradoxical meaning of "not wanted" within her own lineage and life. She began to release the feeling that she was not wanted because she was not meeting outwardly imposed expectations from her family and marriage, and she stopped trying to fit into a pattern that was too small for her. This realization freed her to move into a life she could claim as her own.

Descent—the transformative *nigredo*

In the kabbalistic view, we each carry within us a great light, a Divine spark that is the essence of what Jung called the Self. But when our ego, or conscious awareness, becomes too small to house the light of who we truly are, we may encounter periods of great suffering. We may experience the death of a loved one, the loss of a marriage or a career path. When these things happen, the sense of who we thought we were is blown apart. Yet, if we can trust that this shattering is in service of a greater unfolding, we can open to the growth that such transformative losses carry. Psychotherapist Estelle Frankel reflects that underneath the shards of the shattered vessels of our too-small personalities, we find the hidden light of the Self.[16] As we gather these sparks, these scintillae, of the Self, we begin to shape a new vessel—one that is strong enough to carry this greater light. We become more and more of who we are—which is often vastly different than who we thought we were.

The descent is the encounter with death, decay, despair, darkness, a dark night of the soul, a night sea journey. In alchemy, the alchemical process begins in earnest with the *nigredo*, the blackening, the decomposition of life as we have known it. Our hopes, dreams, images of the future are sacrificed, and we surrender to the unknown. The ego is powerless here. We must learn to see in the dark as we seek to understand the unfamiliar ways of the larger Self.

After Joseph is sold into slavery in Egypt, a leading Egyptian official, Potiphar, recognizes Joseph's light and employs him in his household. When Potiphar's wife seeks to seduce Joseph, Joseph refuses her advances. Potiphar's wife, enraged by Joseph's refusal, falsely accuses him of attacking her, and Joseph is sent to the dungeons of Pharaoh, where he descends into a great darkness. The scorned feminine brings about Joseph's descent, where he must come into relationship with that which has been disowned in himself and his generation.

In the previous generations, the patriarchs and matriarchs carried the poles of masculine and feminine, which were brought into balance through their marriages. Joseph, however, *integrates* masculine and feminine within himself through his deep connection to the feminine quality of receptivity and by using what comes to him in this receptive state to act in the world, an expression of the creative masculine. Joseph heralds a new generation in which it is not the physical union of a man and a woman that brings about wholeness, but the unification of the masculine and feminine energies within a single individual. Joseph offers a new model of integration: the individuated self. This integration is expressed kabbalistically in the figure of Adam Kadmon, or primordial human, who is both male and female.

These years in the darkness are a time of learning for Joseph, as he develops his gifts as a dream interpreter that will ultimately deliver him and allow him to take the next step in his journey. Stanton Marlon writes of the encounter with darkness: "What is not seen by the wounded soul is that what is happening under the surface and in the blackening process is a dying of immature innocence—a *nigredo* that holds a transformative possibility and experience that opens the dark eye of the soul."[17]

Following the Shoah, collective faith was shattered and Jews were thrust into overwhelming darkness and grief. Re-engagement with any concept of the Divine requires coming to terms with the shadow side of life. Our perspective of God can no longer be simplistic or naïve; our spiritual views must acknowledge the existence of cataclysmic evil.

In the Biblical story, the Hebrew slaves lived 400 years without any intervention on the part of God. The hopelessness that many feel today was likely felt by our ancient ancestors who witnessed the murder of their infant children on the banks of the Nile, and the subjugation of the men and women under slavery with no relief or intercession from God. Likewise, the Jews who witnessed the destruction of the First and Second Temples, those who survived the mass expulsion and terrors of the Inquisition as those who would not leave or convert were tortured, and our more recent ancestors who witnessed the massacres and pogroms of Eastern Europe—all had to wrestle with the question of the meaning of God in a world where such cruelty exists.

In our own time, we struggle as we see the earth Herself in the throes of ecological devastation. As in the time of the Great Flood, we are witnessing the quickening losses of entire species, God's beautiful Creation, gone from the planet forever. How are we able to sustain ourselves spiritually in the face of such despair? This is the path of Joseph—to allow ourselves to face the darkness, to dwell within it, to fully experience the grief, and to see what emerges from the unflinching encounter with the depths.

This despair may have been carried in our families for generations. We may experience profound periods of darkness, feeling the suffering not only of our own personal lives, but also the past intergenerational pain that has gone untended. Trappings of ego inflation that may have gotten us through in the past offer no solace and prove useless in the face of the adversities we now encounter. We descend into a dark night of the soul, abandoned like Joseph, abducted into a place where we know no one and no one knows us. The center of the old ego does not hold. A new center, a new way, must be found, and it is not found by force of will, but only through surrender.

This is what Joseph does—he *endures*. He waits. And when the time comes, his gifts come forth in ways that are natural to him. He is a dreamer, a seer, an interpreter of dreams. In finding meaning in the symbolic world, he is freed from prison.

When we stop striving, we give up the ghost, and in the quiet, begin to hear the still small voice within—a voice that speaks in images, in story, in metaphor, in symbols, the voice of dreamtime. That is the heart of the spiritual life—not a belief in some outer transcendent God, but a willingness to listen deeply within and to understand the powerful messengers that come through our dreams and in our meditative visions. We learn there is something more powerful than the ego, something more faithful, more deserving of our time. We make that profound shift to a soul-centered life. Outer trappings matter less as inner visions compel us, perhaps leading us out of the prison of the small self to new fuller expressions of ourselves that reflect our inner light and provide a pathway for that light to come forth in service to the world.

Joseph the dreamer

In the dungeon, Joseph meets the Pharaoh's chief butler and baker, who each have a puzzling dream. Joseph asks them why they look so sad. They respond that none can interpret their dreams. Joseph offers, "Do not interpretations belong to God?"[18] He invites them to share their dreams with him and sees that they foretell that the butler will be released and elevated in Pharaoh's court, but that the baker will be hanged. Both things come to pass.

Pharaoh then has two disturbing dreams—*one of seven fat cows being devoured by seven skinny ones, and of seven stalks of healthy corn being swallowed by seven thin stalks.* The butler, hearing Pharaoh's dreams, which confound his magicians, remembers Joseph and tells the Pharaoh of his gifts. Joseph is called upon and interprets the dreams as foretelling seven years of plenty followed by seven years of famine. He advises Pharaoh to use the fat years to fill the coffers to be prepared for the years of starvation. Following Joseph's counsel, famine is averted. Joseph is elevated to a place of prominence in Pharaoh's kingdom. Through Joseph's leadership, his entire family come to dwell in Egypt and survive the years of drought.

Judaism has long recognized the potency of dreams. Joseph's father Jacob *dreams of a ladder of angels ascending to and descending from Heaven.* The Talmud teaches that a dream that goes uninterpreted is like an unopened letter from God. The dream must be understood, not simply taken at face value, to truly discern the will of God. As a youth, Joseph shares his uninterpreted dreams with his brothers in ways that catalyze their envy and hatred. In prison, Joseph develops the capacity to understand dreams, discerning their meaning through opening to the guidance of Divine wisdom.

Joseph shows us that even with no temple, no access to extended family, no ceremonial objects, ritual, or community, we can still stay connected to the Divine spark within by listening deeply to the symbolic imagination. Although we may despair that the collective memory of Judaism has not been actively transmitted from one generation to the next, we may discover the sacred connection that lives in the depths and finds us in our dreams. Many Jews who have not been raised with Jewish teachings have experienced powerful visions in meditations or dreams that belong to the Jewish mythic imagination. Part of the collective unconscious, Jewish mythic imagination may also open to those drawn to Judaism, some who may become Jews by choice and others who find a meaningful connection to the root metaphors of Western consciousness.

When someone experiences trauma, their symbolizing function can shut down, closing them off from the unconscious. Yet when a person who has been severely traumatized can begin to dream again and to make meaning of the images presented by the unconscious, profound healing can occur. Dreams provide a pathway through which we can hear the voice of Self, lighting the way toward wholeness.

The tsohar—Joseph and the primordial light

According to the kabbalists, before the world was created, God was all that existed. God had to withdraw into Itself, a process called *tzimtzum*, to create a space for the world to come into being, as a mother creates space within her womb for new life to form. Into this void, this vast nothingness, God sent an emanation of primordial light, which was the first act of creation. God uttered, "*Yehi Or*, Let there be light," and the world was born, with the creation of sacred light on the first day. This light was different from the light of the moon and sun and the other luminaries, which were created on the fourth day. The light created on the first day was a spiritual light. It enabled Adam and Eve to see from one end of the world to the other, and "the sun shone like a candle in comparison."[19]

When Adam and Eve ate the forbidden fruit, they lost the light.[20] According to one midrash, God placed the light inside a glowing stone, and the angel Raziel gave this stone to Adam after he left the Garden. The stone was passed down through the generations. God instructed Noah to hang the stone on the Ark.[21] Lighting the way through the 40 days and nights of the Great Flood, the light guided Noah and the family of Creation through the great devastation. Noah lost the light, but it was found by Abraham in an underwater cave and passed down through the generations, coming to Joseph when Jacob gave him the precious stone containing this great light, called the *tsohar*, along with the coat of many colors.[22]

Jacob made Joseph promise to wear the stone at all times, but did not tell him of its power, so that when his brothers threw him in the pit and stole his coat of many colors, they did not take the stone from him. The stone glowed in the pit, protecting him from snakes and keeping him safe, so that he was not afraid. While imprisoned, Joseph made the amazing discovery that placing the stone inside a cup allowed him to interpret dreams and read the future.[23]

In the depths of darkness of Pharaoh's dungeons, Joseph discovers the power of this primordial light. As we descend into our own depths of the unconscious, we may be surprised by the light we find hidden there. From Joseph's journey we gain insight into the Zohar's teaching: "There is no light without darkness, no darkness without light."[24]

All created forms have their origins in no-thing-ness, in the great void that exists before sound or sight, time, or space. When we return to this primordial nothingness, we are impregnated with the seeds of creation, and a slow process begins whereby the emanation we have received begins to find its way, through us, into form. Kabbalah, which means "to receive," teaches that we need an inner receptive vessel, in which our spiritual awareness can develop. The chalice in which Joseph placed the stone containing the light of the tsohar symbolizes this quality of receptivity. Joseph models how the development of the capacities of the feminine, the inner knowing, can lead to psychological liberation.

According to midrash, Joseph placed the chalice with the tsohar in his coffin, and Moses was guided in a dream "to take out the glowing stone and hang it in the Tabernacle, where it became known as the *Ner Tamid*, the Eternal Light."[25]

Myra's journey

On the first day of spring, my mother Myra entered a Catholic hospice in New York City. She was in such a state of agitation, her speech so unintelligible after contracting encephalitis in her brain following surgery two years previously, that the hospice staff thought her to be completely unreachable. When I arrived at her bedside from California two days later, they were surprised to see that I could understand her slurred speech and communicate with her. She calmed down considerably, although she was still highly agitated and combative. For the past two years, she had retreated more deeply into a state of restlessness and isolation, so different from her normal demeanor of kindness and patience.

The day after I arrived, a social worker came and talked with her. She asked my mother if she was afraid. In the two years of watching her suffer, it never occurred to me, or anyone else, to ask her that question. My heart melted as I witnessed her response. "Yes," she said. The social worker asked her what she was afraid of … was she afraid of dying? My mother responded, "I'm afraid …" She paused as she tried to articulate her fear, "I'm afraid … that God won't be there." My heart stood still as I grasped the enormity of the terror she was living with. The social worker said to her, "You know, you can call for God, you can ask God where He is." I thought she meant this as a general insight, but my mother did not hesitate. She began screaming, loudly, in her slurred speech, "Where are you, God? Where are you?"

I watched her, my heart breaking, as I recalled the Hasidic mystic Rabbi Nachman of Bratslav's instructions to his students to call out to God when they were experiencing profound despair. My mother was engaging in this practice, called *hitbodedut*. The social worker sat by her side, encouraging her to notice God's response over the next few days, wisely noting that "God doesn't always respond in words."

About six months before, I had consulted my Native American spiritual teacher, Jeane TuBears Jacobs, about my mother's condition. Without knowing anything about her history, TuBears saw that when my mother was 30 years old, half of her soul passed over to the other side, leaving the other broken half in this world. Her soul needed to reunite with that part that had passed over. I did the math. My mother was 30 in 1966, the year she descended into a profound depression that often left her bedridden. A year later, she left me and my older brother, no longer able to care for us. Months later, I met with her in a hotel room near Washington Square Park, where she was living temporarily, just blocks from where we currently sat at the hospice. She was heavily sedated. I was seven.

The day after the social worker met with my mother, Dr. Charles Gourgey, the music therapist at the hospice, came to see her. My mother, a gifted pianist, loved music, and some of my favorite memories were of sitting with her as she played and sang to me, "Polkadots and Moonbeams" and Ray Charles's "Hallelujah I Love Her So." Charles asked my mother what songs she might like to hear. "Amazing Grace," she said. And the Beatles. And Dylan. He brought his guitar and sang to my mother, and when he learned I also played guitar, he brought an extra one for me to use when he was not there, or for us to play to her together.

Charles was legally blind and had to get close to things to see them. He was not afraid of my mother. He got very close to her face and let her know he was there. They connected. In between music therapy sessions, I spoke with Charles in the family waiting room. He was very concerned about my mother's soul. "If she passes over in the state she is in now, her soul may be wandering for a long, long time. It is very important that she become less fragmented." He saw her agitated psychosis as a defense she used to shield herself from her fear of dying. He was not afraid of it—he seemed to know exactly what was needed. I flashed back on the memory of my mother and me sitting in the hotel room, just after her break-down, not far from where we were now. Finally, it seemed, someone had shown up who just might be able to help us.

Over the next few weeks, the social worker taught me how to meditate with my mother and invite her to relax. I breathed with my mother, inviting her to see herself in a chrysalis becoming a beautiful butterfly. When Charles heard me sing Kate Wolf's "Give Yourself to Love" to my mother, he went and bought a Kate Wolf album and sang "Safe at Anchor" to her. In it Wolf speaks of navigating tumultuous seas, finding the truest, deepest channel, marked by the sky's bright-est stars.[26] That song reflected the truth of my mother's soul, a deep channel that ran true, although she was often tossed about by the raging ocean. Listening to Charles sing to her of surviving the storm and coming to rest safely anchored I felt the possibility of my mother finding her way.

Throughout the weeks my mother was at the hospice, I was fixated on finding a rabbi as her health declined, because of my own experience of being held so profoundly in Jewish Renewal settings. The rabbi assigned to the hospice was never there when I asked, and my mother was not much interested in finding one, having come to find faith in Jesus as her parents had.

Just months before she entered hospice, in one of our last lucid conversations, as I sat with her in her apartment, she looked at me and said intently, "Read the Psalms." She left the room, and I picked up her King James Bible and looked at the Psalms, but could not relate to the heavily Anglicized language. A year after she passed, I attended a workshop on the Psalms with Rabbi Ruth Gan Kagan at a Ruach Ha'Aretz retreat. Through Rabbi Ruth's teachings and Stephen Mitchell's translations, I came to understand the peace the words of the Psalms must have given her. I thought of the many years my mother had wrestled with the dark-ness of her own thoughts and was comforted to know that she found solace in the words of the beautiful poetry of prayer:

Lord, listen to my prayer;
hear me in my hour of need.
I am overwhelmed by my troubles
and terrified by my thoughts.
Guide my feet on your path;

don't let me stop or falter.
Teach me how powerful your love is
and how insubstantial my fears …
Cover me with your mercy;
rock me to sleep in the dark.
And let me, when I awaken,
see nothing but the light of your face.[27]

So concerned was I with finding a rabbi to tend to my mother that I approached a very young Hasidic man in the hospital elevator. I asked him if he was a rabbi. Yes, he said, hesitantly. Could he visit with my mother? Graciously, he came to her room, but within nanoseconds of hearing her screaming in distress, he quickly excused himself.

I called a rabbi in Manhattan that I found through the Jewish Renewal website; she was kind and helpful but out of town. One night, I went to the Kabbalah Center seeking spiritual guidance and a possible contact to a rabbi and was disappointingly pulled into a workshop that resembled an infomercial for financial prosperity.

Eventually I gave up. "Who cares," I thought. If my mother is going to be helped across by the spiritually evolved Catholics at the hospice, maybe I should just go with it. They seemed to be doing just fine. Over the next few days, my mother began to let go of her fear. One afternoon, Charles was playing "Let It Be," and my mother cried out, "Let it be, let it be!" My older brother was there. We all looked at each other knowingly, feeling Myra moving into acceptance. At one point, she grabbed the watch on her left wrist that she had been stubbornly clinging to and pulled it off and handed it to Charles. She was letting go of time, letting go of this world. Her struggle continued but lessened in intensity. One night, I stayed late at the hospice, my heart breaking as I watched my mother screaming in discomfort as the nurses invasively cleared her sinuses. The pain of staying in her body was unbearable.

The next morning, around 10 am, in a meditation, *I saw my mother's body being gathered up lovingly by her Higher Soul, onto a raft floating on a river of light.* I felt that the soul reunification TuBears and Charles spoke of was occurring, profoundly loving and peaceful. My vision was interrupted by the phone ringing—the hospice nurse calling. "Your mother passed away a few minutes ago." She told me that my mother had been listening to a CD of Hawaiian music I had bought her several years before, which she loved. The nurse said she had asked them to put the CD on, and when they came back, she had passed over.

Charles called and said he would be sitting with my mother's body until I got there. When I arrived, he was at her bedside. I felt her spirit still hovering around her body, and there was a sense of deep peace in the room. I acknowledged this feeling and Charles said, "She made it, she's okay." *Safe at anchor.* After a while, I asked Charles if he could find a rabbi that would say the final blessings over my mother's body. "Would you like me to do it?" he asked. "I can grab my prayer book and yarmulke." *Yarmulke*? I thought to myself. "Do you know the bless-ings?" I asked, somewhat stunned. "I'm a cantor," he said. In that moment I felt God's presence with us, acknowledging that throughout her journey Myra had been held so lovingly and skillfully by this Jewish spiritual guide.[28]

Several months after my mother's passing, I listened for the first time to a meditation by Rabbi Tirzah Firestone from *The Woman's Kabbalah*, in which she guides one to enter a river of light.[29] I was floored. This was the same image that came to me at the moment of my mother's passing. That the river of light was an extant image in Jewish mysticism was a synchronicity that brought great solace to me—the river my mother entered existed, in the *imaginatio* of Judaism. Henri Corbin, a scholar of Islamic mysticism, understood the imaginal realm not only as something that arises from our individual imaginations, but also as a realm of consciousness that exists, that can be traveled by those engaged with the cultural cosmology of a shared faith.

Witnessing my mother through her dying process was, I imagine, what it might have been like for Joseph, seeing his mother Rachel on the road. In the midst of agonizing loss, I was shown a cosmic patterning that allowed us to move through the last days of her life with faith.

The Zohar recounts that when the soul is ready to leave the body,

> It will not do so until the Shekhinah reveals herself to it. And the Soul, from joy and love for the Shekhinah, leaves the body behind in order to meet Her. If the person is worthy, the Soul will join and attach itself to Shekhinah. And if not, the Shekhinah departs, and it remains and mourns the separation from the body.[30]

This teaching was offered at a workshop on death and dying presented by psy-chotherapist Alissa Hirshfeld-Flores and Rabbi Irwin Keller. It placed the vision I had at the moment of my mother's death in a new light. While I had thought of her being gathered up by her own *neshama* (soul), I now feel that in her journey of healing during her last days of life, she was able to depart her body in a state of psychic wholeness, gathered into the loving arms of the Shekhinah.

Healing family trauma

Intergenerational trauma impacts families and often causes rifts and divides that may last a lifetime, or more. Understanding how Joseph heals his relationship with his brothers shows us how we may repair painful wounds within the family. In families that have suffered trauma, the individuation of a single family member may transform the way the entire family relates.

After years of estrangement, Joseph meets his brothers again when, because of the famine in their land, Jacob sends his sons to Egypt to buy corn. There is corn in Egypt because the Pharaoh followed Joseph's dream interpretation to store it in anticipation of the seven years of famine. The brothers meet with Joseph, now a powerful leader who can grant their request. Joseph recognizes them, but they do not recognize him. All the brothers arrive except for the youngest, Benjamin, the other son of Jacob's union with Rachel. Jacob demands Benjamin be left at home because, still bereft at the loss of Joseph, he is unwilling to risk losing Benjamin on the dangerous journey.[31]

Though deeply wronged and almost killed by his brothers' cruelty, Joseph does not shun them when he meets them again. He instead devises a scenario that requires them to experience the pain and suffering that they inflicted on him, before revealing his identity to them. Joseph accuses the brothers of being spies. To prove they are not, he asks that they return with their brother Benjamin, while Simeon stays behind to guarantee they will return.

Thinking Joseph cannot understand their language, the brothers discuss among themselves whether the evil that they have done years ago to Joseph is causing them now to be in this predicament. They now consciously suffer the pain of causing Jacob unbearable grief, afraid he will suffer at Benjamin's departure as he suffered when the brothers first threw Joseph into the pit. As he overhears them expressing their remorse, Joseph is moved. He fills their sacks with corn and puts back the money they have paid him, hiding it in their sacks.

The brothers return to Jacob and explain what has happened. Jacob refuses at first to let Benjamin go. Believing Joseph to be dead, he fears the loss of Benjamin will be too much to bear. Judah promises to ensure Benjamin's safety, offering to bear the blame forever if anything should befall him. Jacob allows them to go back, with Benjamin, and instructs them to bring gifts and to return the money that Joseph placed in their sacks.

Here we see the psychological and moral development of the brothers. Instead of envying Jacob's love for Benjamin, Judah feels empathy for his father's suffering, offering to sacrifice his own life for his brother's. He feels the pain he inflicted on his father by casting Joseph into the pit and repents for the wrong he has done. Ann and Barry Ulanov reflect on the power of repentance. Envy is a shadowy response to the good we see in another. As we repent, we recognize the possibility of our own goodness, seeing the God spark inside ourselves.[32] Judah's offering his life places him in touch with his own goodness. Returning the money is also a significant act, symbolizing the repayment of what does not belong to them, perhaps a *tikkun* (repair) for the money the Midianites received when they sold Joseph to the Ishmaelites.

The brothers return to Joseph and present Benjamin, giving back the money that Joseph placed in their sacks. Joseph is moved to tears. Learning that his father is in good health, he again fills the sacks of all the brothers. He has a servant place the same silver chalice in which he divined the dreams by the light of the tsohar in Benjamin's sack. Joseph's servant states, "It is the very one from which my master drinks and which he uses for divination."[33]

As the brothers head out on the road back to their father, Joseph sends his steward after them to confront them about the missing chalice. The brothers protest that there is no reason for them to steal; after all, they have returned the money placed in their sacks on the first trip.[34]

The scene recalls the confrontation between Jacob, Leah, Rachel, and their father Laban as they leave his house. Rachel denies having the holy statuary, although she had secreted them under her seat on the camel. Not knowing that she carried them, Jacob swore that if anyone had the teraphim, he or she would die an early death; Rachel died giving birth to Benjamin.

Now the brothers respond to the accusation that someone has stolen the chalice saying, "With whomsoever of thy servants it be found, let him die." When the chalice is found in Benjamin's sack, the brothers rent their clothes, preparing for Benjamin's death and throw themselves at Joseph's feet, bowing down as they had in Joseph's childhood dream. Judah speaks, begging Joseph to tell them how they can repent.[35]

Here the sons of Rachel and Jacob are engaged in a drama that recalls her life and death. The chalice, a symbol of the feminine, is in Benjamin's pack. But now the possession of the feminine symbol does not lead, as it did with Rachel, to the harsh punishment of death, but to mercy. The feminine qualities of compassion and lovingkindness that Rachel embodied guide the brothers to reconciliation and restoration. The Sacred Feminine energies Rachel once carried secretly in the teraphim are now held within the chalice that passes between her two sons.

Joseph tells the brothers to leave Benjamin with him and return to their home. They know that leaving Benjamin behind will cause their father Jacob an unbearable grief that may well kill him. Judah pleads with Joseph, explaining that Jacob initially refused to let Benjamin go, because his first son with Rachel was "surely torn to pieces," and if Benjamin were to die, the grief would kill him. All these years later, as the energy of the Sacred Feminine begins once again to flow, the brothers now consciously experience the heartache that they refused to feel in their cruelty toward Joseph.

Joseph hears for the first time of the great sorrow that Jacob has suffered and realizes that his brothers have never disclosed their misdeed to their father. Judah offers his own life in Benjamin's place, humbling himself and understanding that he can offer to bring peace to his father in his old age, rather than cause him unbearable grief.

At Judah's transformation, Joseph sees that the *tikkun*, or repair, within the family is complete. Inviting the brothers close, he reveals to them that he is their brother. Weeping openly before them, he is overwhelmed with feeling to learn that his father is still alive. He admonishes them not to be angry with themselves for abandoning him in the pit, because he understands that it was not them, but God, that sent him to Egypt to save their people "for a great deliverance." He asks them to go to Jacob and return with him to Egypt, to dwell in the land of Goshen, with their flocks, to be sustained in the time of famine. Joseph then falls upon Benjamin's neck and weeps, and Benjamin weeps upon his. And Joseph kisses all his brothers and weeps with them.[36]

Pharaoh, learning of the reunion, calls upon Joseph to invite his father and all his brethren to settle and live well in the land of Egypt, "for the good things of all the land of Egypt are yours." Joseph sends his brothers back to Canaan, laden with gifts for each of them and for Jacob, and is especially generous with Benjamin. According to midrash, Serach bat Asher sings to Jacob, with harp and gentle voice, the news that Joseph is alive, lest he die from the shock of hearing the news after all these years of grieving.[37]

The story offers a powerful model of healing in a family that has been torn apart by trauma and its effects. As the scapegoat in his family system, Joseph had to undertake the path of individuation—a solitary journey in which he descended into the depths to find his way to his true self through great trials and pain.

Those who feel things deeply may suffer the disowned pain of their family's traumatic history that has been acted out in unconscious and possibly cruel ways, pain that family members have been unable to integrate or heal. When we undertake the work of individuation, we separate from the family story to gain distance and come into a different relationship to it. Joseph does not get caught up in retribution or anger. Instead, he surrenders to the process, recognizing the hand of God in it. He understands that what transpired was necessary for a larger purpose to unfold. Had he not been sent into Egypt, he would not have been able to save not only the Egyptians, but also his own family, from the devastating starvation caused by the famine.

Joseph helps his brothers move out of the self-recrimination in which they have been caught since their betrayal of him. From this enlightened state, he can offer the tools they need to come to repentance and to understand that they too were actors in a larger story that was destined to unfold in the way that it did.

Yet Joseph does not simply forgive and forget. Instead, he puts events in motion that cause his brothers to consciously experience the pain they have caused both him and his father. This action is central to the concept of *teshuvah*, or repentance. It is not enough simply to seek forgiveness for our wrongdoings; we must feel and understand the pain that we have caused others, gain insight and compassion from that understanding, and make a commitment to grow. Once we become conscious of our shadow, we have a responsibility to contain it, rather than enacting it unconsciously on others. It is through this series of acts that true teshuvah takes place.

When we begin to heal the inherited trauma that we may have carried for much of our lives, we understand the pain and suffering of generations that may have caused unconscious acting out, with power and fear reigning in the family instead of love. This new perspective may enable us to bring healing to our family members, seeing the generational patterns through the eyes of God's compassion, through insight forged in darkness.

The ancient Hebrews have to find Joseph's bones before they can move out of Egypt. They have to come into relationship with their ancestors and with those parts of themselves that have been split off, disowned, devalued, by trauma. In the following chapter, I explore the ways in which turning toward grief can heal the family system. As we allow ourselves to feel the pain, sorrow, and rage that have been split off in the family, we can redeem the fullness of our lineage.

Joseph and Moses bookend a single journey. Before the Hebrew people can leave Egypt, before they can ascend to Sinai, they must summon Joseph's bones from the bottom of the river Nile. As the kabbalists taught, the deeper the depths of darkness we encounter, the greater the light our vessels can contain. Joseph descends alone, for the sake of Moses's ascent with the entire community of Israel. He models how we enter the depths, and learn to consciously value the transformation that suffering brings, opening us to a new internal center that listens to God through dreams and visions.

For the entire 40 years that the people wander through the desert, until they enter the Promised Land, they carry two arks—one containing the Torah, the other containing Joseph's bones—because the entire Torah was revealed to us in the way that Joseph lived.

Notes

1 Psalms 139, *Tanakh* (New York: Jewish Publication Society, 1917), https://www.mec hon-mamre.org/p/pt/pt26d9.htm.
2 Genesis 50:24–26.
3 Louis Ginzberg, *The Legends of the Jews* (Philadelphia: Jewish Publication Society of America, 1969). Bilhah and Zilpah were handmaidens to Rachel and Leah, and together the four of them gave birth to the 12 sons and the daughters (only Dinah is named in the text) that comprised the 12 tribes of Israel.
4 Sotah 13a–13b; cited in Simcha Paull Raphael, *Living and Dying in Ancient Times: Death, Burial, and Mourning in Biblical Tradition* (Boulder, CO: Albion-Andalus, 2015), 47.
5 Erich Neumann, "Stages of Religious Experience and the Path of Depth Psychology," *The Israeli Annals of Psychiatry and Related Disciplines* 8, no. 3 (December 1970), 232–254, 247.
6 Joshua 24:32, Ex. R. 20:19; cited in Raphael, *Living and Dying in Ancient Times*, 48.
7 Genesis 37:5–9.
8 Genesis 37:19–20.
9 Genesis 31:35.
10 Elliot Kiba Ginsburg, *The Sabbath in the Classical Kabbalah* (Albany: SUNY Press, 1989); citing the Zohar 1:60a–b, 235a.
11 Ann Ulanov and Barry Ulanov, *Cinderella and Her Sisters: The Envied and the Envying* (Louisville, KY: Westminster John Knox Press, 1983), 100.
12 Ibid, 107.
13 Joseph Dan, ed., Introduction to *Sefer HaYashar* (Jerusalem: The Bialik Institute, 1986).
14 Genesis 37:28.
15 Sefer ha Yashar, Chap. 42:30–40, 118.
16 Estelle Frankel, *Sacred Therapy: Jewish Spiritual Teachings on Emotional Healing and Inner Wholeness* (Boston: Shambhala, 2004).
17 Stanton Marlan, *The Black Sun: The Alchemy and Art of Darkness* (College Station, TX: Texas A&M University Press, 2005), 23.
18 Genesis 40:8.
19 Howard Schwartz, *Tree of Souls: The Mythology of Judaism* (New York: Oxford University Press, 2004), 85, citing B. Hagigah, 12a, *Zohar* 1:45b.
20 Schwartz, *Tree of Souls*, 84; Wineman, Aryeh. "Wineman, Aryeh. "Metamorphoses of the Hidden Light Motif in Jewish Texts," Hebrew Studies, vol. 60, 2019, pp. 323–332.

of the Red Sea. Lilith symbolizes our capacity to withstand enormous suffering and pain as we open to the truth of who we are. As we make our own inner journey to the Sea's shores, we may find Lilith, who has been waiting there since the dawn of Creation. Rediscovering our ancient original Mother may give us the strength and courage to enter our personal depths, to integrate the unhealed traumas of our ancestral lineage, to grieve, to mourn, to wail and suffer—and to heal.

Lilith is a mythical figure of tremendous power that has often been either overlooked or demonized in Jewish tradition. She symbolizes the chthonic, or earthy, Dark Feminine that has the strength to bear the overwhelming emotions of deep grief. Her wisdom serves us as we, individually and collectively, learn how to bear the collective suffering of our people.

The state of the Hebrews' exile in Egypt, calls to mind the earlier exile of Adam and Eve, cast out of Paradise. They move from a state of profound connectedness to the Divine into the realm of dualistic consciousness, in which they become painfully aware of their separation from God. This story is seen as a template of the human journey—from the original union with the Divine to a state of ego development in which we may forget our interconnectedness with all that is.

Within this story there is an exile that cuts even more deeply in the psyche— the state of being exiled, alone, from Judaism itself. This is the story of Lilith, the first woman, popularized in recent decades by Jewish feminists who reclaimed her as an archetypal image of women's emancipation and autonomy.

There are two accounts of the creation of humans in Genesis. In the earliest account, on the sixth day, "God created man in His own image, in the image of God … male and female created He them."[4] According to the medieval midrash Alphabeta de ben Sira, these first humans were Adam and Lilith, male and female, who were created at the same time, of the same earth (*adamah*).[5] Adam sought dominion over Lilith and wanted to lie above her. Lilith refused, saying to God, "We are made from the same earth, why should he be above me?" Lilith cried out the hidden name of God and flew into the air, and to the shores of the Red Sea. Adam pleaded with God to find Lilith and bring her back. God sent three angels who found Lilith in the midst of the Red Sea "in the raging waters in which one day the Egyptians would be drowned."[6]

The angels asked her to return to the Garden. Lilith inquired, "Will I have to submit to Adam?" When they said she would, she responded, "Well, then, I refuse." The angels imposed a terrible punishment that one hundred of her children would die each day. Lilith chose this fate over subservience.[7]

From this part of the story arose the superstitious practice of families placing an amulet at the crib of newborn babies with the three angels who sought Lilith on it, as a protection against her bringing harm to their children. Lilith is also vilified in patriarchal culture as the embodiment of powerful feminine sexual energy, a she-demon, a succubus who causes men to spill their seed in the night during nocturnal emissions and leads them astray from sexual fidelity. Even the mystical texts venerating the Divine Feminine cast Lilith in this light, forced to carry the projection of men's negative anima, or inner devalued feminine.

Lilith's story reflects a historical reality. Preceding the Biblical story of Adam and Eve, in the Near Eastern cultures of the Fertile Crescent, the Goddess was revered as the Great Mother, giver of life and ruler over death. With the ascendancy of the patriarchal tradition in Judaism, this history became eclipsed. The Jewish midrashic story of Lilith was attributed to Rabbi Abraham ben Sira in the 9th century, acknowledging the powerful chthonic feminine energy that had been suppressed with the ascension of patriarchal values.[8]

Lilith was originally a Sumerian Goddess, whose earthy depths are reflected in the midrashic tale of her as the first woman, made from the earth along with Adam. Lilith carries that part of the Deep Feminine, once represented by the goddesses of the Near East, whose energy is powerful, sensual, and dark as well as light. As detailed in a previous chapter, in the earliest days of Judaism, the Goddess Asherah carried the power of the Great Mother, the giver of life and also the one who receives the dead. The earliest Hebrews worshiped the Feminine aspect as Asherah, along with her daughter Anat (Goddess of War) and Astarte (Queen of Heaven), and continued to honor her for the nearly four centuries during which the First Temple stood. After the destruction of the First and Second Temples, during the rise of rabbinic Judaism, women and the feminine were increasingly exiled from a central role in Jewish practice.

Jungian analyst Siegmund Hurwitz, writing in the mid-20th century, suggests that the appearance of the Lilith midrash in the 9th century served as a compensation for "the one-sided spiritual-patriarchal conscious attitude," corresponding to images of spirit, father, and Heaven.[9] Lilith represents the unconscious aspects devalued by the collective, including aspects of nature, mother, and earth.[10]

Lilith as shadow—the splitting of the Feminine

The rise of kabbalah during the Middle Ages sought to rectify this splitting off of the Feminine aspects of the Godhead by according a central place to the Shekhinah. In kabbalistic thought, the Father, Mother, Son, and Daughter motif replicates earlier observances of God and Goddess as Holy Couple, with their children.[11]

Yet the kabbalists also divided the Feminine into opposites—Lilith represented darkness, and Shekhinah carried the light.[12] The Shekhinah and the Kodesh Baruch Hu (the Blessed Holy One) represented the Feminine immanent and Masculine transcendent aspects of the Godhead that dwelled in union in the Holy Temple in Jerusalem. When the Shekhinah went into exile with the Jewish people after the Temple was destroyed, She was separated from her Beloved. Lilith is said to have taken her place as the Holy One's consort, creating a psychic imbalance in the Creation.

Rabbi Isaac Luria, the great medieval Jewish mystic, interpreted the Book of Isaiah as teaching that Lilith would someday be redeemed, citing the marriage of Jacob and Leah as the symbolic redemption of the love between Adam and Lilith. According to Israeli Rabbi Ohad Ezrahi, Luria taught that Lilith represents that aspect of the Divine Feminine that has yet to be integrated into consciousness.

Lilith represents the chthonic feminine—the earthy, sexual aspect of Feminine power that has been split off from Jewish consciousness and relegated to exile. Ezrahi cites Luria's teachings that suggest that this aspect of the Divine Feminine must be redeemed by being blessed and brought into holy service.[13] As we allow ourselves to consciously experience these opposing poles of dark and light, heavenly and chthonic, we open to the possibility of integrating these energies, thereby expanding our own as well as the collective consciousness of Judaism.

Lilith represents, among other things, the power of female sexuality. In the ancient Sumerian traditions, she was a priestess of the Goddess Ishtar and in other texts, a priestess of Inanna, overseeing the sacred sexual rites.[14] With the ascendancy of patriarchy, feminine erotic power was negatively projected onto the archetypal image of Lilith as a seductress, temptress—a succubus who stole men's semen in the night. Women's innate eroticism was limited to expression within marriage, where it continued to be viewed as holy.[15]

In cutting off the erotic, we lose touch with our innate sense of power. D'vorah Grenn observes that "there is danger to women in ignoring erotic impulses. If we instead learned to appreciate and enjoy without guilt both our sexual pleasures and our ambition—which we have been taught are selfish or inappropriate for women to pursue—they would energize and enrich us."[16]

Lilith carries a painful history, filled with profound meaning for those of us who have felt alienated from Judaism because of the sexism embedded in the tradition. Many of us grew up when Judaism overtly excluded women, gay men, lesbians, and transgender and gender non-binary people from spiritual leadership, and marginalized those who did not comport with conservative political views dominant at the time. For many, the only choice was to leave the tradition and find other ways of connecting with the sacred, or to commit oneself to secular social justice work. Unable to find a place within Judaism, many felt alienated and excluded. Like Lilith, they fled the Garden and, rather than submit to an unconscionable oppression, took refuge elsewhere.

Lilith is *She who was left behind*, in the rich lands of the Fertile Crescent, in the times of powerful Goddesses and rites honoring the Queen of Heaven. Are her rage and bitterness part of her nature, or are they the consequence of her exile?

Many of us know Lilith in our female lineage—women who were denied a voice, denied access to power, whose feminine wisdom was devalued, perhaps hidden even from themselves. Many came to embody the destructive aspects of Lilith—raging, angry, dissatisfied women. Depressed, anxious, terrified women. Sad and disempowered women. Temptresses vying for male attention as the only source of power available to them. The devaluation of the feminine has taken a powerful toll in Jewish spiritual and intellectual life as well as personally, in the life of the family.

Lilith is also a casualty of response to intergenerational trauma. Seeking safety from the overwhelming feelings associated with trauma, we cling to the logical, rational, masculine approach of logos and cut off feminine eros. When under siege, we cannot afford the luxury of feeling, grieving, and fully embodying experience.

Yet the feelings, unlived, do not go away. They get pushed deeper into the unconscious. They fester. They get passed down from one generation to the next in the form of complexes. They get expressed as distortions of our true nature. In this way, Lilith manifests as the intrusive mother who devours her children's autonomy, or who abandons her children through depression and despair, unable to personally metabolize the overwhelming trauma of our collective history.

When Lilith's power is cut off, Hurwitz suggests, she has no choice but to manifest as depression—the numbness that overtakes us when our capacity to connect with our own depths, our feeling self, is exiled.[17] We need to redeem Lilith collectively, to reclaim her, to do the hard work of acknowledging and digesting the despair, grief, rage, terror, and powerlessness that are our inheritance. As we do so, we can begin to heal from transgenerational trauma rather than bequeathing it to our children and descendants.

Entering the darkness—reclaiming psychological wholeness

The Baal Shem Tov, the great Hasidic master, taught that we need to descend to our depths to ascend spiritually.[18] We must move into our dark and frozen places to uncover the Divine spark that has become trapped there, awaiting redemption. In shamanic approaches, this process is referred to as *soul retrieval*.

Facing the Lilith aspect of one's own consciousness requires entering the realm of the Dark Feminine, where grief, rage, and loss dwell.[19] As Lilith's powerful energy has been exiled and repressed, it manifests instead as depression, which differs from grief. Depression is a numbing that cuts off the life force. We are unable to give birth to creative expression; our gifts are devoured by our self-loathing inner critic. Jung observed that the only way to heal depression is to allow ourselves to engage the unconscious through "dreams, fantasies, visions, and especially in active imagination."[20]

Rabbi Lynn Gottlieb recognized that in splitting off and repressing the dark aspects of the feminine, we have lost access to parts of the psyche that are necessary for our healing and our redemption. Lilith and Shekhinah are polarized aspects of the Feminine that are portrayed as enemies, not sisters.[21] Gottlieb suggests that we might imagine Shekhinah descending to the underworld to meet her twin sister Lilith and to listen to hear her suffering, as the Sumerian Goddess Inanna descended to meet her fearsome sister Ereshkigal.[22]

> Those parts of ourself cast off by the patriarchal world are slowly becoming acceptable … We can never return to a myth that does not honor our most sacred quest, the quest to wholeness of being. Our descent to the underworld of our imagination will eventually allow us to give birth to a new vision of wholewoman for our own time.[23]

In the great Sumerian myth of Inanna, the Queen of Heaven must descend to the underworld to find her wholeness. It is only when she meets her dark sister

Ereshkigal in the depths that Inanna is transformed. Ereshkigal is an underworld Goddess who is consumed with the pain she has seen and experienced, and is also in the throes of labor. Turning towards our suffering allows something new to be born in both the individual and collective psyche.[24] When Inanna is able to fully embrace Ereshkigal and to empathize with her, Inanna becomes whole. Like Inanna, we must each surrender our innocence, and experience the depths of suffering of our sister Ereshkigal, or Lilith, to come into our fullness.

The need for re-integration of the Dark Feminine is reflected in the Biblical story of Solomon and the Queen of Sheba. Jungian scholar Rivkah Scharf Kluger sees the Queen of Sheba as a manifestation of Lilith—the "dark sister ... of the Shekhinah, her shadow."[25] Kluger echoes Luria when she suggests that there is "a further development in the divine drama and ... in the human soul. The redemption of Lilith is yet ahead."[26]

Lilith at the shores of the Red Sea

In the midrash we are told that when she flees the Garden of Eden, Lilith dwells by the shores of the Red Sea. Perhaps the Israelites, and each of us making the journey out of our own exilic consciousness, must first encounter Lilith here, because traversing the sea requires integration of the disowned and devalued aspects of ourselves. Before we can surrender to God, before we can walk into the sea, before we can find faith, we must come to terms with our own pain and honor the suffering of our ancestors in the clay pits of Egypt, the pogroms of Eastern Europe, the death camps of Treblinka and Dachau. We carry them with us, as we enter the sea.

Shamanic rabbi Gershon Winkler teaches that Lilith is that aspect of the feminine that allows us to embrace mystery rather than to constrict in the face of the unknown.[27] In the kabbalistic view, Lilith has a dual nature. If we fear uncertainty and cling to stability and the known, she becomes a demon that threatens to destroy us. If we are able to embrace and engage uncertainty, then Lilith becomes a midwife, helping us "break through the barriers that kill what we try to bring forth."[28] Winkler notes that according to kabbalistic sources, when we have spiritually evolved collectively to the state of messianic consciousness, Lilith and Eve shall become one woman, integrating the dual aspects of the feminine.[29]

To enter the Red Sea, to undergo the initiation into the depths and leave behind the constricted consciousness of trauma, we require connection to a holding presence. When our connection to the feminine depths has been cut off, we may feel we do not have the capacity to face whatever may arise. Redeeming Lilith allows her to serve as a midwife to the depths, where we can integrate the grief, rage, and terror that live in our family histories engendered by collective trauma. In so doing, the essential life force that has been constricted in order to survive the trauma may once again begin to flow freely, birthing new psychic life.

Hannah's story continues

As explored earlier, Hannah was raised in an observant household in the South. She loved Judaism as a child, yet eventually turned away because her mother, and the rabbis and teachers at her Temple, could not meaningfully address her spiritual questions about the significance of Jewish ritual, or about death and the afterlife in the immediate wake of the Shoah. All this left her feeling that Judaism lacked deeper meaning. As she reflected on her maternal lineage, she had more insight into how the traumas of her grandfather's childhood impacted her mother and were transmitted to her unconsciously.

Hannah's grandfather was born and raised in Russia. When he was a teenager, he witnessed the incomprehensible horror of his mother being beheaded during a pogrom. He fled to the United States, where he married Hannah's grandmother through an arranged marriage. They had five children. He was a strictly observant and hardworking Orthodox Jew.

It was healing for Hannah to imagine that if he had lived now, he would have had years and years of therapy for the great pain that he carried. But because he did not receive any support for the great trauma he carried, he acted it out in his family, becoming extremely abusive to his wife and children.

By the time Hannah was a child her grandfather lived like a vagabond. She mused, "How he did that and kept kosher, I have no clue." She recalled that he would come to town occasionally, always on Shabbos, and get in touch with her mother. She would go with her mother to meet with him on the street, after morning services, each visit "a horribly painful experience" that brought her mother to tears.

When Hannah was a child, her mother only spoke obliquely about the abuse she and her siblings suffered at the hands her father's rage. When Hannah was in her 30s, her mother told her that her father had raped and impregnated her older sister. Hannah's aunt had to have a backstreet abortion in the 1920s. Her grandfather justified this incestuous rape by referencing the Biblical story of Lot's daughters seducing him when he was drunk to ensure that their people did not die out. Years later, Hannah wondered if her grandfather also molested her mother. Her mother never spoke about it again.

Hannah recalled attending a party where a male psychic approached her and said, "There's someone here." Without her providing any information, the psychic described a man in a uniform with the same first initial as her grandfather, saying he was a shoemaker. Hannah knew it was her grandfather and recalled his narrow escape from conscription into the Russian Army. It was a common practice for young Jewish men to be forcibly conscripted and placed in the most dangerous settings where they would die an early death or, if they survived, never be allowed to leave service.

Hannah asked the psychic what her grandfather wanted, and he responded, "He wants to help you, and he wants to make amends." Hannah left the party feeling upset and greatly pained by trying to discern whether to let her grandfather into her heart.

Hannah recalled a dream she had following a weeklong workshop with Rabbi Tirzah Firestone at a Jewish Renewal gathering. *Two men are pursuing me, and I ran into a house that had a door I was unable to lock. The men came in and I turned to face them—the first time I was able to choose to consciously engage figures in a dream. When I did, one ran off and the other hugged me.*

The dream suggests that Hannah was unable to keep the terror in her family "locked out" any longer, as her mother had to do to survive the suffering of her own childhood. Like the Biblical Jacob on the banks of the river Jabbok, terrified to encounter his brother, Esau, after their long estrangement, Hannah wrestled with what had been disowned in her lineage. As she turned to face the shadowy figures pursuing her in the dream, she had the opportunity to receive a blessing, as Jacob received from the angel he wrestled with the night before he encountered his brother. Hannah's turning toward the figure in the dream may reflect her courageous openness to engage with her grandfather's tormented spirit. Her willingness to face the anguish of her grandfather's life and the suffering he caused allowed her to experience some measure of healing of this painful lineage.

Hannah engaged in an imaginal dialogue with her grandfather. She felt her heart opening, and also felt the challenge of that opening: "Thinking of my grandfather, the pain of opening my heart to him, the pain of the heart opening in general." She recalled the lines to a Psalm she learned in a translation by Rabbi Shefa Gold: "When your heart breaks open and reveals to you its core, and your soul dances like it's never danced before." Hannah painted this prayer on the very first prayer shawl she designed.

Aaron's story continues

Aaron's father left Germany with his family in 1936. Aaron recalled that his father was only 16 when he and his mother and sister were rounded up in September 1938 and sent to a deportation camp in Poland.

> Because they already had papers for sailing and entry into the US from my grandfather who had gone on before, after his own release from Nazi prison in 1936, they managed to bargain their way out of the camp, and passed through their hometown on Kristallnacht, where they were protectively held by police for one night. They then proceeded to the port of embarkment, where my father was nearly arrested at the hotel in a routine check.

The family immigrated to America. Aaron grew up feeling suffocated by the pressure his father exerted on him to conform to conservative views, and to maintain a Jewish identity. He left home at 18 with his non-Jewish girlfriend, which greatly pained his father. They remained estranged for several decades.

In his late 30s, Aaron travelled to Switzerland and Germany for work, where he began speaking German. Aaron learned to speak German in school, but never spoke it with his father or parents, who spoke "an inter-mixture of English-German-Yiddish among themselves." Returning from his travels, he began to speak with his father in his native tongue, which Aaron felt to be a new, profoundly meaningful connection.

Yet they still could not speak directly about the years of painful separation. It was only after he married Julie, whose mother was also a Holocaust survivor, that his parents and in-laws could relate to each other, enabling Aaron to become closer with his father.

Aaron shared a photograph of his father from 1936, at his home in Braunschweig, Germany. His father was 13 years old in the photo and seated next to his two-year-old sister. Aaron also shared a *Yizkor* (memorial) book, given to his family by Julie's mother, compiled in the 1950s about the Braunschweig Jewish community, in which Aaron's extended family was memorialized. As the memory of the once vibrant community was evoked, Aaron felt a longing to apologize to his father for the pain he had caused him by leaving home and marrying outside the tradition and the lack of closeness they experienced for many years. Aaron was moved to tears as he recited the Mourner's Kaddish prayer for his father and his paternal ancestors.

As Aaron worked through the pain of his own family history, his inner world began to open. In meditation he had visions of a shul in Eastern Europe before the war, with five rows of pews. The shul had no ark for the Torah scroll, but there was a wooden *bimah* (podium) in the center and a stained-glass window on the right. Outside he saw green gardens. Aaron was seated in the back and initially there was just an old man and a little boy seated in the second row. Over time in his meditations, souls who had died in the Shoah gathered in.

As Aaron continued revisiting the shul in his meditations over many years, it began to fill. A group of people whose lives had been taken in the Shoah emerged on the left side of the shul. After reading about a diary that had been discovered buried in a box in the Krakow ghetto during the war, Aaron's shul "flooded with souls that wanted to come up and be in the light … Those souls are with me and every once in a while, when I meditate, they're there, all of them … they're mine to see through, they want to come out, they want to help me."

Daniel's story continues

Daniel shared an old photograph of his great-grandfather and great-grandmother and their ten children, his great-aunts and great-uncles. In the photo there was a small photograph hanging on the wall of their home in Poland, of Daniel's paternal grandfather who had already left for America. The rest of his extended family stayed in Poland after his grandfather left. The entire family was killed in the Shoah. Daniel reflected that the photograph had "survived many, many things to make it here."

Daniel's grandfather passed away when Daniel was only eight, shortly before Daniel's father also passed away. He remembered his grandfather as "a wonderful joyful man who loved Judaism so much," but he was surrounded by people who didn't care about it at all. Daniel's father and his siblings all became secular communists. Whenever he visited his grandparents, he saw his grandfather in the morning, wearing tefillin and davening. Daniel marveled that his grandfather was able to maintain his connection to Judaism alone, with no one around him caring for it with him. Strikingly, Daniel later learned that his maternal grandfather, of Syrian Jewish ancestry, hid his deep connection with Judaism from his wife and children who did not support his observance.

In returning to the practice of religious Judaism, Daniel experienced great sadness that the connection he had to both of his grandfathers, who were religious men, was completely lost. "They both passed before I cared at all to receive the transmission of the family history of Judaism, and I'm often very sad about that. I had a dream a couple of weeks ago that my grandfather was alive, and I was rushing to go see him, and I was so excited because I was finally going to get to talk to him about Judaism and to learn from him about that."

Daniel has dedicated himself to meaningful Jewish practice, keeping alive the flame that shone brightly among his ancestors. Finding his own relationship to Judaism despite the absence of it in his childhood home, he carries on the legacy of a deeply religious family that was almost completely extinguished.

Yizkor—remembering

Beginning in the years immediately following the Shoah, survivors began compiling *Yizkor* (remembrance) books to commemorate their families and friends who had perished in the Holocaust. The books were initially private publications, distributed among fellow survivors from a certain town or region. They enabled descendants to honor their relatives during memorial services (Yizkor) held during major holiday observances.

The YIVO Institute for Jewish Research began during the time of the Warsaw ghetto as Jews risked their lives to save sacred texts from destruction. In subsequent years it provided a forum for survivors of the death camps to share what happened during the war. The Yizkor books tell the history of a certain Jewish community, including significant people and events before the war, with photographs as well as eyewitness accounts of life in the ghettos, of deportations and mass murders. A list of all the towns of people who were annihilated, they serve as tombstones for people whose final burial place is unknown.[30]

With the help of the Yizkor books project, we can make meaning of our own histories. Recently a cousin traced my paternal great-grandfather's journey to the United States from the village of Khmelnitski, Ukraine, now Proskurov, in the early 1900s. He came with his immediate family, but grandparents, aunts, uncles, cousins, and friends were all left behind. After my great-grandfather participated in anti-Czarist protests in the early 1900s, he was forced to flee to avoid persecution. In 1920, 20,000 Jews in Proskurov were murdered in a mass pogrom. In 1943, all the remaining Jews were massacred in the Shoah.

In the Yizkor book on Proskurov, Freider Mikhail Sanevich visited the town where his father lived until he fled the Nazis. Citing poet Czeslaw Milosz, Sanevich reflected, "*A heart beats even when it should tear apart.*" I recently visited the Shoah Memorial in Paris and saw a photograph of the mass graves of the Jews in Proskurov in the 1943 massacre. I felt profound grief for the extended branches of my paternal family tree, gone forever, either through mass pogroms or the systematic slaughter by the Nazis. After learning more about my paternal lineage and witnessing the photograph of the mass graves in the Shoah Memorial, I began having dreams about my paternal ancestors, feeling their strength and wisdom.

In recent years, the work of Jewish-German reconciliation—the effort to come to terms with the legacy of Nazism—has extended to the work of Jewish-Polish reconciliation. Louise Steinman witnessed an art project in the village of Lublin, Poland, where the great Hasidic master, the Seer of Lublin, once lived. The town had once been adjacent sections of Jewish and Gentile villages. The Jewish side was now completely covered over by an asphalt parking lot, whereas the Gentile part of the town is still inhabited.

A young Polish artist developed an installation in which the whole town participated. Darkening the lights in the Gentile section, the entire town gathered with candles and walked through a doorway into what was once the Jewish shtetl. The artist noticed that although the village was destroyed, the foundations of the shtetl homes still stood underneath the asphalt. He drilled into the asphalt of the parking lot and placed floodlights at the foundation of the old houses. The lights streamed upward into the sky, emanating a brilliant light emerging from the buried past. People wandered through the shtetl area amid the light, holding candles, and listening to recordings of the stories of those who had once lived there, collected in the Yizkor books.[31]

The Poles, who had lived alongside the Jewish people for a millennium, are able to speak openly now about their experiences during the war for the first time. Following the end of the war, the Communist regime had limited discussion about Polish Jewish history. The guilt, shame, and terror that comprise the collective history of Jews, Poles, Germans, and all those terrorized under the Nazis are surfacing as the work of psychological reconciliation is undertaken by the succeeding generations.

The painful and poignant work of recollecting the histories of these villages touches something powerful within us as our connection to our own past is kindled. Judaism is transmitted generation to generation, *l'dor v'dor*. For Jews who cannot trace their lineage back past their own grandparents or great-grandparents, historical recollection may help fill in the pieces of the long past, through the work of those gathering the shards of the shattered past throughout Eastern and Central Europe.

Arnold Zable, a son of Holocaust refugees who immigrated to Australia, returned to Bialystok to retrace the memories of his father, who had fled Poland during the war. Before his trip, Zable had a dream of being captured and feeling overcome by panic as he was interrogated by guards. "Yet there is one saving grace," Zable said.

> I have in my possession a large volume of stories about the *Tzaddikim*, the early Hasidic masters, who, in the darkest of times, counseled their communities and tried to show them a way back to the light, to the source of Creation.

I look forward to immersing myself in this book as a means of passing time and deriving some comfort while I am imprisoned. But on closer inspection I realize that the book is moth-eaten, and that some of my fellow inmates have ripped out pages to use as cigarette paper.

Then "the partisan" appears, a Gentile family friend who fought with the resistance during the war. He passes Zable a note with instructions about how to escape. "But I cannot quite decipher the scribbled message."[32]

Zable's dream has much to say about the Jewish collective psyche. We are imprisoned in the traumatic memories of the past. The understanding that the Hasidic sages held about how to survive the intolerable by staying connected with the light of the Divine offers guidance, but their wisdom may seem all but lost to us. The partisan appears, offering help, but we are unable to decipher the message.

Bulbes—discovering the rhizome

Recently, I dreamt *that I was at a ritual where various people were engaged in Jewish ceremony. Toward the end of the dream, I feel the presence of my maternal great-grandmother guiding me to bend to the earth and dig. Reaching deep into the soft ground, I find my hands wrapping around a potato infused with a numinous glow. In the dream, I long to know the Yiddish word for potato.* Awakening, I look it up: *bulbes*, from the Lithuanian for "bulbs"—the rhizome from which our lives flower.

When I was growing up, I spent a great deal of time with my maternal grandparents. My grandmother, Emma, was born around 1906 and raised in the Ukraine, immigrating to America when she was around 11 or 12. From the time I was a young child, I was deeply curious about her upbringing, which she adamantly refused to talk about, although she dropped powerful and intriguing hints about her past. When I was around five or six years old, I asked her when her birthday was. "I don't know." I was curious. Birthdays were so important! How could she not know?

Turning her glance to some faraway memory, she told me that the building that held all the records in the town had been burned down and all the birth records were lost. In my young mind I imagined the civic buildings in the town center burning to the ground in a terrible fire, but she did not elaborate. Over the years, when I asked her to explain more about that, or to share anything about her childhood in Russia, she quickly changed the subject, answering variously, "You don't need to know about that," "Let's talk about something happy," or "What's new with you?"

I traveled to Nicaragua in 1985, inspired by the people's revolution, profoundly moved by the graffiti drawn from the iconography of the Spanish Civil War, symbolizing the Nicaraguan people's victory over dictatorship, just as the Spanish Republicans had sought to topple Franco. I spoke by phone with my older brother, who told me that my grandfather was concerned about me and wanted me to call him.

My grandfather always seemed quite conservative, and I was afraid he would be angry at me for traveling to a socialist country. Our phone conversation began mysteriously. He said, "You don't know why you're there, but I know why you're there." I waited silently for him to explain. He continued, "My brother Sol, your great-uncle, died in Spain, fighting Franco." I was floored. I realized that my grandfather understood some powerful force in me that was larger than myself and felt it important to offer me this understanding—a link to my ancestors that contextualized my passion for social justice in a way that my growing up in a moderate, apolitical home never could. My longings had roots—the red and black on the walls of the Nicaraguan villages, the same red and black that inspired the Spanish freedom fighters, also ran in my own blood.

Now, as I understand more about the rich history of the Jews in Spain and the horrors of the Inquisition, I wonder if something ancestral stirred in my great uncle, inspiring him to fight to prevent the rise of dictatorship there. Or perhaps he foresaw how Franco's fascist rule, supported by Hitler, was the first manifestation of the rise of Nazism. Thanks to the preservation work of the Abraham Lincoln Brigade Archives Project at New York University, I recently discovered more about my great-uncle's journey from America to Spain, and how he was one of fewer than 100 Americans who gave their lives fighting fascism in Spain.[33]

My grandparents were not your poster Jewish grandparents. They met in the early 1930s at a Socialist Youth League dance, although they never spoke about their socialist past when I was a child. My grandmother also lost her brother Samuel, who had become a lawyer advocating for the rights of the poor, when he was in his 30s, to a sudden brain aneurysm. The past held tremendous grief for them both, and they rarely talked about it.

My grandmother was considered quite eccentric in the Flatbush neighborhood in Brooklyn where they lived. Suffering with severe agoraphobia, she rarely left the house. She became a spiritual seeker, first drawn to Buddhism in the 1950s and, a few years later, finding Christianity, but never fully converting, maintaining an identity as a Jewish Christian. My grandfather soon followed suit, and they became deeply involved in messianic Judaism. To the outer world, they took on the names Arnold and Emily Ross, but to each other they remained Abe and Emma.

Despite my repeated requests, my grandmother refused to speak about her past. Something in me longed to know my history, my ancestors, and my people. And then the stories came. I do not know why they came when they did. Maybe my grandmother thought I was old enough to understand. Maybe, nearing the end of her life, there was a need to have me carry her history. Maybe I had earned it in some way, with my persistent questions, my longing for understanding.

As she talked, I felt myself carried back to the village in the Ukraine where she had grown up. They were so poor that sometimes, in order to eat, my grandmother would sneak over the walled gardens of those with money to pick potatoes (*bulbes*) to feed her family. I imagined my grandmother as a child, hunched down in the dirt with a spoon digging desperately for potatoes, afraid of being caught. I imagined her carrying them home and giving them to her mother to boil or place in the stove fire.

I listened as my grandmother told me about her father, Moshe, a learned man, the only man in the village who could write in Russian. The villagers would ask him to write letters of petition to the Czar, and later, to government officials. Because of this service, he was much beloved in his community. When the Bolsheviks came to their village, they placed him before the firing squad, along with my grandmother's brother Samuel. Because my great-grandfather was learned in Russian, they labeled him bourgeois, despite the fact that he and his family were quite poor. The villagers pleaded with the soldiers not to kill them, saying that he had done good deeds for them and written letters of petition to the Czar on their behalf. The Bolsheviks let him and my great-uncle escape with their lives.

My grandmother's family quickly gathered themselves up and made their way, traveling for months, first to Italy, then to England, and finally after a long period of waiting, boarding a ship to the United States. My grandmother held these and other stories deep inside herself for decades. She became agoraphobic; she never learned to drive and continued to speak with a heavy Russian-Yiddish accent throughout her life. She never left the house without my grandfather. I wondered about the internalized terror she experienced, and whether her adopting Christianity was an attempt to create more safety for herself in the world.

To the very end of her life, there was not a time I visited when she was not standing at the stovetop, frying potato latkes, dozens at a time, freezing stacks of them, at the ready to be deployed to feed the hungry at their storefront mission or to bring to someone suffering with illness or facing death. When she finally shared the stories of her childhood, I reflected on how by feeding others she also nourished the ravenous child who lived inside her. I had a deeper appreciation of how much she understood what a golden, glistening potato latke might mean to a hungry child.

When I moved from Los Angeles to Mendocino County, I lived on a rural property for the first time in my life. I wanted to plant a garden but felt the need to ask the permission of the Pomo ancestors (the local Native American people) to break ground there. In my meditation, a Pomo grandmother told me, "*You need to plant your feet in the earth.*" She showed me how my own grandmother was ripped from the land of her childhood home in the Ukraine. My grandmother's terror was transmitted to my mother, who struggled with a debilitating depression. She showed me how the women in my family suffered because of being uprooted, of living in a state of psychic exile.

When my mother was in hospice, her sister came to visit her, although they had been long estranged. As we spoke about my mother's suffering, my aunt shared a dream that my grandmother had had long ago. In the dream, *my grandmother saw the whole family on a wagon, escaping from terror, perhaps fleeing Russia as my grandmother had as a girl. As they made their way, the wagon began moving very fast and my mother fell off, and the wagon went on without her.*

After my mother was diagnosed with cancer, she shared with me a dream she had *of walking in a long line of people, a forced march, it seemed, through a seemingly endless, wintry, and brutal night. At one point, she noticed a cabin with a candle burning in the window. She left the line and moved toward the cabin. Inside was her aunt Helen, who had died years before.* I wondered if this dream reflected a release from the painful lives both my grandmother and my mother had endured, and the promise of her finally being welcomed home by the ancestors on the other side.

Lilith in our time

In a meditation, I imagine that this time, when the angels come to the Red Sea seeking Lilith's return to the Garden, she asks, "*Will I still have to lie beneath?*" And the angels respond, "*Well, we've been working on that.*" Lilith returns to *Gan Eden*, now met not only by Adam but also by Eve.

Lilith brings what had been destroying her and lays it down in the Garden, underneath the Tree of Life, and asks for it to be blessed. Her rage, her loss, the tears of grief, the cries of terror, the shame, the unbearable horrors of pogroms, the unspeakable nightmare of the Shoah, the devaluation of women's wisdom for centuries, the loss of the beloved ones tortured and murdered in the Crusades, the Inquisition, Jews, wise women, herbalists, healers, their writings burned, priceless wisdom lost, forever—all of this and more, she lays down underneath the Tree.

And there, cradled by Eve, after all these centuries, she lets go of her rage, and she wails. Adam stands by, surrounded by deer and ibex and wild horses, protected by hawks and eagles, and gives thanks to the Holy One for returning Her, without whom we have been so completely lost.

Notes

1 Victor J. Krebs (2013) "The Power of Ghosts," *Jung Journal Culture & Psyche* 7, no. 4: 35–36.
2 Helene Shulman Lorenz and Mary Watkins, "Silenced Knowings, Forgotten Springs: Paths to Healing in the Wake of Colonialism," paper delivered at the conference of the National Training Laboratory, Bethel, Maine, July 20, 2001.
3 Ibid.
4 Genesis 1:27.
5 Alphabeta de'ben Sira, ed. M. Steinschneider fol. 23a f, Berlin, 1858, cited in Siegmund Hurwitz, *Lilith—the First Eve: Historical and Psychological Aspects of the Dark Feminine* (Einsiedeln: Daimon Verlag, 1992), 119–121. See also Howard Schwartz, *Tree of Souls: The Mythology of Judaism* (New York: Oxford University Press, 2004), 216–226.
6 Hurwitz, *Lilith—the First Eve*, 120.
7 Ibid, *see also,* Raphael Patai, *The Hebrew Goddess* (Detroit, MI: Wayne State University Press, 1967/1978), 223, Schwartz, *Tree of Souls*, 216.
8 Gershon Winkler, personal communication, July 2019. Winkler observes that the actual Ben Sira was Joshua Ben Sira who lived in the 3rd century BCE. The Alphabet of Ben Sira in which the Lilith story appears "was either authored by the same ancient

Ben Sira—as the traditionalists believe—or, as modern scholars believe, it was written anonymously in the 9th century or so in spite of the mention of Ben Sira in its title."

9 Ibid.
10 Ibid.
11 Patai, *Hebrew Goddess*, 118–122.
12 Ibid, 252.
13 Ohad Ezrahi lecture, Santa Rosa, California, August 4, 2005. Ezrahi discovered that Luria designed meditations on how to redeem this powerful aspect of the Feminine.
14 Hurwitz, *Lilith—the First Eve*, 58.
15 Gershon Winkler, *Sacred Secrets: The Sanctity of Sex in Jewish Law and Lore* (Northvale, NJ: Jason Aronson, Inc., 1998).
16 D'vorah Grenn-Scott, *Lilith's Fire: Reclaiming Our Sacred Lifeforce* (Irvine, CA: Universal Publishers, 2000), 80.
17 Ibid, 176.
18 Arthur Green, Introduction to *Hasidism for Tomorrow*, edited by Hava Tirosh Samuelson (Boston, MA: Brill Library of Contemporary Jewish Philosophers, 2015), 43.
19 Hurwitz, *Lilith—the First Eve*, 176.
20 Ibid, 176; citing Jung.
21 Lynn Gottlieb, *She Who Dwells Within: Feminist Vision of a Renewed Judaism* (San Francisco, CA: HarperOne, 1995), 39.
22 Ibid. On the psychological meaning of the Inanna myth, see Sylvia Brinton Perera, *Descent to the Goddess* (Toronto: Inner City Books, 1981), Betty Meador, *Uncursing the Dark: Treasures From the Underworld* (Wilmette, IL: Chiron Publications, 1994).
23 Perera, *Descent to the Goddess*.
24 Betty Meador, *Uncursing the Dark: Treasures From the Underworld* (Wilmette, IL: Chiron Publications, 1994).
25 Rivkah Scharf Kluger, *Psyche in Scripture: The Idea of the Chosen People and Other Essays* (Toronto: Inner City Books, 1995), 99.
26 Ibid.
27 Gershon Winkler, "Lilith and the Demonization of Doubt," lecture presented at Chochmat Ha'Lev, Berkeley, CA, December 2, 2006.
28 Ibid.
29 Ibid.
30 "Groundbreaking Conference to Take Place in November," *YIVO News* 200, no. 5 (Fall): https://docplayer.net/75271695-Groundbreaking-conference-to-take-place-in-n ovember-yivo-awarded-220-000-for-holocaust-archive.html.
31 Louise Steinman, "The Crooked Mirror: A Path to Reconciliation with Self and Other," presented at the Friends of the Jung Institute San Francisco, Sunday, February 1, 2015.
32 Arnold Zable, *Jewels and Ashes* (New York: Harcourt, 1993), 16.
33 Abraham Lincoln Brigade Archives, https://guides.nyu.edu/c.php?g=276867&p =5445937.

Part V

The promise

Chapter 11

The watery initiation and learning to trust the ground of being

"Yukel, which is this land you call Jewish,
which every Jew claims as his own without ever having lived there?"
"It is the land where I have dug my well."
"Yukel, which is this water of our land,
so good against thirst that no other water can compare?"
"It is the water fifty centuries have forgotten in the hollow of our hands."
"Open your hands, brothers," wrote Reb Segre.
"And bury your faces in them.
They will thrive like plants touching water."

Edmond Jabès, The Book of Questions[1]

Grieving all we have left behind, we find ourselves at the shores of the Red Sea. Our monumental choice—to step into a sea that will likely swallow us alive or to be overtaken by the raging Egyptian soldiers in fierce pursuit. This chapter explores the symbolic meaning of the journey across the Red Sea. On a collective level, the loss of faith was profound during the unprecedented assimilation of Jews during the 19th and 20th centuries and in the years following the Shoah. Like the Hebrews after centuries of slavery, many were unwilling to place faith in a God who had been seemingly deaf to their suffering.

On a personal level, the question of putting our faith in the unknown is a developmental leap—we are forced to step beyond the limits of our own egoic consciousness and begin to trust something larger in the psyche, what Jung called the Self. This leap happens again and again as we are continually faced with challenges that call us to marshal both internal and external resources greater than those we have known before.

The holding presence of the Shekhinah enables us to surrender our defenses and enter the unknown, to risk trusting again, even after our trust has been profoundly betrayed. The emergence of a spirituality centered in the feminine marked a profound shift in the landscape of postwar Judaism, a shift to an immanent experience of religious meaning. Leaving behind the constricted consciousness of the cultural complexes, many took the first step into the sea of possibility, finding in the process that the waters parted, opening to a new way of being.

Reb Zalman

The story of Rabbi Zalman Schachter-Shalomi's journey out of Nazi-occupied Europe offers a powerful lived example of how to hold onto one's faith in the midst of catastrophe. Like Sigmund Freud, Reb Zalman descended from a Galician Hasidic Jewish family. Born in 1924 in Poland, in an area that is now the Ukraine, his family moved to Vienna in 1925 and encouraged him to become fluent in German, enrolling him in public school to hasten his assimilation into Austrian society. Although his father took Zalman to the small Hasidic *shtibl* to pray, he did not share with his son the meaning of the practices. Zalman's found his years of assimilated Jewish learning leading up to his Bar Mitzvah uninspiring.[2]

Reb Zalman was 14 when the Nazis annexed Austria in 1938. In the hospital recovering from an appendectomy during Kristallnacht, he witnessed a Nazi officer kill a man, whom he accused of being a Bolshevik, in his hospital bed. Jews were now openly attacked on the streets of Vienna, and Zalman was tormented by Aryan schoolmates who had previously been friends. His father was arrested by the Gestapo and placed on a train to a relocation camp but managed to escape and make his way back to Vienna, staying with friends to avoid capture. The family eventually escaped to Belgium, except for his uncle, Akiva, who chose to return to Poland, despite Zalman's father pleading with him to go west. Akiva returned to the town of Oswiecim, Poland, renamed Auschwitz by the Germans.[3]

As a teenager in Antwerp, Zalman began apprenticing as a furrier, growing bitter as his dreams of becoming a scientist were "as much rubble now as the beautiful stone masonry of our former synagogue in Vienna. Both had been destroyed by the Nazis, and God had let it happen."[4] Zalman recalled going to the local Orthodox youth center to "pick a fight" with someone about his rage at God. A student read aloud from the *Pirke Avot* (Ethics of Our Fathers) that every Jew has a share in the world to come, and Zalman burst out, "Pie in the sky … it's all *narishkeit*, rubbish. Karl Marx was right: religion is the opiate of the masses!"[5] The teacher gently extended his hands to Zalman, asking him, "What else?" Zalman continued to pour out his rage until he felt expended.

The teacher asked if he wanted to hear from someone who agreed with him. Opening the Talmud, he read a passage from *Tractate Sanhedrin*, cautioning against learning Torah in order to earn reward in the world to come.

> For the entire purpose and end of the study of Torah is to know it. There is no other end to the truth but knowing that it is truth, and the Torah is truth … [A] person must believe the truth for its own sake and that a person who does so, we call a "servant of love."

The teacher said, "The *Rambam* (Maimonides, the most renowned Torah scholar of the Middle Ages) agrees with you, and we don't believe in the same God that you don't believe in."[6]

The next few months were times of profound spiritual awakening. Reb Zalman studied diamond cutting with this teacher, Baruch Merzl, singing Hasidic melodies as they worked. As they studied various secular and spiritual texts, Zalman continued to wrestle with the question, "Why is God hiding in the world?" He experienced a luminous brightness as the answer became totally clear: "God bestowed free will to us so that we might grow spiritually, and therefore this is how human life had to be." In that moment, he felt suffused with a sense of "wholeness and unshakable faith," which stayed with him throughout his life.[7]

In 1940, just before his 16th birthday, Zalman's family received permission to travel to the United States and prepared to leave Antwerp. On the day they were to pick up their validated visas, the Germans began their attacks on Belgium and the Netherlands. He and his family waited in line outside the American embassy; eventually they were told no more visas were to be issued. With many other families, they boarded an open-bed coal train headed for Paris. As they arrived at a French border town, the Nazis began strafing the railway station, setting it ablaze, and the family quickly took shelter beneath the train. The engineer was able to get the train into southern France, but not to Paris. This deviation proved to be their salvation, as Paris soon fell under Nazi rule.

Over the next harrowing three months, Zalman and his family were interned at a camp for Jewish refugees. As the Nazis consolidated their conquest of France, Gestapo officers sent his family and others who had obtained passage to the United States to Marseilles, where they were diverted to yet another internment camp. During the difficult days there, Zalman felt guided to create a *shofar* (a ram's horn fashioned into a trumpet-like instrument) as a spiritual act for the community on the Jewish New Year, Rosh Hashanah, when the shofar is sounded. He snuck out of camp and hiked into town, finding a butcher shop whose owner gave him a sheep horn. He boiled the horn and sharpened it on a stone, creating the airway with a makeshift drill he fashioned.

On Rosh Hashanah, he blew the shofar as the community gathered for services. The French camp commander approached and asked what the noise was. Zalman proudly showed him the shofar, the "trumpet of our liberation." The commander replied, "How remarkable!" He began to read an official document and asked Zalman to blow the shofar again, which he did, with deep feeling.

Then the commander announced the names of those whose visas were ready to be picked up in Marseilles, all of whom would be free to leave immediately. Reb Zalman's family's name was among them. He reflected, "I felt sure that in some mystical way, my impassioned act of making that shofar had sparked divine merit for my family and our whole Jewish community incarcerated during Rosh Hashanah in that camp … I had an unforgettable epiphany about faith and right action, blessing and redemption."[8]

The song of the Sea

Reb Zalman's shofar blast in the middle of the refugee camp is like the song Moses offers while crossing the Red Sea. Contrary to common interpretation that Moses sings in gratitude for safe crossing, medieval scholars Nachmanides and

Jacob Seforno believed that Moses sang "*while* the Israelites were still walking on dry land in the midst of the Sea."[9] Biblical scholar Avivah Zornberg observes that this interpretation transforms the meaning of the song from a paean of triumph to "an expression of the terror and faith of those who are still 'in the midst of the Sea.' While they are still walking the precarious passage between massed walls of water, *then*, at this uncanny moment," Moses begins to sing not a victory song, but "a cry from the depths of anguish."[10] According to midrash, Moses and all Israel simultaneously sing the same words and melody; even embryos still in their mother's wombs join in the song.[11]

In the midst of the Red Sea, after centuries of enslavement and devastating losses, Moses and the people sing. They sing not knowing whether this too would end in devastation, whether the walls of the Sea would collapse upon them as it did on the Egyptian soldiers.

Two of the most influential rabbis of the renewal of American Judaism in the 20th century found themselves in the midst of the Red Sea, fleeing from Nazi-occupied Europe. Zalman Schachter-Shalomi and Abraham Joshua Heschel each carried within them the divine sparks of the rabbinic traditions of so many lineages lost in the Shoah. As they sang from the depths of their anguish, their song carried the immanence of God's presence, inviting others to remember the song that came through them as well.

These rabbis exemplified how to not only survive trauma but also to become vessels of holiness and healing, embodying the path of spiritual transformation.[12] Reb Zalman understood personally the rage at a God who did not protect Jews from annihilation by the Nazis. From his own experience of assimilated Jewish life in Vienna, and from his spiritual awakening that opened him to the depths of the mystical in his own Hasidic lineage, he understood that people needed to have a direct spiritual experience of and relationship to God to find their own meaning within Judaism. Theology emerged from direct spiritual experience, not the other way around. Reb Zalman observed:

> We start with wonder, or with thankfulness, or yearning, or even rage, and we ask ourselves: Wonder or rage at what? Thankfulness toward what? Yearning for what? It was simple, searching questions like these that started our ancestors thinking in terms of "God." Torah, Talmud, Hebrew school—that all came later.[13]

Heschel encouraged people to open to the presence of God in experiences of what he called "radical amazement." [14]

Like Moses in the midst of the Red Sea, these rabbis fleeing the flames of the Shoah sang a song of redemption, not knowing whether or how their people would survive. Bringing forth their voices from their own faith and terror, they sang and found themselves among others who also knew the song. Even the embryos were able to sing all the words, as the generations not yet born at the time of the Shoah carried the song in their hearts.

After the Shoah, we as a people have experienced an eclipsing of God as we might have believed Him to be. We can no longer rest in an innocent, childlike conception of God as a protective Father who will deliver us from suffering and evil. Instead, if we are to have a spiritual life, we must come into a mature faith, one that includes awareness of the depth of evil that is possible in the world, and find our way into relationship with the Great Mystery of Being that encompasses this knowing.

Collectively, we are living through a time the alchemists referred to as the *black sun*, when the light of consciousness is completely darkened by experiences of overwhelming despair and loss.[15] From such experiences, we may proceed into a faith that includes awareness of profound and unfathomable suffering, and that acknowledges that God does not prevent atrocities from happening but suffers with us when they do.

The Israelites standing at the shores of the Red Sea faced this same dilemma. They witnessed their deliverance from Pharaoh, but only after surviving centuries of unbearable cruelty. Their ambivalence about placing complete faith in the God who had brought them out of Egypt might be understood as a reasonable response of a traumatized people unwilling to trust the unknown. Like Moses and the Hebrews in the Sea, the great teachers of the post-Shoah era invited the people to cry out in the midst of their anguish, despair, longing, rage, and grief, not knowing what the response, if any, would be.

Psychological rebirthing

At the shores of the sea, we are called to move through the birth canal to a new reality. As we begin to make our way, we are completely disoriented, strangers in a strange land. The contours of our oppression are familiar; the landscape of freedom, vast and unknown. As the Egyptian soldiers fall into the waters of the Red Sea, the voice of our own inner Pharaoh finally loosens its grip on our psyche. In the wilderness of our becoming, we are freed to hear a different voice, to align ourselves to a new reality—that of the emerging Self.

Intergenerational trauma moves in subtle and profoundly damaging ways. When our mothers and fathers do not have a sense of safety and stability in their own bodies, they cannot transmit this sense of safety to us as infants and children. We grow up fearful and distrusting the ground of being itself. We experience a permeating sense of anxiety and dread about life and have difficulty feeling safe. When the trauma manifests in our caretakers in various defenses such as narcissism and shaming, we may take on a profound sense of inadequacy and lack self-worth. These patterns are pervasive and may keep us in a state of anxiety or depression for most of our lives if we do not find ways to address and heal them.

When we have been hurt, when we have been traumatized, how do we find the willingness to risk trusting life again, to have faith that a path may open for us despite previous disappointments and hurts? How do we surrender trying to control every aspect of life to ensure against being hurt or humiliated? The plagues are the contractions, the complexes that make life so restricted, so painful, that we have no choice but to place our foot in the Sea, to move toward a new way of being, and hope against hope that the waters will part. We enter the Sea when the pain of living in fear becomes unbearable. Most likely, we would never take that step into the Sea unless our very lives depended on it.

In one midrash, the Israelites gather at the shores of the Red Sea, the Egyptian soldiers a hair's breadth behind, the raging waters of the Sea in front of them. Nachshon, a descendant of Joseph's brother Judah and his wife Tamar, walks forward and places his foot into the Sea. *Nothing happens.* He walks farther, up to his knees. *Still nothing.* He continues, the water now reaching his belly, his chest, his neck … *nothing!* Willing to risk all, Nachshon walks until his nostrils are filled with water and still he does not stop. As he takes what feels like his last breath … the sea parts, miraculously. Moses raises his staff, and the people follow Nachshon into the parted waters.

Each of us has within us a Nachshon who we may not discover until we are forced to move into the unknown, to trust some force greater than ourselves, which we can only hope will be a benevolent one. Nachshon is descended from Judah, who undergoes a profound transformation in his relationship with his brother Joseph, learning to release his envy and develop humility and compassion. Nachshon symbolizes the consciousness birthed from this humbling. He alone steps forward, trusting that if he fully surrenders his fear, a new way will open.

Later, when the Ark that holds the Torah is assembled, the princes of the different tribes are required to bring their offerings, each on a separate day. Moses does not know who should be the first, but all Israel points at Nachshon, recalling that he sprang first into the Red Sea and brought down the Shekhinah—therefore he should be first to bring an offering.[16] In the Book of Ruth, Ruth's husband Boaz is Nachshon's descendant and carries this new manifestation of the masculine. Boaz's union with Ruth, representing renewed masculine and feminine energies, is the lineage from which the *Mashiach*, or enlightened consciousness, will arise.[17]

The Hebrews standing at the Red Sea are like a pregnant woman whose water has broken; the birth is coming and there is no turning back, only moving forward, into a completely unknown future, or death. The crossing of the Red Sea is a watery initiation to which we must surrender and trust the dissolution of our previous identity, to be formed anew. Jungian analyst Gareth Hill observes that when we have become overly reliant on the masculine outer forms of affirmation for our sense of worth, we must undergo a watery initiation, in which our previous identity dissolves and we are washed in the waters of the larger psyche.[18] Out of this loss of identity, we connect with something essential in ourselves, from which a new personality emerges.

Rabbi Leah Novick notes that the Exodus story is suffused with images of the Shekhinah present in every elemental aspect of the journey through the Sea and during the sojourn in the wilderness. "She manifests in the water of the Red Sea and in Miriam's well; in the air as the clouds of glory; in fire as the pillar of fire; and on earth, where the Israelites gather the miraculous manna."[19] Novick observes, "Metaphorically, the Israelites journey through the watery womb of the Great Mother and emerge reborn on dry land." The pillar of cloud of the Shekhinah arises between the Hebrews and Egyptians, so that the attackers cannot see. The destructive aspect of the Great Mother destroys the soldiers, "fulfilling her assigned role as mobilizer of the armies of God and punisher of the wicked."[20]

In the Red Sea, the Egyptian soldiers are toppled from their mounts and fall into the raging waters. The negative voices that have kept us imprisoned in a narrow way of life give way to a more powerful force. Beginning to trust and depend on the Divine Presence for safety, guidance, protection, and nurturance, the traumatic wounds of the past are transformed.

As the adaptations we have developed to survive trauma dissolve in the watery initiation of rebirth, the core self emerges, sometimes a very young part of us that has not yet had the room to grow into fullness. As old defenses dissolve in the waters of the Red Sea, this emergent self, surrendering into the embrace of the Great Mother, begins the journey into becoming.

Collectively, as the plagues or cultural complexes of the post-traumatic response were worked through, new expressions of Judaism began to emerge. The watery initiation in the post-Shoah generations allowed Jews to move beyond the assimilated, rational approaches of Haskalah Judaism, or the secularism they had grown up with, and to rediscover the depths of the mystical tradition. Traditional forms were also undergoing a rebirth—as patriarchal, hierarchical forms of Judaism that excluded and devalued women's participation and wisdom lost their grip, new forms that honored feminine aspects of spiritual practice developed, forms that invited an opening to the Mystery that sacred ritual was designed to engender.

Joshua's story continues

Joshua's disconnection from Judaism was marked by the separation from his mother just after his Bar Mitzvah, a major event in his life. Without maternal support, he was unable to move forward into a meaningful initiation and instead spiraled down into depression and marijuana addiction.

Joshua described his reconnection with Judaism after decades of estrangement at Rosh Hashanah services at Chochmat Ha'Lev in Berkeley. At the service, he felt his "whole being coming alive" as they sang "*Mi Kamocha*" ("Who Is Like You?"), a song celebrating the miracle of the Red Sea parting. As the congregation began to sing, he had an experience of the awe of God, "of actually standing on a seashore and seeing all of this destruction that had to happen to bring our people to that place."

Joshua also saw how the destruction in his own life had brought him to this moment of crossing. Overcome with tears, his eyes met the congregational leader's, who was also crying. Later they spoke of their shared understanding of the paradox that at this moment of complete destruction, they could be in a state of joy and dancing. Joshua felt his younger, Jewish-identified self return, a soul retrieval, as he was welcomed into the inner circle of the congregation.

As we acknowledge the pain of the traumas we have endured, both individually and collectively, and the devastation that has been wrought in our souls and the souls of our people, we understand the momentousness of taking the first step into the Red Sea. Perhaps it is not so much a question of whether the sea itself will part as it is our own willingness to take that step that is the transformation. Maybe the step itself is the freedom we seek. When we allow ourselves, finally, to trust again, we experience a profound relief. Perhaps we discover that we are not alone, we do not have to carry the world on our shoulders. Perhaps we find that we are held by something greater, something that supports our quest to become our fullest selves.

Miriam and the women

The prophetess Miriam dances with the women as the people make their way across the Red Sea. The dance represents the reconnection with our bodies, our voices, and our joy. We are free to find the movement that emanates spontaneously from our limbs and our muscles. Miriam guides the people, along with her brothers Moses and Aaron, as they journey through the desert. Without her, the Exodus would not have occurred. Her challenge to her father's proposed edict that couples stop procreating led to the night of lovemaking on the shores of the Nile and her parents' conception of Moses. After Moses was born, she safeguarded her brother's reed basket along the Nile, until he was rescued by Pharaoh's daughter Batya.

Now Miriam, whose prophecies have made this collective birth possible, celebrates the crossing of the Red Sea, dancing with the women on the ground that has miraculously opened. Singing, "*This* is my God!," the women recognize that the God who accompanies them as they find themselves in the midst of the Red Sea is the same God who midwifed their infants in the fields of Egypt.

Avivah Zornberg recounts the Talmudic legend of the midwife who safeguards the lives of the Hebrew children, protecting them from Pharaoh's edict. When the enslaved Hebrew women give birth under the apple tree where they had conceived, "God would send from the highest heavens one who would cleanse them and make them beautiful." When the Egyptians came to kill the newborns, the babies were swallowed into the soil, and the Egyptians plowed over the fields with oxen. After they left, "Babies would sprout forth like the grass of the fields." As they grew, the children came in flocks into the homes of the women. And when God "revealed Himself at the Sea—they recognized Him" as the one who had protected their children.[21]

According to another legend, Serach bat Asher was also present at the crossing, and witnessed the collective birth of the Hebrews into new life as they make their way through the Red Sea. She saw "a multitude of angels" accompanying the children of Israel and the Shekhinah with Miriam and the women as they played their timbrels and sang the Song of the Sea. Serach saw "the Holy One commanding the waters of the Red Sea to part. For other than Moses, Serach was the only one alive in that generation who could look upon the Holy One and live."[22]

In the Talmudic era, Rabbi Yohanan explained to his students that the walls of the Red Sea looked like a window lattice. Then they heard a voice saying, "No, it was not like that at all!" The students and Rabbi looked up and saw an old woman's face staring into the study hall. Rabbi Yohanan asked who she was and she responded,

> I am Serach bat Asher … and I know exactly what the walls resembled, I was there, I crossed the Red Sea—and they resembled shining mirrors, mirrors in which every man, woman, and child was reflected, so that it seemed like an even greater multitude crossed there, not only those of the present, but also those of the past and future as well.

When she was done speaking, no one questioned her, for they all knew that she had witnessed the event firsthand.[23]

This passage recalls how the multitudes who left Egypt were conceived when the women brought the copper mirrors to the men, playfully inviting erotic union. The Shekhinah safeguarded the babies who came from this union. Now Serach bat Asher sees each of these souls mirrored by the Divine as they make their way through the Red Sea, reflecting their beauty and courage. This midrash tells us that we were all present—the past, present, and future generations—not only at Sinai, but also here, in the midst of the Red Sea. We each have a living memory of what it was like to have been midwifed and safeguarded by the Divine, finding the courage to surrender to Her capable hands to support us in our rebirth.

Miriam is connected to the waters—from her guidance of Moses's basket down the Nile, to the celebratory dance following the crossing of the Red Sea, to her miraculous powers as a dowser. Her well brings forth water wherever she places it down in the desert. Unlike the Biblical women in previous generations who were defined by their roles as spouses and mothers, Miriam is more like a virgin goddess, one who stands on her own merit. Miriam and Moses represent the renewed feminine and masculine energies that guide the people through the sea and during their wanderings in the desert.

While Moses ascends Mount Sinai alone, Miriam connects with the depths and dances in a sacred circle with the women. Zornberg recognizes that the significance of this act may not yet be fully appreciated. The circle made by our ancestral mothers foretells the feminine structures that may yet emerge as the expression of our connection to the sacred. The great 18th-century Hasidic Rabbi Kalonymous Kalman Epstein observed that Miriam's circle dance offers a kabbalistic image of the feminine, where "all points on the circumference have an equal relationship with the center." He believed that in the messianic era, all forms of masculine hierarchy will be superseded, and "the circle will replace the straight line as the modality of the world to come," as all the dancers will be equally intimate with God.[24]

Miriam represents the leadership that women may have enjoyed in Biblical times and in different incarnations of Judaism in the many eras that followed.

A medieval Spanish Haggadah featuring Miriam and the women dancing may reflect women's spiritual leadership among Sephardic Jews in that time.[25]

Vanessa Ochs observes that Miriam represents every Jewish woman who engages in creating meaningful ritual, transforming sacred texts and ritual objects, and engaging in the active healing of the tradition by widening its arc.[26] In the postwar era, the emergence of Jewish feminism called into question the entire model of hierarchical Judaism and invited the voices of those who had been previously excluded. Both feminism and the *havurah* movements created egalitarian circles in which each person's questions and insights regarding spirituality were valued. The former reliance on an outer authority was largely eschewed in favor of a model of equals searching together for meaning.

Judaism has undergone a complete reorientation in our time, as women have been integrated into every aspect of Jewish life from which they were formerly excluded. Jewish women, first ordained as Reform rabbis in the 1970s, now make up over fifty percent of non-Orthodox rabbinical students and are among the most avid participants in temple life.

Hannah's story continues

As explored earlier, Hannah felt that Judaism lacked depth and meaning. As a teenager, she was disappointed with the inability of her rabbi and teachers to provide meaningful spiritual responses to her questions about death and the afterlife. Turning away from the Judaism she had loved as a child, Hannah sought to find meaning through exploring other spiritual paths and metaphysical approaches. She experienced a series of synchronicities and dreams that ultimately led to her reconnection with Judaism.

In one significant dream, *she was visited by an angelic being that handed her a flier with a date on it*, which she discovered upon waking was an upcoming "Age of Angels" conference. A few days later, on her birthday, she again *dreamt of an angelic presence. This time the angel flew above her. When Hannah asked if she could fly with her, the angel replied, "Then you'll have to open your heart." In the dream, she felt something like a crowbar opening her heart, and she flew up into the air with the angel who began changing into many different female forms.*

Soon after receiving these dreams, Hannah attended a Jewish Renewal retreat in Virginia led by Rabbi Marcia Prager and *Chazzan* (cantor) Jack Kessler. She experienced an electrical current buzzing through her entire body that stayed with her throughout the weekend. She felt she was in the presence of transformation.

Rabbi Marcia explained the spiritual significance of wearing a *tallit*, or prayer shawl. Hannah, raised in the Conservative tradition, had never seen a woman wear a tallit. Rabbi Marcia described it as "wrapping the arms of a loving God around you." The very next Friday, Hannah lit Shabbos candles for the first time since leaving her childhood home and began to observe Shabbat regularly. She bought a necklace around that time with a Star of David and a heart in the center of it, symbolizing her heart coming into her Judaism. Soon after the retreat, Hannah began designing her own *tallitot*, imbuing each with sacred meaning.

Hannah's experience reflects many factors that have enabled Jews alienated from Judaism to find a pathway to reconnection. As detailed in the previous chapter, her grandfather suffered tremendous trauma when he witnessed his mother being murdered in a pogrom in Russia. He continued to observe Orthodox Judaism, but he suffered from severe mental illness. He enacted the trauma he experienced on his children, abusing them emotionally, physically, and sexually. Although Hannah's mother practiced Judaism, her observance was cut off from feeling, likely because observance was fraught with many conflicted feelings about her own childhood.

The lack of meaning that Hannah experienced in her temple as she became a teenager likely reflected the inability of the elders around her to have easy answers—or *any* answers—about the meaning of life in the aftermath of the Shoah. They, like many of that era, had great difficulty responding to questions of faith.

For Hannah, the gateway back came through a dream of an angel encompassing many archetypal manifestations of the feminine and from a female rabbi who could impart a felt understanding of the tradition, allowing her to connect with the symbols and rituals of her childhood. As Reb Zalman noted, spirituality rooted in direct experience can provide a profound basis for faith. Hannah experienced a reintegration of meaning that enabled her to develop a deeply felt heart connection with the tradition.

The immanent Divine—dwelling in presence

Transformation of consciousness may be heralded by a direct experience of the sacred, but may require ongoing practices that enable us to grow and develop new awareness. The 40 years spent wandering in the desert have less to do with the distance traveled geographically than the amount of time needed for the people to establish a new state of being. As the people open their awareness to the greater expanse of the Self, they are given practices—commandments, or *mitzvot*. This section explores feminine practices that support connection with the immanent Divine, the Shekhinah.

The following chapter explores more active practices that enabled the newly liberated slaves to become a people free from the psychological distortions imposed by centuries of trauma. These same practices sustained our ancestors' connection to the Source as they endured millennia of exile, and guide us in growing into a state of expanded consciousness following trauma.

Shabbat—sacred time

When the people come to the other side of the Red Sea, the first experience they are given is that of Shabbat, the rest day. Shabbat is when we welcome in the presence of the Sabbath Bride, the Queen, the Shekhinah, the Indwelling Presence. The medieval Spanish kabbalists and the Safed mystics spoke of the Shekhinah as the embodied Feminine, the consort of the Holy One. In this personified form, she was welcomed at each Shabbat gathering, as the mystics in their white linens gathered in the fields and called her Presence to them.

The connection between Shabbat and the Divine Feminine reaches deep into the ancient roots of our psyches. As Esther Harding reflects in her book *Woman's Mysteries*, the word for *Sabbath* comes from Near Eastern traditions in which all activities ceased during the monthly period when the Moon Goddess was menstruating.[27] As in traditional Jewish observance, during this ancient lunar Sabbath observance, our foremothers in the Fertile Crescent refrained from making fires, cooking, and other usual daily activities.

On Shabbat, we taste *Mashiach* consciousness, a future time of fulfillment when the transcendent and the immanent will be unified. This corresponds to psychological wholeness, of a consciousness that is aligned with and actualizes the wisdom of the Self, which guides our spiritual longing and development. On the Sabbath, all the souls of Israel receive a *neshamah yeterah*, a second soul, that blooms forth from the Tree of Life. Rabbi Abraham Joshua Heschel recognized that Sabbath is "spirit in the form of time." Eternal life "is planted within us," growing beyond us.[28]

In the loving embrace of the Shekhinah in the desert, the people are reborn into a new reality, a new consciousness, a new beginning. Each week as we rest in the fullness of Shabbat, we dwell within this lived experience of wholeness, in which we are resourced, again and again.

For the Hebrews who were enslaved for over 400 years, Shabbat carried the essential aspect of freedom—freedom from doing and resting in being. In our own lives, we may have inherited patterns of striving and overdoing that are responses to traumatic deprivation and anti-Semitism, patterns of needing to create material safety and a place in a new world, after centuries of displacement. The gift of Shabbat offers a refuge in which to dwell in stillness, in holiness; it is a space of inner replenishment, of being rather than doing, where we can feel the soul that blooms forth from the Tree of Life taking root within.

The Mishkan—sacred space

In the desert, God tells the people to build a mishkan so the Holy Presence can dwell among them. It is from *mishkan* that the word *Shekhinah* comes. The *mishkan* is the sacred tabernacle in which the soul encounters the presence of the Divine. In this tent of meeting, God brings the Shekhinah, the Divine Presence to dwell with the people. The Shekhinah leads the people by day with a pillar of fire. When the camp is at rest, the people must keep the fire burning and tend it through the night.

Creating a mishkan in the center of our beings, a vessel in which we can deepen and cultivate our relationship with God, sustains an inner temenos for ongoing transformation. Seeing ourselves through God's eyes as valuable, as sacred, as worthy beings may be, for some of us, the first relationship that has made us feel strong and safe enough in ourselves to risk relationships with others. We may heal the unmet needs of our childhoods by coming into relationship with the Source, what Jung called the Self, which provides what we need for our own fulfillment and growth. In this way, we move toward spiritual adulthood and develop a secure base deep within ourselves. Opening to a deeper trust, our relationships with others may also begin to feel less defended, gradually transmuting into holy spaces in which the Divine Presence dwells.

When the Israelites gather to decorate the mishkan, all the precious symbols of the journey out of Egypt are brought to adorn it. The decorating of the tabernacle symbolizes the sanctification of a spiritual vessel that will hold the transformative space of our becoming. To decorate the mishkan, we gather the most significant symbols of our journey—those that help us birth the unfolding of our deepest Self, that remind us of the courage it took to get here, as well as reminders of the losses and suffering we have incurred along the way.

According to midrash, when the Blessed Holy One tells Moses to build the mishkan, the men bring silver and gold and carnelian and other stones. The women ask themselves what they might have to offer and choose to bring the mirrors used in the clay pits of Egypt, on the night of erotic play with the men, revivifying the life force of the people. Moses rages when he sees the mirrors, and he tells the men, "Take sticks and break their thighs! Who needs these mirrors?"

God reprimands, saying "Moses! Do you disdain these? These mirrors produced all these multitudes in Egypt! Take some of them and make out of them a bronze basin with its stand for the priests, from which the priests will purify themselves." God guides the women to use the mirrors to create the basin the priests will use for purification, reflected in the true light of love that the mirrors represent.

In medieval kabbalistic literature, these mirrors of the women who ministered (*mar'ot hazove'ot*) were associated with the sefirot of the Tree of Life and with the Shekhinah. The sefirah of Malkhut "is a cosmic mirror reflecting all of the higher Sefirot, the forms of all being. Because She contains them all and displays them, She herself is called *mar'ot hazove'ot*."[29]

Miriam's well—connection with the depths

The Talmud recounts that Moses, Aaron, and Miriam were the leaders of Israel as they wandered through the desert. God provided three gifts because of their merits—the well by the merit of Miriam, the pillar of cloud due to Aaron's merit, and manna due to the merit of Moses.[30] The Biblical text reflects that after Miriam died, the people had no water.[31] They began attacking Moses for bringing them to the desert.

God advised Moses to go to Mt. Horeb in the desert, from which water flowed abundantly. God told Moses to speak to the rock.[32] Moses could not contain his anger at the rebelling people, and instead of speaking to the rock, struck it instead. Because of his frustration and anger with the people, Moses was denied the right to enter the Promised Land.[33] A commentary by Rashi suggests that Moses was so overcome with grief for his sister, who had safeguarded his life from the time of his conception, that he was unable to contain his anger at that moment.[34] The sacred well ceased to flow, and in the wake of Miriam's death, we see the resurfacing of enmity and anger that arises in the absence of relatedness, such as occurred among Joseph's brothers after the death of Rachel.

Yet rather than allow the enmity to devolve, after Moses struck the rock and water flowed forth from it, in the merit of Miriam, according to midrash, God gifted the people with her well. The midrash offers a vision of its abundant flowing waters. In answer to the people's prayers, water would gush up in high pillars, forming great navigable streams on which "the Jews sailed to the ocean, and hauled all the treasures of the world therefrom." Women would cross the rivers that separated the encampments in ships, to visit one another. As the water stretched out beyond the camp, it formed a great plain, where every conceivable plant and tree grew, and fresh fruits appeared each day.[35]

Midrashic legend recounts that throughout the many years of wandering in the desert, the Hebrews had fresh water to drink from the enchanted well God gave the people in the merit of Miriam. The well followed the people everywhere, ascending the mountains and descending into the deep valleys with them. "Some say that well was created at the beginning of Creation, while others say that the patriarchs … dug it." Some say it accompanied the people until they reached the Holy Land. Some say the well "can still be found traveling from place to place, wherever Jews can be found. Whenever a *minyan* gathers, it is possible to drink from the well."[36]

No less than Moses, Miriam's fierce commitment to the continuation of the life of the Jewish people makes possible their journey into freedom. In her merit, the wellsprings of renewal now travel with the people. No longer tied to a particular place, the connection to the deep Feminine accompanies the people throughout their wandering. This is a dynamic symbol for our own journey of faith. As we venture forth into the unknown, we cannot know whether we will be sustained. Miriam teaches us how to draw water wherever we are.

Finding my way out of exile

As a young woman, *Jewish feminism* seemed like an oxymoron, an irreconcilable conflict. I wrestled with the idea of whether the Divine was feminine or masculine. In a meditation on the Big Sur coast, a clear voice showed me that God was beyond gender; that male and female were simply ways we had of conceptualizing the Divine so that we could fathom It. Years later, when I encountered the idea of the *Ein Sof* in kabbalah, the transcendent Divine that is "beyond knowing," I understood that my experience on the beach was an insight into the Jewish mystical view of the nature of God.

While I was finding my way in Goddess circles and Native American sweat lodges, others who felt the same disenchantment and alienation from Judaism that I did, had been busy wrestling with the outmoded forms and incarnating a rebirth of Jewish spirituality. Rather than being blinded by the seemingly irreconcilable contradictions between Judaism and feminism, these women—rabbis, scholars, feminists—had confronted the conflicts directly, asking whether it was possible for women's voices to be heard in Judaism, to overcome more than 2,000 years of almost exclusively male voices that have defined the tradition, or whether what they were up to might necessitate the formation of an entirely new religion—a religion of recovered women's wisdom.

A new generation of Reconstructionist and Renewal rabbis and spiritual leaders arose, as well as Orthodox, Conservative, and Reform women, feminist men and gender non-binary teachers, reclaiming embodied forms of practice such as meditation, chanting, movement, and a deep recognition of the Sacred Feminine. Rabbis Jane Litman, Debra Orenstein, and others designed non-hierarchical rituals that reflected Miriam's circle dance. Rabbi Shefa Gold infused the liturgy with chants that helped Jews unfamiliar with Hebrew to resonate deeply with the poetry of Biblical verse; Rabbi Marcia Praeger helped people find deep meaning in the prayers and rituals of Jewish practice; Rabbis Leah Novick, Tirzah Firestone, and Jill Hammer opened and deepened the understanding of the Shekhinah in the kabbalistic tradition.

The mirrors of these women who ministered reflected the light of the Ein Sof in new ways, reclaiming the beauty and depth of the mystical in forms that included expressions of the Feminine as seen and experienced by women. As I stepped into the Red Sea trusting the unknown, I, along with many others, allowed myself to be birthed into a new reality. Re-engaging with new forms of Jewish expression, I drank deeply from the waters of the well they had drawn up from the ancient depths, restoring the Sacred Feminine at the heart of Judaism.

My meeting with Reb Zalman

I had the honor of meeting with Reb Zalman in 2013, a year before his passing, to discuss my work exploring the experiences of those deepening into Judaism through Jewish Renewal practices and communities. I spoke with him about the Hebrew goddess Asherah, sharing the conflict I felt inside for many years with the Biblical prohibitions against Her worship. He quietly reflected that what had been the Canaanite quaternity of El, Asherah, Baal, and Anat was absorbed into kabbalistic mysticism as Mother, Father, Son, and Daughter because it is a deep archetypal pattern in the psyche and must be expressed. I felt his wisdom as a scholar of comparative religions helping me move out of a constricted way of seeing that now gave way to a larger understanding.

He asked me about my own process of reconnection, and I discussed with him my journeying visions with my ancestors. "And who do you talk to about such things?" he wondered. I shared some of my experiences at the San Francisco Jung

Institute and in my own analysis with a Jewish analyst. A light came across his face as he discussed his strong desire to work with Erich Neumann. "I wanted to see Neumann," he said, and arranged to move to Israel in the late 1950s to become his analysand. "But he died just a year later." I sensed the sadness and loss in his statement and felt it echoing my own, as I was just now having the opportunity to meet personally with Reb Zalman in his advanced years.

He encouraged my explorations with an inner teacher and expressed how important it is that Judaism allow people to access their embodied experience. He asked me if I was familiar with the work of Colette, a mystical teacher in Jerusalem who shared the lineage that came through her maternal line, and the work of Jewish Renewal Rabbi Nadya Gross, who also transmitted the teachings from her maternal line of mystics. I felt his encouragement of this women's way of knowing, of listening to the ancestors and receiving their message through meditation and guidance, as I have felt my own grandmothers guiding me.

He offered, "The reality map to which our magisterium is connected has to be revised."

What I heard was, "The same God that you don't believe in, I don't believe in either."

What I understood was, the mirrors of the women who minister reflect the reality of the upper worlds in ways that are constantly unfolding.

The inner scroll

To be in exile, to be without the Mother, is to be separated from the ground of existence itself. This is the legacy of trauma. In families where parents or grandparents survived anti-Semitic violence, pogroms, displacement, loss of home and community, there was often a lack of mothering or maternal presence. Not only were the ecstatic practices of Judaism that offered a pathway to direct experience of the sacred absent, but few growing up in the post-war era were aware that such practices even existed.

Trauma shatters the psyche; the scattered sparks are woven back together through story. Judaism has enabled Jews to survive the trauma of diaspora for millennia by including a central and cohering story that provides a way of making meaning—of reminding us of who we are and by giving us a mythic framework for surviving overwhelming realities.

Each of us has an individual story that is a scroll unto itself. It is the scroll of our personal history, our lineage, the story of how it was passed down to us under tremendous adversity, and how we almost didn't receive it, how we almost missed it, and how the power of it sought us out. The inheritance finds us, and perhaps in a moment of cracking, enough light penetrates to awaken our curiosity, to explore what this treasure is that we have been gifted.

Perhaps there is sufficient holding so that the light does not get blown out by the winds of postmodernity, of distraction, of nihilism, of despair. Perhaps we sit with it long enough, get quiet enough, to hear. "*Shema, Yisrael.*" Listen, Israel. Listen, wrestling one. Holding a shell to our ear, perhaps we get quiet enough to hear the lapping waters of the Red Sea. Perhaps we trust enough to put our foot in the sea and watch how the water parts for us, and how, by simply walking forward, we may be birthed into a new reality of connectedness, of coming home— to a home we have never known, yet never forgotten.

Notes

1 Edmond Jabès, *The Book of Questions*, Vol. I (Hanover: Wesleyan University Press, 1972), 59.
2 Zalman Schacter-Shalomi, *My Life in Jewish Renewal: A Memoir* (Lanham, MD: Rowman & Littlefield Publishers, 2012), 7–11.
3 Ibid, 19–23.
4 Ibid, 26.
5 Ibid.
6 Ibid, 30.
7 Ibid, 31.
8 Ibid, 41–42.
9 Avivah Zornberg, *Bewilderments: Reflections on the Book of Numbers* (New York: Schocken, 2015), 101.
10 Ibid.
11 Ibid, 102.
12 John P. Wilson, *The Posttraumatic Self: Restoring Meaning and Wholeness to Personality* (New York: Routledge, 2006), 45.
13 Zalman Schacter-Shalomi and Joel Segel, *Jewish with Feeling: A Guide to Meaningful Jewish Practice* (Woodstock, VT: Jewish Lights Publishing, 2006), 7.
14 Abraham Joshua Heschel, *I Asked for Wonder: A Spiritual Anthology*, edited by Samuel H. Dresner (New York: The Crossroad Publishing Company, 1983).
15 Stanton Marlon, *The Black Sun: The Alchemy and Art of Darkness* (College Station, TX: Texas A&M University Press, 2005).
16 Numbers 7:12; Louis Ginzberg, "The Gifts of the Princes," in *The Legends of the Jews* (Philadelphia: Jewish Publication Society of America, 1969).
17 Yehezkiel Kluger, *A Psychological Interpretation of Ruth* (Einsiedeln: Daimon Verlag, 1999).
18 Gareth S. Hill, *Masculine and Feminine: The Natural Flow of Opposites in the Psyche* (Boston: Shambhala, 1992), 24–26.
19 Leah Novick, *On the Wings of Shekhinah: Rediscovering Judaism's Divine Feminine* (Wheaton, IL: Quest Books, 2008), 25.
20 Ibid.
21 Zornberg, *Bewilderments*, 103; citing Talmud B. Sotah 11b.
22 Howard Schwartz, *Tree of Souls: The Mythology of Judaism* (New York: Oxford University Press, 2004), 380; citing Pesikta de-Rav Kahana 11:13.
23 Ibid, 381; citing Pesikta de-Rav Kahana 11:13.
24 Zornberg, *Bewilderments*, 106.
25 Vanessa Ochs, "Ritualizing the Presence of Miriam," in *Women Remaking American Judaism*, edited by Riv-Ellen Prell (Detroit, MI: Wayne State University Press, 2007), 262.
26 Ibid.
27 Esther Harding, *Woman's Mysteries: Ancient and Modern* (Boston: Shambhala, 2001), 62–63.

The word *sabattu* comes from Sa-bat and means Heart-rest; it is the day of rest which the moon takes when full, for at that time it is neither increasing nor decreasing. On this day, which is the direct forerunner of the Sabbath, it was considered unlucky to do any work or to eat cooked food or to go on a journey. These are the things that are prohibited to the menstruating woman. On the day of the moon's menstruation everyone, whether man or woman, was subject to similar restrictions, for the taboo of the menstruating woman was on all. The Sabbath was at first observed only once a month, later it was kept at each quarter of the moon's phases.

28 Abraham Joshua Heschel, *The Sabbath* (New York: Farrar, Straus and Giroux, 1951), 74.
29 Daniel Chanan Matt, "David Ben Yehudah Heḥasid and His 'Book of Mirrors.'" *Hebrew Union College Annual* 51 (1980): 129–172, 134. www.jstor.org/stable/23507684.
30 Talmud Bavli Ta'anit 9a
31 Numbers 20:1-2.
32 Exodus 17:6.
33 Numbers 20:8–12.
34 Ismar Schorsch, "The Death of Miriam," *Jewish Theological Seminary online,* http://www.jtsa.edu/the-death-of-miriam, June, 1994.
35 Ginsberg, "The Gifts of the Princes," 129, 133.
36 Schwartz, *Tree of Souls*, 387, citing *Targum Pseudo-Yonathan* on Numbers 21:16-20.

Chapter 12

The fiery initiation and moving toward the Promised Land

Who is Jewish? Perhaps the person who, while
never sure of it, by and by discovers his
Jewishness in the probability.
Judaism is conjugated in the future.
To read in yourself—not only for yourself—
The book you are carefully deciphering.
To read the erasures
Under the writing.

Edmond Jabès, The Book of Shares[1]

After crossing the Red Sea, the Israelites begin their 40-year journey through the desert. Before they can reach the Promised Land, old ways of being and thinking must be transformed in the wilderness. The ten plagues represent the distortions of the ten sefirot of the Cosmic Tree of Life and of our own personal and collective psyche. The Ten Commandments that the people receive at Sinai represent the new consciousness that the people must adopt to move to a higher state of awareness and to come into alignment with the Divine. Symbolically, the 40 years represent how the ten sefirot must be transformed on all four worlds of consciousness—physical, emotional, mental, and spiritual. A complete transformation must take place before we can live in the new reality.

Freeing ourselves from the complexes that trauma creates is a process that requires both insight and sustained discipline to stay connected to this new way of experiencing life. In the desert, the people are guided to develop practices that enable them to deepen their relationship with the Divine. Psychologically, this corresponds to developing an ongoing relationship between the ego and the Self, what Erich Neumann termed an ego-Self axis, that guides the process of individuation.

Moses's solitary encounter with the burning bush is now experienced collectively as the Hebrew people encounter the fiery mountain together at Sinai, and learn to tend the spiritual fire in the mishkan. We too move from an initial moment of spiritual awakening to maintaining regular practices, or *mitzvot*, that facilitate ongoing relationship with *Ehyeh Asher Ehyeh*, the God of Becoming. By loosening the constrictive hold of defenses engendered by traumatic experience, we come more fully alive.

Lillian: re-consecrating the cornerstone

Lillian recalled celebrating *Sukkot*, the fall harvest festival, at a retreat with Jewish Renewal founder Rabbi Zalman Schachter-Shalomi. Lillian's decision to turn away from Judaism also occurred during a Sukkot gathering at her temple when she was a young teen, disappointed by the lack of meaning in the ritual offered at Hebrew school. Yet years later, her soul awakened when she was able to experience the holy day's meaning in spiritual community.

Sukkot, along with Passover and *Shavuot* (the receiving of the Torah at Sinai), is one of three ancient agrarian festivals around which the Jewish calendar is structured. On Sukkot, people build small sukkahs, or huts, celebrating the fall harvest, symbolizing the dwellings of the ancient Hebrews as they wandered through the desert. Throughout the seven days of Sukkot that culminate the New Year High Holiday season, prayers offered to the highest realms on Rosh Hashanah and Yom Kippur flow down as blessings integrated through the seven lower sefirot of the Tree of Life.

Lillian's spiritual awakening took place on top of a mountain near Santa Cruz. She was part of a group that circled the sukkah with the sacred species—a *lulav* (palm, willow, and myrtle branches) and *etrog* (a fragrant citron fruit)—for several days. During one of the last processions, the group chanted the psalm, "This is the day the Lord has made, rejoice and be glad."[2] Lillian recalled how she just completely opened and started to cry. "It was that moment on the deck with Zalman, and I knew I was just going to change my whole life right then."

Lillian remembered that her father, a professed agnostic, would wistfully recall at Passover that all Jews who ever lived were present at Mount Sinai when Moses received the Torah. Now, at a mountaintop retreat in Santa Cruz, Lillian experienced an encounter with the numinous that was completely transformative. She began to make her life into a spiritual vessel, studying Hebrew and attending services at Aquarian Minyan in Berkeley, joining a communal Jewish household, and eventually becoming a leader in her community. After her childhood experience with a rabbi who told her that he would eventually get everyone to agree with his point of view, she became fiercely dedicated to defending congregants' right to disagree with the rabbi.

In Psalm 118, the psalm that changed Lillian's life, we find these powerful words: "The stone that the builders rejected has become the cornerstone." Jung cited this line from the Psalms when discussing the shift from the ego-centered existence that is forever altered by the numinous encounter with the Self. The stone that is the foundation of the Self is often discarded or devalued earlier in life, especially when trauma has cut off connection to the soul. The trauma Jews suffered often resulted in a devaluation of Judaism itself, an internalized anti-Semitism, subtle but pernicious. Gershom Scholem noted that Jewish mysticism was a stone that the builders rejected during the enlightenment Haskalah, but its riches became the cornerstone of a renewed Judaism.[3] The experience of reconnecting with Judaism after a lifetime, or generations, of turning away from it may provide a cornerstone that can house the foundation of the Self.

The draw that Lillian felt toward Judaism as a child was strong, but without the support from her secular parents, compounded by her experiences in a temple that failed to convey deeper meaning, her longing went underground, until it was reawakened as an adult. Finding this Divine spark reignited, she was able to turn toward and cultivate the flame of her spiritual life.

When we rediscover this rejected stone through ritual that opens us up to the cultural collective unconscious of Judaism, we may be overwhelmed by the numinous intensity of the experience. In that stone lives our connection to ancient wellsprings of life-sustaining wisdom, and to a spiritual fire that does not consume but instead continuously transforms us. With this cornerstone we can build a new inner temple, a mishkan in which we engage in an ongoing conversation with our soul's unfolding, guided by our dreams, ancestral wisdom teachings, and *Ehyeh Asher Ehyeh*, the Holy One of being and becoming.

Mount Sinai—initiation into a new consciousness

Following the watery initiation at the Red Sea, the people's meeting with God at Sinai is an initiation by fire.[4] The encounter with the numinous is, according to Jung, the essence of religious experience. "Religion … is a careful and scrupulous observation of what Rudolf Otto aptly termed the 'numinosum,' that is, a dynamic existence or effect, not caused by an arbitrary act of will. On the contrary, it seizes and controls the human subject," altering consciousness.[5]

As the Hebrew people prepare to encounter the presence of the living God at the fiery mountain, they are overcome with terror. The ego, or small self, is face to face with an overwhelming power. The meeting at Sinai is an initiatory ordeal associated with the rites of the Father.[6] Jungian analyst Joseph Henderson observes, "Such initiations are always sacral in character: they are meant to impart religious belief of the highest order."[7]

Initiations are terrifying by nature—we encounter a force that has the potential to overwhelm our consciousness completely. The Hebrew people initially hope to ascend the fiery mountain with Moses. As the time draws close, overcome with fear, they plead with Moses to ascend on their behalf while they wait for him below. Moses ascends halfway up the mountain, and God descends halfway to meet him. In a meeting of above and below, the mountain and everything in its reach resonates with the awesome power of the revealed Presence of the transcendent living God. It is a time of synesthesia—the people hear the sights and see the sounds. The entire psyche is thrown into a state of disorientation, a gateway to a new reality.

One midrash recounts that when Moses first encounters the Divine Presence at the burning bush, he sees the 22 letters of the Hebrew *aleph-bet* "written before him with devouring fire."[8] In these letters, Moses perceives the presence of the Divine. God created the world from the blueprint of the primordial Torah, written with letters of black fire on white fire. When Moses ascends the mountain at Sinai, he sees the burning letters spelling out the Holy Name, YHVH, followed by the remaining letters of the aleph-bet. "The letters danced, joined into hundreds of permutations of the name of God." Then the letters joined into one long Name, revealing the Torah as a "single, holy, mystical Name."[9]

Other midrashic texts reveal that Moses was met by angels guarding the throne of God. Some angels questioned why a man was on the mountain. God responded that he had come to receive the Torah. The angels protested—how could such a treasure pass into the hands of a mere mortal? God admonished them that it was for this very purpose that the Torah was created.[10]

Another midrashic legend recounts that as God uttered each of the Ten Commandments, the people assembled at the base of the mountain retreated ten miles, completely blown back by experiencing God's voice so directly. It took a legion of angels to walk the people back the ten miles they had retreated, so they could again stand at the base of the mountain. And with the issuance of the next utterance from the Divine Source, they again retreated ten miles and again were accompanied back by the angels to the mountain. And so on, until they had traveled 200 miles back and forth as the Ten utterances were received.[11] At Sinai, the people were blown away as they encountered the Living God, and were restored under the guidance of the angels. Creating a vessel capable of containing numinous experience without being destroyed by it is a monumental task.

Reorientation of the psyche

If the ten plagues reflect our awareness of ways in which the sefirot were profoundly disrupted by the trauma of exile, the Ten Commandments represent the realignment of the Cosmic Tree so that each of us may grow to fullness. Coming into relationship with the ever-unfolding reality takes an inordinate amount of courage. Trauma keeps us stuck in a hell where an ever-repeating past projects itself onto every present and future situation. Yet as we begin to trust, a larger pattern may reveal itself that allows us to perceive the Divine spark, the *numinosum* that inhabits all life. Thankfully, the midrash teaches, angels accompany us to provide us with strength and comfort.

The people encountering the presence of the living God at Sinai powerfully experienced what Martin Buber called the I–Thou relationship. We, like them, are invited through the teachings of Torah to experience the Thou-ness of others and of the Divine.[12] The first two Commandments concern the primacy of God, the centrality of the Divine Reality, or the Self, as the orienting point of our psyches, so we are not derailed by addictions or in thrall to material wealth, power, status, or other false idols. The Ten Commandments imparted to the people at Sinai help us learn how to live in awareness of alignment with the ethos of the Divine Reality by engaging in right speech (not bearing false witness), right relationship (not indulging our envy by coveting what belongs to others or by committing adultery, honoring our mothers and fathers), and right action (honoring Shabbat consciousness, not harming others).

The *Shema*, the central prayer in Judaism, affirms that the God that manifests itself as the many is the One. This prayer is followed by a prayer spoken in a whisper: "*Baruch Shem K'vod Malchuto L'olam Vaed*." ("Blessed is the Name, God's Glory inhabits all of creation through all time and space.") When we have moments of profound illumination, we can see that underlying the multiplicity of manifest existence is a unified field of consciousness. Jung referred to this field as the *unus mundus*, reflecting his understanding that "the multiplicity of the empirical world rests on an underlying unity. Everything divided and different belongs to one and the same world."[13]

In the *merkavah* mystical tradition from the 1st century CE, the *k'vod* refers to the supernal light emanating from God's throne, through which Creation is manifested. This k'vod is continuously reverberating through time and space in each moment. Creation is not a historical event, but the continual emanation of the supernal light of the Creator. As Jung found in his work with quantum physicist Wolfgang Pauli, the essential metaphors of the mystical traditions anticipated the scientific revelations of quantum theory—the waves and particles that bring existence into being are in continual motion, the supernal light infusing life into creation in each moment.

Jung noted that this underlying pattern makes itself known to us in experiences of synchronicity, in which outer events line up in an uncanny and arresting way that demands our attention. He wrote that behind such synchronicities "lies the operation of a cosmic Eros which corresponds to an individual's urge to individuation and which, paradoxically, leads men in the end to a state of universal relatedness with existence."[14]

The sacred marriage

When the people encounter God at Mount Sinai, the transcendent aspect of God descends the mountain, uniting with the Shekhinah, representing the collective soul of the people, who ascends with Moses. This *hieros gamos*, or sacred marriage, is expressed in Jewish cosmology as the mystical union of the Divine Feminine and the Sacred Masculine, a central theme in kabbalah.

Sinai as a sacred marriage marks the next stage in the development of consciousness—the union of the transcendent Masculine with the immanent Feminine. The Biblical story begins with a *coniunctio* between Adam and Eve, but this is a lesser *coniunctio* that exists solely in the unconscious. When they are expelled from the Garden, Adam and Eve leave this state of unconscious union with the Divine and the generations that follow develop consciousness through the travails they undergo.

At Sinai, a new relationship between humans and the Divine becomes possible through the difficult work of transformation by each individual. The covenant is no longer passed through one individual patriarch or matriarch. Now each person assumes the mantle of consciousness and relationship with the Divine Reality. This union is a greater *coniunctio* that arises from the developed consciousness of the people who have themselves been forged in fires of great adversity.

On Shavuot, we celebrate the giving of the Torah at Sinai. Medieval kabbalists developed the practice of *Tikkun Leyl Shavuot*, involving all-night study representing the adornment of the Bride, the Shekhinah, as she prepares for her union with her Beloved. In the morning, "She enters the bridal canopy, illumined with the radiance of sapphire, which shines from one end of the world to the other."[15] God pledges to the Shekhinah, the representative of the Jewish collective soul, to be Her shelter and refuge. God offers the Torah, guiding the people to live "in health and tranquility. The Covenant shall be valid and binding forever and ever."[16]

This sacred marriage is the union of lovers spoken of in the Song of Songs. Marie-Louise von Franz noted that the Song of Songs reflected coming into connection with the Self, "experienced as a union of the cosmic opposites." Such an experience "frees the human being into cosmic expanse."[17]

Postmodern consciousness and the re-engagement with Torah

The mystical marriage between human consciousness and the Divine Other, requires a strongly developed ego lest it be overcome by the powerful pull of the unconscious. For many Jews, the differentiation from the collective in which they or their parents were raised may be viewed as a necessary development. The post-Shoah era required a more strongly developed individuated consciousness that could engage with the Divine in the wake of collective devastation and a concomitant loss of faith.

In the early 20th century, German and other European Jews were concerned with the preservation of Jewish collective memory in the face of cultural genocide. Martin Buber, Gershom Scholem, Walter Benjamin, Erich Neumann, and Reb Zalman Schachter-Shalomi were all raised in assimilated homes. They each dedicated their lives, in different and profound ways, to recovering meaning and preserving the connection to Jewish collective memory.

These great thinkers came of age in a time when Jews were increasingly engaged with *Haskalah*, a Jewish expression of rational Enlightenment thinking. This valuing of differentiated consciousness enabled them to look back on the tradition with fresh eyes and to see things that had not been recognized before. Scholem saw kabbalah as a comprehensive system that arose alongside and informed much of established rabbinic Judaism. Walter Benjamin, a leading cultural theorist, recognized how the belief in messianic deliverance and the connection to collective memory enabled Jews as a people to survive and sustain their culture in the face of millennia of historical oppression and exile.

Buber explored the spiritual and psychological depths of Hasidic mysticism. Erich Neumann saw that Jewish symbols and practices could be experienced in the individual psyche as a path to personal and collective transformation. Reb Zalman gathered the wisdom of these teachers and translated it into practices that he and his colleagues developed into a new way of engaging Judaism as a lived spiritual practice in the post-Shoah era.

In the text, when Moses first came down from Mount Sinai with the tablets containing the Torah, he saw the people, who had lost faith and patience, worshiping the golden calf. Angered at their inability to experience the sacred transmission at the level he had received it, he smashed the tablets on the ground. After Moses smashed the tablets, God had Moses fashion two more tablets, upon which God rewrote the commandments. God's transmission was comprehended by Moses but had to be given in a new form for the people as a whole to be able to receive and integrate it.

Reb Zalman's son, Rabbi Barya Nadiv Schachter, offered this poignant reflection of his father in his eulogy:

> It's no surprise that my father chose the month of Tamuz to ascend to heaven. In a few days we will mark the smashing of the First Tablets, the end of sacrificial service, the breaching of the walls of Jerusalem, the burning of the Torah and the violation of the Temple. In all these events we see that when the Covenant with the Living God becomes obscured, the symbol of that covenant must be destroyed, forcing us to return to the reality which it represents.
>
> After the Holocaust the protective limits of *halacha* (Jewish law) became a prison for so many Jews ... My father dared to smash the Tablets of *Halacha*, setting free both the alienated Jews and *HaKadosh Baruch Hu* (the Blessed Holy One) and introduced them to one another again ... But that's not the end of the story. There were Second Tablets.[18]

For Jews to come back into relationship with the sacred following the Shoah, the very conception of God had to undergo a profound transformation. Jung recognized that "transformations of the God-image ... run parallel with changes in human consciousness."[19] Edward Edinger recognized that in times of transformation in collective consciousness, the image of God is also transformed.

> All God images are modes of expression of humanity's experience and understanding of the autonomous psyche ... The God-image is not a static entity. The archetype of the God-image—what we live whether we know it or not—is part of a dynamic process ... that unfolds, that develops and undergoes transformation ... and is part of the "divine drama."[20]

The golden calf is a symbol of the Great Mother, and her worship at a time when people were losing faith perhaps represents their longing for Her protection. At the time of Sinai, the Hebrew people had recently emerged from worship of the Hebrew Goddess in the material form of teraphim statues that allowed them to experience the corporeality of the Divine.

Yet, this Sinai moment of consciousness perhaps required a leap of faith to a new understanding of the Divine as transcendent, the *Ein Sof*, beyond human comprehension, not reducible to physical form. A new conceptualization of the Divine was emerging. This may also reflect the shift in the collective psyche from the primacy of the feminine as Great Mother, to the development of the anima, or the feminine as Beloved, who calls us into a relationship between conscious awareness and the depths of the Self. Yet the ascendancy of patriarchy largely eclipsed the Sacred Feminine altogether, which had yet to be redeemed, in medieval kabbalistic mysticism, in Hasidism, and in a new and profound way, through the voices and experiences of women in our own time.

In the profound shift of consciousness in the post-Shoah era, an ethos of egalitarian structures emerged, along with a distrust of all-encompassing narratives. In feminist, queer, and diversity scholarship, the voices of those who had been disempowered and dispossessed by the dominant culture challenged the singular story that had been told by those who held power. Following the Shoah, the idea of an omnipotent God was difficult to relate to, and many left it behind completely, either for secular pursuits or for less hierarchical structures—for example, Eastern cosmologies such as Buddhism and Hinduism, or earth-based practices such as Wicca and indigenous, shamanic rituals.

Many Jews who had given up looking for God in Judaism were profoundly surprised when they felt the Beloved calling them to the garden of pomegranates. Synchronistic experiences and encounters with the Divine astounded them, and drew them closer, as Moses was drawn to the uncanny light of the fire that burned but did not consume the bush on the mountainside. God arose spontaneously within their souls. Yet had Judaism not evolved to meet them, it is likely that many would not have found a way to reconnect with it.

Sarah—choosing, not chosen

Today more than any other time in history, Jews are free to choose not only whether to be Jewish, but also *how* Jewish, as we inhabit multiple identities and can freely engage in an array of spiritual practices. Jews who integrate secular and spiritual consciousness find that developing Judaism as a spiritual practice opens a gateway into the ancestral psyche. Developing a relationship with the mythic imagination of Judaism is a commitment to tending the spiritual fire.

Sarah spent several years living in Berlin in the late 1980s and early 1990s. She had already been involved with Jewish Renewal and missed her connection with it. The Jewish community of Berlin presented a huge celebration of Judaism with a featured panel on California Jewish life that included Reform Rabbi Laura Geller, a left-wing Orthodox rabbi, and David Biale, a historian of Jewish life and culture, each speaking about their own relationship to their Jewish identity. She heard an inner voice asking, "If not now, when?"

Sarah understood immediately: "If I don't now, at the age of 53, really pursue my interest in Jewish learning, when am I ever going to do it?" She immediately sought out a Hebrew teacher and took out books from the Jewish library. She discovered that the line she had heard in her head was from the ancient Jewish text *Pirke Avot* (*The Wisdom of Our Fathers*). She subsequently co-founded an egalitarian Jewish congregation and a women's *Rosh Chodesh* (new moon) group.

Sarah also experienced the movement to deepen her Jewish spiritual life in a dream in which she was visiting her parents' study. Her mother, who died when Sarah was just a teenager, was in the dream. It was rare for her to dream about her. *In the dream her mother showed her that there was another window above the window she was looking through.* Sarah felt her mother was "affirming my spiritual yearnings, that they were something to be pursued."

Jungian analyst Rivkah Scharf Kluger invites us to reframe the concept of the "chosen people" as *our* choosing to enter a covenant, choosing to be in an ongoing relationship with God, a covenant that demands commitment to developing moral and spiritual consciousness. Kluger notes, "Here begins the history of suffering for the sake of consciousness. [Being chosen] proves to be a tremendous task, reaching to the limits of human capacity."[21]

Kluger recounts the Talmudic legend in which God tilts Mount Sinai over the people of Israel like a bucket and says, "If you're willing to receive the Torah, good; but if not, here is your grave."[22] Had the Israelites refused the covenant, the world would have reverted to the unformed void that existed at the beginning of Creation, or the angels would have destroyed it.[23]

As we choose to come into relationship with the Jewish cultural collective unconscious, the covenant brings soul growth and redemption. Refusal may lead to the loss of the storehouse of riches that has been safeguarded for us for millennia. Engaging in an ongoing relationship with the living God ensures that this world will survive within us as a sacred treasure. As the number of those engaging with Jewish spiritual practice faces startling rates of attrition, our continued engagement with the tradition also ensures the continuation of this world in the larger collective psyche. As we each choose to develop and strengthen our vessel as a vehicle of receiving and transmitting collective memory, we become a conscious link in the *shalshelet*, the chain of Jewish souls.

Journeying to the Promised Land

The Hebrews wandering in the desert have left behind the constricted perspective of mitzrayim, but they still have a long way to go before reaching the Promised Land. Like our ancestors, we must wander in the psychological desert, learning the ways of this new reality. We undergo the travails of becoming conscious, the challenges of the path of individuation. The struggles enumerated in the stories of the Hebrews wandering in the desert offer guidance in helping us understand how to become conscious as we strive toward wholeness.

The ego, or consciousness, is continually required to bow before the larger reality of the Self and to understand that it is only through the relationship with the Self that we are blessed. God tells the people, *"You shall become holy because I am holy.*" The ego becomes the servant of the Self, as our lives and actions reflect an increasing psychological wholeness and complexity.

In the desert *mishkan*, the illuminating Pillar of Fire carries the light of consciousness first encountered at the burning bush and again at Sinai, which now accompanies the people through their journey. As we tend to the spiritual fire, we undertake the work of transformation. The Zohar teaches that God's longing for humanity and the bestowal of God's grace must be awakened by the longing from below.[24] The sacrifices that are offered on the fire altar of the mishkan, and later in the Holy Temple, carry the longing of the lower worlds up through the smoke to the upper worlds, replicating the state of Divine union entered into at Sinai.

If we do not tend the spiritual fire, we will not invite the blessing or participation of the Holy One. When the Temple in Jerusalem was destroyed, the practice of sacrifice was replaced with the prayers of the Amidah. In this prayer, we bring ourselves into the presence of the living God, inviting the spiritual fire to burn away the inflatedness of the ego. We sacrifice the idea that we alone know how to control our lives and our destinies and recall that our lives are a co-creation with the unfolding of the Mystery. We invite the wisdom of the Self to guide us.

Spiritual transformation requires a relinquishment of familiar psychological territory and a courageous opening to the unknown. As we move into a new state of consciousness, we experience a period of mourning for the loss of what is familiar, even if it has been hurtful. In the desert journey, the Hebrews are constantly falling into states of doubt and distrust—angry at God, angry at Moses, longing for the comfort of mitzrayim, afraid that they have been brought out from Egypt only to meet a certain death in the barren desert. Regardless of the miracles that God performs for them, regardless of the constant and abiding presence of the Shekhinah providing manna and Miriam's well bringing forth water, the people are quick to anger and doubt.

As the Hebrews approach the Promised Land, Moses sends out scouts to see what the land that they are about to inhabit will hold for them. The scouts return and all except Joshua and Caleb fill the people with stories of fear and dread. In response, the people once again rebel against Moses. As we approach the threshold of new awareness, the Promised Land, a land in which we may live in ongoing and deepening connection with the Source, we may be filled with fear and lack of trust. We may find ourselves retreating under the sway of the familiar, annihilating voice of the inner Pharaoh.

In the text, the generation that has traveled out of Egypt will not live to enter the Promised Land. The story reflects the psychological truth that unless and until the part of us that remains in traumatized consciousness gives way to a new psychic center, we will not be able to inhabit this new state of consciousness. In the vicissitudes of the desert wanderings, the Hebrews undergo a transformational journey of death and rebirth, in which the attitudes of the old ego formed under the harshness of slavery yield to a new way of being. Metaphorically speaking, the part of us that lives according to the laws of the inner Pharaoh must die, so that a new self can be born, one aligned with the Cosmic Reality. We can never know fully the expanse of the Self. Like Moses, we can glimpse the Promised Land but cannot fully inhabit it. Yet we are always moving toward it.

Harvesting the fruits of an individuated Judaism

Reb Zalman observed that when Jews left the Old World of the shtetl, the Tree of Life sent forth new seedpods that could adapt to life in the new realities of the diaspora. These seedpods developed in the fertile soil of feminism and social justice, depth psychological understandings, and scientific insights about the interconnectedness of all life. Although these seedpods differed from earlier expressions of Judaism, they represent the development of a new Jewish identity that integrates the emergent consciousness of the time. The seedpods took root, and new branches emerged, widening to bear fruit that reflected a new, individuated Judaism, integrating the insights gleaned from the rational worldview of Haskalah Judaism with the collective wisdom of the ancestral tradition.

For many, Judaism is no longer experienced as a fixed set of laws to be rigidly followed, but a sacred technology of practices and teachings that allows one to grow spiritually. Jewish identity is not a reified state, but a continual process of moving out of constricted small mind (*mochin d'katnut*) to a state of expanded consciousness (*mochin d'gadlut*), allowing the unfolding of Self. Jewish ritual and sacred practice assist the process of individuation. As we deepen our relationship with Torah, the mythic imagination of Judaism, we are transformed by it.

Working through our relationship to Judaism may allow us to arrive at a renewed individuated Judaism—one chosen, not out of obligation, but out of love and the soul's yearning. As I explored this journey with individuals who had reclaimed their connection to Judaism, they each offered fruits that symbolized the harvest of their spiritual development.

Julie, Ruth, and Lillian felt that the pomegranate best symbolized the fruit of their engagement with Judaism. The pomegranate is said to contain 613 seeds, a mystical symbol of the number of the *mitzvot*, or sacred commitments, that guide Jewish spiritual practice. Julie's mother was a Holocaust survivor, who descended into depression following Julie's paternal grandmother's suicide. Her father lost his faith in God. Julie's personal work of healing the shattered soul of her family allowed her to develop a new and engaged spirituality that included artistic expression and training in spiritual direction, offering others a way of finding soul healing in Judaism. The pomegranate's roundness represents a complete unity, but Julie observed it also has an opening that could also take her beyond Judaism.

Both Ruth and Lillian were raised by secular and intellectual parents at a time in which Jewish women were excluded from leadership, but felt deeply drawn to the legacy of their observant ancestors. They found ways to develop their spiritual gifts in the secular world. Now each bring their combined gifts as psychological and spiritual leaders to their communities, offering the feminine nourishment symbolized by the pomegranate as they devote themselves to their own and others' deepening connection to the wisdom tradition.

Elaine's spirituality was represented by a Fuyu persimmon, signifying her re-engagement with Judaism after years of feeling that it lacked meaning. The persimmons she grew up with "were kind of yucky," and nobody actually ate them. Then she discovered the Fuyu, a completely different, delicious persimmon. It represented "a renewal of a persimmon," symbolizing the transformation of her relationship with the Judaism she had experienced as a child, oppressive and frightening, to the engagement with Jewish Renewal, which was alive and inspiring. She recently asked for a Fuyu persimmon tree as a birthday gift, which she has since planted. Representative of her own burgeoning relationship to a meaningful Jewish practice, she observed that the tree faced some challenges. It is small and not producing fruit, "but it's still alive, and I keep nurturing it and there's a real hope in it."

Yehiel's spiritual journey was also symbolized by a Fuyu persimmon, because its short growing season reflected "the mindfulness and the savoring and appreciating what's in my life at the moment and not thinking about when it's not going to be there anymore." The persimmon with no shell is symbolic of her own journey. As a leader of a small Jewish meditation group in her community, she has been able to open to the unknown by losing the hard shell of the rigid Orthodoxy with which she was raised, relishing the sweet inner fruit of the deep wisdom tradition of her ancestors.

Aaron brought grapes to symbolize "the Judaism I feel these days, which is, it's contained, it's easy for me, I can take it anywhere, I can offer it in bits, in relative amounts to anybody I meet." He has transmuted the pain and alienation of his childhood experience of Judaism and, acknowledging the tremendous strength and gift of his legacy, is making it his own in a way that he can openly share with others. Aaron offered an "extemporaneous aboriginal blessing" over the fruit, reflecting his relating to Judaism authentically rather than through rote observance. "*Baruch Atah*, Source of all blessing are You, *Yah*, Who Was, Is, and Will Be, *Eloheinu Ruach Ha'olam*, Whose every breath creates existence anew, for transforming sun, earth, water into this fruit that we eat."

Joshua and Daniel both completed a three-year Jewish meditation teacher training, and each spoke about the gifts they were harvesting and the ways in which they hoped to share these with others. Joshua's journey was symbolized by a mandarin orange. He explored its intricate beauty: The rind was a garment that hid the unity of the fruit underneath, a unity that would not function "unless it was composed of separate elements." The separate elements were joined by "white connective stuff," which he likened to "the connective ability of Jewish community." As he stepped into the role of a Jewish meditation teacher, he was hoping to bring a gift "of being able to see the Divine in anything, of seeing the underlying unity in anything."

Joshua's image of the rind as a garment recalled his childhood memory of standing together with his sister and father beneath their fathers' tallit, chanting at services. The connective tissue that had been the gift of his childhood experience of Jewish family, torn apart by his parents' divorce and his subsequent withdrawal, was rediscovered in the family he had found in the Jewish community.

Daniel's journey was symbolized by an apple, "a completely ordinary fruit that one can get anywhere, in so many varieties. I kind of feel like that with the everydayness of my Jewish practice, which is ordinary, but that miraculousness is in potential in any moment and is contained within that experience." Daniel's choice to share the simplicity of the apple echoed his childhood memory witnessing his grandfather praying in the hallways of his home, wrapped in tefillin, and how deeply affected he had been by the beauty of this simple daily practice.

Hannah's journey was symbolized by candied ginger. "The raw ginger is just a little bit too intense" but is edible when prepared with sugar and "very, very spicy! And it is sweet as it can be." The ginger reflected the aliveness of Judaism Hannah felt after a childhood in which she was unmet by her parents and rabbis, who had been deeply impacted by trauma. She courageously turned toward the repressed trauma in her own family, allowing her heart to be broken open in the process. After recovering meaning through Jewish Renewal practices, Hannah developed her work as an artist making ritual objects, imbuing them with the sweetness that grew from her own journey of transformation.

Sarah's journey was symbolized by a kiwi, which, she explained, appears unattractive on its surface, but "once you get inside, it's very juicy and succulent." She reflected that its skin was like the garments "in which my own spirit is pretty well hidden a lot of the time." The sweetness of the fruit represented "the delights of Jewish practice," whereas "the seeds represent text, all those little problems in studying text." The "sourness of the kiwi represents … all my anger and struggles with the patriarchal nature of the text and the liturgy."

Sarah spoke of claiming her place in the lineage as a student of the great texts of Judaism, a path just recently opened to women, thanks to the work of many devoted Jewish feminists like her. Her sharing reflected that much of the bitterness over women's exclusion has been worked through, and we are now collectively harvesting the sweetness of the tradition, meaningfully reinterpreted to honor the Sacred Feminine and the long-ignored gifts and insights of women.

Morphic fields and the 23rd letter

The Jewish collective psyche is a morphogenetic field that is constantly evolving.[25] Because the Torah is written without vowels, it is open to myriad interpretations—there are as many interpretations of Torah as there are humans engaging with it. When we encounter passages that trouble us, we are invited to wrestle with them, infusing them with meaning reflecting our current stage of consciousness, which may not have been available to earlier generations.

In the Book of Isaiah, God states, "A new Torah shall come forth from me," suggesting that the Messiah will bring a new understanding—one that can emerge as we each develop *Mashiach* consciousness. The Hebrew alphabet contains 22 letters, but the midrash teaches that the new Torah will be comprised of an alphabet with 23 letters. According to a Talmudic legend, the extra letter was invisible when it first accompanied the other 22 letters. When we read the text with this additional letter, "the letters of the Torah will combine in a different way, and new meanings will emerge."[26]

Judaism is a panchronistic conversation across generations. Joseph Dan, a chronicler of Jewish mystical experience, explains that no one can claim to glean the final word of God. We can only search together, "digging deeper into the infinite layers of divine wisdom, never reaching the end."[27] Jewish prayer is a "treasury in which the people of Israel, generation after generation, have deposited things of exquisite beauty. Each generation chooses its own pearls of wisdom and emotion, stringing them together to form verses of prayer."[28]

Reb Zalman recognized that each person must come into relationship with Judaism in a way that has personal meaning—in essence, in an individuated, rather than a collectively prescribed, relationship with the Divine.

> The definitions we had of God that were the old ones had to be discarded. No person can really have a real relationship with God unless they have been an iconoclast first. Abraham had to smash the idols of his father, and so we have to go through the same thing. We have to smash the idols of our childhood in order to get to a more mature God.[29]

Some of the most difficult language in the text comes as the Hebrews enter the Promised Land and are enjoined to destroy the Asherah groves and the sacred places of the other peoples who live there. We live in a time in which the cradle of civilization in the Middle East has been decimated by seemingly endless wars, resulting in the loss or devastation of countless thousands of lives, traditional communities, and ancient archeological treasures. The Biblical injunction to denigrate, devalue, and destroy the holy places and practices of others, or the groves dedicated to the worship of the Great Mother, cannot continue as we recognize the interconnectedness of all life.

We often speak of Jews and Muslims as brothers, born of the same father, Abraham. But as we learn more about the Great Mother religions of the Fertile Crescent, the correspondences between the Hebrew Goddesses Asherah and Astarte Canaanite and Mesopotamian Goddesses Ashtaroth, Ishtar and Inanna, we may see that as we go even further back, we all come from the same Mother. Wrestling deeply with questions of ethical responsibility and social justice, today Jews in Israel and around the world are working to create cultural exchanges and pursuing policies for peaceful reconciliation between Israeli Jews and Palestinians. As we wrestle with these and other passages in the Torah, we generate new collective consciousness.

As women, gay and lesbian, transgender and gender non-binary rabbis, scholars, and participants increasingly bring their perspectives to the text, we wrestle with the difficult language and generate new insights, evolving the Torah and our understanding of it. Jews of color are inviting increasing awareness of the privileging of whiteness within Judaism and challenging assumptions of Ashkenormativity that eclipse the experiences of non-European Jews. The growth of interfaith families and Jews by choice is widening the understanding and acceptance of the depth of Judaism in the larger culture.

We are continually receiving and making meaning of the synesthetic revelation at Sinai. As our capacity to understand the transmission develops, we glean new insights. By coming into relationship with a Judaism that has itself been renewed, we may find that the part of us that may have felt the most exiled is the cornerstone that carries our spiritual essence. We are surprised to find our exiled part welcomed, even invited, to add our perspective to the ongoing panchronistic conversation. As each new generation brings its awareness drawn from its own experiences of life to bear on the words, new meanings can surface. As we widen our understanding to include the perspectives that have been exiled, we get glimpses of the 23rd letter.

The Talmud describes the words of the Torah as black fire written on white fire. The written words of the Torah are the black fire. The white fire is the consciousness with which we interpret them. Today, in many congregations we are humbled to read words of Torah from scrolls salvaged from the Shoah, scrolls that once belonged to vanished communities of Europe. We carry their memories, the traces of their fingers on the parchment, as we find our own way into the white fire.

Notes

1 Edmond Jabès, *The Book of Shares*, translated by Rosemarie Waldrop (Chicago, IL: University of Chicago Press, 1987, 1989), 22.
2 Psalm 118.
3 Gershom Scholem, *On the Possibility of Jewish Mysticism in Our Time and Other Essays* (Philadelphia: The Jewish Publication Society, 1997), 77.
4 Gareth Hill, *Masculine & Feminine: The Natural Flow of Opposites in the Psyche* (Boston: Shambhala, 2001), 54–55.
5 C.G. Jung, *Psychology and Religion* (New Haven, CT: Yale University Press, 1938), 4.
6 Joseph Henderson, *Thresholds of Initiation* (Middletown, CT: Wesleyan University Press, 1967), 92; Theodor Reik, *Mystery on the Mountain: The Drama of the Sinai Revelation* (New York: Harper & Brothers Publishers, 1959).
7 Henderson, *Thresholds of Initiation*, 92.
8 Howard Schwartz, *Tree of Souls: The Mythology of Judaism* (New York: Oxford University Press, 2004), 257–258; citing Memar Markah 6:3 (Samaritan) and Jarl E. Fossum, *The Name of God and the Angel of the Lord* (Tübingen: J.C.B. Mohr, 1985).
9 Ibid, 265; Genesis Rabah 1:1; Zohar 1:134a, 3:36a; Ta'amei ha-Mitzvot 3a; Y. Shekalim 6:1; Perush Rambam al ha-Torah, 6–7; Maggid Devarav le-Ya'akov 50; Sefer Ba'al Shem Tov, Bereshit, 8.
10 Ibid, 261–262; B. Shabbat 88b–89a; B. Menahot 29b; B Sukkah 5a; B. Yoma 4a; Exodus Rabbah 28; Pseikta Rabbati 20:4; Mekhilta de-Rabbi Ishmael, ba-Hodesh 4:55–58; Ma'ayan Hokhman in Beit ha Midrash 1:60–61; Otzrot Hayim; Memar Marka 5:3 (Samaritan); IFA 16628.
11 Avivah Zornberg, *The Particulars of Rapture: Reflections on Exodus* (New York: Doubleday, 2001), 263.
12 Martin Buber, *I and Thou* (Edinburgh: T. and T. Clark, 1947).
13 C.G. Jung, *The Collected Works of C.G. Jung, Mysterium Coniunctionis*, Vol. 14 (Princeton, NJ: Princeton University Press, 1970), paras. 767–770.

14　C.G. Jung, cited in Marie Louise von Franz, *Number and Time: Reflections Leading Toward a Unification of Depth Psychology and Physics*, translated by Andrea Dykes (Evanston, IL: Northwestern University Press, 1974), 299.

15　Schwartz, *Tree of Souls*, 304, citing Zohar 1:8.

16　Ibid, 305; citing Deuteronomy Rabbah 3:12; Pesikta Rabbati 31:10; Ketubah le-Shavuot from the Sephardi Mahzor, Israel Najara, 16th century.

17　Gustav Dreifuss, *Studies in Jungian Psychology 1965–2002* (Haifa, Author, 2003), 199.

18　Barya Nadiv Schachter, Eulogy for Zalman Schachter-Shalomi, https://www.facebook .com/121083714615628/posts/a-eulogy-given-by-rabbi-shlomo-barya-nadiv-schac hter-reb-zalmans-son-who-recentl/746299112094082/.

19　C.G. Jung, *The Collected Works of C.G. Jung*, Vol. 9ii, *Aion: Researches into the Phenomenology of the Self* (Princeton, NJ: Princeton University Press, 1978), 194.

20　Edward Edinger, *The New God Image: A Study of Jung's Key Letters Concerning the Evolution of the Western God-image* (Wilmette, IL: Chiron Publications, 1996), xv.

21　Kluger, *Psyche and Bible*, 39.

22　Ibid, 42; citing Trakt. Sabbath 88a.

23　Ibid; citing Aboda sara 3a; Midr. Tehillim 68, 10.

24　Gershom Scholem, *Zohar: The Book of Splendor* (New York: Schocken, 1966), 9–10.

25　Rupert Sheldrake, *The Presence of the Past: Morphic Resonance and the Memory of Nature* (New York: Park Street Press, 2012).

26　Schwartz, *Tree of Souls*, 522–523; citing Midrash Tehillim, Genesis Rabba, Alpha Beta de-Rabbi Akiva, Zohar, Sha'arei Gan Eden, Sefer ha-Temunah, Se'udat Gan Eden.

27　Joseph Dan, *The Heart and the Fountain: An Anthology of Jewish Mystical Experience* (Oxford: Oxford University Press, 2002), 11.

28　Ibid.

29　Susan Goldstein, "Rabbi Schachter-Shalomi Extended Interview," *Religion & Ethics NewsWeekly*, September 30, 2005, Public Broadcasting Service, https://www.pbs.org/ wnet/religionandethics/2005/09/30/september-30-2005-rabbi-zalman-schachter-shalo mi-extended-interview/9753/.

Index

Heschel, Susannah 79
Hirshfeld-Flores, Alissa 172
history 178
hitbodedut 169
Hitler 39
Hitler-Stalin non-aggression pact in 121
Hoffman, Edward 39
Hoffman, Eva 101
Holocaust 10, 129; survivors of the xxii,
    51, 90, 101, 186, 225
Holocaust Remembrance service
    (*Yom HaShoah*), meaning of 1–2
Holub, Margaret xiii, 2–4, 79
"Holy of Holies" 77
holy person (*tzaddik*) 110
Holy Temple 180; and the Queen of
    Sheba 151
human consciousness, and the Divine
    Other 220
human history, mapping of 48–49
humanistic psychology 39, 50, 51
Hurwitz, Siegmund xix, xxii, xxiv, 38,
    50, 182; and the Analytical Psychology
    Club of Zurich 46; and Jung 44, 45; on
    Lilith 180, 182

"I See You in the Foothills, Oma"
    (Lowinsky) 139
Idel, Moshe xix
imagination: loss and reclamation of the
    117–118; second plague 117–118
Immanent Divine 207
"In the Synagogue" (Ozick) 59
Inanna 181–183
individual soul 37; *see also* soul
individual spiritual development xvi
individuation 13, 42, 72, 98, 215, 219;
    Christ as a symbol of 48; Jewish rituals
    and 225; Joseph and 160, 163, 175;
    journeys of 12, 95–96, 223; Judaism as
    a pathway 50
Indwelling Presence 208; *see also* Divine
    Presence
inner Pharaoh 103, 109
inner scroll, the 212–213
Inquisition, the 3, 12, 128, 190; women
    healers and 78
instinctual self 122
intergenerational trauma 123; healing from
    51, 127, 172–176; Julie and 89; and
    unhealed trauma 125–126
internalized anti-Semitism xxiii, 50, 105,
    119–120; *see also* anti-Semitism

inversion experience 52, 118
Ishtar 228
Isis 228
Isle of Apples 5
Israel, tribes of 158
Israelites 215
I–Thou relationship 218

Jabès, Edmond: *The Book of Questions*
    197; *The Book of Shares* 215
Jacobs, Jeane TuBears xiv, 1, 4, 143,
    169, 171
Jacobson, Burt xix
Jacobson, Yosef 114
Jaffé, Aniela 46
Jellinek, Adolf 40
Jewish activists 121–122
Jewish assimilation xvii, xx, xxii,
    12, 49, 60, 84–85, 99, 197; into
    American culture 72, 132; in Central
    Europe 18; *kelipot* of 72; Lillian's story
    and 102; Reb Zalman and 198; and
    social status 119–120, 122; in Western
    Europe 37
Jewish collective memory xx–xxi, xxii, 10,
    132, 140–141; break in transmission of
    70; preservation of 220; soul loss 10
Jewish collective psyche xxiii, 38, 109,
    227; healing of the 109
Jewish cosmology 81
Jewish cultural collective unconscious xix;
    reconnecting with 50
Jewish Enlightenment xviii, 18
Jewish feminism/feminists 79, 210–211;
    hierarchical Judaism 206; feminist
    spirituality xx; feminist theologians 5
Jewish identity 10, 99, 225; the author's
    61–64; conflicted 50; exile and
    conflicted 60–61; forming a new 72;
    Jewish summer camp and 62; loss and
    reclamation of 50; in modern times 60;
    unfolding of 149
Jewish immigrants 121
Jewish memory xvi; Serach bat Asher
    and 150
Jewish mysticism xvii, xx, xxii, 5, 29,
    38; in the face of devastation 10;
    Jung and 38, 47–48; psychoanalysis
    and 38; Rabbi Arthur Green and 29;
    reclaiming 20–21; reclamation of xvii,
    xviii–xx; re-emergence of xix; Sacred
    Feminine xxii
Jewish national affair 37, 39